MUSEUM COMPANION to

LOS ANGELES

Copyright © 1996 Borislav Stanic
Photographs Copyright © 1996 Borislav Stanic, Mihailo Stanic

Copy Editor:
Catherine Selfridge
Maps and plans:
David Shiigi
Cover Design:
Marek Djordjevic
Marketing:
David Shiigi

First Edition
5 4 3 2 1

Printed and bound in the United States of America

Publisher's Cataloging-in-Publication

Stanic, Borislav
Museum Companion to Los Angeles : a guidebook to museums, historic houses,
libraries, special collections, botanical gardens and zoos in LA county.
267p.   23cm.
Includes index
ISBN 1-889224-01-1
1. Museums—Los Angeles (Calif.)—Guidebooks.
2. Historic Buildings—Los Angeles (Calif.)—Guidebooks.
3. Los Angeles (Calif.)—Descriptions—Guidebooks.
I. Title
917.9493'074—dc20   96-77668

Bulk purchases of this book are available at special discounts for sales promo-
tions or premiums. Custom editions can be provided with personalized covers
and corporate imprints for special needs. For more information write to the
publisher at the address below.

Every effort has been made to ensure accuracy of the information in this book.
All contents are based on data available at the time of publication. However,
time brings change and the publisher can accept no responsibility for any loss or
inconvenience sustained by any visitor as a result of information contained in
this book.

Readers are invited to write to the publisher with their comments, suggestions
and ideas. We would be grateful if you would advise us of any institutions you
know that are currently omitted, so we can include them in the next edition.

Please send your letters to:
MUSEON Publishing,
P.O. Box 17095
Beverly Hills, CA 90209-2095

MUSEUM COMPANION to

LOS ANGELES

A Guidebook to Museums, Historic Houses, Libraries, Special
Collections, Botanical Gardens and Zoos in LA County

Borislav Stanic

MUSEON
PUBLISHING

CONTENTS

INTRODUCTION

Los Angeles, often called the entertainment capital of the world, has long been known for its theme parks and attractions related to the movie industry. What is less known is that **Los Angeles has more museums than any other city in the world!** Nearly 300 museums, historic buildings, libraries with special collections, botanical gardens and zoos make LA an important and exciting international cultural center. This book reflects the huge cultural diversity and depth that no other city in America, and just a few in the world can equal.

This well-researched book is a guide for Angelenos and visitors alike, for anyone interested in exploring all the cultural resources Los Angeles has to offer. *Museum Companion to Los Angeles* for the first time lists in one place all famous as well as hidden treasures. It is the only complete reference guide to the great variety of institutions in Los Angeles, from the smallest one-room museums with a few display cases to world-class collections.

One of the criteria for inclusion in this book was the definition accepted by ICOM (International Council of Museums). A museum is recognized as 'any permanent institution which conserves and displays for purposes of study, education and enjoyment collections of objects of cultural or scientific significance'. Botanical gardens, arboreta, aquariums and zoos fall within this definition as collections of 'living displays'. Another criterion was that the institution also had to be open to the public on some regular schedule. The size of an institution, quality and the nature of the collections were not criteria for selection. Some of the organizations listed here are rather small and mainly of local interest.

In addition to providing necessary practical information for the visitor, the book features a description of every institution and its collections, with interesting historical and architectural details, as well as collection highlights. All essentials are included: addresses, phone and fax numbers, hours, reservation requirements, directions (the Thomas Guide page and grid numbers), parking information, admission prices, membership and public transportation. Visitors unfamiliar with the city's public transportation system should call 1-800-COMMUTE for schedule and rate information.

All entries contain information about programs and activities offered by each institution, including classes/courses, events, educational and school programs, guided tours, lectures and workshops. Facilities such as bookstores, gift shops, libraries and restaurants are listed as well. Information about wheelchair access and activities for sight- and hearing-impaired visitors is also provided.

Museums are rarely static. They are constantly acquiring new pieces and changing the way they present their collections. Because the exhibits on display are often rotated, loaned to other museums or removed for study or conservation, some of them mentioned in the book may not be on view at the present time. Certain institutions may be closed to the public due to renovation or repair, others may relocate or even cease to exist.

Every effort has been made to ensure the accuracy of the information in this book. All hours, fees, days closed and phone numbers are based on information available at the time of publication. However, time brings change and the publisher cannot responsibility for any loss or inconvenience sustained by visitors as a result of information contained in this book. We urge you always to call ahead and verify particulars.

Readers are invited to write to the publisher with their comments, suggestions and ideas. We would be grateful if you would advise us of any institutions you know that are currently omitted, so we can include them in the next edition.

HOW TO USE THIS BOOK

Museum Companion to Los Angeles is divided geographically into 16 sections, so that users can explore specific areas more easily. Each section is preceeded by its own map. The numbers on the map correspond to the numbers of the text entries, indicating the location of every institution featured in the section.

Comprehensive indexes found at the end of the book make this guide particularly easy to use: an index listing all institutions alphabetically, a geographical index grouping entries by city and an index arranging them by category. Other indexes list institutions by governing authority, activities/programs, facilities and features. For the serious reader, a collection focus index with ample cross-references and a complete general index are included.

The guide is lavishly illustrated with 800 photographs, many taken specifically for this book, 17 city and area maps and detailed floor and garden plans.

Special symbols used in the guide are shown below:

✉	Mailing address	$	Admission	◻	Photography policy
☎	Phone	P	Parking	♿	Handicapped facilities
🚍	Public transportation				

The following abbreviations appear in the text:

Assn	Association	Corp	Corporation	N	North
Ave	Avenue	Dept	Department	Pl	Place
Bldg	Building	Dr	Drive	Rd	Road
Blvd	Boulevard	E	East	S	South
Bros	Brothers	Fwy	Freeway	St	Street
Co	Company	Hwy	Highway	W	West

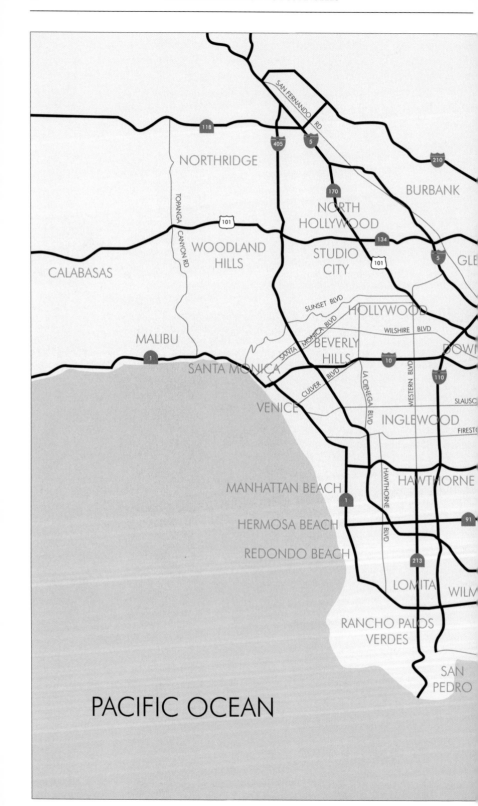

LOS ANGELES COUNTY

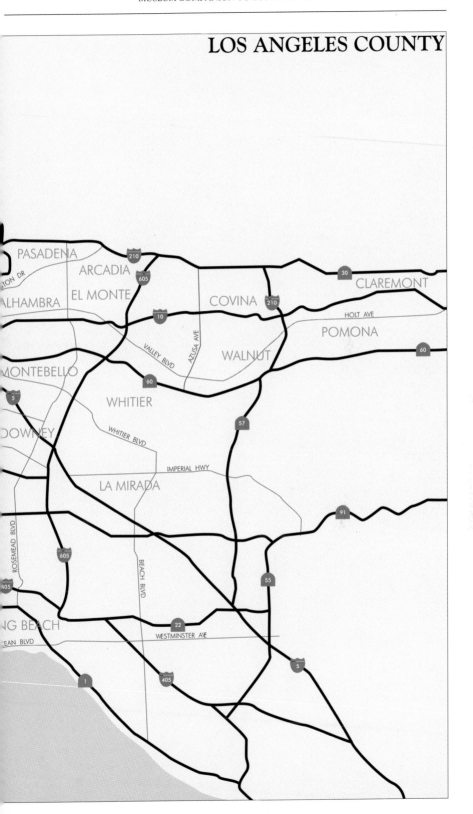

PASADENA
ARCADIA
...TON DR
ALHAMBRA EL MONTE
COVINA
CLAREMONT
HOLT AVE
POMONA
VALLEY BLVD
AZUSA AVE
WALNUT
MONTEBELLO
WHITIER
DOWNEY
WHITIER BLVD
IMPERIAL HWY
LA MIRADA
ROSEMEAD BLVD
BEACH BLVD
NG BEACH
EAN BLVD
WESTMINSTER AVE

MALIBU AND SANTA MONICA

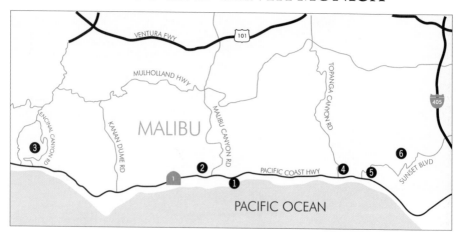

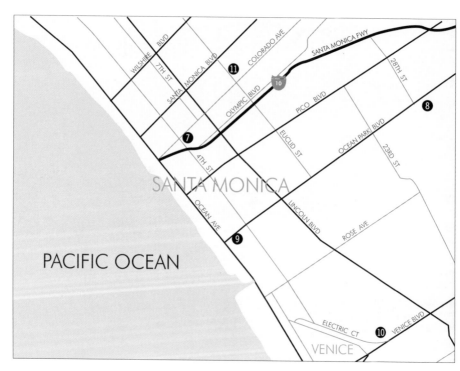

❶ Adamson House/Malibu
   Lagoon Museum
❷ Frederick R. Weisman
   Museum of Art
❸ Charmlee Nature Preserve
   Study Center

❹ The J. Paul Getty Museum
❺ Self-Realization Fellowship
   Lake Shrine/Museum
❻ Will Rogers State Historic
   Park
❼ Angels Attic Museum

❽ Museum of Flying
❾ California Heritage Museum
❿ Social and Public Art
   Resource Center (SPARC)
⓫ Santa Monica Historical
   Society Museum

Adamson House, east façade

1 Adamson House

23200 Pacific Coast Hwy, Malibu, 90265. ✉ PO Box 291, Malibu, 90265. ☎ (310) 456-8432. **Thomas Guide:** 629 B7. 🚌 bus. **Hours:** Wed-Sat 11am-3pm (last house tour: 2pm); Tue only: bus tours with reservations. $ $2 house tour; grounds and museum free. **Reservations:** necessary for large bus tours. [P] $6 in front of grounds; free street parking. 📷 grounds OK; not in house. **Membership:** available. **Year founded:** 1981. **Year opened:** 1983. **Research fields:** Malibu Potteries tile. **Publications:** *Ceramic Art of the Malibu Potteries.* **Governing authority:** state. **Category:** historic building/site open to the public. **Activities/programs:** docent programs, guided tours, volunteer programs. **Facilities:** bookstore, gift shop, picnic area. ♿ strollers permitted, parking, wheelchair accessible. **Collection focus:** architecture, clothing and dress, decorative and applied art, domestic utensils, furniture and interiors, local history, mural painting and decoration, painted and stained glass, period rooms, personal history, porcelain and ceramics, railways, textiles.

The Adamson House occupies one of the most beautiful locations on the southern California coast, with views of the lagoon, Malibu Pier and the surfer's paradise, Malibu State Beach. The house was designed by architect Stiles O. Clements in Moorish-Spanish Colonial Revival Style, and built in 1929 for Rhoda Rindge Adamson and her husband, Merritt Huntley Adamson. She was the daughter of Frederick Hastings Rindge, the last owner of the 17,000-acre Rancho Malibu Spanish Land Grant.

The 10-room Adamson House is renowned for its lavish use of decorative ceramic tiles, produced at the Malibu Potteries Tile Company. The company was owned by the Rindge family and during its short life from 1926 to 1932, it developed a wide range of world-famous glazed tiles.

Each room in the house is embellished with tiles of different patterns: The kitchen features Native American motifs, the living room is accented with rooster figures and bath tiles bear flowers and plants. A tiled Persian rug covers the loggia floor, and the pool, bathhouse and several fountains all utilize Malibu tiles.

Peacock fountain

The Spanish-style furniture was designed especially for the house, which also contains magnificent examples of ironwork, lead-framed windows and hand-carved teakwood doors. Artists from Denmark were invited to paint the molded ceilings, beams and walls.

The 13 acres of landscaped grounds, restored to their former beauty, feature well-kept gardens with more than 100 species of perennials, shrubs, vines and trees.

The Adamson House was designated California Historical Landmark No. 966 and placed on the National Register of Historic Places.

Adamson House dining room

Malibu Potteries tile

Malibu Lagoon Museum

Adjacent to the Adamson House, this museum provides an account of life in Malibu from before the Spanish conquest to the present. The exhibit on the Chumash Indians, who lived along the coast and in the interior, illustrates early local history. On display are artifacts such as arrowheads, bowls, fishhooks, beads and pendants. One interesting object is a cloud blower, used by medicine men to blow air (spirits) to the clouds. Chumash heritage is visible today in the names of their villages that are still used: Malibu, Simi, Ojai.

The Rancho Malibu exhibit offers the view of the first four owners of the ranch, showing branding irons, deeds, wills and family photos. The collection includes a rare document: the original land title search on Rancho Malibu, tracing the ownership from 1804 to 1892. There is also a small exhibit on early explorers who visited the area: Cabrillo in 1542 and Vancouver in 1714.

Guns from the Rindge Colt Collection are on display, as are fine examples from the Frederick Hastings Rindge Collection of early Greek and Roman coins. There is a noteworthy display of Malibu Potteries, with examples of manufactured tiles, pages from production and sales catalogues and a salesman's miniature sample kit. The Malibu surfing exhibition illustrates the history of the sport from its early days (surfing was introduced in California in 1909 by George Freeth of Hawaii — the first surfer in the US). Also shown is the development of the famous Malibu movie colony.

❷ Frederick R. Weisman Museum of Art

Pepperdine University, 24255 Pacific Coast Hwy, Malibu, 90263. ☎ (310) 456-4851. Recorded information: (310) 317-EVNT. Fax: (310) 456-4556. Thomas Guide: 628 G6. 🚌 bus (limited). Hours: Tue-Sun 11am-5pm. Closed: holidays. Ⓢ free. Ⓟ free on campus lots. 📷 allowed. Year founded: 1992. Primary focus: contemporary art. Major exhibitions: "Dynaton" (1992). Governing authority: college/university. Category: art museum. Activities/programs: changing exhibitions, guided tours, outreach programs, performances. Facilities: exhibit space/gallery. ♿ strollers permitted, parking, wheelchair accessible. Collection focus: modern and contemporary art.

The museum collection consists of pieces of contemporary art received through the Frederick R. Weisman Art Foundation. It includes works by Christo, John McLaughlin, Donald Teague, Charles Arnoldi and Alison Sarr, among others. The museum rotates exhibitions of works from its small permanent collection together with long-term loans and selections from the F. R. Weisman Art Foundation. It also features changing exhibitions on selected themes.

❸ Charmlee Nature Preserve Study Center

2577 S. Encinal Canyon Rd, Malibu, 90265. ☎ (310) 457-7247. Fax: (310) 457-4386. Thomas Guide: 626 F4. Hours: 8am to dusk daily; study center, 1pm-5pm Sun. Closed: holidays. Ⓢ free. Reservations: necessary for groups. Ⓟ $3 on weekends. 📷 allowed. Membership: available. Primary focus: environmental education, outdoor recreation. Research fields: insects and other invertebrates of the Santa Monica Mountains, birds and wildlife, native plants. Publications: Scat 'N' Chat docent newsletter. Governing authority: municipal, nonprofit. Category: nature center/wildlife refuge. Activities/programs: classes/courses, concerts, docent programs, educational programs, events, guided tours, lectures, outreach programs, school programs, slide presentations, summer programs, volunteer programs, workshops. Facilities: gift shop, picnic area. ♿ parking. Garden features: peak time: spring, dogs allowed on leash, small pond, butterfly garden, restrooms. Collection focus: biology, birds, botany, ecology, insects, mammals, reptiles, zoology.

The preserve consists of 524 acres of natural open space in the Santa Monica Mountains. Charmlee is noted for its displays of spring flowers, and some endangered native plants can be seen here, including the Santa Susana tar plant and the Catalina Mariposa lily. Here also can be found a full range of mammals and over 240 bird species, including rare and endangered black-shouldered kites and golden eagles.

A small nature study center has displays of local lore and natural history artifacts, as well as static exhibits of birds, insects, moths and butterflies of the Santa Monica Mountains. Among the live animal exhibits are: birds, reptiles, frogs, insects and small mammals. A large educational mural portrays hundreds of plants and animals.

Ecology lecture presented before the *Environmental Education* mural

Main Peristyle Garden and museum façade with columns of south colonade

❹

The J. Paul Getty Museum

17985 Pacific Coast Hwy, Malibu, 90265-5799. ✉ PO Box 2112, Santa Monica, 90407-2112. ☎ (310) 458-2003. **Fax:** (310) 454-6633. **TDD:** (310) 394-7448. **Thomas Guide:** 630 F5. 🚌 bus. **Hours:** Tue-Sun 10am-5pm. **Closed:** holidays. Ⓢ free, but advanced parking reservation is required. Visitors without reservations may be dropped off at the front gate guardhouse or arrive by motorcycle, bicycle, taxi or MTA bus 434 (request a museum pass from the driver); walk-in traffic is not permitted. 🅿 free. 📷 commercial photography not allowed. **Year founded:** 1974. **Primary focus:** to acquire, preserve, study, exhibit and interpret works of art of the highest quality within the fields of its collecting. **Publications:** *Calendar*, quarterly; books and exhibition catalogs. **Governing authority:** private, nonprofit. **Category:** art museum. **Activities/programs:** educational programs, events, internship programs, lectures, storytelling, interpretive galleries and interactive videodiscs. **Facilities:** bookstore, cafe-

Kouros, Greek, ca. 530 BC or modern forgery

teria/restaurant, conservation center, research library, sculpture garden. ♿ strollers permitted, parking, sign-language interpretation, wheelchair accessible. **Garden features:** herb garden. **Collection focus:** classical archaeology and antiquities, European art, Greek and Roman art, decorative and applied art, drawing, furniture and interiors, manuscripts, Dutch and Flemish painting, French painting, Italian painting, 17th-, 18th- and 19th-century painting, photography, sculpture.

The J. Paul Getty Museum is one of seven programs of the J. Paul Getty Trust, a private foundation dedicated to the visual arts. Other programs include the Getty Center for the History of Art and the Humanities, the Getty Conservation Institute, the Getty Art History Information Program, the Getty Center for Education in the Arts and the Getty Grant Program. The J. Paul Getty Trust Endowment is at present valued at $4.1 billion.

The founder of the museum, J. Paul Getty (1898-1976) was born in Minneapolis, Minnesota, the only child of wealthy attorney and oil businessman George F. Getty. When the family moved to southern California in 1906, J. Paul Getty entered the oil business and by age twenty-three became a millionaire. After his father's death in 1930, he became president of the firm, expanding its operations overseas and making it one of the strongest oil companies in the world.

Getty's interest in art developed during his numerous trips to Europe, where he visited museums, archaeological sites and art

dealers whenever possible. His collecting began in 1931 with a purchase of a landscape by Jan van Goyen, and in the years that followed, through intense buying, he formed the core of today's collection. The museum was established in 1953 at Getty's ranch house in the Santa Monica Mountains in Malibu, bought for his retirement. Realizing that the house could no longer exhibit his vastly grown collection, Getty commissioned a new building on the ranch site, and the present museum was opened to the public in 1974.

The building is a reconstruction and adaptation of the ancient Roman Villa dei Papiri, built outside the walls of the city of Herculaneum on the Bay of Naples. The city and the villa were buried in a catastrophic eruption of Mt. Vesuvius in AD 79. The villa was discovered by chance in the middle of the 18th century, and the floor plans made by archaeologists at that time were used as the basis for the layout of the new museum.

Main Peristyle Garden

The museum grounds include five gardens: the Main Peristyle, the Inner Peristyle, the Herb, the East and the West. Featured plants include shrubs, herbs, flowers and trees that probably grew in Roman gardens two millennia ago. Some seeds and bulbs were even imported from Italy. Wall paintings and floor and ceiling decorations are replicas of the designs found in various houses in Herculaneum and Pompeii. Bronze statues in the gardens are copies of the originals found at the Villa dei Papiri.

The museum's holdings are divided into seven curatorial departments. Besides the three primary and oldest collections — Antiquities, Decorative Arts and European Paintings — there are also new collections of Drawings, Manuscripts, European Sculpture and Photographs.

The collection of Greek and Roman Antiquities dating from 3000 BC to AD 300 is the largest in the museum and the third most important of its kind in the United States. It consists of Greek sculpture and vases, Roman portraits, Cycladic figures and vessels, Hellenistic metalwork and arts of the Greek colonies. There is also a small collection of Egyptian portrait paintings. Among the highlights are the bronze Victorious Athlete from the late 4th or early 3rd century BC; the limestone and marble Aphrodite, end of the 5th century BC; a marble group of two griffins attacking a fallen doe from the late 4th century BC; and the red-figured kalpis, attributed to Kleophrades Painter, ca. 480 BC.

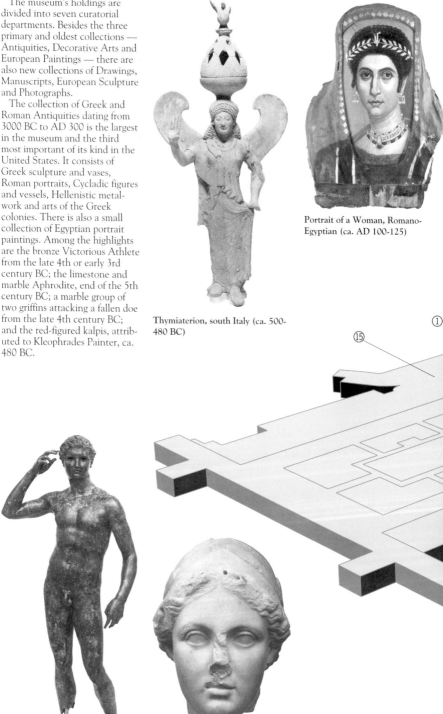

Portrait of a Woman, Romano-Egyptian (ca. AD 100-125)

Thymiaterion, south Italy (ca. 500-480 BC)

Victorious Athlete, Greek (last quarter of 4th century BC)

Head of Athena, Greek, Asia Minor (mid 2nd century BC)

Black-figured Hydria, Caeretan (ca. 525 BC)

Harpist, early Cycladic II (ca. 2500 BC)

The J. Paul Getty Museum

Main Level

1. Early Mediterranean
2. Classical Greek
3. Fayum Portraits
4. Greek Vases
5. Getty Kouros
6. South Italian
7. Roman Decorative Arts
8. Basilica
9. Etruscan
10. Roman
11. Greek and Roman Vases
12. Cycladic
13. Atrium
14. Main Peristyle Garden
15. Herb Garden
16. West Garden
17. Inner Peristyle Garden
18. East Garden

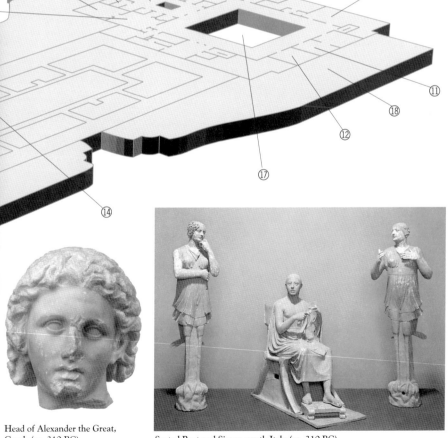

Head of Alexander the Great, Greek (ca. 310 BC)

Seated Poet and Sirens, south Italy (ca. 310 BC)

The Decorative Arts collection contains mainly pieces made in Paris between 1660 and 1815. It consists of furniture, tapestries, carpets, clocks, porcelain, and small objects — chandeliers, wall lights and inkstands. Furniture made in Germany, Italy and Northern Europe is also on display. Major works include a ca. 1680 cabinet made for Louis XIV and a ca. 1744 corner cupboard made by Jacques Dubois.

The European Paintings collection, particularly rich in French, Italian and Dutch works, covers the period from the early 14th to the late 19th centuries. The most important works include Rembrandt's *Saint Bartholomew* (1661), Jan Steen's *Drawing Lesson* (ca. 1665), Pontormo's *Portrait of Cosimo I de' Medici* (ca. 1537) and Veronese's *Portrait of Man* (ca. 1560); Impressionist and Post-Impressionist paintings: Monet's *Still Life with Flowers* (1869), Renoir's *La Promenade* (1870), Manet's *Rue Mosnier with Flags* (1878) and van Gogh's *Irises* (1889).

The Drawings collection features more than 400 works spanning the period from the second half of the 15th century to the end of the 19th century. Works by Rubens, Leonardo, Raphael, Dürer, van Dyck, Goya, Watteau, Ingres, Cézanne and van Gogh are represented.

The core of the Manuscript holdings consists of the Ludwig Collection of 144 illuminated manuscripts purchased in 1983. Ranging from the 9th to the 17th centuries, collection highlights include Ottonian, Byzantine, Romanesque, Gothic and Renaissance manuscripts.

The collection of Photographs, one of the best in the United States, covers the medium from the early 1840s to the 1950s. Among the important European and American artists whose works are included are Talbot, Cameron, Nadar, Bayard, Cunningham, Man Ray, Kertész and Weston.

European Sculpture from the Middle Ages to the end of the 19th century is represented by works of Giambologna, Bernini, Clodion, Houdon and Carpeaux, among others.

The J. Paul Getty Museum

Upper Level

1. Neoclassical Sculpture
2. Dutch and Flemish Painting
3. Renaissance Bronzes
4. Medieval and Renaissance Painting
5. Maiolica and Glass
6. Baroque Painting
7. Régence Room
8. Rococo Room
9. Neoclassical Room
10. Decorative Arts
11. Drawings
12. Silver
13. Manuscripts
14. 19th-Century Paintings
15. Photographs
16. South Terrace
17. West Terrace

Portrait of Agostino Pallavicini (early 1620s) by Anthony van Dyck

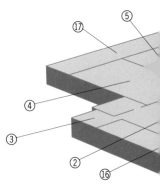

Bathsheba (1571-3) by Giambologna

Portrait of Cosimo I de'Medici (1537-8) by Pontormo

Venus and Adonis (ca. 1555-60) by Titian

Corner cupboard, made by Jacques Dubois, French (ca. 1755)

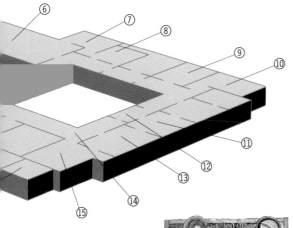

Two Shells (1927) by Edward Weston

Decretum Gratiani (ca. 1170-80), fol. 228: *Tree of Affinity*

Nude Woman with a Snake (ca. 1637) by Rembrandt van Rijn

Waterfall with Krishna statue

❺

Self-Realization Fellowship Lake Shrine

17190 Sunset Blvd, Pacific Palisades, 90272-3099. ☎ (310) 454-4114. **Thomas Guide:** 630 G5. **Hours:** Tue-Sat 9am-4:45pm, gardens; 11am-4pm, museum and gift shop. **Closed:** holidays; occasionally Saturdays. $ free. P free. 📷 non-commercial allowed in gardens, no photography inside buildings. **Year founded:** 1950. **Primary focus:** presenting the teachings of Paramahansa Yogananda. **Governing authority:** church. **Category:** specialized museum. **Facilities:** bookstore, gift shop, sculpture garden, visitor's center. ♿ strollers permitted, parking, wheelchair accessible. **Garden features:** Japanese garden, sunken garden, water garden, restrooms; peak times: spring and fall. **Collection focus:** personal history.

Lake Shrine was opened to the public in 1950 by Paramahansa Yogananda, one of the great spiritual leaders of our time. Born and educated in India, where he started his training, Sri Yogananda spent thirty years in America, devoting his life to helping people of all races and cultures on their spiritual search. He traveled extensively in America, Europe and India, giving lectures and introducing thousands of followers around the world to the science and philosophy of yoga and his techniques of meditation. His best-known book, *Autobiography of a Yogi*, has been translated into eighteen languages.

Highlights of the 10-acre grounds include the Court of Religions, where each of the five major religions of the world is represented by its symbol; and the Windmill Chapel, an authentic reproduction of a 16th-century Dutch windmill, for services and lectures. Other attractions include the Golden Lotus Archway, a "wall-less temple"; the double-deck houseboat (originally used for movie sets); the Gandhi World Peace Memorial, containing a portion of Mahatma Gandhi's ashes; the island bird refuge; and the sunken gardens.

The site is a natural amphitheater, featuring ponds, waterfalls and gardens. The spring-fed natural lake has many varieties of water birds and colorful fish. The grounds are beautifully maintained, and visitors can take a scenic walk along a path meandering around the lake, enjoying the picturesque beauty of this peaceful environment.

Self-Realization Fellowship Lake Shrine Museum

This small museum offers exhibits on the life and work of Paramahansa Yogananda and the history of the Lake Shrine. On display are some unique artifacts given to him by grateful friends and students: an early Kodak camera, given to Yogananda by George Eastman; a mother-of-pearl inlaid dresser that belonged to Sarah Bernhardt; a *veena* (Indian string instrument), a gift from Leopold Stokowski; a Japanese bronze phoenix from the Meiji period; a 16th-century brass table and vase, engraved with passages from the *Koran*; and Indian and Persian miniatures, among others.

God Vishnu, one of the Hindu Trinity (Brahma, the Creator; Vishnu, the Preserver; Shiva, the Destroyer-Renovator). Khmer Civilization, Cambodia (11th or 12th century)

A pictorial exhibit, "Wherever You Go You Will Find Friends," shows photographs of Sri Yogananda with such dignitaries as George Eastman, botanist Luther Burbank, opera singer Amelita Galli-Curci and Mahatma Gandhi. One photograph was taken in 1935 during Yogananda's visit to India, when he instructed Gandhi in the spiritual science of *Kriya Yoga*.

A gift shop with arts and crafts from India also offers books and tapes by and about Paramahansa Yogananda.

The Golden Lotus Archway, a "wall-less temple," surrounding the Mahatma Gandhi World Peace Memorial

6

Will Rogers State Historic Park

1501 Will Rogers State Park Rd, Pacific Palisades, 90272. ☎ (310) 454-8212. **Thomas Guide:** 631 C4. **Hours:** 10am-6pm daily (the house sometimes closes earlier). **Closed:** Thanksgiving, Christmas and New Year's Day. Ⓢ free. **Reservations:** recommended. Ⓟ $5. **Year founded:** 1945. **Primary focus:** Will Rogers's film career. **Governing authority:** state (division of Dept of Parks and Recreation). **Category:** historic building/site open to the public. **Activities/programs:** audio guides, docent programs, guided tours, internship program, volunteer programs. **Facilities:** visitors' center. ♿ parking. **Collection focus:** Western art, furniture and interiors, personal history, textiles.

Will Rogers' ranch house

The cowboy, trick roper, rodeo performer, comedian, actor, newspaper columnist, radio commentator, author and humorist Will Rogers lived on this 186-acre ranch with his wife and their three children from 1928 until 1935. Rogers started his career as a roper in traveling rodeos. His talent brought him to the New York vaudeville stage and the Ziegfeld Follies and later on to Hollywood, where he became a star in the "talkies" and held all the box office records of his day. His newspaper column, *Will Rogers' Remarks*, appeared on the front page of over 500 news-

Fireplace in the living room

papers nationwide. A passionate aviator and promoter of air travel, Will Rogers was killed in a plane crash in Alaska in 1935.

The living room of the ranch house features a porch swing and a mounted calf, given to Rogers to rope instead of roping his friends. On exhibit in the living room is a collection of Indian rugs, baskets and costumes, as well as ropes, bolas and saddles. There are also numerous drawings and paintings, including two Charles Russell watercolors, and Frederic Remington bronzes. This room best reflects Rogers' personality and his love for the American Southwest. The north wing of the house includes the library, his study, the sunroom and family bedrooms, with displays of photographs, statues and memorabilia.

Will Rogers' branding iron

Cigar Stone Indian

The ranch is maintained so that it looks as it did when the family lived there. The grounds feature a polo field, the only outdoor polo field in Los Angeles County, and the only field that is regulation size. Occasional polo matches are still held on weekends (check with the ranger). There are also renovated stables, corrals, a riding ring, a roping arena, tennis courts

and a golf course. Riding and hiking trails offer visitors scenic views of the ranch and surroundings — including the Pacific Ocean and the Santa Monica Mountains.

The visitors' center, which once was a guest house, tells the story of Will Rogers' life through displays of photographs and memorabilia. Of special interest is a short film showing him with politicians, statesmen, celebrities and common people alike. It also features highlights of his career and many variations of his astonishing skills, including roping a galloping horse and rider with three ropes at the same time.

Among the most beloved Americans of his time, famous for his wit and humor, Will Rogers will be best remembered for his saying: "I have never met a man I didn't like."

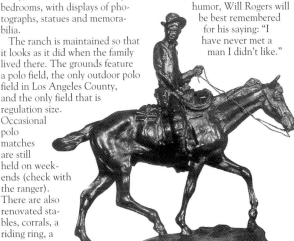

Will Rogers by Tex Wheeler

7

Angels Attic Museum

516 Colorado Ave, Santa Monica, 90401. ☎ (310) 394-8331. **Thomas Guide:** 671 E2. Hours: Thu-Sun 12:30-4:30pm. **Closed:** Easter Sunday, July 4, Thanksgiving, Christmas, New Year's Day. $ $4 adults, $3 seniors, $2 children under 12. [P] metered street parking, handicapped parking/access in rear. 📷 not allowed. **Membership:** available. **Year founded:** 1984. **Governing authority:** non profit. **Category:** specialized museum. **Activities/programs:** changing exhibitions. ♿ wheelchair accessible. **Collection focus:** dolls and puppets, miniatures.

Angels Attic Museum

The museum is in a 2-story restored Queen Anne Victorian house. Built in 1895, it is one of only two Victorian houses remaining in Santa Monica. The 7 galleries hold a large collection of dollhouses, miniatures, dolls and toys dating from the late 18th century up to the present.

The over 60 antique dollhouses on display vary in size and country of origin, and the majority are furnished. Among the most interesting is the Shoe House, a unique 58-in-high and 45-in- long doll house based upon the straight-laced form of a Victorian lady's boot. It contains a toy shop, a nursery, a bedroom, a dining room, a bathroom and a mysterious sun room, whose secrets are revealed by pulling an outside lever. Also on display are an early American keeping room, with chairs and pewter dating back to late 1700s or early 1800s; a baby house from the first half of the 19th century, with its dolls and Golden Oak furniture from Germany; and a spectacular miniature Versailles, commissioned by Angels Attic, featuring numerous small rooms, halls and courtyards. The palace, never done before in miniature, is 5 feet tall, over 6 feet across and over 3 feet from back to front. It took over 2 years to complete and includes the work of 8 specialized artists from England and France.

Galleries on the second floor are filled with display cabinets containing a range of dolls in their original or period clothes. An array of toys on exhibit consists of tin trains, turn-of-the-century steam locomotives and electric trains, model and pedal cars, carousels, toy soldiers and teddy bears. A 19th-century carved-wood Noah's Ark with a variety of animals is also included.

The museum alternates exhibitions from its own collection and loans from other museums and collections. It also organizes the annual Santa's Workshop from November till January. Afternoon tea is served to visitors for a fee on the veranda.

Shoe House. The only one of its kind in the world, built by Rod Forss, England (1979).

Shirley Temple doll (1930s)

Carousel

[8]

Museum of Flying

Museum of Flying, interior

2772 Donald Douglas Loop North, Santa Monica, 90405. ☎ (310) 392-8822. **Fax:** (310) 450-6956. **Thomas Guide:** 672 A2. 🚌 bus. **Hours:** Tue-Sun 10am-5pm. $ $7 adults, $5 seniors, $3 children. [P] valet parking/street parking. 📷 allowed for personal use only. **Membership:** available. **Year founded:** 1989. **Primary focus:** protecting, restoring and exhibiting historic aircraft and artifacts from aviation history. **Governing authority:** nonprofit. **Category:** specialized museum. **Activities/programs:** changing exhibitions, concerts, docent programs, educational programs, events, school programs, volunteer programs, workshops. **Facilities:** available for rent, bookstore, gift shop, library, theater. ♿ strollers permitted, parking, wheelchair accessible. **Collection focus:** aerospace.

The museum is housed in the contemporary, 53,000-square foot Supermarine building, designed by local architect Richard Solberg, on the grounds of Santa Monica municipal airport and almost on the exact site where Donald Douglas founded his Douglas Aircraft Company in 1922. From these grounds, then known as Clover Field, on March 17, 1924, four Santa Monica-built Douglas World Cruisers took off on the first around-the-world flight. The *New Orleans*, one of the original aircraft that circled the globe for the first time, is housed here.

The museum displays its extensive collection of aircraft and aviation memorabilia on three open levels. The first level serves as the main exhibit area for over 40 of the museum's aircraft, both propeller and jet powered. It contains vintage planes such as a restored Beachley Little Looper (1914), the first airplane to loop the loop in the US; the replica of the Curtiss JN-4D *Jenny*, the principal US and Canadian trainer of WWI; a replica of the Fokker DR-1 Triplane, made famous by German WWI ace pilot Manfred von Richthofen, the "Red Baron"; an open cockpit biplane Waco GXE (1927); and a Curtiss B-1 Robin (1928).

Republic P-47 Thunderbolt

The museum features an impressive display of WWII aircraft, including a ground-attack fighter Bell P-39 Airacobra (1938), a dive bomber Douglas AD-6 Skyraider (1945), the famed 1935 transporter Douglas R4-D (DC-3), and the British torpedo plane Fairey Swordfish (1936). Among the fighter aircraft are a Supermarine 361 Spitfire HF. IXe; a Hawker Hurricane Mk. XII; a North American P-51 Mustang, and a Republic P-47D Thunderbolt. Many of the aircraft are in flyable condition, and some are occasionally flown, using the runway outside the museum for takeoff and landing.

The museum also features some aircraft used in the movies, such as the smallest jet-powered aircraft in the world, Bede BD-5J Micro (1973), which appeared in the James Bond movie *Octopussy* (1983); and a replica of the 1931 Gee Bee Model Z Super Sportster seen in the opening scenes of *The Rocketeer* (1991).

A children's interactive area offers hands-on educational programs with a flight simulator, model building stations and actual cockpits. Video kiosks show short films of historic planes in action. The second level features the Donald Douglas Board Room and a model display area with over 120 production models of concept planes, along with an exciting collection of over 300 model aircraft, illustrating the history of aviation from its early days to the present. A screening room and theater on the third level show classic aviation films and booths on the first level show newer footage, including clips of the B-2 Stealth Bomber.

Museum of Flying

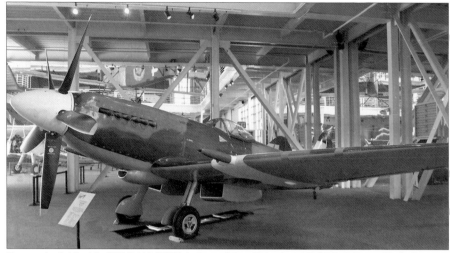

Supermarine Spitfire Mk. XIV. British WWII single-seat fighter. Using the 2,050 HP Rolls-Royce "Griffon" engine, this fighter was the most successful of all Spitfire variants in downing the V-1 Flying Bomb, accounting for 300.

Museum of Flying

1st Level

① Main Exhibit Area
② Outdoor Exhibit Area
③ Flight Simulator
④ Children's Interactive Area

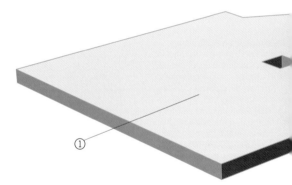

Yakovlev YAK-3. Soviet WWII fighter (1943). This aircraft is thought to be the only one in the world in its original condition.

North American P-51 Mustang. Single-seat fighter, built in Inglewood, California (1940).

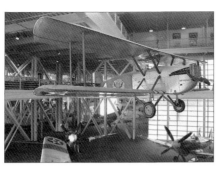

Douglas World Cruiser *New Orleans.* One of two airplanes that made the first around-the-world flight (1924).

Curtiss JN-4 *Jenny.* The greatest aviation contribution the United States made to WWI.

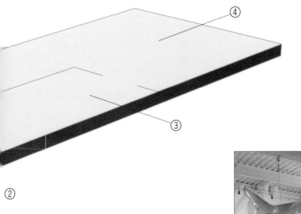

Douglas A-4 Skyhawk. Standard attack plane, painted in Blue Angels colors.

Douglas AD-6/A-1H Skyraider. Single-seat attack aircraft (1945).

Fuji LM-2 "Super Nikko." Japanese military liaison aircraft (1958).

9

California Heritage Museum

2612 Main St, Santa Monica, 90405. ☎ (310) 392-8537. **Thomas Guide:** 671 F4. [bus] bus. **Hours:** Wed-Sat 11am-4pm; Sun noon-4pm. [$] $2 adults, children free. [P] free parking in rear lot. 📷 allowed. **Membership:** available. **Year founded:** 1977. **Year opened:** 1980. **Primary focus:** history of California and display of decorative collectibles. **Major Exhibitions:** "Mission Memories"; "Monterey: California Rancho Furniture, Art and Pottery"; "Toy Boats: The Bathroom Fleet"; "Myrna Loy"; "Home on the Range: American Indian-style Blankets." **Governing authority:** nonprofit. **Category:** historic building/site open to the public. **Activities/programs:** changing exhibitions, docent programs, outreach programs, school programs. **Facilities:** exhibit space/gallery, gift shop, photo archives, picnic area. ♿ parking, wheelchair accessible. **Collection focus:** architecture, furniture and interiors, local history, period rooms.

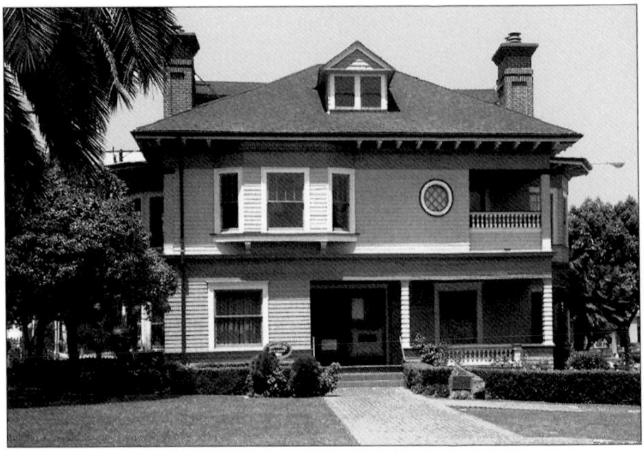

California Heritage Museum

The museum is a 2-story house built in 1894 for Roy Jones, son of Santa Monica's founder, Senator John Percival Jones. It was designed by architect Sumner P. Hunt, whose other works include the Southwest Museum and the headquarters for the Automobile Club of Southern California. The house was restored and moved to its present site in 1977.

The first-floor rooms are restored to reflect different periods of the life of the house. The dining room is decorated to reflect life in the 1890s, with original woodwork, fireplace and cabinets. On display is period furniture, silverware, French and German china and accessories. The living room recounts the turn of the century and early 1900s through furniture and artifacts. The museum's kitchen and pantry relate to the 1920's and 1930's, with fully restored working stove and authentic water heater. The kitchen is modeled after one owned by Merle Norman, Santa Monica's first businesswoman and founder of the world famous cosmetics company. She started her business in the kitchen of her home, just a few blocks from the museum. On display in the pantry is Mrs. Norman's own complete set of china from England.

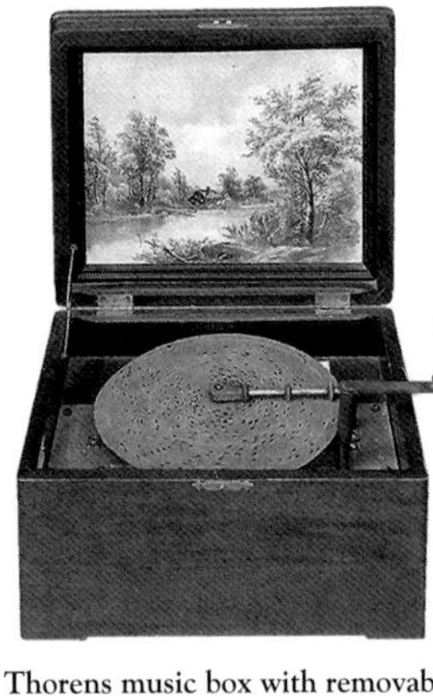

Thorens music box with removable discs (1890s)

Exhibitions showing California production-line pottery are frequently organized. The museum also features historical exhibitions and shows by local artists.

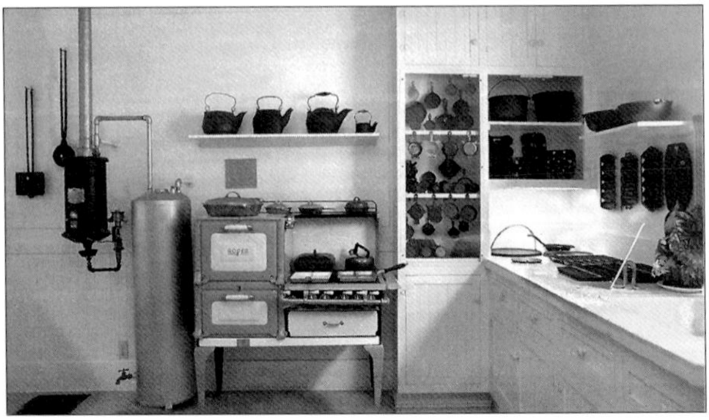

1920s-style kitchen in the California Heritage Museum

10

Social and Public Art Resource Center (SPARC)

685 Venice Blvd, Venice, 90291. ☎ (310) 822-9560. **Fax:** (310) 827-8717. **Thomas Guide:** 671 J5. Hours: Mon-Fri 10am-5pm. [$] free. [P] free. 📷 by appointment only. **Membership:** available. **Year founded/opened:** 1976. **Primary focus:** public art. **Governing authority:** nonprofit. **Category:** art museum. **Activities/programs:** artist talks, changing exhibitions, competitions, educational programs, gallery talks, installations, lectures, performances, retrospectives, school programs, workshops. **Facilities:** bookstore, exhibit space/gallery, slide registry. ♿ strollers permitted; parking; wheelchair accessible. **Collection focus:** mural painting and decoration.

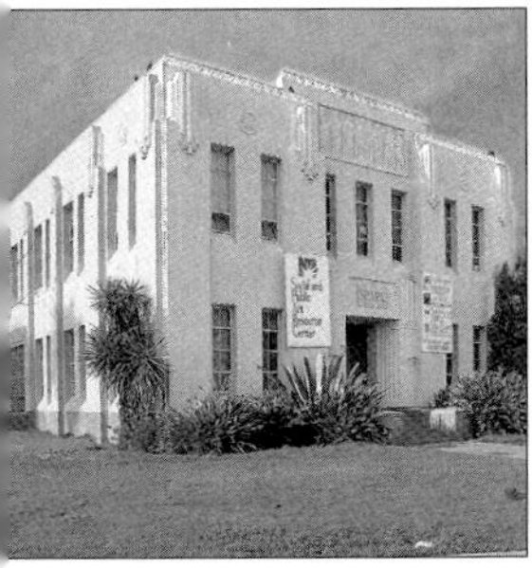

Social and Public Art Resource Center (SPARC)

The SPARC is a multicultural arts organization that produces, exhibits, distributes and preserves public artworks. It administered the "Great Walls Unlimited: Neighborhood Pride" mural program, which began in 1988 and produced over 60 murals across the city. Its collection consists of murals SPARC commissioned, including seven mural panels painted by Judith Baca for the "World Wall" traveling project. The Mural Resource Center has the most extensive collection of material about 20th-century muralism in the country. There are 20,000 slides of murals from around the world, as well as numerous photographs, transparencies and historical documents relating to mural production.

A historic 2-story 1929 Art Deco building previously used as the Venice police station and city jail has served as SPARC's headquarters since 1978.

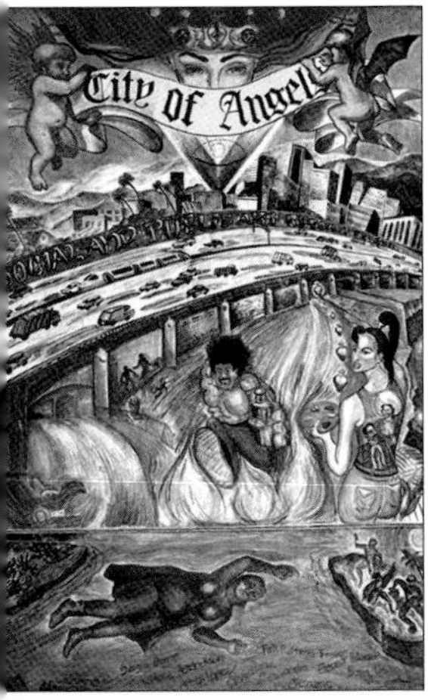

City of Angels (1987), mural on the SPARC building

11

Santa Monica Historical Society Museum

1539 Euclid St, Santa Monica, 90404. ✉ PO Box 3059, Santa Monica, 90408-3059. ☎ (310) 394-2605. **Recorded information:** (310) 395-2290. **Fax:** (310) 453-0302. **Thomas Guide:** 671 F1. **Hours:** 2nd and 4th Sun each month 1-4:30pm. $ $2 adults, children free. **Reservations:** for group and school tours. [P] free parking behind the building; street parking. 📷 with permission. **Membership:** available. **Year founded:** 1975. **Year opened:** 1987. **Primary focus:** to collect, preserve and display the artifacts relating to the history of the Santa Monica Bay area. **Research fields:** art, history and culture of the Santa Monica Bay area. **Special collections:** the Dr. Earl Dible Collection; the Bill Beebe Collection. **Major exhibitions:** "Indian Painting" (1993). Publications: *Santa Monica — Jewel of the Sunset*; newsletter. **Governing authority:** nonprofit. **Category:** history museum. **Activities/programs:** awards, changing exhibitions, docent programs, educational programs, events, guided tours, internship program, lectures, outreach programs, performing arts, school programs, slide presentations, volunteer programs, workshops. **Facilities:** bookstore, exhibit space/gallery, gift shop, 7,000-volume research library, photo archive with over 15,000 photos and slides and over 25,000 negatives, theater. ♿ parking, wheelchair accessible. **Collection focus:** clothing and dress, domestic utensils, local history.

The museum is maintained by the Santa Monica Historical Society, founded by the City's Centennial Committee in 1975. Its collection is displayed in seven rooms, each of them exploring different themes related to local history. The main gallery contains photo panels illustrating the history of Santa Monica and nearby communities; original letters written by actor Stan Laurel, who was a Santa Monica resident; cases with memorabilia including a guest book from the first hotel built in the city; and military items from WWI onward. Other exhibits include: medical instruments and operating equipment; early photographs of local businesses, such as Douglas Aircraft; maps of the early ranchos and sets of tools over 100 years old; household items and kitchen appliances; vintage clothing and accessories, including dresses, hats and lingerie from the late 1800s to the 1930s; and antique and collectible dolls and toys.

Historical films are shown in the museum theater, which also features photo displays of many celebrities who lived in Santa Monica, including Clark Gable, Greta Garbo, Stan Laurel and Oliver Hardy, Cary Grant and Joan Crawford.

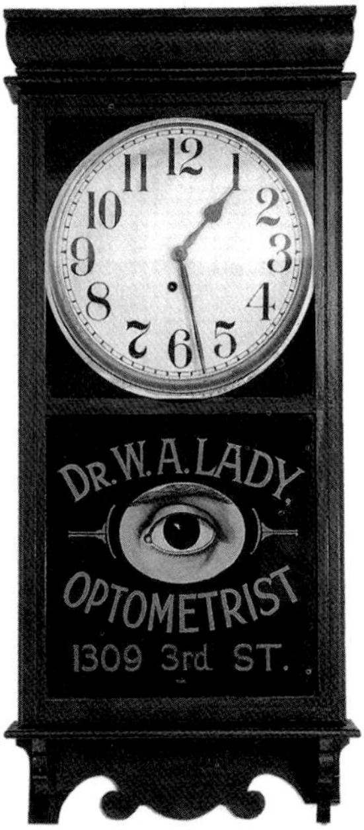

Dr. W. A. Lady's clock

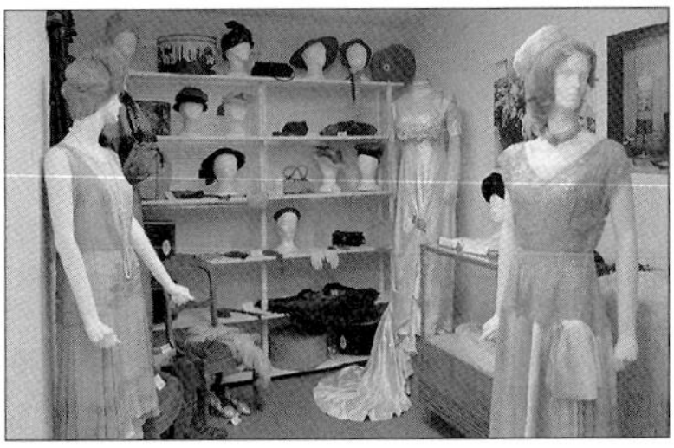

Fashion room (1920s)

WEST LOS ANGELES

1. UCLA at the Armand Hammer Museum of Art
2. Grunwald Center for the Graphic Arts at UCLA
3. Franklin D. Murphy Sculpture Garden
4. UCLA Fowler Museum of Cultural History
5. Mildred E. Mathias Botanical Garden
6. UCLA — Louise M. Darling Biomedical Library: History and Special Collections
7. UCLA — Athletic Hall of Fame
8. Hotel Bel-Air Garden
9. Sondra and Marvin Smalley Sculpture Garden
10. The UCLA Hanna Carter Japanese Garden
11. Los Angeles Temple Visitors' Center

UCLA at the Armand Hammer Museum of Art

❶

UCLA at the Armand Hammer Museum of Art

10899 Wilshire Blvd, Los Angeles, 90024. ☎ (310) 443-7000. **Fax:** (310) 443-7099. **Thomas Guide:** 632 B3. 🚌 bus. **Hours:** Tue-Sat 11am-7pm, Thu 11am-9pm, Sun 11am-5pm. **Closed:** July 4, Thanksgiving, Christmas and New Year's Day. **$** $4.50 adults; $3 seniors, non-UCLA students and UCLA faculty/staff; $1 UCLA students; free for museum members and children; free for everyone on Thu 6-9pm. **P** $2.75 for the first 2 hours with validation; $1.50 for each additional 20 minutes thereafter. **📷** not allowed. **Membership:** available. **Year opened:** 1990. **Primary focus:** to serve as a vital cultural center, presenting historical and contemporary art exhibitions and a variety of educational and cultural programs. **Research fields:** 19th- and 20th-century painting and sculpture. **Special collections:** the Armand Hammer Collection; the Armand Hammer Daumier and Contemporaries Collection; a small historical painting collection held by UCLA. **Major exhibitions:** "Kazimir Malevich, 1878-1935" (1990); "Catherine the Great: Treasures of Imperial Russia from the State Hermitage Museum" (1991-2); "Splendors of the Ottoman Sultans" (1992). **Publications:** exhibition catalogs. **Governing authority:** college/university. **Category:** art museum. **Activities/programs:** art rental gallery, artist talks, hanging exhibitions, classes/courses, concerts, docent programs, educational programs, gallery talks, guided tours, inter-museum loan,

internship program, lectures open to the public, outreach programs, performances, retrospectives, school programs, storytelling, traveling exhibitions, volunteer programs. **Facilities:** bookstore, cafeteria/restaurant, checkroom, exhibit space/gallery, lecture hall. **&** strollers permitted, parking, wheelchair accessible. **Collection focus:** European art, modern and contemporary art, North American art, bronzes, European painting, 19th- and 20th-century painting, sculpture.

Juno (ca. 1662-5) by Rembrandt van Rijn

Opened on November 28, 1990, just two weeks before its founder's death, the Armand Hammer Museum and Cultural Center raised controversies from the very beginning of its construction. They started when Hammer announced his decision to withdraw his collection from the Los Angeles County Museum of Art, which he had promised as a gift long before. The stockholders of Occidental Petro-

leum Corporation, of which Armand Hammer was chairman, had objections to using company money for financing a personal museum. The dispute was eventually settled in court, allowing Hammer to complete his plans.

The 2-story black-and-white-marble museum building, attached to Occidental's corporate headquarters, was designed by New York architect Edward Larabee Barnes. It features several galleries with 14,000 square feet of exhibit space for the permanent collection and temporary exhibitions, along with an open-air landscaped courtyard used for outdoor performances.

The museum collection on display is actually Hammer's third collection. His second one, consisting of Old Master paintings, was given to the University of Southern California in 1965. The first collection was assembled in Russia during the 1920s, where Armand Hammer, who was a doctor of medicine, traveled in 1921 to help fight a typhus epidemic. He was already a millionaire, his fortune made in his family's pharmaceutical business. When he arrived in Russia, he found starvation the main cause of suffering and decided to buy cheap American wheat and feed the local population. This soon brought him in contact with Soviet leaders, including Lenin, who became Hammer's close friend. Having obtained Soviet concessions, he developed a successful import-export business and stayed in Russia for another 9 years. During that time he amassed a collection of furniture, rugs and china, cheaply bought from the impoverished Russian aristocracy.

View of Bordighera (1884) by Claude Monet

Boulevard Montmartre, Mardi Gras (1897) by Camille Pissarro

Hammer's investment in Occidental Petroleum during the 1950s was his most successful venture, enabling him to form the present museum collection. It consists of over 100 works, with

Unfruitful Search for the Planet Leverrier, a lithograph by Honoré Daumier

an emphasis on Old Masters, French Impressionists and Post-Impressionists, with significant holdings of prints and drawings. Highlights of the collection are Rembrandt's *Juno* (ca. 1662-5), a memory portrait of his mistress Hendrickje Stoffels and *Portrait of a Man Holding a Black Hat* (ca. 1637). Among the 18th-century paintings are Goya's *El Pelele* (ca. 1791) and Fragonard's *Education of the Virgin* (1748-52).

Impressionism and Post-Impressionism are represented by *Grape Pickers at Lunch* (ca. 1888) by Pierre-Auguste Renoir, *Boy Resting* (ca. 1887) by Paul Cézanne, *Lilacs* (1887) by Vincent van Gogh and *Three Dancers in Yellow*

Skirts (ca. 1891) by Edgar Degas. Other 19th-century paintings include *Portrait of a Girl* (ca. 1860) by Camille Corot and *Salome Dancing Before Herod* (1876) by Gustave Moreau.

Works by Americans include Thomas Eakins' *Sebastiano Cardinal Martinelli* (1902), Gilbert Stuart's *Portrait of George Washington* (1822), Mary Cassatt's *Summertime* (1894) and John Singer Sargent's *Dr. Pozzi at Home* (1881). *Tete de Femme* (1930) by Pablo Picasso and paintings by John Constable and other masters from UCLA's collection are also on display.

The museum houses one of the most important private collections of drawings and watercolors in America, consisting of Dürer's watercolor and drawings by Michelangelo, Raphael, Correggio and Rembrandt. It is particu-

Bonjour M. Gauguin (1889) by Paul Gauguin

larly strong in the 18th-century French school, with drawings by Watteau, Fragonard and Boucher, as well as in the works by the 19th-century artists Ingres, Degas, Millet, Seurat and Toulouse-Lautrec, among others.

The Armand Hammer Daumier and Contemporaries Collection consists of approximately 7,000 works by 19th-century French satirist Honoré Daumier and his contemporaries. It is the largest collection of works by these artists in the United States. Highlights include *Don Quixote and Sancho Panza* (1866-8), *A Hero of July* (1831), *Lawyers (The Bar)* (ca. 1860) and 36 small busts of the Parliamentarians. The museum rotates exhibitions comprised of paintings, sculpture and lithography from this collection.

Hospital at Saint Rémy (1889) by Vincent van Gogh, painted during his hospitalization at this institution

UCLA and the Armand Hammer Museum and Cultural Center signed the operating agreement on April 1, 1994, under which the university assumes management of the museum. UCLA's Wight Art Gallery and Grunwald Center for the Graphic Arts have moved into the Hammer Museum. The museum oversees the Franklin D. Murphy Sculpture Garden and the independent Grunwald Center for the Graphic Arts.

he Triumph of Mordecai (1515), an engraving by Lucas van Leyden

A comprehensive collection of 19th- and 20th-century works includes *The Bathers* (1896) by Paul Cézanne, *Harbor* (ca. 1913) by Emil Nolde, *The Burial of Pierrot — Plate VIII* from *Jazz* (1947) by Henri Matisse, and works by other major artists such as Henri de Toulouse-Lautrec, Ernst Ludwig Kirchner, Kathe Kollwitz and Pablo Picasso, along with contemporary artists Jasper Johns, Richard Diebenkorn, June Wayne and Joyce Treiman.

The center houses a collection of 20th-century artists' books and a substantial number of 20th-century American photographs. The Richard Vogler George Cruikshank Archives consist of more than 3,000 prints, drawings and

Grunwald Center for he Graphic Arts at JCLA

0899 Wilshire Blvd, Los Angeles, 0024. **Hours:** Mon-Fri 9am-5pm. free. **Reservations:** mandatory; all (310) 443-7076 to schedule an ppointment. **Membership:** available. **Year founded:** 1956. **Cate-

ing from the Renaissance to the present. **Special collections:** the Fred Grunwald Collection; the Frank Lloyd Wright Collection of Japanese Prints; the Richard Vogler George Cruikshank Archives; the Schneider Old Master Prints; the Feitelson Old Master Drawings; the Rudolf Baumfeld Collection; the Norton Simon Matisse Prints; Tamarind Lithography Archives. **Major exhibitions:** "Words and Images" (1978); "Politics and Polemics: French Caricature and the French Revolution" (1988); "The French Renaissance in Prints from the Bibliothéque Nationale de France" (1994). **Collection focus:** European art, Japanese art, book arts, books, drawing, graphic arts, photography.

This is one of the finest university collections of graphic arts in the country. The center's holdings consist of more than 35,000 prints, drawings, photographs and artists' books dating from the 13th century to the present. The center's particular strength is its collection of over 5,000 prints and drawings from the Renaissance through the 18th century, including works by Dürer, Mantegna, Rembrandt and Tiepolo. There is also a collection of European ornament prints and costume design.

The Small Horse (1505), an engraving by Albrecht Dürer

illustrated books by the renowned English caricaturist, including a hand-colored etching titled *Snuffing Out Boney!* (1814).

he Actors Nakamura Kiyosaburo nd Onoe Kikugoro as Lovers Playing Shamisen (ca. 1750), a voodcut by Ishikawa Toyonobu

ory: art museum. **Primary focus:** to erve as a primary resource for eaching and research; independently and in association with major nuseums and libraries in the world, he Grunwald Center organizes exhiitions and publishes catalogues. Research fields: works on paper dat-

Landscape with Three Gabled Cottages Beside a Road (1650), an etching by Rembrandt van Rijn

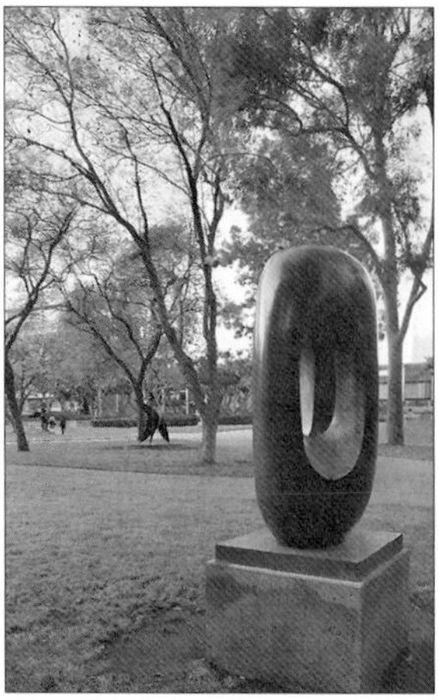

Franklin D. Murphy Sculpture Garden

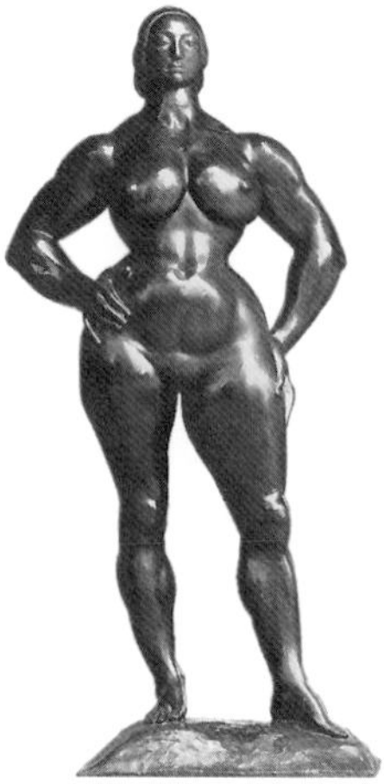

Standing Woman (1932) by Gaston Lachaise

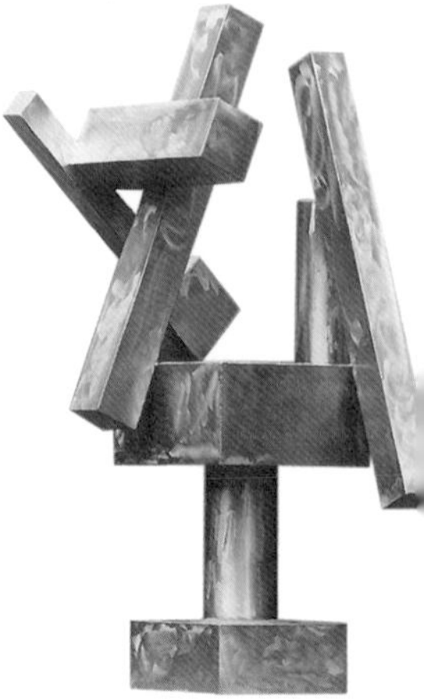

Cubi XX (1964) by David Smith

[3]

Franklin D. Murphy Sculpture Garden

405 Hilgard Ave, Los Angeles, 90024. ☎ (310) 443-7000. **Thomas Guide:** 632 B1. **Hours:** open daily. **Closed:** never. [$] free. [P] $5 on campus parking lots. 📷 allowed. **Year founded:** 1967. **Governing authority:** college/university. **Category:** art museum. **Facilities:** sculpture garden. ♿ strollers permitted, parking, wheelchair accessible. **Collection focus:** bronzes, modern and contemporary art, sculpture.

Situated on UCLA's North Campus, this remarkable garden is the creation of former UCLA chancellor Franklin D. Murphy and landscape architect Ralph Cornell. It was dedicated in 1967 and since then has assembled a fascinating collection of pieces by some of the greatest European and American sculptors of the 19th and 20th centuries.

There are over 70 works on display on five landscaped acres, including *Bas-Reliefs I-IV* (1909-30) by Henri Matisse, *Song of the Vowels* (1931-2) by Jacques Lipchitz, *Two-Piece Reclining Figure, No. 3* (1961) by Henry Moore, *Ptolemy III* (1961) by Jean Arp, *Garden Elements* (1962) by Isamu Noguchi, *Button Flower* (1959) by Alexander Calder and *Reclining Nude* (1970) by Francisco Zuñiga.

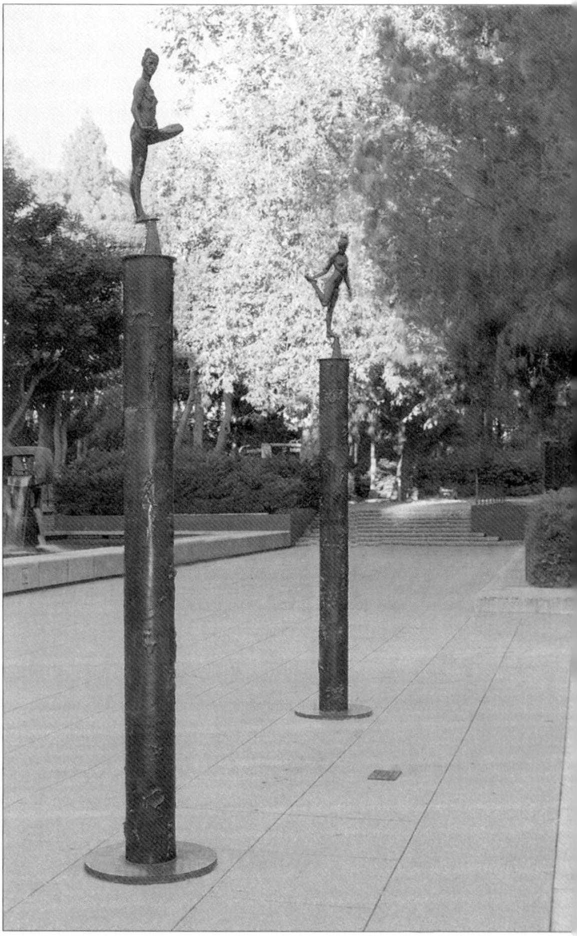

Dance Columns I and II (1978) by Robert Graham

UCLA Fowler Museum of Cultural History

05 Hilgard Ave, Los Angeles, 0024-1549. ☎ (310) 825-4361. ax: (310) 206-7007. **Thomas** Guide: 632 B1. 🚌 bus. **Hours:** Ved-Sun noon-5pm, Thu noon-pm. 💲 free. 🅿 $5 on campus arking lots 4 and 5. 📷 not llowed. **Membership:** to be nnounced. **Year founded:** 1963. **ear opened:** 1992. **Primary focus:** celebrate the diverse cultures and ch visual arts found throughout the orld. The museum collects, preerves, interprets and exhibits the arts nd material cultures primarily of frica, Native and Latin America, Oceania and Asia in a cultural cont, encompassing past and present. **esearch fields:** anthropology. **Special collections:** the Francis E. Fowler r. Collection of Silver; the Jerome L. oss Collection; the Sir Henry Wellome Collection; the George G. elinghuysen Collection; the utch Collection of Indian Texles; the Cordry Collection; r. and Mrs. Herbert L. ucas Jr. Collection; the uhn Collection; the ulryan and Meiers ollection. **Major exhiitions:** "Royal Tombs of pan" (1993). The useum organizes six to ght exhibitions each year. ublications: catalogs with most xhibitions. **Governing authority:** ollege/university. **Category:** pecialized museum. **Activies/programs:** changing xhibitions, educational rograms, lectures, perormances, school prorams, traveling exhibiions, volunteer prorams, workshops. **Facilies:** bookstore, conservation center,

UCLA Fowler Museum of Cultural History

Rasputin chalice from the Francis E. Fowler Collection of Silver

ift shop, lecture hall, research brary with 7,500 volumes on ethnic nd ancient art and archeology. ♿ arking, wheelchair accessible. **Collection focus:** anthropology, African rt, Afro-American art, American ndian art, Asian art, European art, ispanic art, Japanese art, Latin merican art, Mexican art, modern nd contemporary art, Oceanic art, e-Columbian art, baskets, clothing nd dress, domestic utensils, festials, folk art, folk life and traditions,

fur and leather, furniture and interiors, gold, headdresses, masks, music and musical instruments, performing arts, religious art, sculpture, silver, textiles, weaving, woodcarvings.

The museum was established in 1963 as the Museum and Laboratories of Ethnic Arts and Technology, to consolidate UCLA's various departmentally dispersed collections. In 1971 it was renamed the UCLA Museum of Cultural History. The museum moved from Haines Hall to its present location in 1992 to be renamed again, this time in honor of one of its benefactors and donors. The new 3-story building, designed by Arnold C. Savrann in association with John Carl Warnecke and Associates, contains four galleries, seminar rooms, an auditorium, a conservation laboratory and a library.

The Fowler Museum is considered one of the nation's four leading university-based anthropological museums. It houses a collection of over 750,000 objects that represent contemporary, historic and pre-historic cultures. The objects are as diverse as weapons, figures, masks and marionettes, pottery, jewelry, textiles and musical instruments.

The African art collection is one of the largest in the world.

Works from Oceania (primarily Melanesia) are very strongly featured. Mostly European Neolithic and Paleolithic materials are extensive. The museum contains folk art from around the world, although the greatest concentration is from Latin America. There is also a good collection of ethnographic materials from the tropical rain forests of South America. Pre-Columbian materials are well represented, with particularly strong sections from Chupicurao, Mexico. One of the most important collections is Indonesian. Sections focusing on the Near Eastern, ancient Egypt, Greece and Italy are in development. Museum highlights include English, European and American silver, Peruvian ceramic vessels, sculpture and textiles from Indonesia and Northwest Coast Indian painted boxes.

Inner courtyard

UCLA Fowler Museum of Cultural History

1st Floor

1. The J. Paul Getty Trust Gallery
2. The Francis E. Fowler Jr. Collection of Silver
3. The Lucas Family Gallery
4. The Jerome Lionel Joss Gallery
5. The Elizabeth W. Thomas Dave Courtyard

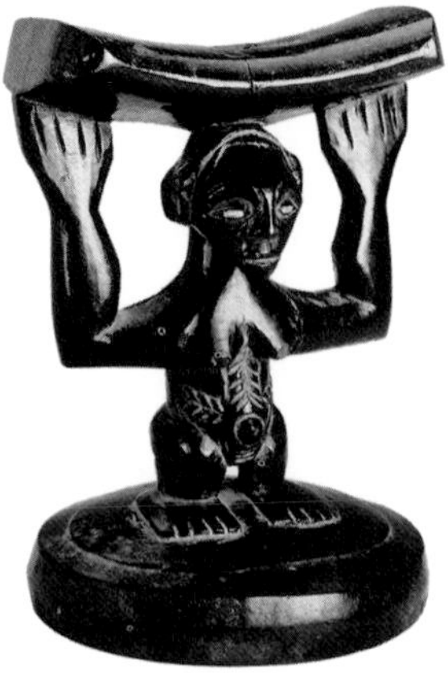

Headrest (*kambaandzia tsiinda*). Hemba, Zaire

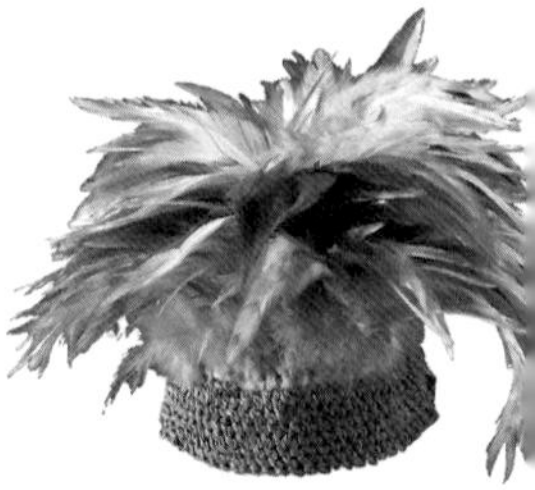

Headdress (*idumbi*). Lega, Lualaba River, eastern Zaire

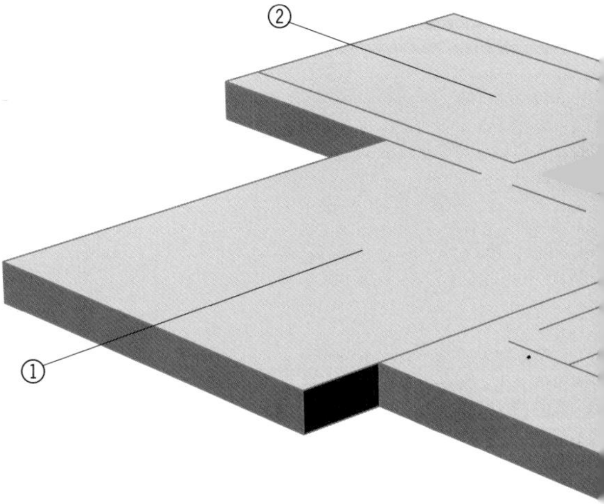

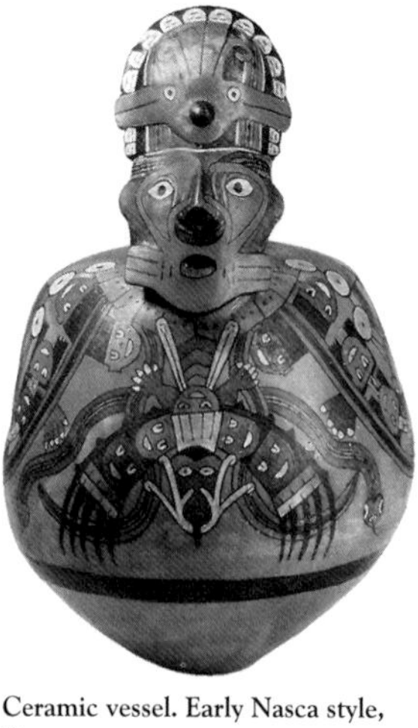

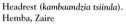

Ceramic vessel. Early Nasca style, Peru

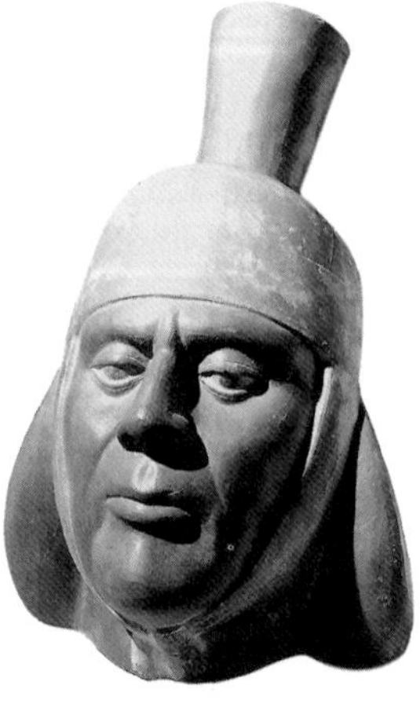

Portrait head jar. Moche, Peru

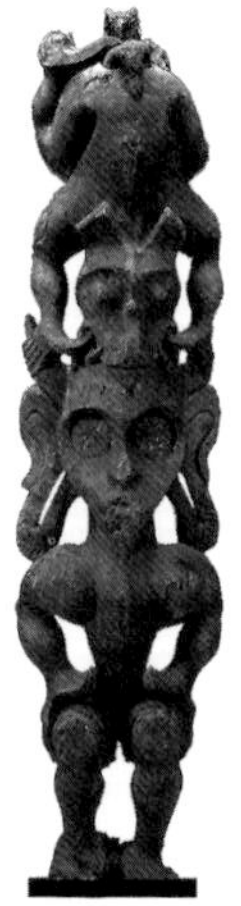

Bahau Dayak figure

Mortar. Kuba, Zaire

Charm post. Yaka or Nkanu, Zaire

Shield

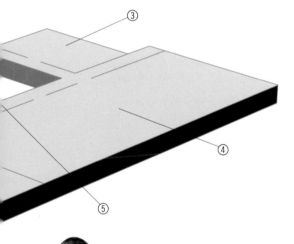

Spoon. Timor

Museum interior

5

The Mildred E. Mathias Botanical Garden

405 Hilgard Ave, Los Angeles, 90095-1606. ☎ (310) 825-1260. **Fax:** (310) 206-3987. **Thomas Guide:** 632 B2. 🚌 bus. **Hours:** Mon-Fri 8am-5pm, Sat-Sun 8am-4pm. **Closed:** university holidays. $ free. **Reservations:** necessary for groups. [P] $5 on campus parking lots. 📷 allowed. **Year founded/opened:** 1930. **Primary focus:** long-term repository for unusual plants, a refugium for biodiversity. **Research fields:** horticultural research, testing the persistence of plants growing in this climate. Plant records are computerized and available for research by professional botanists around the world. **Special collections:** Malesian rhododendrons, cycads, lilies, Mediterranean-type shrubs, ferns, endemics of the Hawaiian Islands, bromeliads. **Governing authority:** state. **Category:** botanical garden/arboretum. **Activities/programs:** docent and volunteer programs. ♿ wheelchair accessible (limited). **Gardens features:** greenhouse (not open to the public), herb garden, labels/descriptions, pond, rare and endangered species, seed store, water garden, dogs allowed with leash. **Collection focus:** biology, botany.

The botanical garden is a living museum, offering its educational contents to the campus community, residents of Los Angeles and visitors to enhance learning about plants and promote greater appreciation for their relevance to the community. It was established in 1930 to assist the undergraduate teaching mission at UCLA. Due to campus development, today only 7 of the original 31 acres remain. Despite its relatively small size, the garden comprises an interesting and prized set of plant species from around the world. The greater part of that collection was assembled by Professor Mildred E. Mathias, who was a botanist at UCLA and director of the botanical garden for 18 years. The garden was named for her in 1979 to honor her outstanding contribution.

The botanical garden displays a diverse collection of vascular plants, with an emphasis on uncommon forms and plants from exotic lands or narrowly restricted ranges. Subtropicals and tropicals, rare in other gardens in the United States, were chosen because freezing temperatures are rare here. Over 4,000 species in 225 families are grown in the grounds and in the lath-house and greenhouse.

The garden is divided into 14 sections, their design based on major groups of plants or their adaptations to similar environments. A wide variety of true lilies (*Liliales*) from around the world is exhibited in the Lily Beds. The Cycad Section has about a dozen of the only 100 cycad species now left in the world. Once widely distributed, they are presently considered "living fossils."

The Tropical American Highlands section features shrubs from the mountains of tropical South and Central America. Native plants are grown in the Hawaiian Section and Malesian Rhododendron Beds. Many species of *Eucalyptus*, a genus almost completely restricted to Australia, are planted in the Australian Section. Gymnosperms (plants with exposed seeds) are represented with pines, cedars and the maidenhair tree (*Ginkgo*), along with dawn redwood (*Metasequoia*), a plant considered extinct prior to 1941. Living specimens were discovered in Szechuan that year, and the dawn redwoods in the garden are grown from seeds brought from China.

The Palm Section consists of about 25 palm species (*Arecaceae*) from every tropical region and ferns planted in the lower section. The plants in the Aquatic Section illustrate adaptations to aquatic life. The Mediterranean and California Sections contain native species of the chaparral and coastal sage scrub habitats. The Experimental Garden is closed to the public and grows plants for horticultural and scientific research. The Desert Garden exhibits plants from desert areas around the world. Bromeliads are the latest addition to the garden.

1. Lily Beds
2. Cycad Section
3. Tropical American Highlands
4. Hawaiian Section
5. Malesian Rhododendron Beds
6. Australian Section
7. Gymnosperms
8. Palm Section
9. Aquatic Section
10. Mediterranean Section
11. California Section
12. Experimental Garden
13. Desert Garden
14. Bromeliads
15. Fern Section

Palm Section

Cycad Section

Fern Section

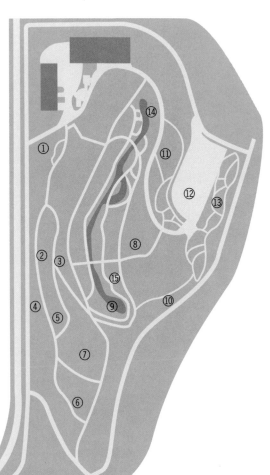

Malesian Rhododendron Beds

Lily Beds

George Shaw's *General zoology* (1804)

❻
UCLA — Louise M. Darling Biomedical Library: History and Special Collections

10833 Le Conte Ave, Los Angeles, 90024-1798. ☎ (310) 825-6940. **Fax:** (310) 825-0465. **Thomas Guide:** 632 B2. 🚌 bus. **Hours:** Mon-Fri 8am-5pm. **Closed:** holidays. 🛈 free; reference card requested to use rare book collection. **P** $5, on campus parking lots. 📷 handheld cameras only; supervised photo shoots require appointment and fee. **Year founded/ opened:** 1964. **Primary focus:** history of medicine, history of biology. **Special collections:** the John A. Benjamin Collection; the S. Weir Mitchell Collection; the Florence Nightingale Collection; the Maurice N. Beigelman Collection; Barlow Medical Library. **Major exhibitions:** "Aid to the Ailing: Medicine in Two Worlds Before 1500 — Mexico and Europe" (1993). **Governing authority:** state. **Category:** library with collections other than books. **Activities/ programs:** changing exhibitions, lectures, outreach programs. **Facilities:** 500,000-volume research library, micro holdings. ♿ parking, wheelchair accessible. **Collection focus:** Japanese art, books, book arts, manuscripts, printing, woodcuts.

The History and Special Collections Division of the Louise M. Darling Biomedical Library was established in 1964. Today it has 28,000 rare books and also contains manuscripts, prints, portraits and museum objects. The division's collection is divided into two broad subject areas: health sciences and life sciences. The health sciences collection comprises rare works on medicine and allied fields dating from the earliest times to the early 20th century. Among the most important medical classics are Vesalius's *De humani corporis fabrica* (1543) and William Harvey's *Exercitatio anatomica de motu cordis* (1628). Georg Bartisch's illustrated *Augendienst* (1583) provides significant information about Renaissance eye surgery. Also included are a collection of Japanese and Chinese medical books and prints, as well as a splendid collection of Arabic and Persian manuscripts.

Bernhard Siegfried Albinus's *Taulae sceleti et musculorum corporis humani* (1747)

The life sciences collection consists of more than 10,000 books and over 7,000 photographs and slides. Among the most important are Mark Catesby's illustrated *Natural History of Carolina, Florida, and the Bahama Islands* (1731-43) and Daniel Giraud Elliot's *Monograph of the Felidae* (1883).

Among the library's new acquisitions is Joseph Banks' *Florilegium*, with 738 copperplate engravings of plants collected during Captain James Cook's first voyage around the world from 1768-1771.

❼
UCLA — Athletic Hall of Fame

J. D. Morgan Center, 405 Hilgard Ave, Los Angeles, 90024. ☎ (310) 206-6662. **Recorded information:** (310) 825-8699. **Fax:** (310) 206-7728. **Thomas Guide:** 632 A2. **Transportation:** bus. **Hours:** Mon-Fri 8am-5pm. **Closed:** holidays. 🛈 free. **P** $5 in parking lots 4, 6 or 8. 📷 with permission. **Year founded/ opened:** 1984. **Governing authority:** college/university. **Category:** specialized museum. **Activities/programs:** guided tours. ♿ parking, wheelchair accessible. **Collection focus:** sports and recreation.

Those interested in sports will find this place impressive. It houses trophies and awards collected by UCLA Bruin athletes, who have won 70 NCAA championships and over 100 individual titles, along with numerous conference and Pac-10 trophies. In 1982 UCLA became the first university to win five NCAA championships (men and women) in a single year. Bruins have dominated the NCAA championships in tennis (15 titles), volleyball (15 titles) and basketball (11 titles). Photo displays highlight Bruin basketball and football history, with a special section devoted to coach John Wooden and his record 10 NCAA basketball championships. Other exhibits include Bruin Olympians, a panel of all Bruins appearing on Sports Illustrated magazine covers, and boards dedicated to each sport in which UCLA competes.

UCLA — Athletic Hall of Fame.
Los Angeles Championship Trophy

Garden pond

8

Hotel Bel-Air Garden

701 Stone Canyon Rd, Los Angeles, 90077. ☎ (310) 472-1211. **Fax:** (310) 471-6267. **Thomas Guide:** 592 A6. **Hours:** open daily. **Closed:** never. $ free. [P] complimentary valet parking. **Year founded:** 1922. **Year opened:** 1946. **Governing authority:** private. **Category:** botanical garden/arboretum. **Garden features:** herb garden, labels/descriptions, ponds, restrooms, dogs permitted. **Collection focus:** botany.

Courtyard

Located in the wooded canyon of the fashionable Bel-Air district, the main structure 2-story Bel-Air Hotel was built by oil millionaire Alfonzo E. Bell in 1922 as his office building, with stables and a riding ring. It was converted to a hotel in 1946 by its new owner, Joseph Drown, who hired architect Burton Shutt to design a cluster of villas around the original building, preserving its Spanish Revival, Mission-style architecture.

The hotel's 11.5-acre grounds are lavishly landscaped with over 200 plant species. Many of the garden's trees and shrubs are rarely seen in southern California, including coastal redwoods, 15-foot-tall white-flowering birds of paradise and an Irish ewe tree. There is a 60-year-old lonchocarpus tree, indigenous to the East Indies and the only one in California. A yellow-blossoming tipu tree, ancient sycamores and a 200-year-old California live oak are also featured. One of the garden's highlights is a magnificent 50-foot-tall floss silk tree, planted in the 1920s by Alfonzo E. Bell. Native to Brazil, it is the largest species of its kind to be found in California.

View of the garden

Flowers that enhance the garden include primroses, hyacinths, camellias, roses, bougainvilleas, pansies and azaleas, as well as blossoming orange, peach and apricot trees. The grounds feature over 10,000 bulbs — irises, tulips and daffodils — planted every year. The chef's herb garden grows aromatic basil, oregano, bay leaf, tarragon, fennel, rosemary, mint and sage.

Smalley Sculpture Garden

9

Sondra and Marvin Smalley Sculpture Garden

University of Judaism, 15600 Mulholland Dr, Los Angeles, 90077. ✉ 1076 Brooklawn Dr, Los Angeles, 90077. ☎ (310) 476-9777. **Thomas Guide:** 591 G1. **Hours:** open daily. **Closed:** never. [$] free. [P] free on the street; campus lot. **Year founded:** 1981. **Governing authority:** private, nonprofit. **Category:** art museum. **Collection focus:** bronzes, modern and contemporary art, sculpture.

This small sculpture garden, dedicated in 1981 and located at the University of Judaism, was named after its founders, Sondra and Marvin Smalley. It contains works created during the second half of the 20th century. Among the sculptures on display are: *Balanced-Unbalanced "Wedge Arc"* (1983) by Fletcher Benton, *Juncture* (1965) by Aldo Casanova, *Action Causes More Trouble...* (1988) by Jenny Holzer, *Spiral 123456789* (1980) by Sol Lewitt, *Two Open Triangles Up Gyratory* (1983) by George Rickey and *Undetermined Line* (1991) by Bernar Venet.

10

The UCLA Hanna Carter Japanese Garden

10619 Bellagio Rd, Los Angeles, 90024. ✉ UCLA Community Relations, 405 Hilgard Ave, Los Angeles 90024. ☎ (310) 206-6632. **Fax:** (310) 206-5792. **Thomas Guide:** 592 A7. **Hours:** Tue 10am-1pm, Wed noon-3pm. [$] free. **Reservations:** necessary. [P] free (only 2 parking spots are available). **Year founded:** 1961. **Governing authority:** college/university. **Category:** botanical garden. **Activities/programs:** docent programs. **Garden features:** Japanese garden, pond. **Collection focus:** botany.

This garden was created by Verabelle and Gordon Guiberson to be reminiscent of the gardens of Kyoto, the ancient Japanese capital. Designed by landscape architect Nagao Sakurai, it incorporates three key symbolic elements: water, stones and plants. Most of the garden structures — the main gate, teahouse, bridges and family shrine — were built in Japan and reassembled here by Japanese craftsmen. Symbolic rocks, antique stone carvings and water basins were also transported from Japan. With the exception of the coast live oaks and plants in the Hawaiian Garden, all species grown here are found in Japan: pines, azaleas, mondo grass, liriopes, Japanese maples and magnolias.

Along with a traditional koi pond, five-tiered pagoda and lanterns, the garden contains a 1,000-year-old carved stone depicting Buddha seated in 16 different positions. There are zig-zag stepping stones that help deter demons who, being unable to follow the path across the water, may fall in and drown. A bamboo device, self-filling with water, is meant to scare off a wild boar. Other attractions include a family shrine with an antique hand-carved Buddha decorated with gold leaf and a teahouse with furnishings and tea ceremony utensils.

11

Los Angeles Temple Visitors' Center

10777 Santa Monica Blvd, Los Angeles, 90025. ☎ (310) 474-1549. **Fax:** (310) 470-0213. **Thomas Guide:** 632 C4. 🚌 bus. **Hours:** 9am-9pm daily. **Closed:** never. [$] free. [P] free on temple grounds. 📷 permitted. **Year founded:** 1967. **Primary focus:** Mormon religion. **Governing authority:** church. **Category:** park museum/visitor center. **Activities/programs:** films, foreign-language tours, guided tours, multimedia presentations, performances, school programs, slide presentations. **Facilities:** audiovisual holdings, sculpture garden, theater. ♿ parking, wheelchair accessible. **Collection focus:** bronzes, religious art, religious history and traditions.

With its focus on the religious history, doctrine and practice of the Church of Jesus Christ of Latter-day Saints (Mormon), the visitors' center features displays and paintings depicting the ministry of Christ. There is also an impressive 12-foot-tall marble replica of Thorvaldsen's resurrected *Christus*. The sculpture garden contains Florence Peterson Hansen's bronzes honoring women and family values.

Christus by Thorvaldsen

BEVERLY HILLS AND MIRACLE MILE

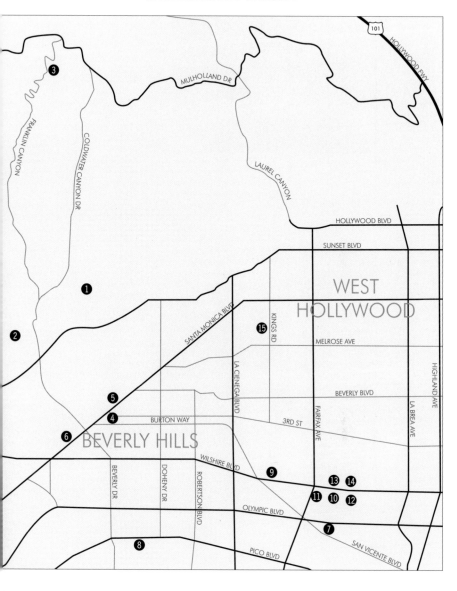

1. Greystone Mansion and Park
2. Virginia Robinson Gardens
3. Mountains Education Program — Sooky Goldman Nature Center
4. Beverly Hills City Library — Art Collection
5. Beverly Hills Historical Society
6. Beverly Hills Cactus Garden
7. My Jewish Discovery Place
8. Simon Wiesenthal Center's Museum of Tolerance
9. Martyrs Memorial and Museum of the Holocaust
10. Carole and Barry Kaye Museum of Miniatures
11. The Petersen Automotive Museum
12. The Craft and Folk Art Museum (CAFAM)
13. Los Angeles County Museum of Art (LACMA)
14. George C. Page Museum of La Brea Discoveries
15. Schindler House
16. California Museum of Ancient Art (no facility for exhibits at this time)

Curving stairway at Greystone Park

❶

Greystone Mansion and Park

905 Loma Vista Dr, Beverly Hills, 90210. ✉ 455 N. Rexford Dr, #100, Beverly Hills, 90210. ☎ (310) 550-4796. **Fax:** (310) 858-5965. **Thomas Guide:** 592 F5. **Hours:** daily 10am-5pm (winter); 10am-6pm (summer). **Closed:** Thanksgiving, Christmas, New Year's Day. ⑨ free. **P** free. 📷 by permit only. **Year founded:** 1927. **Year opened:** 1968. **Primary focus:** cultural resource for the city of Beverly Hills. **Governing authority:** municipal. **Category:** historic building/site open to the public. **Activities/programs:** concerts, performances, summer programs, volunteer programs. **Facilities:** available for rent, picnic area. ⚿ strollers permitted. **Garden features:** ponds, restrooms. **Collection focus:** architecture.

Lily pond

In his youth, Edward L. Doheny was an adventurer and gold miner. With his friend Charles Canfield, he was the first to discover oil in Los Angeles in 1892. Their local holdings, together with later discoveries in southern California and Mexico, eventu-

ally made them the largest oil producers in the world. Having amassed a fortune in the oil business, Doheny began to purchase land, and his 429-acre ranch was the largest estate in the history of Beverly Hills. In 1925 he gave 12.58 acres to his only son, Edward Jr., to be the site of his residence.

Greystone Mansion

Designed in 1927 by architect Gordon B. Kaufman, the 55-room English Tudor mansion was built of steel-reinforced concrete with 3-foot-thick walls faced with Indiana limestone. Roofed in Welsh slate, it was named Greystone for its somber gray look.

The mansion features elaborate hand carvings; a living room with a balcony for performing musicians; a movie theater; a card room with a marble floor and a fountain; a bar hidden behind the ceiling; and a room that was used only for wrap-

ping Christmas presents. Each of the seven chimneys was handmade by a different artist.

The Greystone grounds, designed by landscape architect Paul G. Thiene, originally included a lake, brooks, fountains, garden art, an eighty-foot waterfall, an elaborate outdoor lighting system and what was at the time the world's largest sprinkler system.

Today, the grounds, courtyard and terrace are open to the public (the mansion, however, is not). Although the grounds have changed significantly over the years, visitors can still enjoy the magnificent vistas and manicured gardens with their stone terraces, shadowy walkways, flower beds, lawn and fountains.

Niche

The family sold the house and grounds in the mid-fifties, and it was used as a movie location. More than 40 productions were filmed there — until 1965, when the City of Beverly Hills purchased the estate to build a 19-million-gallon reservoir. Today the grounds are still used for filming; recent productions include *Murder, She Wrote*; *The Winds of War*; *The Witches of Eastwick*; and *Ghostbusters II*.

The mansion was placed on the National Register of Historic Places in 1976.

Formal gardens in the Greystone Park

Virginia Robinson Gardens, main entrance

❷ Virginia Robinson Gardens

1008 Elden Way,
Beverly Hills, 90210.
☎ (310) 276-5367.
Fax: (310) 276-5352.
Thomas Guide: 592 E6.
Hours: open for guided walking tours by appointment only: Tue-Thu 10am and 1pm, Fri 10am. 💲 $5 adults; $3 seniors, students and children. **P** free. 📷 allowed for personal use only. **Membership:** available. **Year founded:** 1911. **Year opened:** 1982. **Primary focus:** botanical garden. **Governing authority:** county. **Category:** botanical garden/arboretum. **Activities/programs:** educational programs, guided tours, school programs. **Garden features:** labels/descriptions, ponds, rose garden. **Collection focus:** botany, furniture and interiors, textiles.

This is the oldest estate in Beverly Hills, built in 1911 for Harry Robinson, heir to the Robinson's department store chain, and his wife, Virginia. The house was designed by the bride's father, architect Nathaniel Dryden, as a wedding gift. The 6,000-square-foot Mediterranean Classic Revival house was the site of Mrs. Robinson's fabulous parties, with famous guests such as Clark Gable, Carole Lombard, Mary Pickford, Charlie Chaplin and Amelia Earhart. The interiors remain as they were when Mrs. Robinson lived there, with all of its original furnishings and memorabilia.

Virginia Robinson died in 1977, having survived her husband for 43 years. Having no heirs, she bequeathed the estate to the County of Los Angeles. The home is listed in the National Register of Historic Places.

Covering more than 6 acres, the original gardens were designed by renowned landscape architect Charles Gibbs Adams. Among the over 1,000 varieties of plants, mainly subtropicals, the gardens contain azaleas, gardenias, kaffir lilies, southern magnolias, roses, ear pod trees, various

Main residence, morning room

fruit and citrus trees and the largest monkey hand tree in California. Over 50 varieties of Mrs. Robinson's favorite flower, the camellia, grow in the garden, including the *Camellia japonica cv. Virginia Robinson*, named for her by Nuccio's Nursery in 1957. A magnificent palm grove features several hundred mature palms, including the largest stand of king palms outside Australia and the world's largest collection (more than 60 varieties) of *Chamaedorea* palms.

Central Courtyard

Back of the main residence with lawn

Virginia Robinson Gardens

[1] King Palm Jungle
[2] Tropical Foliage Garden
[3] Palm Collection
[4] East Overlook
[5] Flowering Trees East
[6] Aviary Garden
[7] Rose Garden
[8] Central Courtyard
[9] Camellia Garden
[10] Citrus Garden
[11] Tropical Fruits
[12] Flowering Trees West
[13] Residence
[14] Guest House
[15] Pool

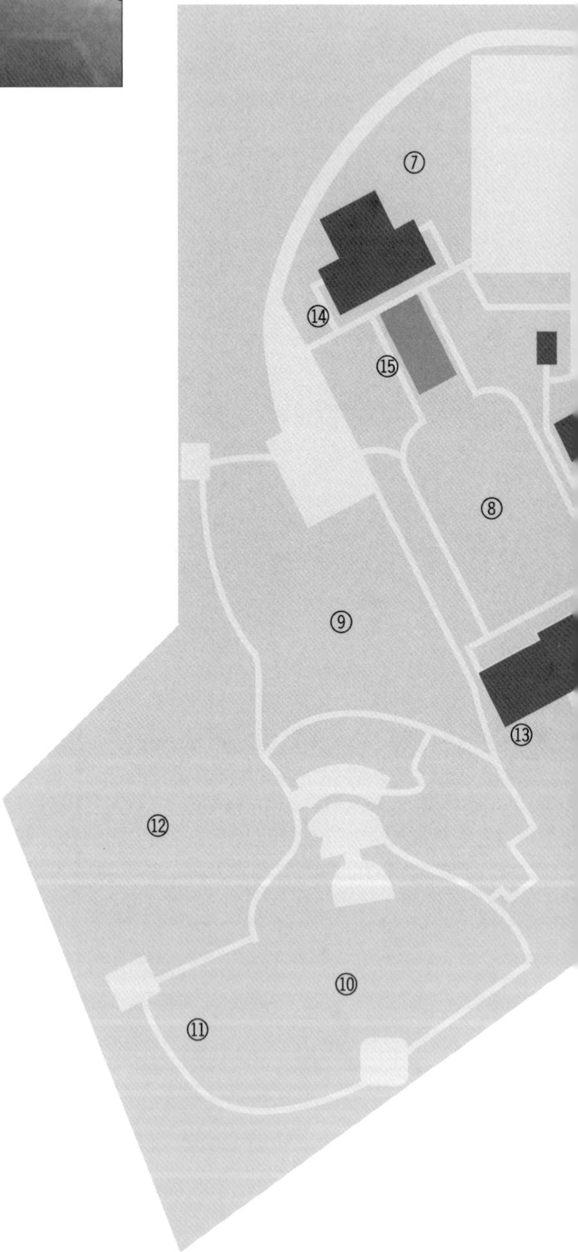

Fountain sculpture in the Aviary Garden

East terrace of the Camellia Garden

View of the Citrus Garden

60-foot-tall stand of king palms

Lantern

❸ Mountains Education Program — Sooky Goldman Nature Center

2600 Franklin Cyn, Beverly Hills, 90210. ☎ (310) 858-3090. Fax: (310) 858-0117. Thomas Guide: 592 E1. Hours: daily 9am-5pm. Ⓢ free. Ⓟ free. 📷 not allowed. Year founded: 1991. Primary focus: to increase awareness of the tremendous natural and cultural resources of the Santa Monica Mountains among the residents of Los Angeles and Ventura counties. Governing authority: private, nonprofit. Category: nature center/wildlife refuge. Activities/programs: docent programs, educational programs, volunteer programs. Facilities: bookstore, exhibit space/gallery, lecture hall. Collection focus: ecology, zoology.

California mountain lion

As part of the Mountains Educational Program, which provides hands-on environmental education, the Sooky Goldman Nature Center features exhibits about the use and conservancy of water and ways to save energy. Dioramas depict scenes from the everyday life of the Indians of central and southern California. On display are many mounted animals, including the California mountain lion; mammal skeletons; pine cones and birds' eggs commonly found in Franklyn Canyon.

The Mountains Educational Program also organizes 2-hour nature walks that utilize games and activities to convey ecological concepts, increase awareness of and sensitivity to nature and incorporate cultural history.

George Bernard Shaw by Auguste Rodin from the Beverly Hills City Library Art Collection

❹ Beverly Hills City Library — Art Collection

444 N Rexford Dr, Beverly Hills, 90210. ☎ (310) 288-2201. Fax: (310) 278-3387. Thomas Guide: 632 G1. Hours: Mon-Thu 10am-9pm, Fri-Sat 10am-6pm, Sun noon-5pm. Closed: holidays. Ⓢ free. Ⓟ free. Governing authority: municipal. Category: library with collection other than books. ♿ parking, wheelchair accessible. Collection focus: modern and contemporary art.

A small collection of sculptures, paintings, prints and photographs is housed in various parts of the library. There are over 30 works on display, including: "DNA" Molecule by Claire Falkenstein; Marble Sculpture by Jean Arp; Monumental Torso of the Walking Man by Auguste Rodin; and Spring Dance by John Matthew Richen.

❺ Beverly Hills Historical Society

444 N. Rexford Dr, Beverly Hills, 90210-4877. ✉ PO Box 1919, Beverly Hills, 90213. ☎ (310) 246-1914. Thomas Guide: 632 G1. Hours: by appointment only. Ⓢ N.A. Ⓟ free. Membership: available. Year founded: 1984. Primary focus: recording, collecting and preserving that which is pertinent to the history of Beverly Hills. Research fields: history of Beverly Hills. Publications: The Illustrated History of Beverly Hills. Governing authority: private, nonprofit. Category: history museum. Activities/programs: changing exhibitions, events, guided tours, lectures. Facilities: audiovisual holdings, photo archive. ♿ parking, wheelchair accessible. Collection focus: local history.

The historical society, located on the second floor of the Beverly Hills Public Library, maintains an archival collection of early photos, films, maps, records and documents related to Beverly Hills. A display case on the main floor of the library exhibits various items from the collection.

Beverly Hills City Hall. Photograph in the Beverly Hills Historical Society collection.

⑥ Beverly Hills Cactus Garden

Santa Monica Blvd, between Camden Dr and Bedford Dr. ✉ 455 N. Rexford Dr, Beverly Hills, 90210. ☎ (310) 285-2537. **Thomas Guide:** 632 F1. 🚌 bus. **Hours:** open daily. **Closed:** never. 💲 free. P street parking. 📷 allowed. **Founded:** mid-1930s. **Governing authority:** municipal. **Category:** botanical garden/arboretum. **Garden features:** desert garden. **Collection focus:** botany.

Beverly Hills Cactus Garden

Dragon's blood tree, bear grass tree, century plant, yucca, Indian pencil plant, night-blooming cereus and a variety of cacti and succulents grow in this small garden (just over one-half acre) along the northern edge of Santa Monica Boulevard.

⑦ My Jewish Discovery Place

5870 W Olympic Blvd, Los Angeles, 90036. ☎ (213) 857-0036, ext. 2257. **Fax:** (213) 937-9426. **Thomas Guide:** 633 B3. 🚌 bus. **Hours:** Wed & Sun 12:30pm-4pm; group hours: Tue & Thu 10am-noon, Sun 9:30am-11am. 💲 $7 adults and children over 7, $2 children 2-7; free for children under 2. **Reservations:** necessary for groups. P free. 📷 with permission only. **Membership:** available. **Year founded/opened:** 1992. **Primary focus:** to

Giant Torah scroll (7 ft x 16 ft)

offer adults and children a unique opportunity to discover jointly the wonders of their Jewish heritage. **Governing authority:** Jewish Community Centers of Greater Los Angeles. **Category:** children's museum. **Activities/programs:** changing exhibitions, classes/courses, concerts, docent programs, educational programs, events, internships, lectures, outreach programs, school programs, storytelling, summer programs, volunteer programs, workshops. **Facilities:** gift shop. ♿ strollers permitted, parking, sign-language interpretation. **Collection focus:** Judaica.

Housed on the top floor of the Westside Jewish Community Center, this museum was developed for children 3-11 years old and their families to learn through its interactive displays about Jewish history, tradition, religion, customs and folklore.

Among the museum's hands-on exhibits are "A Walk Back in Time," a re-creation of Sephardic communities in Spain in the early 1400s; "People Helping People"; a miniature model synagogue; and "The Many Faces of Israel," with a costume center and life-size dolls of children from Israel.

⑧ Simon Wiesenthal Center's Museum of Tolerance

9786 W Pico Blvd, Los Angeles, 90035. ☎ (310) 553-9036. **Recorded information:** (310) 553-8403. **Fax:** (310) 553-4521. **Thomas Guide:** 632 F4. 🚌 bus. **Hours:** Mon-Thu 10am-5pm (last tour), Fri 10am-1pm (last tour), Sun 11am-5pm (last tour). **Closed:** Sat, major and Jewish holidays. 💲 $8 adults, $6 seniors, $5 students, $3 children. **Reservations:** recommended for groups. P free underground. 📷 not allowed. **Membership:** available. **Year founded:** 1977. **Year opened:** 1993. **Primary focus:** the dynamics of racism and prejudice in America, and the history of the Holocaust. **Major exhibitions:** "Abram Games: The War Posters" (1994); "Appeal to This Age: Photography of the Civil Rights Movement, 1954-1968" (1994). **Governing authority:** nonprofit. **Category:** history museum. **Activities/programs:** changing exhibitions, classes/courses, docent programs, educational programs, films, guided tours, multimedia presentations, school programs, storytelling, traveling exhibitions. **Facilities:** audiovisual holdings, bookstore, cafeteria/restaurant, exhibit space/gallery, gift shop, library, sculpture garden, theater. ♿ strollers permitted, parking, sign-language interpretation, wheelchair accessible; tour for the hearing impaired 1st Mon of each month at 4pm. **Collection focus:** modern history; Judaica.

Beth Hashoah Museum of Tolerance

Civil rights wall

This $50-million experiential museum was founded to increase awareness of bigotry and racism in American life and to present the Holocaust in both historic and contemporary contexts. It enables visitors to witness the

World War II and Anti-Semitism. Touch-screen technology helps visitors browse through 5,700 entries; 57,000 photos; film and video clips; maps; music and documents.

The library and archival collection contains 10,000 original documents, tens of thousands of photographs, over 1,500 artifacts and memorabilia, rare books and more than 350 original works of art. Collection highlights include Anne Frank's original letters; medical instruments used for experiments on inmates; original bunk beds from the Majdanek death camp; a passport issued by Raoul Wallenberg; and a rare piece of 17th-century anti-Jewish propaganda, *Entdecktes Judenthum*

Collection of artifacts

horrors of recent history through high-tech exhibits, hands-on computer stations, interactive displays, graphics, films and video.

The museum is divided into several major areas, starting with the Tolerancenter, with its 35 exhibits focusing on hatred and intolerance in everyday life. It features "Timeline: Understanding the Los Angeles Riots"; the "Other America" exhibit, with documentation and location of 250 hate groups in the United States; the Whisper Gallery, for experiencing

insults and name-calling; and a multimedia presentation on a 16-screen video wall titled "Ain't You Gotta Right?" about the struggle for civil rights in America.

Holocaust exhibits occupy the larger part of the museum's permanent display. Among the highlights are a reconstruction of a street in prewar Berlin; an exhibit illustrating the Wannsee Conference, where fourteen Nazi leaders planned "The Final Solution of the Jewish Question" and the Hall of Testimony, where visitors can see and hear stories of Holocaust survivors.

The multimedia learning center consists of 30 workstations that provide access to information and historical data on the Holocaust,

Replica of the gates of Auschwitz

(Judaism Unmasked), which is believed to have influenced Hitler in his anti-Semitic policies.

Cafe street scene

Plan of the Sobibor death camp

⑨

Martyrs Memorial and Museum of the Holocaust

6505 Wilshire Blvd, Los Angeles, 90048-4906. ☎ (310) 852-3242. **Fax:** (310) 951-0349. **Thomas Guide:** 633 A2. 🚌 bus. **Hours:** Mon-Thu 9am-5pm, Fri 9am-3pm, Sun 1pm-5pm. **Closed:** Sat. 💲 free. **Reservations:** recommended for groups. Ⓟ available (with validation). 📷 allowed. **Membership:**

The Torah scroll, produced in Czechoslovakia in 1830

available. **Year founded/opened:** 1978. **Primary focus:** to memorialize the victims of the Holocaust and to educate people of all ages about this unprecedented period of history. **Research fields:** Holocaust. **Major exhibitions:** "Anne Frank in the World" (1985); "In the Shadow of the Holocaust" (1988). **Publications:** *Viewer's Guide to Schindler's List; Zachor,* quarterly newsletter. **Governing authority:** Jewish Federation Council of Greater Los Angeles (nonprofit). **Category:** history museum. **Activities/programs:** changing exhibitions, docent programs, educational programs, films, gallery talks, guided tours, installations, lectures, outreach programs, school programs, traveling exhibitions, workshops. **Facilities:** cafeteria/restaurant, exhibit space/ gallery, research library. ♿ parking, wheelchair accessible. **Collection focus:** modern history, Judaica, personal history.

Founded by Holocaust survivors, the museum is located on the first two floors of the Jewish Community Building. Devoted to the history of the Holocaust and the modern phenomenon of genocide, this collection illustrates the destruction of European Jews through historical documents, artifacts, memorabilia, artworks and multimedia exhibits.

The permanent photo-narrative exhibits on the first level begin with the history of German Jewry up to 1933 and proceed through events and movements (such as National Socialism, the myth of racial purity, anti-Semitism, the Nazi policy toward the Jews, the establishment of ghettos and the deportation to death camps) that culminated in the Nazi's Final Solution. There is an exhibit recounting the story of the Warsaw Ghetto uprising, when 7,000 Jews died during the revolt and the survivors were immediately deported to the Treblinka death camp. Another exhibit focuses on the medical experiments conducted by Nazis on concentration camp inmates (over 7,000 men, women and children were used as guinea pigs in medical labs).

Video monitors show vintage newsreels from WWII, featuring themes such as the invasion of Europe, resistance, ghettoization, camps and rescue, along with oral testimonies from Holocaust survivors. There is a scale model of the Sobibor death camp, made by a victim who managed to escape.

Die Bonke by Eli Leskly

Second-level exhibits are devoted to the liberation of the camps and the Nuremberg trial. Highlights of the collection are Eli Leskly's watercolors of Terezin Ghetto life. Painted during his captivity and hidden under the floor boards of his barrack, these satiric cartoons were recovered after the liberation.

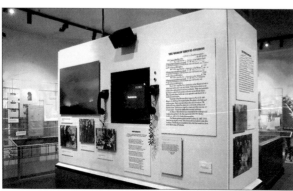

The Warsaw Ghetto Uprising exhibit

Carole and Barry Kaye Museum of Miniatures

Carole and Barry Kaye Museum of Miniatures

5900 Wilshire Blvd, Los Angeles, 90036. ☎ (213) 937-6464. **Fax:** (213) 937-2126. **Thomas Guide:** 633 B2. 🚌 bus. **Hours:** Tue-Sat 10am-5pm, Sun 11am-5pm. 💲 $7.50 adults, $6.50 seniors, $5 students, $3 children. **Reservations:** recommended for groups of 20 or more. P under building, lot across

Fontainebleau Palace

the street, limited metered and free street parking. 📷 not allowed. **Membership:** available. **Year opened:** 1994. **Governing authority:** private. **Category:** specialized museum. **Activities/programs:** artist's talks, audio guides, awards, changing exhibitions, classes/courses, competitions, inter-museum loans, lectures. **Facilities:** bookstore, gift shop, lecture hall. ♿ strollers permitted, parking, sound augmentation systems, wheelchair accessible. **Collection focus:** dolls and puppets, miniatures.

Trying to find ways to entertain her grandchildren, Carole Kaye started building and collecting dollhouses just a few years ago. Her hobby soon grew to more

than 100 exhibits displayed at the Petite Elite Gallery in Century City. With further acquisitions and commissions, it turned into the largest collection of contemporary miniatures assembled by a single individual in the world. This spectacular collection is now housed in the newly opened Carole and Barry Kaye Museum of Miniatures.

The museum features incredibly detailed and accurate exhibits, all true-to-scale (1/12 or less), spanning from the 4th century BC to the present day. Among the collection highlights are the rococo palace Fontainebleau, with 215 working lights and hand-done paintings, created by London-based miniaturist Kevin Mulvaney; Susan Hendrix's China Shop, with a golden Buddha and numerous vases and sculptures; and Peter Brown's Soda Shop by Bill Lankford, a re-creation of a turn-of-the-century soda fountain, with minuscule silver spoons. There is

a miniature Hollywood Bowl complete with representations of Louis Armstrong and his orchestra, as well as Ella Fitzgerald, Nat King Cole and Sarah Vaughan; a stately Southern mansion, with a fabulous wedding in the ballroom; and a magnificent Japanese Royal Palace.

The Kupjack Gallery displays 16 works by renowned artists Eugene and Henry Kupjack, including a banquet hall from Domus Augustana, Emperor Domitian's ca. 100 AD state residence, and the French Empire Salon, complete with rare wood inlays reflecting the imperial tastes of Napoleon I.

The George Stuart Gallery features 18-inch-tall historical figures, including Marie Antoinette, Mme Pompadour, Katherine the Great and King Charles II, among others. There is a collection of Galia Bazylko's 44 First Ladies, from Martha Washington to Nancy Reagan, each with exact replicas of their original inaugural ballgowns. Antique automobiles on display include a 1933 Duesenberg Twenty Grand, a 1925 Rolls-Royce Silver Ghost and a 1985 Lamborghini Countach 5000S.

Louis XIV by George Stuart

An authentically decorated room at the Fontainebleau Palace

Petersen Automotive Museum

ECO Tireflator

⓫
The Petersen Automotive Museum

6060 Wilshire Blvd, Los Angeles, 90036. ☎ (213) 930-CARS. **Fax:** (213) 930-6642. **Thomas Guide:** 633 B2. 🚌 bus. **Hours:** Tue-Sun 10am-6pm. **Closed:** Mon, except holidays; Thanksgiving; Christmas and New Year's Day. 💲 $7 adults; $5 seniors and students; $2 ages 5-12; children under 5 free. **Reservations:** recommended for groups, call (213) 964-6356. 🅿 $4 security parking in the attached garage. 📷 for personal use only; no flash. **Membership:** available. **Year opened:** 1984. **Primary focus:** dedicated to collecting, preserving and interpreting the role of the automobile and its technology in shaping American culture. **Governing authority:** county. **Category:** specialized museum. **Activities/programs:** changing exhibitions, educational programs, guided tours, school programs. **Facilities:** bookstore, cafeteria/restaurant, exhibit space/gallery, gift shop. ♿ parking. **Collection focus:** transportation, vehicles.

Opened in 1994 as a member of the Natural History Museum of Los Angeles County, the Petersen Automotive Museum is the largest and most innovative automotive museum in the world. The $40 million facility, designed by Marc Whipple of the Russell Group, encompasses over 300,000 square feet of what was once the Ohrbach's department store building. The museum is named after Robert E. Petersen, chairman and founder of Petersen Publishing Company, a leading publisher of specialized magazines and books, including *Hot Rod* and *Motor Trend*, among the world's largest automotive magazines.

The museum recounts the history of the automobile and its link to Los Angeles, the only major city in the world to be almost entirely shaped by the automobile. Through its multitheme exhibits, it traces the evolution of the car

1932 Duesenberg, Model J Roadster Murphy

culture through the 20th century and its influence on the city, the country and the rest of the world.

The idea behind the museum's unconventional planning was not just to exhibit vintage cars (although there are more than 200 vehicles on display at any given time), but to relate the automobile to everyday life. The visitor's unusual experience is enhanced by the astonishing sights, sounds and smells of the galleries.

Each of the 30 permanent exhibits of the first floor's "Streetscape" is organized around one of five underlying themes.

The first, "How People Travel," is devoted to the evolution of cars and the road and freeway system, showing how the development of trolleys and other transportation alternatives led to competition between the automobile and mass transit. The second theme, "How People Live," shows settlement patterns and domestic life in southern California, with examples of houses with attached garages from the 1920s through the late 1950s. "How People Consume" is the third theme. It covers new forms of businesses and buildings developed in response to specific demands created by the automobile, such as a new-car showroom, modeled after a dealership on Hollywood Boulevard in 1932. The fourth theme, "How People Have Fun," features recreational touring, the pursuit of speed and drag racing. The fifth theme, "The Public Cost of Private Transportation," shows how the automobile stimulated the construction of roads and bridges and generated the creation of new government agencies, such as the California Highway Patrol and the Department of Motor Vehicles. A separate section covers the history of Los Angeles and its growth from an outpost at the end of the continent to one of the world's leading cities.

LA Autotude depicts bizarre and eccentric cars seen on the streets of Los Angeles

Case Study: Mazda RX-7. One of 16 design studios open by major car manufacturers in southern California.

Alternative Propulsion. The 1989 Solar Eagle built by Cal State Los Angeles student engineers.

The Petersen Automotive Museum

1st Floor

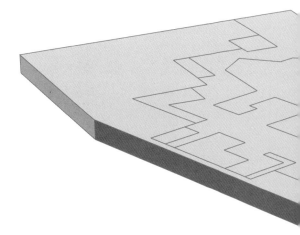

Stutz Racer. Earl Cooper's 1915 "White Squadron" racer shown on the Playa del Rey board track.

California Highway Patrol. An officer and his 1934 Harley Davidson hidden behind an authentic billboard.

Dog Cafe. Scale model of the 1928 roadside landmark.

A classic scene from the 1930 movie *Hog Wild* shows Laurel and Hardy trapped in a Ford Model T crushed between two trolley cars in central Los Angeles.

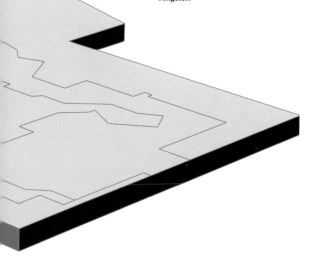

Wrecked Car. This safety exhibit features a wrecked 1993 Toyota Supra with deployed air bags.

Richfield Gas Station. A full-scale replica of a 1929 service station.

1985 Lola T900

"suitcase car." Also on display is a 1957 BMW 507. Industrial designer Raymond Loewy had this BMW built by Pichon et Parat of Sens, France for his personal use.

The Otis Chandler Motorcycle Gallery recounts the history of motorcycles, ranging from the 1903 Orient and the1916 Excelsior to the 1993 Gilera. Highlights include the motorcycle of world champion motocross racer Jeremy McGrath and other bikes frequently seen in California, such as the 1962 Harley Topper.

The third floor is devoted to art and education, containing galleries, a library and classrooms. Galleries feature changing exhibitions of works by famous artists, architects and photographers who were inspired by the automobile.

The second floor is divided into five large galleries that feature rotating exhibitions presenting the automobile as an object of art, design and technology. The exhibitions show classics, movie cars, early motorcycles, race cars, prototypes, technology, design and marketing.

The Hollywood Gallery displays "cars-of-the-stars" and "cars-as-stars." Among the automobiles on display that were owned by celebrities are the 1925 Lincoln originally owned by Greta Garbo, Joan Crawford's 1933 Cadillac and a 1956 Mercedes 300SC Coupe owned by Clark Gable.

Cars featured in movies and television include a 1920 Moon from *Lucky Chances* and 1963 Aston Martin DB5 Prototype, the original James Bond vehicle.

The second gallery covers automotive innovation, technology and styling, focusing on five selected time periods.

The third gallery offers changing exhibitions of world-famous car collections. The premiere exhibition featured

Mullin-Hull's private collection of 1930s and 1940s French luxury cars. The Bruce Meyer Gallery

Otis Chandler Motorcycle Gallery

presents concept, custom and dream cars of the last 40 years, including a 1963 Chrysler turbine car, a 1975 Dale and the 1994 Mazda

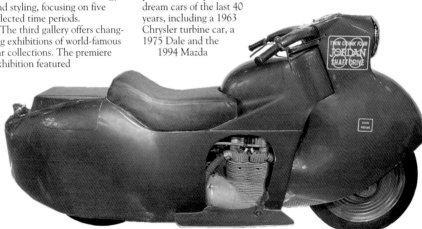

1947 Jordan, Twin Crank Four

The Craft and Folk Art Museum

⑫

The Craft and Folk Art Museum (CAFAM)

5800 Wilshire Blvd, Los Angeles, 90036. ☎ (213) 937-5544. **Fax:** (213) 937-5576. **Thomas Guide:** 633 C2. 🚌 bus. **Hours:** Tue-Sun 11am-5pm, Fri 11am-8pm. 💲 $4 adults; $2.50 students and seniors. 🅿 pay parking behind building; limited metered street parking. 📷 call for info. **Membership:** available. **Year founded:** 1972. **Year opened:** 1975. **Primary focus:** to study, preserve and celebrate cultural expressions through the objects people throughout the world use for everyday living — crafts, folk arts and design. **Publications:** over 30 catalogs. **Governing authority:** private, nonprofit. **Category:** art museum. **Activities/programs:** artist's talks, changing exhibitions, classes/courses, docent programs, educational programs, events (the annual Festival of Masks), gallery talks, guided tours, installations, inter-museum loans, internships, lectures, outreach programs, performances, retrospectives, school programs, slide presentations, storytelling, summer programs, traveling exhibitions, volunteer programs, workshops. **Facilities:** audio-visual holdings, giftshop, bookstore, research library, slide registry. ♿ elevator. **Collection focus:** crafts, folk art, masks, product design, textiles.

Rocker (1988) by Sam Maloof

CAFAM's permanent collection of over 3,000 objects comprises contemporary fine craft (fine art using craft media), folk art (culturally traditional arts), product design and masks from around the world. The folk art collection is representative of the variety of ethnic and cultural customs found in the immigrant and ethnic populations of Los Angeles. It features Hispanic (Mexican, Guatemalan, Bolivian) and Asian (Japanese, Chinese, Indian, Korean, Balinese) traditional objects.

Other portions of the folk art collection include toys, tools, basketry and dolls; 19th- and 20th-century textiles and costumes from India, Indonesia and Uzbekistan; Eastern European costumes; Guatemalan huipiles; and Amish and other American quilts. The museum possesses an impressive array of masks from Africa, Burma, China, Japan, Sri Lanka, Indonesia, Nepal, Italy, Finland, Mexico and Guatemala, and it includes some rare Korean masks.

The contemporary crafts collection emphasizes works by craftspeople living in and near Los Angeles, including fiber construction by Olga De Amaral, ceramic sculpture by Beatrice Wood, glass sculpture

Guitarron player by **Pedro Linares/Linares Family**

Ikebana basket, 19th century

by Richard Marquis and John Lewis, ceramics by Laura Anderson, wood and a leather jewelry box by John Cederquist, a pine needle basket by Sharon Robinson, and works by John Garett, Raoul Coronel and Melinda Farver. The collection highlight is a set of functional tableware consisting of wine goblets, water glasses, ceramic place settings, centerpiece, napkin rings and a program box. It was commissioned by Rosalynn Carter for the White House to honor American craftspeople.

The museum recently acquired an international industrial-design collection of lighting fixtures from Ron Rezek. A collection of utilitarian design products consisting of household items, tools and toys was donated by the Arango Design Foundation.

International Festival of Masks

View of LACMA's Anderson Building

Los Angeles County Museum of Art (LACMA)

5905 Wilshire Blvd, Los Angeles, 90036. ☎ (213) 857-6000 (general); (213) 857-6010 (tickets); (213) 857-6108 (tours); (213) 857-6139 (educational programs); (213) 857-6130 (handicapped). **TDD:** (213) 857-0098. **Fax:** (213) 931-7347. **Thomas Guide:** 633 B2. 🚌 bus. **Hours:** Tue-Thu 10am-5pm, Fri 10am-9pm, Sat-Sun 11am-6pm. **Closed:** Thanksgiving, Christmas and New Year's Day. 💲 $6 adults, $4 students and seniors, $1 children 6-17, free for children 5 and under; admission free to all on second Wed of every month. **Reservations:** necessary for school groups and for groups of 20 or more. [P] parking lot across the street, limited metered street parking. 📷 allowed for handheld film or video cameras. **Membership:** available. **Year founded:** 1910. **Year opened:** 1965. **Special collections:** the Nasli and Alice Heeramaneck Indian, the Nepalese and Tibetan Collection; the Heeramaneck Near Eastern Collection; the Heeramaneck Collection of Islamic Art; the John Wise Collection; the Phil Berg Collection; the Heeramaneck Far East Collection; the Arthur and Rosalinde Gilbert Collection; the Gilbert Collection of Post-Renaissance Mosaics; the B. Gerald Cantor

Collection; the David E. Bright Collection; the William Preston Harrison Collection; the Paul Rodman Mabury Collection; the George Gard de Sylva Collection; Kleiner Foundation Collection; Shin'enkan Collection. **Major exhibitions:** "Emil Nolde: The Painter's Prints" (1995); "Painting the Mayan Universe: Royal Ceramics of the Classic Period" (1994); "The Peaceful Liberators: Jain Art from India" (1994); "Italian Panel Painting of the Early Renaissance" (1994). **Publications:** At the Museum, monthly magazine; catalogs with most exhibitions; books: American Art; The Ahmanson Gifts; Rodin in His Time; Indian Painting; Indian Sculpture; Art of Nepal, etc. **Governing authority:** county. **Category:** art museum. **Activities/programs:** art rental gallery, audio guides, changing exhibitions, classes/courses, concerts, docent programs, educational programs, films, gallery talks, guided tours, inter-museum loans, outreach programs, performances, retrospectives, scholarships and fellowships, school programs, sketching, storytelling, summer programs, traveling exhibitions, volunteer programs. **Facilities:** audiovisual holdings, bookstore, cafeteria/restaurant, checkroom, conservation center, exhibit space/gallery, gift shop, lecture hall, research library, micro holdings, sculpture garden, slide registry, theater, visitor's center. ♿ strollers permitted, wheelchair accessible, restrooms. **Garden features:** Japanese garden. **Collection focus:** entire range of the history of art.

LACMA, one of the largest art museums in the United States, started as part of the Los Angeles County Museum of History, Science and Art, founded in 1910 in Exposition Park. The art collection was separated in 1965 and opened three years later at the present location, occupying three buildings designed by Pereira & Assoc. The museum

complex was enlarged by the addition of the Anderson Building in 1986 (Hardy Holzman Pfeiffer, architects) and the Japanese Pavilion in 1988 (Bruce Goff and Bart Prince, architects).

The Ahmanson Building features objects from a wide range of cultures as well as the permanent collection of paintings, sculpture, graphic arts, costumes, textiles and decorative arts. Special loan exhibitions are presented in the Hammer Building, which also contains the print, drawing and photography collections. The Robert O. Anderson Building houses 20th-century paintings and sculpture, along with special loan exhibitions. The Bing Center features the 600-seat Leo S. Bing Theater and the 100-seat Dorothy Collins Brown Auditorium. The Art Research Library, the William J. Keighley Slide Library and the Robert Gore Rifkind Center for German Expressionist Studies are also housed there. The Pavilion of Japanese Art contains the museum's impressive Japanese collection. The B. Gerald Cantor Sculpture Garden features bronzes by Auguste Rodin and his contemporaries, and the Director's Roundtable Sculpture Garden has large-scale contemporary sculptures.

LACMA's remarkable holdings of 250,000 works cover the entire range of the history of art. The collections are organized into ten curatorial departments.

The American Art Collection, covering the early-18th through late-19th centuries, is represented by John Singleton Copley's Portrait of a Lady (1771); the Neoclassical Portrait of Jacob Gerard (ca. 1827) by Rembrandt Peale; the realistic and sensitive Cotton Pickers (1876) by Winslow Homer; and Mother About to Wash Her Sleepy Child (1880) by Impressionist Mary Cassatt.

The Ancient and Islamic Art Collection contains examples of Egyptian, Near-Eastern, Greek and Roman, Islamic and Pre-Columbian art. Egyptian objects include tomb reliefs, small figures such as a ca. 1500 BC gilded-wood statuette of Osiris and a monumental quartzite royal head, possibly of King Nectanebo I

(380-362 BC). Greek and Roman works include The Hope Hygeia, a 2nd-century AD Roman copy of the Greek original; and a ca. 435 BC Greek red-figure neck-amphora attributed to the Hector Painter. Islamic art is represented by a ceramic bowl from Iran (9th-10th century), and a page from the *Diwan* of Sultan Husain Mirza, a fine example of Iranian calligraphy from the late-15th or 16th century. Pre-Columbian art is illustrated by the crouching figure of Man-Jaguar from the Olmec civilization (ca. 900-300 BC); numerous ceramic vessels, figures and gold masks are also displayed.

The Textiles and Costumes Collection, one of the largest in the United States, is made up of antique and modern textiles and period costumes, representing ancient Egypt, Persia, the Far East and Europe. Highlights include a burial mantle from Peru (300 BC-AD 300); the "Ardabil" carpet from Persia (1539) and an 18th-century emperor's silk hunting cape from China.

The Decorative Arts Collections include two great cathedral windows from 14th-century Le Mans; French Gothic chests; Italian Renaissance cassone and majolica; German glassware and Meissen; 18th-century French tapestries, furniture and Sévres; and English Jacobean furniture and porcelain. There is an outstanding collection of British silver, featuring the "lost" Methuen Cup, a silver-gilt Scottish piece from the 16th century. The American Collection includes early glass, silver and furniture dating from 1675 to 1820.

The European Painting and Sculpture Collection ranges from the early-14th through the late-19th centuries. Examples of early Italian Renaissance and Renaissance art include *Madonna and Child* (ca. 1465) by Jacopo Bellini, Titian's *Portrait of Giacomo Dolfin* (ca. 1531) and El Greco's *The Apostle Saint Andrew* (ca. 1600). Dutch and Flemish art of the 17th century is well represented with portraits, landscapes and genre scenes, including *Portrait of Marten Looten* (1632) by Rembrandt, *Landscape with Dunes* (1649) by Jacob van Ruisdael and *The Card Players* (1659) by Gerard Terborch. European painting and sculpture from the 19th century includes Jean François Millet's portrait *A Norman Milkmaid at Gréville* (1871) and Jean-Jacques Feuchère's bronze *Satan* (ca. 1850). Among the Impressionist and Post-Impressionist works are *The Bellelli Sisters* (1862-64) by Edgar Degas, *Place du Théâtre Français* (1898) by Camille Pissarro, *The Huntsman* (1910) by Renoir and *Still Life* (1883-87) by Paul Cézanne.

The Far Eastern Collections comprise works from China, Korea, Japan and Central Asia. The Chinese Collection spans 3,000 years and encompasses bronzes, pottery, porcelain, calligraphy and paintings. The Japanese Collection consists of paintings, sculpture, lacquer ware,

Japanese Pavilion

ceramics and textiles, along with painted screens and scrolls, and a splendid collection of netsuke (small ivory carvings).

The Collection of Indian and Southeast Asian Art is considered the finest in the Western world. It contains Indian stone and bronze religious sculpture, wood carvings, decorative arts, fascinating Mogul miniatures and many fine examples of Buddhist art from Nepal, Tibet and Cambodia, including sculpture, manuscripts and paintings.

The Photographs Collection includes works by both Europeans and Americans, including Alfred Stieglitz, Laszlo Moholy-Nagy, Clarence John Laughlin, Eileen Cowin and John Pfahl, among others.

The Prints and Drawings Collection is made up of representative etchings and woodcuts by Dürer and prints by Schongauer, Lucas Cranach, Mantegna, van Dyck and Goya. Important works include van Gogh's drawing *The Postman Roulin*, a watercolor *Strolling Players* by Eugène Delacroix and works by Toulouse-Lautrec, Modigliani, Rodin, Gauguin, Picasso, Matisse and Stuart Davis.

The Collection of 20th-Century Art includes works by Europeans, such as *Still Life with Violin* (1914) by Georges Braque; Picasso's *Portrait of Sebastan Juner-Vidal* (1903) and *The Treachery of Images* (ca. 1928) by Belgian Surrealist René Magritte. American art is represented by Mark Rothko's *White Center* (1957), Richard Diebenkorn's *Ocean Park Series No. 49* (1972) and Frank Stella's *St. Michael's Counterguard* (1984).

View of the Gerald Cantor Sculpture Garden

Los Angeles County Museum of Art (LACMA)

Ahmanson Building Lower Level

- [1] Early Chinese Art
- [2] Korean Art
- [3] Late Chinese Art

Plaza Level

- [4] Pre-Columbian Art
- [5] 20th-Century Ceramics
- [6] Early 20th-Century American Art
- [7] Late 19th-Century American Art
- [8] American Glass
- [9] Mid-19th-Century American Art
- [10] American Painting and Decorative Art
- [11] English Painting, Sculpture and Decorative Art
- [12] European Painting and Decorative Art
- [13] Gilbert Silver
- [14] Gilbert Mosaics
- [15] European Decorative Art

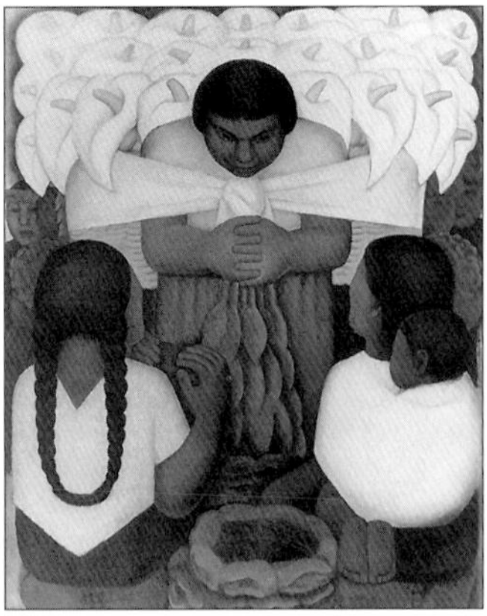

Flower Day (1925) by Diego Rivera

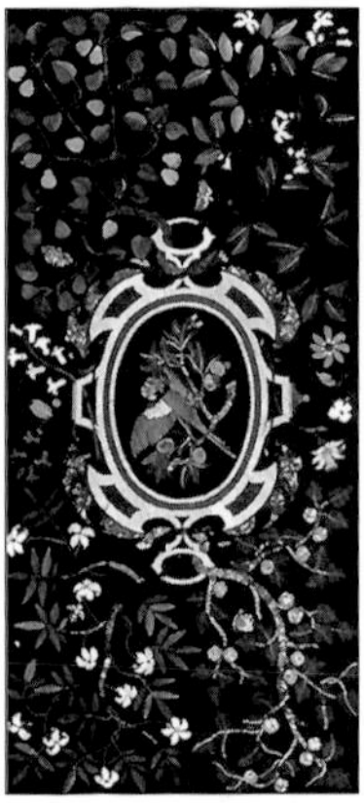

Tabletop with parrot. Italy, 17th century

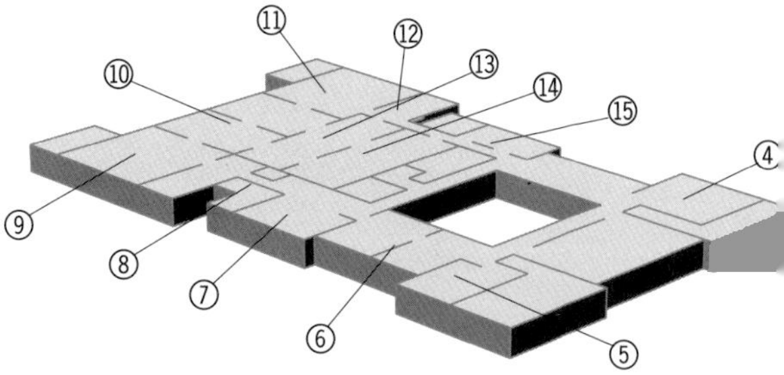

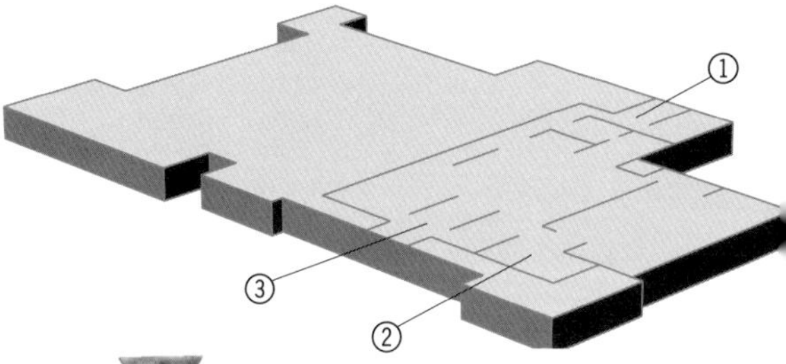

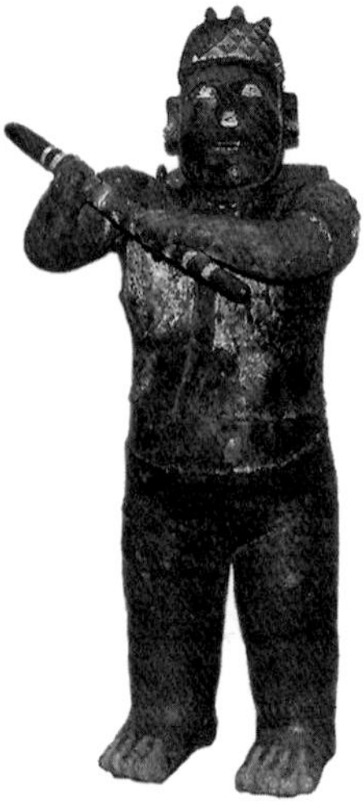

Standing Warrior. Mexico, ca. 200 BC-AD 500

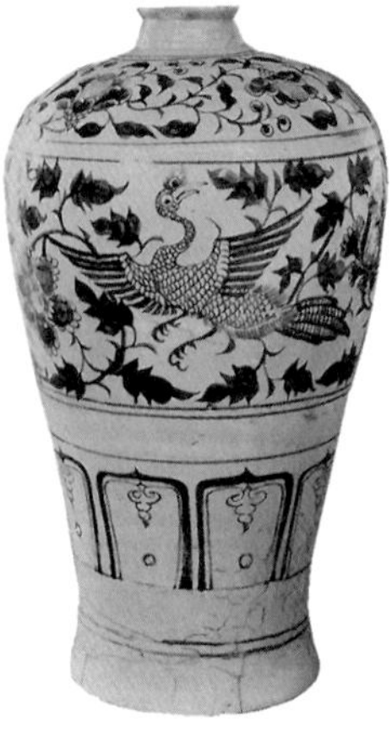

Mei P'ing Vase. China, Ming Dynasty (14th century)

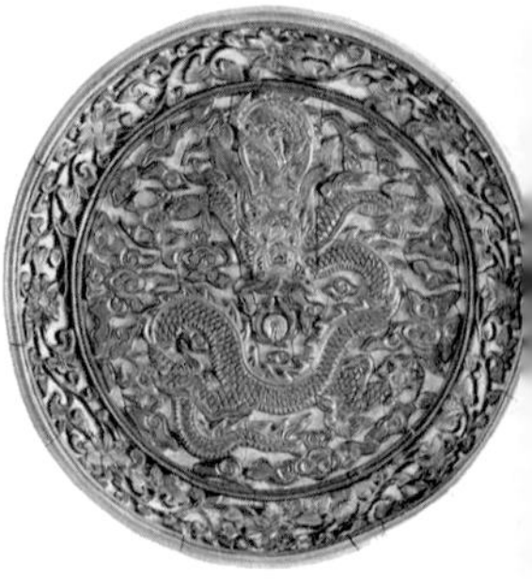

Circular dish. China, Ming Dynasty (1573-1619)

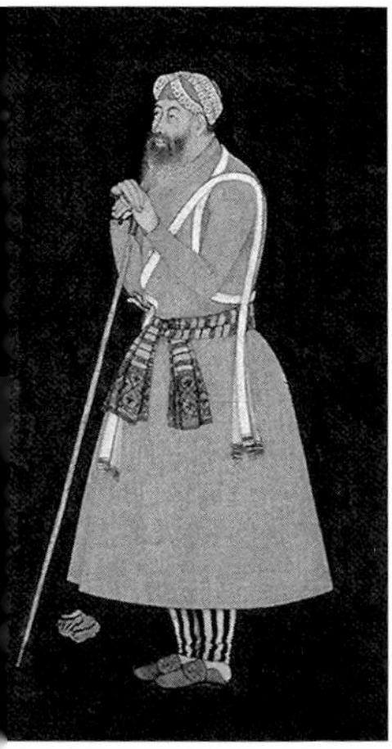

Mirza Rustam Safavi. Mogul, ca. 1635

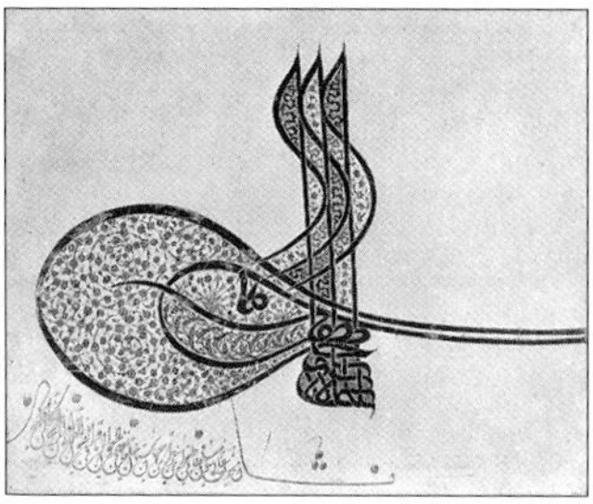

Tughra of Sulayman I. Turkey, ca. 1550

Ahmanson Building 2nd Level

1 Egyptian Art
2 Ancient West Asian Art
3 Art of Ancient Iran
4 Ancient Glass
5 Greek and Roman Art
6 Medieval European Art
7 Early Renaissance Art
8 Renaissance Art
9 Renaissance and Mannerist Art
10 Medals
11 European Decorative Arts
12 17th-Century Dutch and Flemish Art
13 18th-Century European Art
14 Early 19th-Century European Art
15 Romantics and Realists
16 19th-Century European Sculpture
17 17th-Century Spanish, Italian and French Art
18 Rodin Sculpture
19 European Glass

3rd Level

20 Costumes and Textiles
21 Islamic Art
22 Indian Painting and Decorative Arts
23 Himalayan Art
24 Southeast Asian Art
25 Indian Sculpture

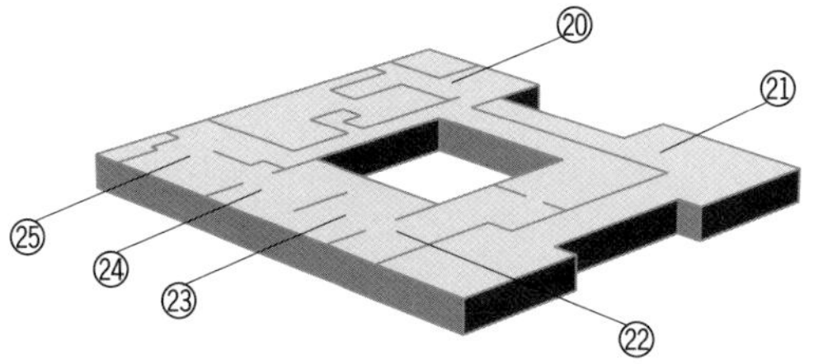

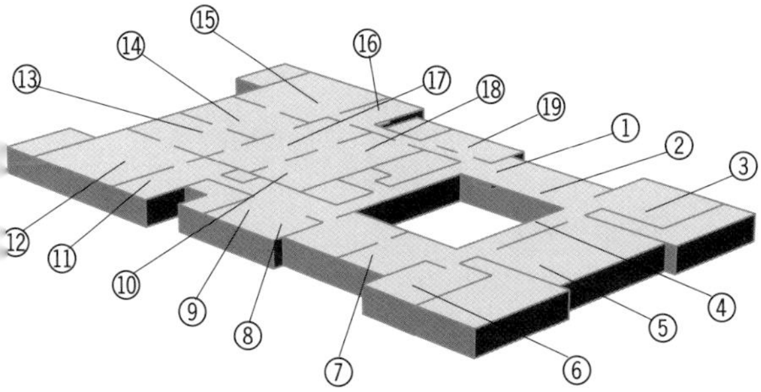

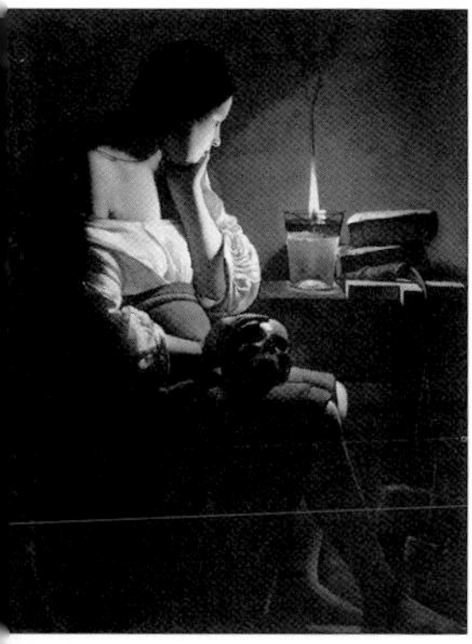

Magdalen with the Smoking Flame (ca. 1640) by Georges de La Tour

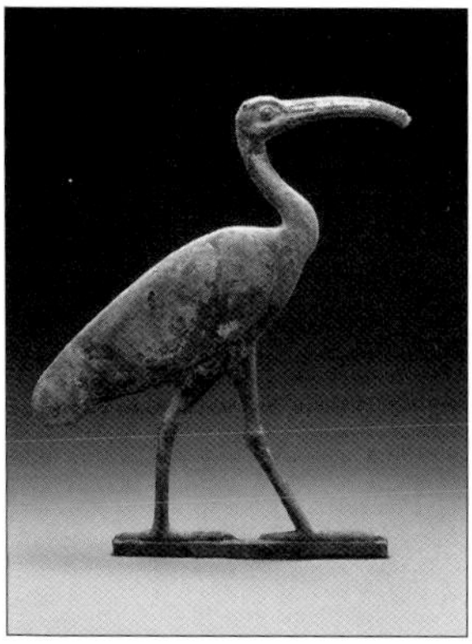

Ibis. Processional standard. Egypt, Late Period (712-332 BC)

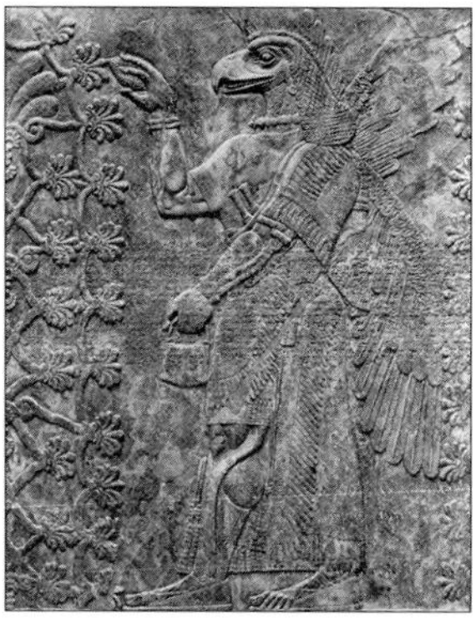

A Bird-Headed Deity Touches a Purifier to a Sacred Tree. Relief from the Palace of King Ashurnasirpal II of Assyria. Calah (now Nimrud, Iraq), ca. 870 BC.

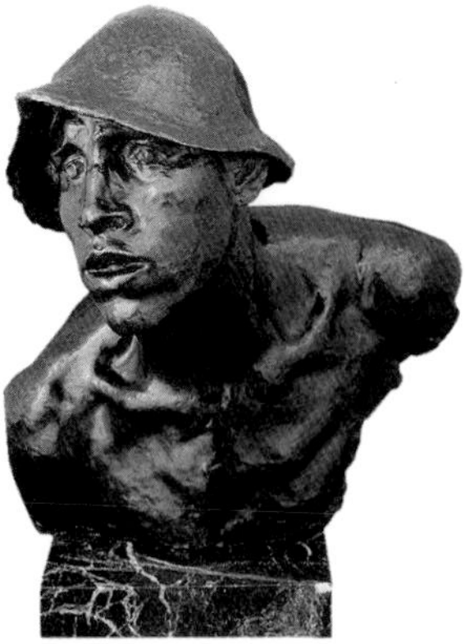

Bust of a Peddler (ca. 1895) by Constantin Meunier

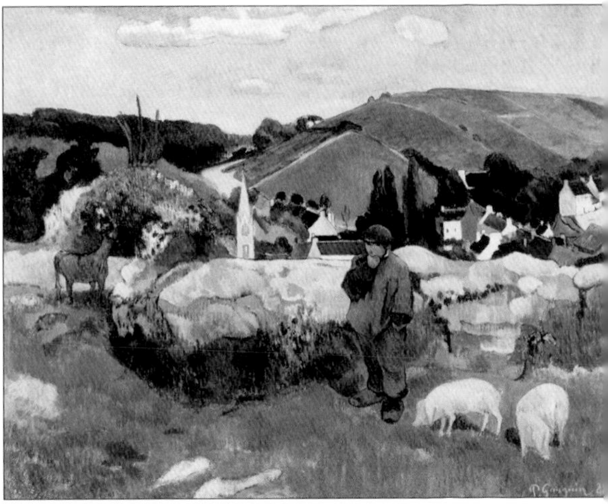

Swineherd, Brittany (1888) by Paul Gauguin

Los Angeles County Museum of Art (LACMA)

Hammer Building 2nd Level

1. Photography
2. Prints and Drawings
3. Impressionism and Post-Impressionism
4. Photography
5. Late 19th-Century European Art
6. German Expressionist Prints and Drawings

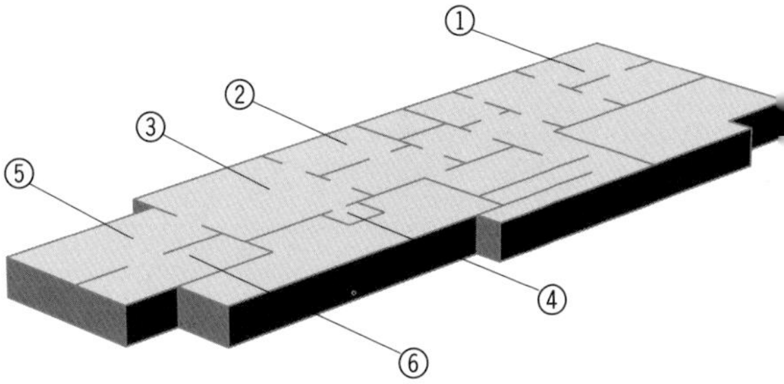

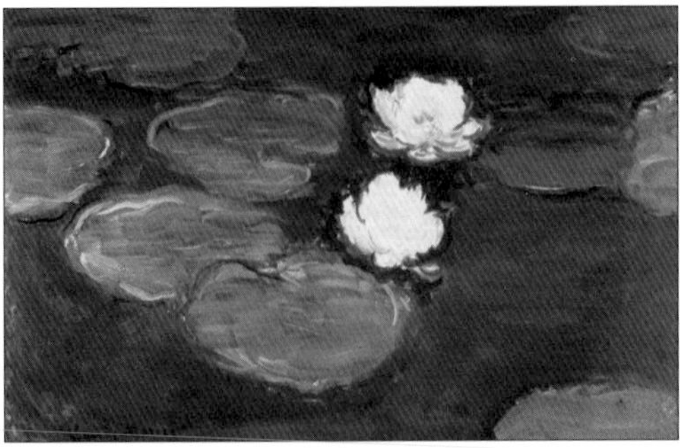

Water Lilies (1897-98) by Claude Monet

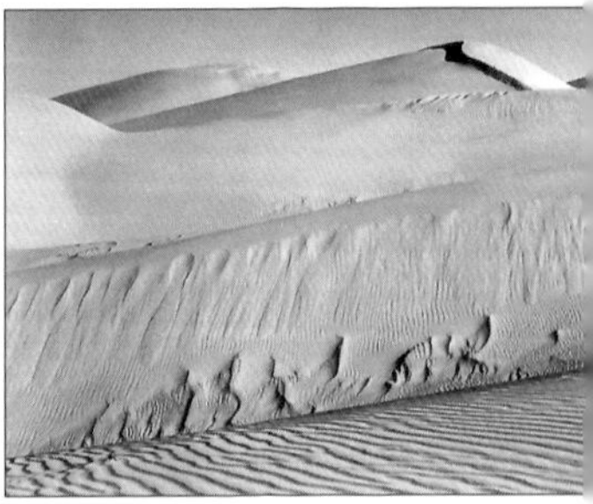

Dunes, Oceano (1936) by Edward Weston

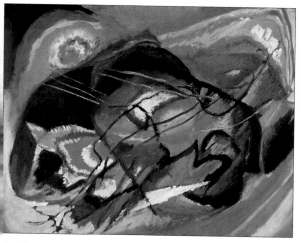

Untitled Improvisation III (1914) by Vasily Kandinsky

Young Woman of the People (1918)
by Amedeo Modigliani

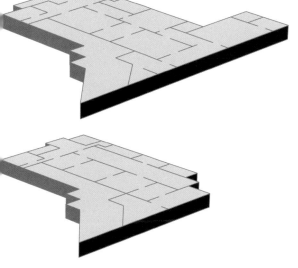

Anderson Building
2nd Level

20th-Century Art since 1960

3rd Level

20th-Century Art 1900-60

he Book (1985) by Anselm Kiefer

Video Flag Z (1968) by Nam June Paik

Los Angeles County Museum of Art (LACMA)

Japanese Pavilion

Plaza Level

① Netsuke Gallery

2nd Level

② Sculpture, Decorative Art and Textiles
③ Prints
④ Painting Galleries

Interior of Japanese Pavilion

Seated Warrior. Japan, Tumulus period (ca. 6th century)

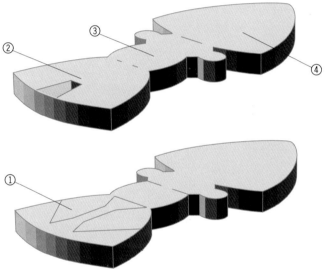

Mt. Fuji at Dawn (from "36 Views of Mt. Fuji") by Katsushika Hokusai

Vase. Japan, Kamakura period (13th-14th centuries)

14

George C. Page Museum of La Brea Discoveries

5801 Wilshire Blvd, Los Angeles, 90036. ☎ (213) 857-6311. **Recorded information:** (213) 857-6306. **Fax:** (213) 933-3974. **Thomas Guide:** 633 C2. 🚌 bus. **Hours:** Tue-Sun 10am-5pm. **Closed:** Thanksgiving, Christmas and New Year's Day. $ $6 adults, $3.50 students and seniors, $2 children 5-10 years old, free for children under 5. [P] parking lot behind the museum, metered street parking. 📷 flash and videos OK, battery operated only. **Membership:** available. **Year opened:** 1977. **Primary focus:** to exhibit fossils, plants and animals of extinct birds and mammals from the Rancho La Brea Tar Pits in Hancock Park. **Research fields:** paleontology, geology, biology, archaeology. **Publications:** *Rancho La Brea: Treasures of the Tar Pits* (1985); newsletter. **Governing authority:** county, nonprofit. **Category:** natural history museum. **Activities/programs:** classes/courses, docent programs, educational programs, films, guided tours, inter-museum loans, internships, lectures, outreach programs, school programs, summer programs, traveling exhibitions, volunteer programs. **Facilities:** audiovisual holdings, bookstore, gift shop, research library, picnic area, theater. ♿ strollers permitted, parking, wheelchair accessible. **Garden features:** atrium, labels/descriptions, restrooms, dogs allowed. **Collection focus:** North American archaeology and antiquities, biology, birds, bones, botany, fossils, geology, local history, insects, mammals, mollusks, prehistory, reptiles, zoology.

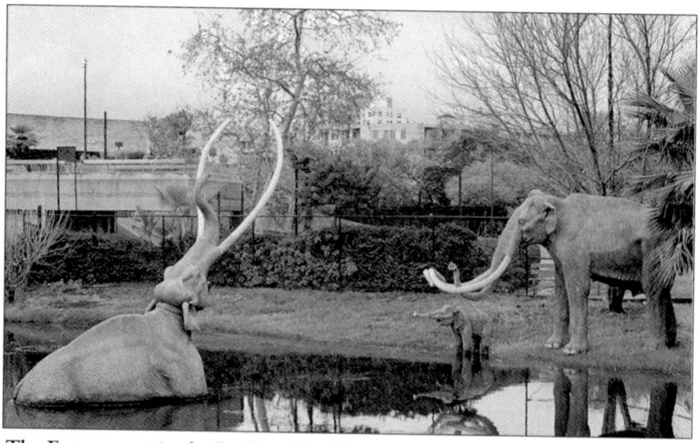

The Entrapment in the La Brea Tar Pits

The La Brea Tar Pits at Hancock Park is one of the world's richest Ice Age fossil sites. The tar (*brea* means tar in Spanish) is actually asphalt in which unwary animals were trapped. The fossils were preserved by asphalt impregnation over thousands of years, which caused the bones to turn a distinctive brown color. Most of the fossils were removed from the asphalt between 1906 and 1915, but digs continue to the present day. More than 625 species of animals and plants from more than 100 pits have been identified. The fossils found at La Brea are possibly the most perfect in the world, ranging in size from microscopic plants to giant mammoths.

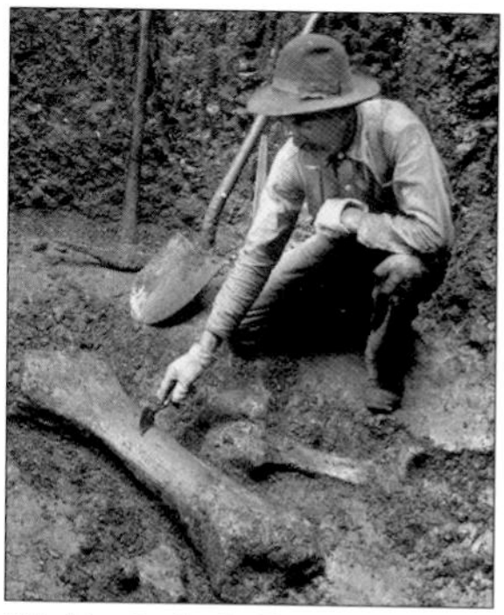

Working in the La Brea Tar Pits

Through its vivid exhibits, the George C. Page Museum of La Brea Discoveries illustrates life in the Los Angeles area during the Ice Age, some 4,000 to 40,000 years ago. The museum structure, designed by architects Willis Fagan and Frank Thornton, was built by entrepreneur and philanthropist George C. Page. It houses over one million prehistoric specimens recovered from the asphalt deposits in the Rancho La Brea tar pits. The museum features more than 30 exhibits, holographic displays, fossil storage areas and a glass-walled paleontology laboratory. Visitors can watch bones being cleaned, repaired, identified and sorted. *The La Brea Story*, an orientational film, and other films about dinosaurs are shown in two theaters.

Among the fossils on display are skeletons of many extinct species including Harlan's ground sloth, American lion, western horse, long-horned bison and saber-toothed cat. An exhibit of 404 dire wolf skulls is especially impressive. With over 3,600 individual skeletons recovered at La Brea, dire wolf is the most abundant find. Besides mammals, there are fossils of plants, pollen, seeds, leaves and small creatures such as insects, fish, frogs, snakes, turtles and birds. The remains of only one human have been recovered: a woman who lived about 9,000 years ago.

The museum is situated within the 23-acre Hancock Park, which features observation pits, sculptures of extinct animals and plants that grew during the last Ice Age.

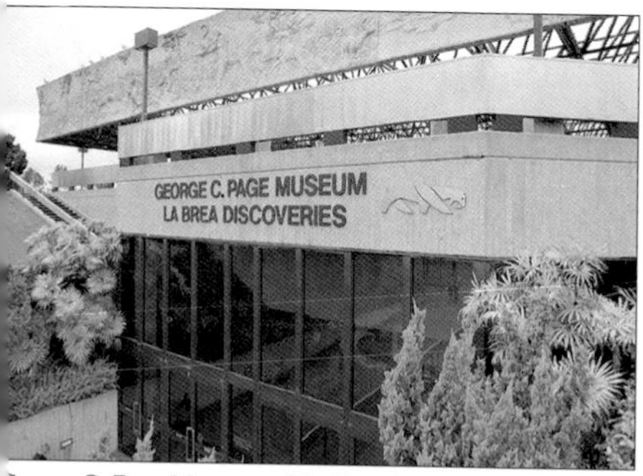

George C. Page Museum of La Brea Discoveries

George C. Page Museum of La Brea Discoveries

[1] Inner Courtyard
[2] Paleontology Laboratory
[3] Dinosaur Theatre
[4] Time Wall La Brea
[5] La Brea Story Theatre

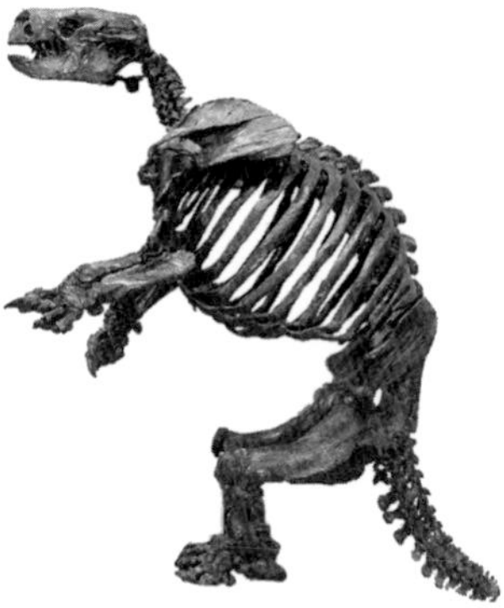

Harlan's ground sloth (*Glossotherium harlani*). Ground sloths are primitive mammals related to present-day armadillos and the small tree sloths of Central and South America.

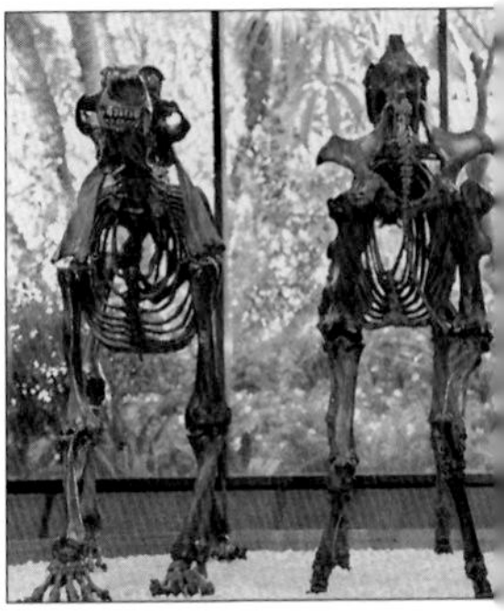

Western horse and short-faced bear exhibit

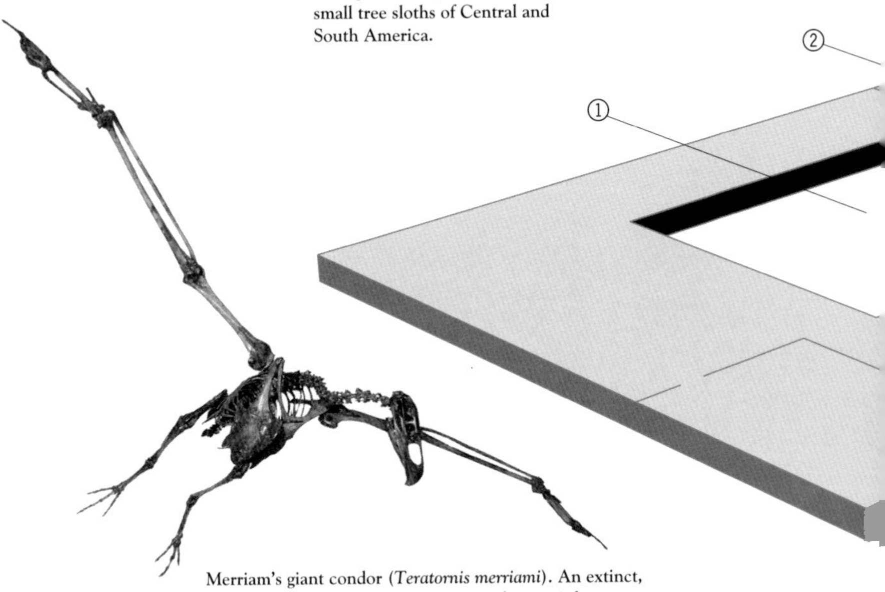

Merriam's giant condor (*Teratornis merriami*). An extinct, condorlike scavenger had a wingspan of over 12 feet.

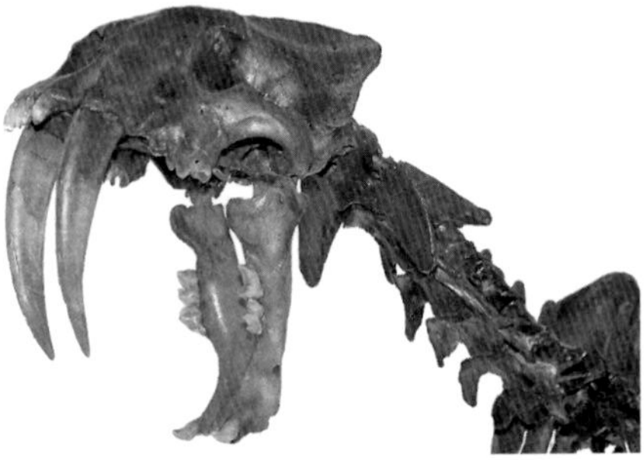

Skull of California saber-toothed cat (*Smilodon californicus*), the state fossil of California

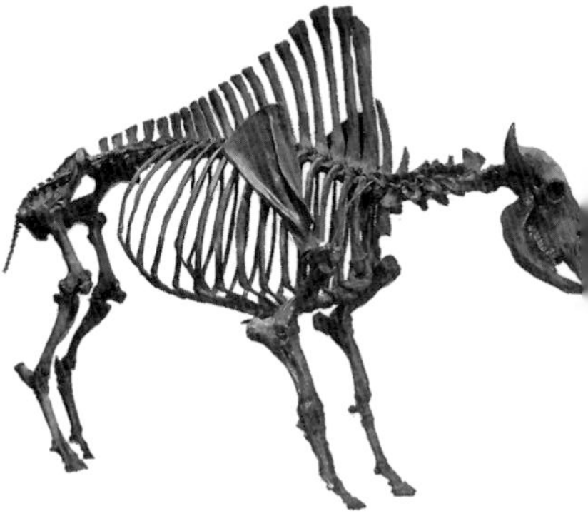

Antique bison (*Bison antiquus*), the most common plant-eater found at Rancho La Brea

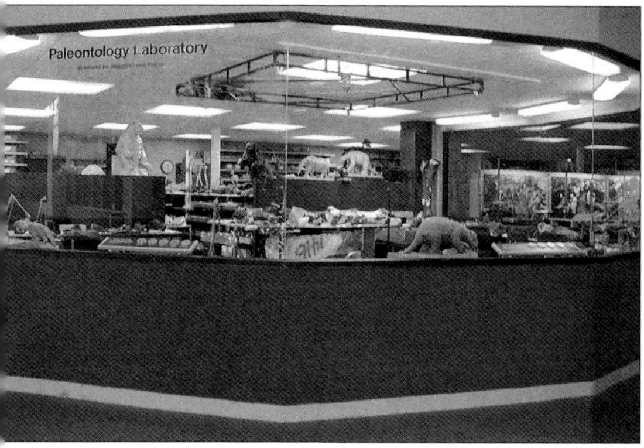

leontology laboratory

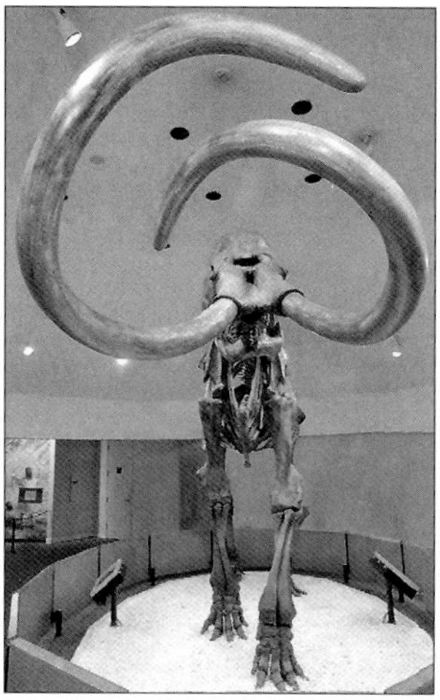

12-foot-tall skeleton of imperial mammoth (*Mammuthus imperator*), the largest of the elephants that lived in North America during the Ice Age

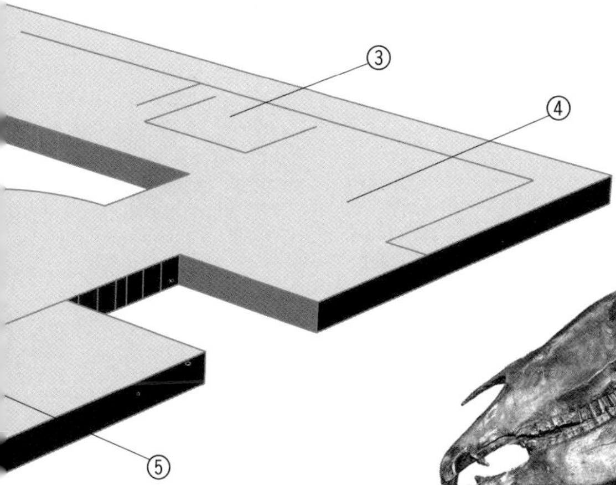

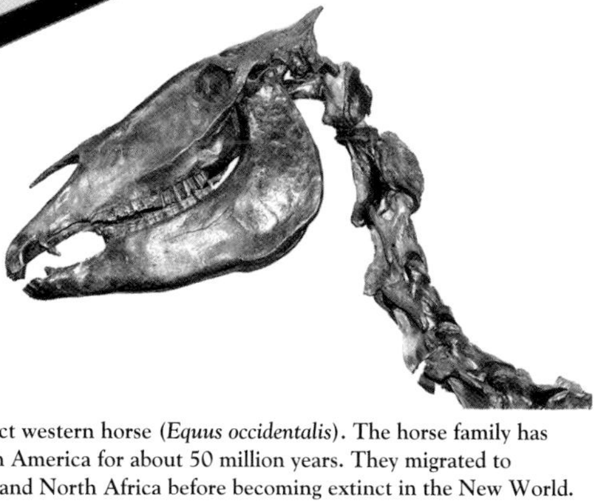

Skull of extinct western horse (*Equus occidentalis*). The horse family has lived in North America for about 50 million years. They migrated to Europe, Asia and North Africa before becoming extinct in the New World.

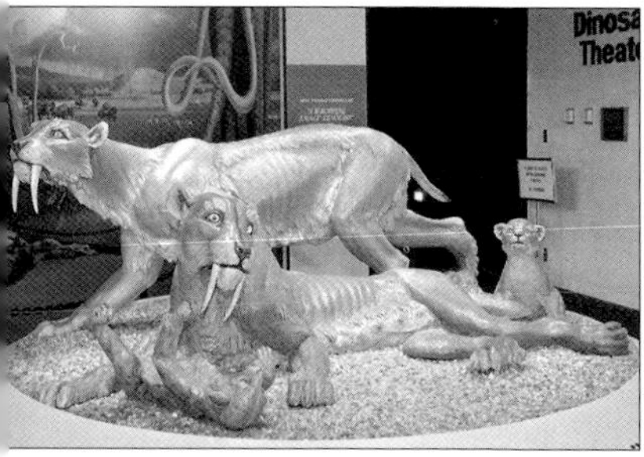

ber-toothed cat family

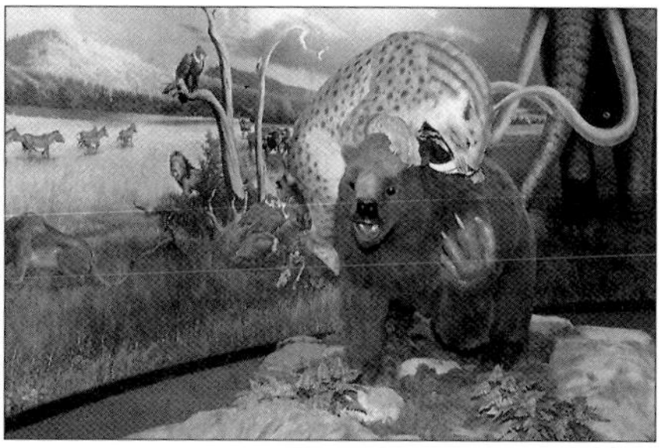

Saber-toothed cat attacking Harlan's ground sloth

15

Schindler House

835 N. Kings Rd, West Hollywood, 90069. ☎ (213) 651-1510. **Fax:** (213) 651-2340. **Thomas Guide:** 593 A6. 🚌 bus. **Hours:** Sat-Sun 1pm-5pm. **Closed:** major holidays. $ $5 for adults, free for children under 18. Admission free on Sep 10, May 24 and Dec 1. **Reservations:** required. [P] free on street. 📷 allowed. **Membership:** available. **Year founded:** 1922. **Year opened:** 1980. **Primary focus:** to preserve the Schindler House and operate it as a center for the study of 20th-century art, architecture and design. **Publications:** *R. M. Schindler House 1921-22.* **Governing authority:** private, nonprofit. **Category:** historic building/site open to the public. **Activities/programs:** changing exhibitions, docent programs, guided tours. **Facilities:** bookstore. ♿ strollers permitted, wheelchair accessible. **Collection focus:** architecture, furniture and interiors.

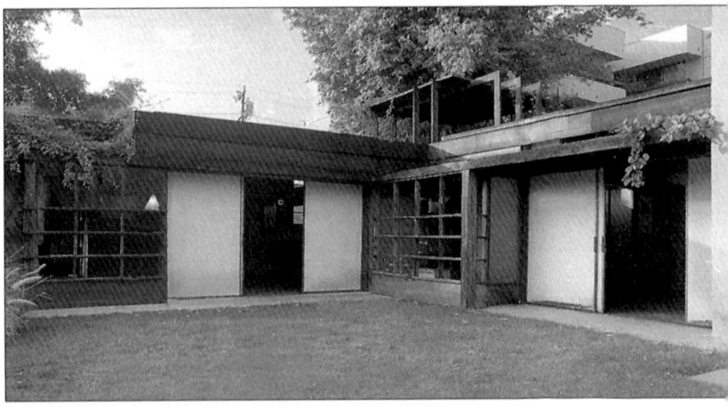

Schindler House, view from the east patio

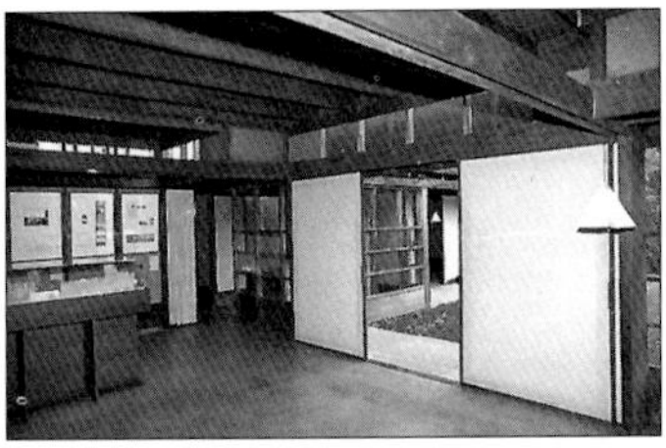

Sliding doors connecting patios and studios

Hidden behind a densely planted garden and almost invisible from the street stands the first house built in Los Angeles by architect Rudolph M. Schindler. Born and educated in Vienna, Schindler moved to the United States in 1914 to work as a draftsman in Chicago. After joining the office of Frank Lloyd Wright in 1918, he came to Los Angeles with his wife, Pauline, to supervise the construction of Hollyhock House. In 1921 he designed his own house, which was completed in 1922.

The unconventional design of the building manifests both Schindler's European and American experiences. While responding to the specific climate of California, it calls upon both Japanese and Hispanic traditions. Schindler's design was particularly influenced by a camping vacation in Yosemite, incorporating "the basic requirements for a camper's shelter: a protected back, an open front, a fireplace, and a roof." Planned as a group of four artist's studios, the house was shared by another couple, Clyde and Marian Chace, who were artists from Chicago. As Schindler wrote in a letter to Pauline's parents, the basic idea was "to give each person his own room — instead of the usual distribution — and to do most of the cooking at the table — making it more a social 'campfire' affair...."

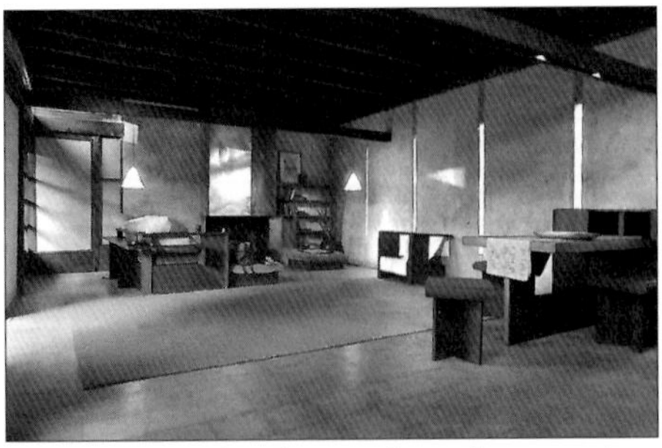

Sophie Pauline studio. The vertical space between each slab of the tilt-slab concrete wall is filled with glass.

The house was constructed of concrete, redwood and canvas. The integration of the building and the landscape make it arguably the most innovative residence in modern architecture. It features courtyards level with the concrete-slab floors of the studios, sliding doors, two open patios with outdoor fireplaces and flat roofs used as open sleeping porches.

After the Chaces moved from the house in 1924, Richard Neutra, a friend of Schindler's from Vienna, moved in with his family

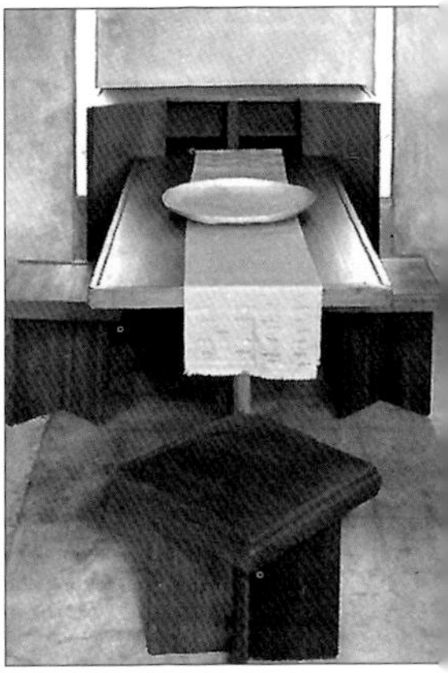

Original furniture by Rudolph Schindler

and stayed until 1930. During the following years the house was a meeting place for numerous artists, including painter Galka Scheyer, novelist Theodore Dreiser, photographer Edward Weston and composer John Cage. Schindler lived in the house until his death in 1953. After Pauline's death in 1977, a private, nonprofit organization called Friends of the Schindler House purchased the building and started a program of restoration. The house is on the National Register of Historic Places and is now operated by the MAK-Center for Art and Architecture, Los Angeles.

California Museum of Ancient Art

✉ PO Box 10515, Beverly Hills, 90213. ☎ (818) 762-500. **Hours:** no facility for exhibits at this time. ⓢ N.A. **Membership:** available. **Year Founded:** 1983. **Primary focus:** to collect, exhibit and educate the public about the art and cultures of the ancient Near East: Egypt, Mesopotamia and the Levant. **Research fields:** Egyptology, ancient Near Eastern studies, Biblical archaeology. **Major exhibitions:** one or two temporary exhibits per year. **Publications:** *Ancient News*, newsletter. **Governing authority:** nonprofit. **Category:** art museum. **Activities/programs:** educational programs, lectures, international archaeological tours. **Collection focus:** Egyptian archaeology and

Elamite black chlorite vase with two unicorn humped bulls in archetypal garden or riverbank setting. Elam, Sumerian Period, ca. 2250 BC

Coptic limestone relief of Apollo and Daphne. Sheikh Ibada, Egypt, Christian period, ca. 500 AD

antiquities, Middle and Near Eastern archaeology and antiquities.

Spanning the period from 3000 BC to 500 AD, the museum's unique collection consists of approximately 2,000 ancient artworks and artifacts from the cultures and people of Sumer, Babylon, Assyria, Hittite, Canaan, Israel, Judea, Philistine, Pharaonic Egypt and Coptic Egypt. Although the museum does not yet have a facility to display its holdings, plans for building a permanent home for these materials are under way. When the facility opens, the California Museum of Ancient Art will be the first museum of the ancient Near East in the western US. The museum plans to use modern audiovisual technology, with life-size, walkthrough environments that will allow visitors to directly experience past cultures with all of their senses.

Objects from Egypt in the collection include a limestone relief of a pharaoh, perhaps Ramses the Great, dating from the 19th Dynasty (ca. 1250 BC); a large, indurated limestone sarcophagus lid (ca. 300 BC); and a black granite block statue of a priest (ca. 400 BC). There is also a painted wooden sarcophagus of Namenkhamun, the young songstress of Amun, depicting scenes from *The Book of the Dead*, that dates from the 26th Dynasty (ca. 600 BC).

Egyptian indurated sandstone statue of Osiris, god of the afterlife. Egypt, New Kingdom, ca. 1300 BC

Syro-Hittite bronze statue of Baal Haddad, Old Testament god of war and weather. Syria or Anatolia, ca. 1300 BC

Sumerian culture is represented by a ca. 2500 BC alabaster head of a female orant and a black steatite head of a bull-man (ca. 2150 BC). There is a large Mesopotamian terracotta dog with a Kassite cross from about 1400 BC. Amazing finds from Assyria include a ca. 700 BC limestone relief fragment from King Sennacherib's monumental palace at Nineveh, showing two Elamite women captives approaching an Assyrian soldier. Other artifacts include a ca. 650 BC Phoenician shell carving of a goddess and a ca. 1200 BC Philistine temple libation vessel in the form of a woman.

Egyptian monumental limestone temple capital in the form of the head of Hathor, the cow-eared goddess of fertility. Egypt, ca. 300 BC

HOLLYWOOD

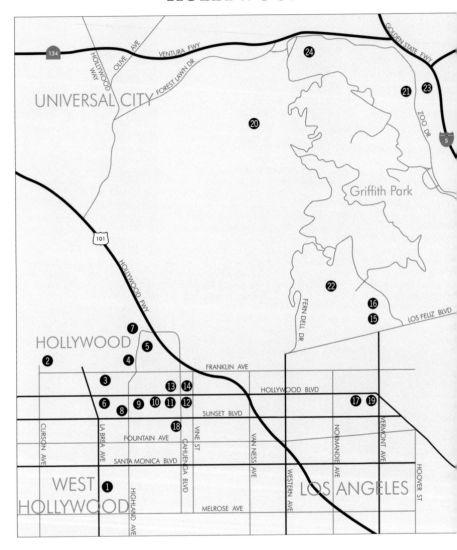

1. Mole-Richardson Moletown
2. Wattles Mansion
3. American Society of Cinematographers (ASC)
4. Freeman House
5. Hollywood Studio Museum
6. Hollywood Historical Review
7. Hollywood Bowl Museum
8. Hollywood High School Alumni Museum
9. Max Factor Museum of Beauty
10. Ripley's Believe It or Not!
11. Guinness World of Records Museum
12. Frederick's of Hollywood Lingerie Museum
13. The Hollywood Wax Museum
14. L. Ron Hubbard Life Exhibition
15. The Fantasy Foundation
16. Ennis-Brown House
17. Hollyhock House
18. Dr. Blyth's Weird Museum
19. International Child Art Collection (ICAC)
20. Forest Lawn — Hollywood Hills
21. Los Angeles Zoo
22. Griffith Observatory
23. Gene Autry Western Heritage Museum
24. Travel Town Transportation Museum

Type 214 5K Senior Solarspot (1935) and Type 218 2K-18" Sunspot (1927-31)

❶ Mole-Richardson Moletown

900 N La Brea Ave, Los Angeles, 90038-2384. ☎ (213) 851-0111. Fax: (213) 851-7854. **Thomas Guide:** 593 D6. 🚌 bus. **Hours:** Mon-Fri 11am-6pm, Sat 11am-5pm. **Closed:** holidays. Ⓢ free. Ⓟ free. 📷 allowed. **Year founded:** 1927. **Primary focus:** motion picture lighting. **Governing authority:** company. **Category:** company museum/corporate collection. **Facilities:** exhibit space/gallery, gift shop. **Collection focus:** lamps and lighting, motion pictures.

The Mole-Richardson Company was founded in 1927 by Peter Mole, an electrical engineer and developer of incandescent lighting used for motion-picture production. He also designed many electrical and mechanical devices still used in Hollywood Studios.

This small museum presents the history of the company through its displays of Solarspots, Sunspots, Handilamps, Spotlamps and other studio electrical equipment manufactured by the Mole-Richardson Company from the 1920s onward. There is also an exhibit of early movie and photography cameras. The museum gallery features early photographs of the company's shops and plants, along with scenes showing some of Mole-Richardson's lighting equipment used on major movie productions: Universal's *Broadway* (1929), Warner Bros' *The Desert Song* (1929), and 20th Century Fox's *Ladies in Love* (1936), among others.

❷ Wattles Mansion

1824 N Curson Ave, Los Angeles, 90046. ✉ PO Box 2586, Los Angeles, 90028. ☎ (213) 874-4005. **Fax:** (213) 465-5993. **Thomas Guide:** 593 C4. **Hours:** Mon, Wed, Fri noon-5pm; by appointment only. Ⓟ on street, metered. 📷 allowed. **Year founded:** 1907. **Primary focus:** preservation of architecture. **Parent institution:** Hollywood Heritage. **Category:** historic building/site open to the public. **Activities/programs:** events, volunteer programs. ♿ wheelchair accessible. **Collection focus:** architecture.

Wattles Mansion

Built in 1907 in the Hollywood Hills as a winter home for Omaha businessman Gurdon Wattles and his family, the estate is today the last remaining example of the lifestyle that prevailed in Hollywood's pre-movie years. The mansion was designed by Myron Hunt and Elmer Grey as a modified Mission Revival house, and it features beamed ceilings, elegant arches, hand-painted moldings and roof tiles.

The 49-acre grounds include a lawn, a public park, a community garden and a Japanese teahouse (not open to the public). The estate's extensive terraced gardens were a main tourist attraction in Hollywood's early years, and they are presently being restored.

❸ American Society of Cinematographers (ASC)

1782 N Orange Dr, Los Angeles, 90028. ✉ PO Box 2230, Los Angeles. 90078. ☎ (213) 969-4333. **Fax:** (213) 882-9361. **Thomas Guide:** 593 D4. 🚌 bus. **Hours:** weekdays 9am-5pm. **Closed:** holidays. Ⓢ free. **Reservations:** by appointment for groups. Ⓟ free. 📷 with permission. **Year founded/opened:** 1919. **Primary focus:** to promote the art of cinematography. **Special collections:** the Joseph Westheimer Collections, the Stephen Chamberlain Library. **Publications:** *American Cinematographer* magazine. **Governing authority:** nonprofit. **Category:** specialized museum. **Activities/programs:** awards, events. **Facilities:** available for rent; bookstore, research library. **Collection focus:** cameras, motion pictures.

The ASC is a honorary society of distinguished directors of photography. Chartered in 1919, it is the oldest continuously active film society in the world. ASC membership is conferred only by invitation and to those cinematographers whose body of work warrants recognition. Its headquarters is a 1902 Mediterranean-style mansion, the only remaining building of its kind in Hollywood. It houses the museum, which displays antique cameras, related items and movie memorabilia. Among the highlights are an 1891 Edison kinetoscope, the first motion picture machine to use 35 mm film; an 1896 Lumiere projector; an 1860 zoetrope; the original 1888 Kodak; and a 1909 mutoscope.

Magic lantern projector, England, turn of the century

Freeman House

❹
Freeman House

1962 Glencoe Way, Los Angeles, 90068. ☎ (213) 850-6278. **Recorded information:** (213) 851-0671. **Fax:** (213) 874-7392. **Thomas Guide:** 593 E3. **Hours:** Sat only, guided tours at 2 & 4pm. **Closed:** Christmas, Thanksgiving, New Year's Day. ⑤ $10 general, $5 students. **Reservations:** required for groups. Ⓟ free parking at Methodist Church (at Highland and Franklin) or on Hillcrest Dr. noncommercial only. **Membership:** available. **Year founded:** 1986. **Year opened:** 1989. **Primary focus:** to educate students, professionals and the public about the house's design and its architect, Frank Lloyd Wright, its historically accurate renovation, as well as restoration itself. **Research fields:** historic preservation, Frank Lloyd Wright, Rudolph Schindler. **Special collections:** household furnishings designed by Schindler as well as by Wright. **Governing author-**

Living room, south view

ity: college/university. **Parent institution:** School of Architecture, USC. **Category:** historic building/site open to the public. **Activities/programs:** classes/courses, directed research studies, events, guided tours, school programs, slide presentations, workshops. **Collection focus:** architecture, carpentry, decorative and applied arts, furniture and interiors, local American history, lamps and lighting, personal history.

This remarkable house was designed in 1923-24 as the third of four Frank Lloyd Wright structures in Los Angeles built in his textile-block construction method. It was an experiment in low-cost housing appropriate for the southwestern climate. The house was built for newlyweds Samuel and Harriet Freeman, members of Los Angeles's artistic circles. He was a jewelry salesman, and her inter-

ests included modern dance and social issues. Soon after construction, their home became the site of an avant-garde salon.

The 2-story house was constructed on a small and steep lot of some 12,000 solid and perforated concrete blocks cast on site. It contains some memorable spaces, including the living room that extends to the balcony, offering a spectacular view of Hollywood. The most astonishing features are the two-story mitered windows at each of the south corners, used for the first time in residential architecture.

Original furnishings in the living room consist of a pair of floor lamps (ca. 1924) and a small dining table (ca. 1924, later altered), by Wright; and a couch, library table and storage unit (ca. 1928); couch and shelving (ca. 1950) by Schindler. The bedroom suite in the master bedroom (ca. 1930) and the partition between the living room and kitchen (ca. 1928) were also designed by Schindler.

The house was donated to USC in 1986 by Harriet Freeman. It is designated as a City of Los Angeles Cultural Monument and listed on the National Register of Historic Places. (All four of Wright's concrete-block houses were designated as a single California State Historic Landmark.)

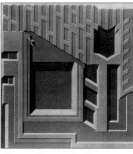

Freeman House 16-inch concrete block

Floor lamp designed by Frank Lloyd Wright (ca. 1924)

Two-story mitered corner window

Hollywood Studio Museum

[5]
Hollywood Studio Museum

2100 N Highland Ave, Los Angeles, 90068. ☎ (213) 874-2276. **Thomas Guide:** 593 E3. **Hours:** Sat-Sun 10am-4pm. $ $4 adults, $3 students and seniors, $2 children 6-12, children under 6 free. [P] Fairfield parking - free. 📷 no restrictions. **Membership:** available. **Year founded:** 1982. **Year opened:** 1985. **Primary focus:** silent film era, beginnings of film industry, Cecil B. De

Mary Pickford's make-up case

Mille, Jesse L. Lasky, Adolph Zukor, Samuel Goldwyn. **Research fields:** musical accompaniment to silent film, locations of silent film, studios. **Special collections:** the Albert Rosenfelder Still Collection. **Major exhibitions:** "Ten Commandments Set" (1993); "Hollywoodland" (1989); "Lon Chaney" (1988). **Publications:** *Shadowland*, annually. **Parent institution:** Hollywood Heritage. **Category:** historic building/site open to the public. **Activities/programs:** changing exhibitions, docent programs, films, lectures. **Facilities:** gift shop, library. ♿ wheelchair accessible. **Collection focus:** local American history, motion pictures.

The structure that houses the Hollywood Studio Museum was originally a 1895 horse barn on Jacob Stern's Lemon Ranch, located at Vine Street and Selma Avenue. Part of it was used to house a small film lab, Burns & Revier, when Cecil B. De Mille discovered it in 1913. After brief negotiations, he rented the hall, but the owner continued to keep his horses in the other half of the barn. De Mille, Jesse Lasky and Samuel Goldwyn used it as a set, office and dressing rooms for *The Squaw Man (1914)*, the first feature-length motion picture made by a major company in Hollywood. Its success made the Jesse L. Lasky Feature Play Company an industry leader. After the merger with Adolph Zukor's Famous Players Corporation, the structure was transferred in 1926 to the site of today's Paramount Pictures. It was declared California State Landmark No. 554, the first state landmark linked with the movie industry. In 1983 the barn was finally moved to its current site, where it was restored and opened as a museum.

Helmet worn in *Cleopatra* (1934)

The museum explores the early history of the movie industry in Hollywood through its displays of photographs, props, costumes and equipment. Among the exhibits are Beverly Bane's cape from *Romeo and Juliet* (1913), Rudolph Valentino's shirt from *Son of the Sheik* (1926) and Mabel Normand's 1930s trunk. The motion picture camera collection includes a 1908 Prestwich 35mm, a 1909 Williamson 35mm Tropical Model and the 1916 Karl Brown camera used to shoot *Intolerance*. On display is a 1917 Bell & Howell camera used by the Charlie Chaplin Studio until 1939. The "Double Cross" marks on the camera case are Chaplin's parody version of the Nazi swastika and indicate its use in *The Great Dictator* (1940). There is a 1913 Power Cameragraph projector, which used a dry-cell battery power source and a carbon arc light source. Also on display is the original painted furniture from Grauman's Egyptian Theater, built in 1922.

Chariot from *Ben Hur* (1926)

Camera used in *The Great Dictator*

Re-creation of Cecil B. De Mille's 1913 office

❻ Hollywood Historical Review

Hollywood Roosevelt Hotel, 7000 Hollywood Blvd, Los Angeles, 90028. ☎ (213) 466-7000. **Fax:** (213) 462-8056. **Thomas Guide:** 593 D4. 🚌 bus. **Hours:** daily. **Closed:** never. 🛈 free. P free on street, validated hotel parking. 📷 allowed. **Primary focus:** Hollywood of the 1930s and 40s. **Governing authority:** company. **Category:** specialized museum. **Facilities:** cafeteria/restaurant, gift shop. ♿ strollers permitted, parking, wheelchair accessible. **Collection focus:** motion pictures.

Hollywood Historical Review

The 12-story landmark building was designed in 1926 by architects Fisher, Lake and Traver. Named after Theodore Roosevelt, the 26th president of the United States, the hotel was a center of glamorous activity. In 1927 the first Academy Awards ceremony took place there. At the mezzanine level, the Hollywood Historical Review presents a pictorial history steeped in the atmosphere of the 1930s and 40s — the Golden Era of Hollywood. Photographic panels feature such themes as Theaters, Restaurants, Nightspots, Architectural Classics, the Birth of Hollywood and From Movies to Talkies. Other displays include the original Technicolor 3-strip movie camera used to film *Gone With the Wind* (1939), a 35mm hand-crank silent-movie projector (ca. 1915) and other vintage equipment.

View of the Hollywood Bowl (1945)

❼ Hollywood Bowl Museum

2301 N Highland Ave, Los Angeles, 90078. ☎ (213) 850-2058. **Fax:** (213) 851-5617. **Thomas Guide:** 593 E3. **Hours:** Tue-Sat 10am-4pm (winter), 10am-8:30pm (summer). 🛈 free. P free before 4pm. 📷 permitted for private use. **Year founded:** 1983. **Year opened:** 1984. **Primary focus:** music, performing arts, Hollywood Bowl history, musical culture. **Research fields:** music, ethnomusicology, cultural history. **Major exhibitions:** "Music in Films: The Sound Behind the Image" (1994); "New Sounds in New Shapes" (1992); "Exiles in Paradise" (1991). **Publications:** *Exiles in Paradise; The Vo Family: A Vietnamese Musical Odyssey.* **Governing authority:** private, nonprofit. **Parent institution:** Los Angeles Philharmonic Association. **Category:** specialized museum. **Activities/programs:** artist talks, changing exhibitions, concerts, docent programs, educational programs, internship program, lectures, multimedia presentations, performances, performing arts, retrospectives, school programs, summer programs, traveling exhibitions, volunteer programs. **Facilities:** exhibit space/gallery, gift shop, picnic area. ♿ parking; wheelchair accessible. **Collection focus:** music and musical instruments, performing arts.

The museum's permanent exhibition presents the history of the Hollywood Bowl and its role in the development of the performing arts in Los Angeles through photographs, documents, programs and artifacts. Its collection contains original drawings of the Hollywood Bowl concert shell structure by Lloyd Wright. The museum also organizes changing exhibitions of loaned objects on the performing arts. Visitors can watch a short video recounting the evolution of the Hollywood Bowl and listen to recordings of remarkable Bowl performances.

❽ Hollywood High School Alumni Museum

1521 N Highland Ave, Los Angeles, 90028. ☎ (213) 461-3891. **Fax:** (213) 957-0238. **Thomas Guide:** 593 E4. 🚌 bus. **Hours:** by appointment only. 🛈 donations accepted. P street parking. **Year opened:** 1993. **Governing authority:** municipal. **Category:** specialized museum. **Facilities:** lecture hall. **Collection focus:** education, photography.

Hollywood High School Alumni Museum

Located in Hollywood High School's 1907 library building, this small museum's pictorial exhibits feature photographs of famous alumni of the school, including Lana Turner, Judy Garland, Mickey Rooney, Carol Burnett, Stephanie Powers, Linda Evans, James Garner, Barbara Hershey and Warren Christopher. The museum includes memorabilia donated by former students, along with sport photos and uniforms.

Museum entrance

⑨
Max Factor Museum of Beauty

1666 N Highland Ave, Los Angeles, 90028. ☎ (213) 463-6668. **Fax:** (213) 463-0952. **Thomas Guide:** 593 E4. 🚌 bus. **Hours:** Mon-Sat 10am-4pm. $ free. P free. 📷 not allowed. **Year founded:** 1932. **Year opened:** 1983. **Primary focus:** Max Factor cosmetics company. **Governing authority:** company; nonprofit. **Category:** company museum/corporate collection. **Activities/programs:** films, gallery talks, guided tours. **Facilities:** exhibit space/gallery, theater. **Collection focus:** cosmetics.

The museum is housed in the former Max Factor Hollywood Makeup Salon. The building was originally constructed in 1915, and architect S. Charles Lee remodeled it in 1935, creating the Art Deco façade. Over 8,000 people attended the premiere opening of the Max Factor Studio, including every big name in the movie industry. Each celebrity was invited to sign a large genuine parchment, known as The Scroll of Fame, which became one of the largest collections of screen stars' autographs in existence.

The museum fills nine rooms and spans 80 years of cosmetic innovation and Hollywood glam-

Kissing machine (ca. 1939)

our. Through early photographs and artifacts the exhibitions trace Max Factor's career from his first cosmetics shop and later positions as a wig maker and makeup artist for the royal ballet in Czarist Russia, to Los Angeles, where he opened the store in the city's theater district.

In 1914 Max Factor perfected the first makeup specially created for motion picture use — a thin greasepaint in cream form, made in 12 precisely graduated shades. It was worn for the first time by actor Henry B. Walthall, who served as a model for screen tests. Factor's most important invention was color harmony, a principle that certain combinations of women's complexions, hair and eye coloring were most effectively complemented by specifically prescribed makeup shades. This concept is demonstrated in four museum makeup rooms, filled with artifacts and memorabilia, all originally designed in 1935 and dedicated to certain periods of makeup and Hollywood history: the Mint Green Redhead Makeup Room, dedicated to the time period 1928-35; the Powder Blue Blonde Makeup Room, dedicated by Jean Harlow in 1935, now devoted to the 1940s; the Dusty Pink Makeup Room for Brunettes Only, dedicated by Claudette Colbert in 1935, now devoted to the 1950s; the Peach Tone Makeup Room for Brownettes Only, now dedicated to the 1960s and 1970s.

Among the most interesting exhibits is the beauty calibrator, a face-measuring device invented in 1932. It enabled Hollywood makeup artists to pinpoint facial corrections that had to be made. Although Max Factor measured hundreds of screen beauties, he never found a perfect face. Also on exhibit is a mechanical osculator, a replica of Max Factor's "kissing machine," designed to test the relative adhesion powers of experimental lipstick formulas.

Max Factor created the first wig used in a motion picture; it was fashioned completely of human hair. When actor Dustin Farnum fell in the water wearing it during the shooting of *The Squaw Man* (1914) and nearly drowned, the wig was saved first. Max Factor also created the first pair of human hair false eyelashes in 1919 for actress Phyllis Haver. His revolutionary hairlace wigs for women and men created the illusion of natural-looking hairlines for the first time. Wigs on display include those worn by Rudolph Valentino in *Monsieur Beaucaire* (1924), Norma Shearer and John Barrymore in *Marie Antoinette* (1937) and Marlene Dietrich in *Manpower* (1941).

Max Factor checking the makeup of actress Joan Blondell

Wig blocks of famous personalities molded to the exact size and shape of the individual's head are also exhibited, including those made for Elizabeth Taylor, Barbra Streisand, Charlton Heston and John Wayne.

At one point 97% of all the actors and actresses in Hollywood used hairpieces, wigs and cosmetics by Max Factor.

Beauty calibrator

Robert Ripley with a genuine shrunken human head from the Jivaro Indians of Ecuador

⑩

Ripley's Believe It or Not!

6780 Hollywood Blvd, Los Angeles, 90028. ☎ (213) 466-6335. **Fax:** (213) 466-6512. **Thomas Guide:** 593 E4. 🚌 bus. **Hours:** daily 10am-11pm. **Closed:** never. Ⓢ $8.95 adults, $5.95 children 4-11, children under 4 free. Ⓟ on street; metered parking lots nearby. 📷 allowed. **Year founded/opened:** 1992. **Primary focus:** strange and bizarre. **Research fields:** authentic artifacts of the world that are unusual and hard to believe. **Governing authority:** private. **Category:** specialized museum. **Activities/programs:** events, multimedia presentations, school programs. **Facilities:** bookstore, exhibit space/gallery, gift shop. ♿ wheelchair accessible. **Collection focus:** curiosities, money.

For over forty years Robert Ripley, artist, traveler, reporter and collector, searched worldwide for wonders and curiosities. Called the Modern Marco Polo, he visited 198 countries, exploring the unknown, witnessing the peculiar and collecting the unusual. His first *Believe It or Not!* cartoon, covering unusual sporting achievements, appeared in 1918 in the *New York Globe*. At one point, his cartoons were published in over 300 newspapers worldwide and translated into 17 different languages, with a readership of over 80 million people.

Ripley's Believe It or Not! Hollywood Museum houses over 300 unusual items from around the world collected by Robert Ripley or his organization. Among the

Shock machine used for self-treatment. In the 1800s it was popularly believed that small doses of electricity could cure many ailments, from rheumatism to baldness

rarities are the skeleton of a twoheaded human baby, an Egyptian mummified hand and a six-legged cow. There is a 14-piece vampire killing kit (ca. 1850), containing everything one would need to vanquish a vampire — from a cross to a garlic-based "wonder serum." A tobacco enema kit for resurrecting the dead was used in the 19th century, when doctors pumped tobacco smoke into drowning victims to stimulate them back to life. Also on display is a collection of medieval torture instruments, 18th-century bloodletting instruments and thumbscrews occasionally used by American police officers at the turn of the century.

The Old Favorites exhibits feature strange people from around the world, including Liu Ch'ung,

the double-eyed man of China, who was born with double pupils in each of his eyes; Danish astronomer Tycho Brache, known as the Man With the Golden Nose; the giraffe-necked Paduang woman of Burma; and Three Ball Charlie, who could put three balls

Quarter-Million-Dollar Marilyn

in his mouth and whistle at the same time.

The Money Room features Alaskan walrus-tooth money, grass skirt money and boar's tusk money from New Guinea, an iron chain-link currency belt used by the Ushashi tribe of East Africa and German inflation money. Works of art made of everyday objects include the *Button Child*, a statue created entirely of 8,000 common garment buttons and the *Quarter-Million-Dollar Marilyn*, sculpture made from over $264,000 in worn-out dollar bills that the government had thrown in the garbage.

Phineas P. Gage survived having a 4-foot-long crowbar, which weighed 14 lbs, driven completely through his head by an explosion

Two-headed goat

⓫ Guinness World of Records Museum

6764 Hollywood Blvd, Los Angeles, 90028. ✉ 6767 Hollywood Blvd, Los Angeles, 90028. ☎ (213) 463-6433. **Thomas Guide:** 593 E4. 🚌 bus. **Hours:** Sun-Thu 10am-midnight, Fri-Sat 10am-2am. **Closed:** never. 💲 $8.95 adults, $6.95 children 5-10, children under 5 free. 🅿 metered street parking; valet parking nearby. 📷 allowed. **Year opened:** 1990. **Governing authority:** private. **Category:** specialized museum. **Activities/programs:** school programs. ♿ wheelchair accessible. **Collection focus:** curiosities.

Michael Jackson's *Thriller* is the No. 1 selling album of all time

Located at the former Hollywood Theater, Hollywood's first movie house and National Register Landmark, the Guinness World of Records Museum features the greatest facts, the wildest feats and the most outstanding achievements of all time. It contains over five million pieces of information displayed through photographs, life-size replicas, videos and interactive exhibits. The museum is divided into several sections featuring different themes, such as human beings, the living world, space exploration, the sports world, science and technology, structures and machines, and arts and entertainment. Designed and produced in London, all exhibits in this 15,000-square-foot museum were shipped to and assembled in Hollywood.

Visitors can discover that St. Simeon the Younger (ca. 521-597 AD) spent the last 45 years of his life on a stone pillar. The Message in a Bottle exhibit reveals

Sports World exhibit

that the longest recorded interval between drop and pickup is 73 years. The oldest man in the world was Shigechiyo Izumi, who lived 120 years and 237 days. Visitors can climb on the scales and compare their weights to the world's heaviest man, Robert Earl Hughes, who weighed 1069 lbs (485 kg). At 24 inches (61 cm) high, Pauline Musters was the world's smallest lady. The world's tallest man was Robert Wadlow, who stood 8 feet 11-1/10 inches (275,5 cm). The fastest animal in the world is the peregrine falcon, which can fly 217 mph (350 km/h). Carl Lewis is the fastest man on earth; his top speed is 26.95 mph (43,37 km/h).

Visitors can personally test the world's longest echo, play best-selling recordings, find details about record-breaking movies and box office successes and learn that the youngest Oscar winner was Shirley Temple at age 5. Walt Disney garnered the most Oscars (20 statuettes) and Bob Hope holds the most honorary degrees (44).

In 1933 Mickey Mouse received 800,000 letters, a fan mail record that has never been broken

⓬ Frederick's of Hollywood Lingerie Museum

6608 Hollywood Blvd, Los Angeles, 90028. ☎ (213) 466-8506. **Thomas Guide:** 593 E4. 🚌 bus. **Hours:** Mon-Thu & Sat 10am-6pm, Fri 10am-9pm, Sun noon-5pm. 💲 free. 🅿 metered. **Year founded:** 1946. **Year opened:** 1989. **Governing authority:** company. **Category:** company museum/corporate collection. **Collection focus:** clothing and dress.

Madonna's black bustier with tassels from the *Who's That Girl?* world tour (1987)

When Frederick Mellinger began his company in 1946 with the motto: "Fashions may change, but sex appeal is always in style," he hardly dreamed that Frederick's of Hollywood would make fashion history. The company opened the world's first lingerie museum at its flagship store, a purple and pink 1935 landmark Art Deco building designed by Frank Falgien and Bruce Marteney.

The Celebrity Lingerie Hall of Fame salutes more than 40 stars of stage, screen and television who "glamorized" lingerie. Among the famous objects on display are Marilyn Monroe's bra from *Let's Make Love* (1960), Lana Turner's black camisole from *Merry Widow* (1952), Zsa Zsa Gabor's bra and lace panty from *Lili* (1952), Tony Curtis's black lace bra from the classic *Some Like It Hot* (1959) and Elizabeth Taylor's hoop skirt from *Raintree County* (1959).

⑬

The Hollywood Wax Museum

6767 Hollywood Blvd, Los Angeles, 90028. ☎ (213) 462-8860. **Thomas Guide:** 593 E4. 🚌 bus. **Hours:** Sun-Thu 10am-midnight, Fri-Sat 10am-2am. **Closed:** never. 💲 $8.25 adults, $7.50 seniors, $6.95 children 6-12, free for children under 6. Ⓟ metered street parking; valet parking nearby. 📷 allowed. **Year opened:** 1964. **Governing authority:** private. **Category:** specialized museum. **Facilities:** gift shop. ♿ wheelchair accessible. **Collection focus:** waxworks.

This Hollywood attraction displays over 220 wax replicas, ranging from film and television stars to politicians, sport heroes and other celebrities. The main section contains scenes from such hits as *The Guns of Navarone*, *Bonanza*, *Star Trek*, *Superman*, *The Terminator*, *Batman* and *Rambo*. It includes Judy Garland following the Yellow Brick Road in *The Wizard of Oz*, Michael Douglas and Kathleen Turner in *Romancing the Stone*, the cast of M.A.S.H., Michael J. Fox and Christopher Lloyd going *Back to the Future* and Robert Redford and Paul Newman in *Butch Cassidy and Sundance Kid*.

Celebrities from the entertainment world include Elvis Presley, Frank Sinatra, the Beatles, Bruce Springsteen, David Bowie, Ann Margret, Eddie Murphy and Bill Cosby. The most renowned part of the museum is The Chamber of Horrors, containing re-creations of some thrilling scenes

Elvis Presley

from *The Silence of the Lambs*, *The Exorcist*, *Phantom of the Opera*, *Hellraiser III* and *Aliens*. There are world-famous movie monsters, such as Frankenstein, Dracula, the Wolfman and the Hunchback of Notre Dame.

Famous figures in the museum's Sports Hall of Fame include boxers Mike Tyson and Muhammad Ali, and basketball greats Kareem Abdul-Jabbar and Magic Johnson. The Presidents' Gallery features George Washington, Abraham Lincoln, Ronald Reagan and JFK. Another section is devoted to religious representations, including the *Crucifixion*, Leonardo's *The Last Supper* and Michelangelo's *Pieta*.

A special exhibit features weapons and curios from the savage Gows, headhunters of the South Pacific, including skulls, beheading clubs, double-edge flying kreis, war shields, killer boomerangs and musical instruments.

⑭

L. Ron Hubbard Life Exhibition

6331 Hollywood Blvd, Los Angeles, 90028. ☎ (213) 960-3511. **Fax:** (213) 960-1959. **Thomas Guide:** 593 F4. 🚌 bus. **Hours:** daily 9:30am-10pm. **Closed:** Christmas. 💲 $5 adults, children under 12 free. **Reservations:** recommended. Ⓟ metered parking; many parking lots nearby. **Year opened:** 1991. **Primary focus:** to illustrate the extraordinary life of L. Ron Hubbard, his works and discoveries. **Governing authority:** church, nonprofit. **Category:** specialized museum. **Activities/programs:** guided tours. **Facilities:** audiovisual holdings, bookstore, theater. ♿ sign-language interpretation, wheelchair accessible. **Collection focus:** personal history.

Exhibit of L. Ron Hubbard's books

This exhibition, housed in the 1923 Hollywood Guaranty Building, has more than 30 audiovisual and interactive displays, including photographs, books and artifacts. It presents the life and accomplishments of L. Ron Hubbard, writer of both fiction and non-fiction, explorer, researcher of the human mind and founder of the Church of Scientology. He is one of the most widely read authors of all time, his books having been published in 31 languages in more than 85 countries. His self-help book *Dianetics* has sold 15 million copies since its first appearance in 1950. Hubbard's other works include *Battlefield Earth*, the largest science-fiction novel ever written, and its sequel, the 10-volume *Mission Earth*.

Wax figures of Hedy Lamarr, Humphrey Bogart, Rudolph Valentino, Stan Laurel and Edward G. Robinson

Main exhibit room with Ultima Robotrix recreation from *Metropolis* (1927)

⑮
The Fantasy Foundation

2495 Glendower Ave, Los Angeles, 90027-1110. ☎ (213) MOON FAN. **Fax:** (213) 664-5612. **Thomas Guide:** 594 A2. **Hours:** daily 10am-4pm. **Closed:** never. Ⓢ free. Ⓟ free on street. **Year founded/opened:** 1946. **Primary focus:** to create the world's greatest collection of science fiction, horror and fantasy memorabilia. **Research fields:** science fiction, fantasy, film, art, history of sci-fi. **Special collections:** Frankenstein, Dracula, space stamps, autographs. **Major exhibitions:** Los Angeles County Museum of Art (1970), Tokyo (1978), Madrid (1983), Verona (1985), Smithsonian Institution (1986), Berlin (1985/1995). **Governing authority:** private. **Category:** specialized museum. **Activities/programs:** films, foreign language tours (Esperanto), gallery talks, guided tours, lectures, school programs, slide presentations.

Facilities: audiovisual holdings, bookstore, gift shop, 20,000-book research library. **Collection focus:** books, hobbies, masks, miniatures,

motion pictures, personal history, postage stamps, posters, toys and games.

This is the largest collection of science-fiction, horror and fantasy books, artifacts and memorabilia in the world. It was assembled by Forrest J. Ackerman, a legend in the genre of sci-fi, a term he invented in 1954. "Mr. Science Fiction," as Ackerman is known, was the editor of *Famous Monsters of Filmland* magazine for 25 years, from 1958 to 1983. In 1953 he received the first Hugo Award, the greatest honor in science fiction, for his distinguished contribution to the field.

His fascinating collection is housed in the 4-story, 17-room estate, known as Ackermansion, which once belonged to actor Jon Hall, a horror-movie star of the 1940s. It encompasses the entire history of the genre, consisting of more than 300,000 items, including over 125,000 sci-fi movie stills and posters, 18,000 movie lobby cards, original movie scripts and countless recordings, paintings and unusual props. Among the 100,000 books and magazines are 275 editions of *Frankenstein* and almost as many of *Dracula*, numerous volumes of *Tarzan*, complete collections of

Frankenstein bust

Amazing Stories and other sci-fi magazines, and the first *Buck Rogers* comic strip. Highlights include an edition of *Frankenstein* signed by teenage author Mary Shelley; a 1897 first edition of *Dracula*, autographed by author Bram Stoker, famous film vampires Christopher Lee, Vincent Price and Bela Lugosi, and even the curator of Dracula's castle in Transylvania!

On display are Lon Chaney's makeup kit, Bela Lugosi's ring and cape from the 1931 film *Dracula*, together with several of his scrapbooks, pieces of the Krell lab from *Forbidden Planet* (1956) and Lon Chaney's teeth and top hat worn in the lost silent film *London After Midnight* (1927).

Cover design for sci-fi book by French artist Druillet

The exhibits of old movie props include a reconstructed Ultima Robotrix from Fritz Lang's 1927 movie classic *Metropolis*, the creature from the *Black Lagoon* (1954), the only remaining model of the Martian flying machines from *War of the Worlds* (1953), animated dinosaurs from *King Kong* (1933) and a head from one of the aliens in *Close Encounters of the Third Kind* (1977).

Nautilus from *20,000 Leagues Under the Sea* (1954)

The first issue of *Amazing Stories* magazine (October 1926)

Living room looking north. Above the fireplace is a mosaic panel.

16

Ennis-Brown House

2655 Glendower Ave, Los Angeles, 90027-1114. ☎ (213) 660-0607, reservations (213) 668-0234. **Fax:** (213) 660-3646. **Thomas Guide:** 594 A2. **Hours:** by reservation only. **$** $10 adults; $5 students, seniors and children. **P** info provided with tour reservation. **📷** permitted of exterior only. **Membership:** available. **Year founded/opened:** 1980. **Primary focus:** architecture of Frank Lloyd Wright. **Publications:** *The Ennis Brown House.* **Governing authority:** nonprofit. **Category:** historic building/site open to the public. **Activities/programs:** docent programs, guided tours, school programs, volunteer programs. **Facilities:** available

for rent, gift shop (mail order). **Collection focus:** architecture.

"You see, the final result is going to stand on that hill a hundred years or more. Long after we are all gone it will be pointed out as the Ennis House and pilgrimages will be made to it by lovers of the beautiful — from everywhere." Forecasting the future, Frank Lloyd Wright wrote these words in a letter to Charles and Mabel Ennis, who commissioned from him a residential building in 1923.

The Ennis-Brown House is one of the most outstanding architectural landmarks in Los Angeles. It is the last, largest and most complex of Wright's four textile-block houses designed in the area. The house was built in 1924 for the Ennises, owners of a men's clothing store in downtown Los Angeles. Despite their apparent affluence, they led a quiet life, far from the public eye. The house was first sold in 1936 and subsequently changed ownership several times. Its last owner, August O. Brown, donated it to the Trust for the Preservation of Cultural Her-

itage, a nonprofit organization established to restore and maintain the building. To honor Brown's outstanding contribution, its name was changed to the Ennis-Brown House.

The house was constructed of 24 different forms of precast concrete blocks joined with steel rods. A low, dark entrance hall on the ground floor leads up a marble stairway to the second level and all the principal rooms. They are unified by a 100-foot loggia, creating a space Wright called the great room. It features stained-glass windows and a glass-tile mosaic above the living room fireplace.

Located on a 1/2-acre site in the Hollywood Hills, the house commands spectacular views of the mountains to the north and

Hall landing

the city to the south. It has been the set for numerous movies and TV productions, including *The Day of the Locust* (1975) and *Blade Runner* (1982).

Ennis-Brown House entrance

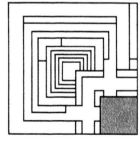

Ennis-Brown House concrete textile-block motif

⑰
Hollyhock House

4800 Hollywood Blvd, Los Angeles, 90027. ☎ (213) 485-4581. **Recorded information:** (213) 662-7272. **Fax:** (213) 485-8396. **TDD:** (213) 660-4254. **Thomas Guide:** 594 A4. 🚌 bus. **Hours:** Tue-Sun, public tours conducted hourly noon-3. **Closed:** holidays. 💲 $2 adults, $1 seniors, children under 12 free. **Reservations:** necessary for groups. P free in Barnsdall Park. 📷 for noncommercial use only. **Membership:** available. **Year opened:** 1976. **Primary focus:** to promote public awareness of Frank Lloyd Wright, Aline Barnsdall and Olive Hill, and the need for historic preservation. **Governing authority:** municipal. **Category:** historic building/site open to the public. **Activities/programs:** docent programs, educational programs, events (F. L. Wright Birthday Celebration — each Jan), guided tours, school programs. **Facilities:** bookstore, research library, picnic area. ♿ parking, sign-language interpretation. **Collection focus:** architecture, furniture and interiors; local American history.

Hollyhock House, western façade. The living room with balcony and pool.

The living room, furnished with reproductions of original Frank Lloyd Wright furniture.

The Hollyhock House was Frank Lloyd Wright's first commission in Los Angeles, built between 1919 and 1921. It was designed for oil heiress Aline Barnsdall, an unconventional person whose interests included the arts, poetry, education, and social and women's issues. Her greatest passion was theater: she was the producer and codirector of an experimental theater company. Impressed with Wright's Midway Gardens in Chicago, Barnsdall appointed the architect to develop a dramatic arts community center she envisioned for Los Angeles.

It was planned as a complex of structures, consisting of residences, a theater, a director's house, a dormitory for actors, studios for artists, shops and a motion picture theater. This elaborate plan never materialized as conceived, and only the Barnsdall home and two secondary residences were finally built. Wright was rarely on site during construction of the house, spending most of his time overseeing the building of the Imperial Hotel in Tokyo. He consequently invited Rudolph Schindler and his son Lloyd Wright to supervise the completion of the project.

The house was built of hollow tile, stucco and wood, and its most notable feature is the way it connects the interiors to the exterior space, flowing freely, uninterrupted by thresholds. It was named after a geometric motif based on the hollyhock, Barnsdall's favorite flower, which Wright incorporated into the roof eaves, walls, columns and furniture. The house contains the original dining room furniture designed by Wright, and replicas of his living room furniture were installed in 1990.

In 1927 Aline Barnsdall donated Hollyhock House and the surrounding site to the City of Los Angeles, and it is now administered by the Cultural Affairs Department.

An upper-level bridge with a semicircular amphitheater and a circular pool.

⑱
Dr. Blyth's Weird Museum

1641 N Cahuenga Blvd, Los Angeles, 90028. ☎ (213) 462-7078. **Fax:** (213) 462-6700. **Thomas Guide:** 593 F4. 🚌 bus. **Hours:** Mon-Sat 11am-7pm, Sun 1-5pm. **Closed:** never. Ⓢ $3 general, children under 12 with adult free. **P** on street, metered. 📷 not permitted. **Year founded/opened:** 1970. **Primary focus:** entertainment and education. **Governing authority:** private. **Category:** specialized museum. **Facilities:** gift shop. **Collection focus:** curiosities.

Human oddities in Dr. Blyth's collection of horrors include a Cyclops baby, a dwarf fetus, Siamese twins and a 23-pound tumor. There is a Hand of Glory, one of only three in existence. This mummified left hand of an executed murderer is one of the most powerful occult tools in the world. Also on display is a head that belonged to one of the ax-murder victims of the infamous Mad Butcher of Kingsbury Run, active in Cleveland, Ohio. Other exhibits include Henri Landau, known as the Bluebeard murderer; a mummy of an Egyptian priest from 1350 BC; a Haitian voodoo devil mask, drums and a necklace of human bones.

One of the most unusual exhibits is a moldering corpse, purportedly of Vlad Tepes Dracula, but Dr. Blyth was unable to prove without a doubt that this was indeed the body of "the Impaler." A short video made for the anatomy department at USC shows Dr. Blyth exercising total muscle control.

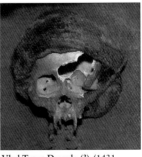

Vlad Tepes Dracula (?) (1431-1476)

⑲
International Child Art Collection (ICAC)

4814 Hollywood Blvd, Los Angeles, 90027. ☎ (213) 485-4474, 660-3362. **Fax:** (213) 485-7456. **Thomas Guide:** 594 A4. 🚌 bus. **Hours:** Mon-Sat 10am-5pm. Ⓢ free. **P** free in designated areas. 📷 by permission. **Year founded/opened:** 1967. **Primary focus:** to provide opportunities for multicultural understanding, aesthetic appreciation and art experiences with children's art. **Major exhibitions:** "Children's Art From the Hobby Craft Center, Baroda, India" (1994); "Play Ball" World Cup '94 International Soccer Art (1994). **Governing authority:** municipal, nonprofit. **Category:** art museum. **Activities/programs:** classes/courses, outreach programs. ♿ parking, wheelchair accessible. **Collection focus:** juvenile art.

Painting by Vishal D. Shah

The International Child Art Collection forms the permanent collection of the Junior Arts Center, a Barnsdall Art Park Facility, which provides extensive art and educational programs. Founded by UNESCO in San Francisco in the 1960s and later entrusted to the Junior Arts Center, the International Child Art Collection contains over 3,500 works by children from over 50 countries. Ranging in scope from domestic scenes and cultural and sporting events to world images, the artworks include prints, paintings, collage, fabric, murals, drawings and metal reliefs.

The Liberty Museum

⑳
Forest Lawn — Hollywood Hills

6300 Forest Lawn Dr, Los Angeles 90068. ✉ 1712 S. Glendale Ave, Glendale, 91205. ☎ (800) 204-3131. **Fax:** (213) 344-9035. **Thomas Guide:** 563 G5. **Hours:** daily 10am-4:30pm. **Closed:** never. Ⓢ free. **P** free. 📷 not allowed inside buildings. **Year founded:** 1944. **Year opened:** 1951. **Primary focus:** American and Pre-Columbian history. **Governing authority:** company. **Category:** history museum. **Activities/programs:** changing exhibitions, concerts, educational programs, multimedia presentations. **Facilities:** lecture hall, sculpture garden. ♿ strollers permitted, parking, wheelchair accessible. **Collection focus:** Hispanic art, Mexican art, Pre-Columbian art, American history, mosaics, sculpture.

The Hall of Liberty, located on the southeastern side of Forest Lawn Memorial Park, houses two historical museums. The Liberty Museum features manuscripts, paintings, uniforms and other historical objects dating from the years of America's struggle for independence. The Museum of Mexican History contains photographs, ceramic figurines, instruments, native costumes and other objects of the early cultures of Mexico. The Plaza of Mexican Heritage is an outdoor sculpture garden containing 18 replicas of sculpture from the earliest civilizations of North America.

A highlight of the collection is *Birth of Liberty*, the world's largest historical mosaic, composed of 25 scenes that depict the most important events in American history from 1619 to 1787. It is 162 feet long by 28 feet high and contains more than 10 million pieces of Venetian glass.

㉑
Los Angeles Zoo

333 Zoo Dr, Los Angeles, 90027.
☎ (213) 666-4650. **Recorded infor-**
mation: (213) 666-4090. **Fax:** (213)
662-9786. **Thomas Guide:** 564 A4.
🚌 bus. **Hours:** daily 10am-5pm.
Closed: Christmas. Ⓢ $8.25 adults,
$3.25 children 3-12, chilldren under
2 free. Ⓟ free. 📷 no restrictions.
Membership: available. **Year**
founded: 1966. **Primary focus:** to
nurture wildlife and enrich the
human experience. **Research fields:**
Species Survival Plan programs to
breed endangered species, California condor breeding program. **Spe-**
cial collections: great ape families,
reptiles, koalas. **Publications:**
ZooView, quarterly magazine;
ZooScape, monthly newsletter. **Gov-**
erning authority: municipal.
Category: zoo. **Activ-**
ities/programs:
classes/
courses, con-
certs, docent
programs,
educational
programs, guided **Tarantula**
tours, lectures,
outreach programs, school programs, slide presentations, storytelling, summer programs, volunteer
programs, workshops. **Facilities:**
bookstore, cafeteria/restaurant, gift
shop, lecture hall, picnic area,
research department. ♿ strollers
permitted, parking, wheelchair
accessible. **Zoo features:** endangered species, labels/descriptions,
rare species. **Collection focus:** birds,
mammals, reptiles, zoology.

Los Angeles Zoo entrance

The first zoo in Los Angeles
was the Selig Zoo and Amuse-
ment Park, which opened in
1885. It was owned by silent film
producer William N. Selig, who
rented out animals for use in
motion pictures. Its
successor, the Grif-
fith Park Zoo,
opened in 1912,
and by the
1950s, with
700 animals, it
was outgrowing its site.
The Los Angeles Zoo
opened in 1966 at its
present location in the northeast-
ern section of Griffith Park, on 80
acres of lushly landscaped
grounds and gardens.

This is one of the ten
largest zoos in the
United States, hous-
ing approximately
1,600 mammals,
birds, amphibians and
reptiles. They represent more
than 400 different species, almost
70 are rare and threatened. The
zoo participates in more than 30
cooperative programs for endangered species. Among zoo-bred
animals that have been returned
to the wild are Arabian onyx,
golden lion tamarin, Bali mynah,
California condor and Andean
condor. The first successful birth
in captivity of a mountain tapir
took place here, as well as the
first birth of a Verreaux's sifaka
(lemur) outside its native Mada-
gascar.

Arranged according to the animals' native habitats, the zoo collection is divided into five geographical areas. The Australian
Region features wallabies, Tasmanian devils, kangaroos, and
that rare and beautiful land bird,
the cassowary. One of the high-

lights is the Koala House, a natural twilight setting inhabited by
nocturnal animals. North America is represented by thick-billed
parrots, coyotes, red wolves and
warthogs. The African Section
contains gerenuks, Jentink's duik-
ers (the most endangered antelope) and the nearly extinct
Sumatran rhinos. The primate
section, with 30 different varieties, is one of the largest displays
in the United States. The Eurasia
Region features island hornbills,
sloth bears and endangered
orangutans. The South American
Section has an impressive collection of monkeys, including sakis
and uakari, rare mountain tapirs
and Andean condors.

The exhibits in the
Aquatic Section

Inhabitant of the Reptile House

include California sea lions,
black-footed penguins and polar
bears. Hillside animals include
zebras, Rocky Mountain goats
and rare Japanese serows. One of
the most interesting displays is
found in the Reptile House, with
gila monsters, crocodiles and
Egyptian cobras. The zoo's newest
attraction is Adventure Island,
the children's zoo, which features
animals of the American Southwest exhibited in five environments: Cave, Desert, Meadow,
Mountain and Shoreline.

Giraffe

Los Angeles Zoo

1. Adventure Island
2. Meerkats
3. Flamingos
4. Monkey Island
5. Aviary
6. Reptile House
7. Koala House
8. South America
9. Eurasia
10. Hillside Animals
11. Africa
12. North America
13. Australia
14. Aquatics

Koala

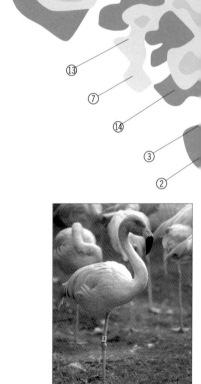

Baby pudu (the world's smallest deer)

Emperor tamarin

Flamingo

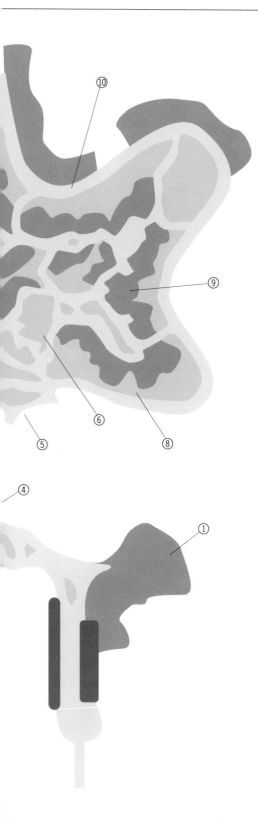

Ring-tailed lemur

Indian fruit bat

Tiger Falls exhibit

[22]

Griffith Observatory

2800 E Observatory Rd, Los Angeles, 90027. ☎ (213) 664-1191. **Recorded information:** (213) 663-8171 (updated weekly); (818) 997-3624 (Laserium recording) **Fax:** (213) 663-4323. **Thomas Guide:** 593 J2. **Hours:** daily 12:30-10pm in summer; Tue-Fri 2-10pm, Sat-Sun 12:30-10pm in winter. $ Hall of Science and telescope: free; planetarium: $4 adults, $3 seniors, $2 children 5-15; Laserium: $7 adults, $6 children 5-12. (Children under 5 are free to planetarium but only are allowed into certain shows.) [P] free. 📷 noncommercial allowed. **Membership:** available. **Year opened:** 1935. **Primary focus:** astronomy, space and related sciences. **Research fields:** ancient and prehistoric astronomy. **Publications:** *Griffith Observer*, monthly magazine. **Governing authority:** municipal. **Category:** planetarium/observatory. **Activities/programs:** educational programs, gallery talks, lectures, multimedia presentations, outreach programs, school programs, planetarium presentations. **Facilities:** bookstore, gift shop, research library. ♿ parking, some sound augmentation systems. **Collection focus:** astronomy.

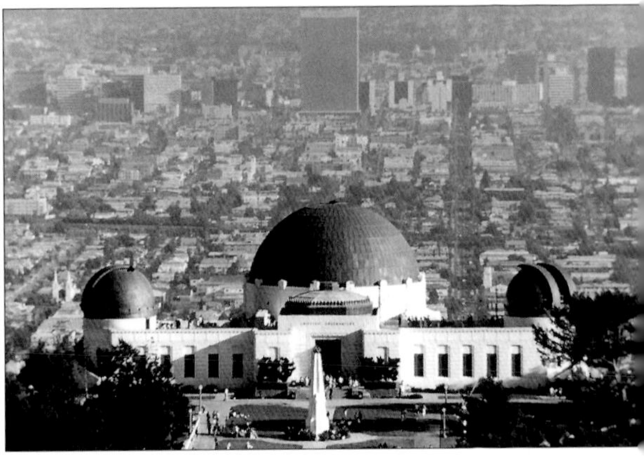

Griffith Observatory

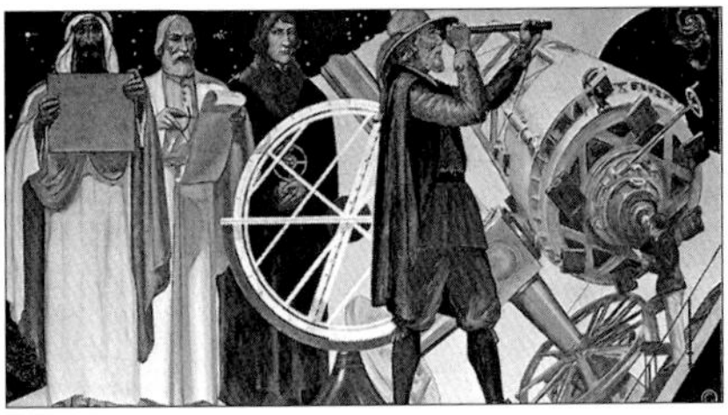

***Astronomy* by Hugo Ballin. The mural depicts four historic astronomers: the Arabic Arzachel, the English John Holywood, the Polish Copernicus and the Italian Galileo Galilei.**

Griffith Observatory is one of LA's major attractions, with nearly two million visitors each year. It was built as a gift to the city by Col. Griffith J. Griffith, a wealthy real estate developer whose other donations include the Greek Theatre and the surrounding park bearing his name. With more than 4,000 acres, it is one of the largest city parks in the United States. The Art Deco observatory, with its three large copper domes, was designed by F. M. Ashley and John Austin and constructed in 1931-35.

The observatory's main rotunda contains a Foucault pendulum, its 240-lb brass ball suspended by a 50-foot-long wire that swings in a constant direction, demonstrating the earth's rotation. The eight Hugo Ballin mural panels, painted in 1934, depict highlights of aeronautics, astronomy, civil engineering, geology and biology, mathematics and physics, time, metallurgy and electricity.

The east hall contains a geochron, a clock that shows the current time around the world, together with the sunset and sunrise lines. Camera obscura ("dark chamber" in Latin) illustrates how a lens focuses light, and a 6-foot globe shows the detailed surface of the moon. A demonstration seismograph records floor vibrations. The east rotunda features a 12-inch Zeiss refracting telescope and a 6-foot-diameter globe of the earth with detailed topography. The meteorite exhibit includes two large pieces weighing several hundred pounds each.

On view in the west hall is a Tesla coil, a step-up transformer that increases voltage from 110 V to 500,000 V, with sparks that leap more than 4 feet. Other exhibits address galaxies, radio astronomy and cosmic rays. The focus of the west rotunda is the sun, and it houses a triple-beam solar telescope, a WWII vintage periscope and a model of Palomar Observatory's 200-inch Hale telescope. The theme of the south gallery is planets, with a gravity well whose parabolic shape reproduces the effect of the sun's gravitational pull on the planets. There is also an orrey, a mechanical device that shows the planets' rotation around the sun. On display are scale models of the planets, as well as large color transparencies, most of them taken by spacecraft.

The planetarium is a large theater that features live multimedia sky shows projected onto a 75-foot-diameter dome with the aid of a 1-ton Zeiss projector and more than 100 special-effects projectors. Laserium offers impressive light and sound shows. From the observatory terraces, visitors can enjoy a stunning panoramic view of the city, from downtown to the ocean, and a close-up view of the HOLLYWOOD sign.

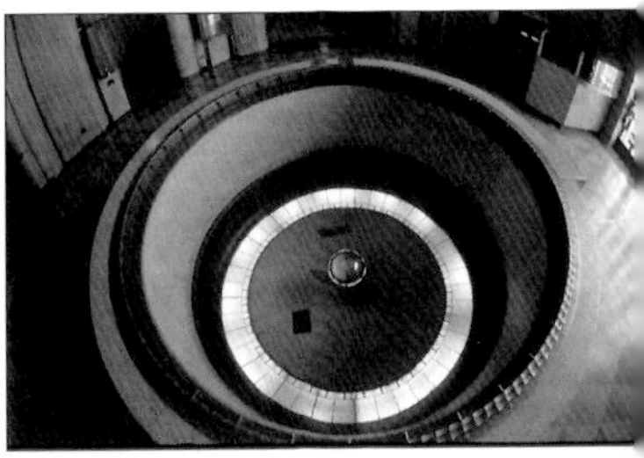

Foucault Pendulum

23

Gene Autry Western Heritage Museum

4700 Western Heritage Way, Los Angeles, 90027-1462. ☎ (213) 667-2000. **Fax:** (213) 660-5721. **Thomas Guide:** 564 B4. 🚌 bus. **Hours:** Tue-Sun 10am-5pm. **Closed:** Thanksgiving and Christmas. $ $7 adults, $5 seniors and students, $3 children 2-12, under 2 free. **Reservations:** recommended for groups. [P] free. 📷 allowed. **Membership:** available. **Year founded:** 1987. **Year opened:** 1988. **Primary focus:** to acquire, preserve and interpret artifacts that document the history of the American West. **Special collections:** Colt Gun Collection. **Major exhibitions:** "Walt Disney's Wild West" (1995); "Thundering Hooves" (1995); "Western Masters: Treasures from the Gilcrease Museum" (1994). **Governing authority:** nonprofit. **Category:** history museum. **Activities/ programs:** changing exhibitions, classes/ courses, concerts, docent programs, dramatic programs, educational programs, events, films, guided tours, lectures, outreach programs, performances, school programs, slide presentations, storytelling, summer programs, volunteer programs, workshops. **Facilities:** audiovisual holdings, bookstore, cafeteria/ restaurant, conservation center, exhibit space/gallery, gift shop, lecture hall, research library, picnic area, theater. ♿ activities for the visually impaired, strollers permitted, parking, wheelchair accessible. **Collection focus:** carriages and carts, American Indian art, American Western art, Hispanic art, Mexican art, clothing and dress, criminology, decorative and applied arts, expeditions and explorations, folk art, folk life and traditions, folklore, gold, handicraft, headdresses, general and local American history, horses, military and naval history, motion pictures, North American painting, 17th — 20th-century painting, performing arts, personal history, posters, sculpture, silver, social conditions, textiles, transportation, military uniforms, vehicles, weaving.

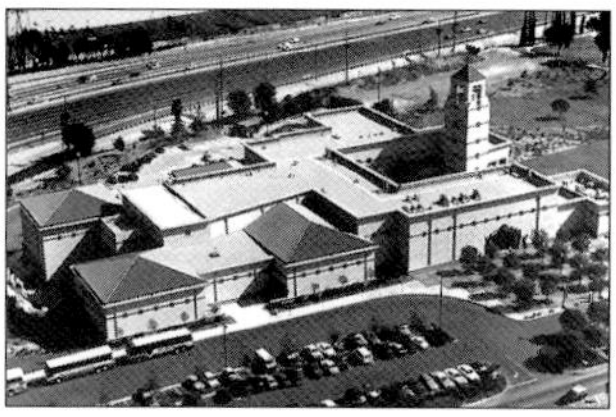

Aerial view of the museum

Founded by the famous singing cowboy Gene Autry in 1987, this $54-million museum celebrates the people, cultures and events that have shaped the rich history of the West from prehistoric times to the present. The 3-level, 140,000-square-foot structure designed by Windom, Wein and Cohen includes galleries for both permanent and changing exhibitions, a garden, a movie theater, research facilities and an educational center.

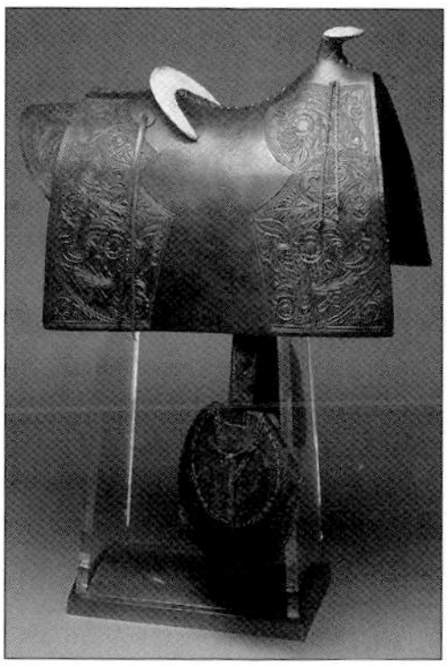

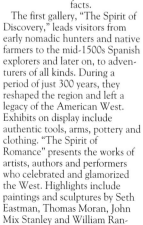

Vaquero saddle, made by Main and Winchester, San Francisco, about 1860

The museum's permanent collection of 16,000 artifacts, artworks and other materials is displayed in 7 thematic galleries designed by Walt Disney Imagineering. They feature interactive displays and multimedia exhibits, pioneering a fiber-optic lighting system to better preserve the artifacts.

The first gallery, "The Spirit of Discovery," leads visitors from early nomadic hunters and native farmers to the mid-1500s Spanish explorers and later on, to adventurers of all kinds. During a period of just 300 years, they reshaped the region and left a legacy of the American West. Exhibits on display include authentic tools, arms, pottery and clothing. "The Spirit of Romance" presents the works of artists, authors and performers who celebrated and glamorized the West. Highlights include paintings and sculptures by Seth Eastman, Thomas Moran, John Mix Stanley and William Ranney. "The Spirit of Imagination" illustrates the influence of radio, television, film and advertising on the formation and dissemination of the image of the mythical West throughout the world. Among the exhibits are a re-creation of a Wild West movie set, posters, photographs, props and movie stars' memorabilia, such as the US Marshall badge worn by James Arness in *Gunsmoke* and a toupee worn by Gary Cooper.

"The Spirit of Cowboy" traces the roots of one of the West's most popular figures and displays the equipment and attire the cowboy used at work and in the rodeo: hats, bridles, saddles and chaps from the 1700s to the mid-1900s. "The Spirit of Community" focuses on social life and law and order in the West, with portraits of some of its famous lawmen and outlaws: Pat Garrett, Billy the Kid, Wyatt Earp and Doc Holliday. The exhibits include a Los Angeles pattern saloon bar built around 1895, and objects from saloons and gambling houses, including a device used for cheating at cards. "The Spirit of Conquest" describes how the face of the West was altered by the arrival of settlers and the subsequent destruction of the land's native peoples. Exhibits show both the Indian and the soldier ways of life, a buffalo hunt, the clash of cultures, the Pony Express and the telegraph and railroad systems. "The Spirit of Opportunity" explores why settlers, traders, miners, trappers and other travelers were drawn to the West — the search for land, gold and glory. The displays aim to recapture the settler's life and experiences on the Oregon, Santa Fe and other trails, using tools and artifacts from daily life.

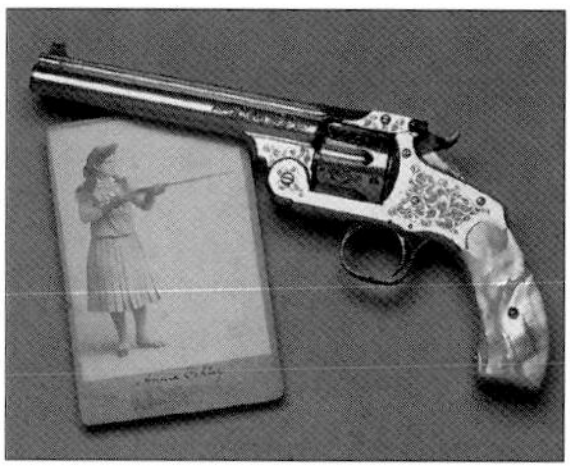

Annie Oakley's gold revolver. Skilled at shooting glass target balls tossed into the air, she once shattered a record of 4,775 out of 5,000 balls.

Gene Autry Western Heritage Museum

Main Level

① Spirit of Discovery Gallery
② Spirit of Romance Gallery
③ Spirit of Imagination Gallery

"Western chase scene, take one." A child's image is superimposed over footage of a chase scene.

Frank James' Remington revolver. Frank surrendered soon after his brother Jesse was killed in 1882 for a reward by gang member Robert Ford.

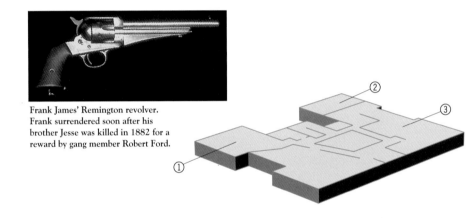

Movie poster *Oh, Susannah!* (1936)

Indian Overlooking a Precipice (1847) by Charles Deas

Foot soldier. Spanish, 16th century. The Spanish came to America equipped for European warfare, with lances, swords and armor.

Lower Level

Vaquero, predecessor of the US cowboy

Exhibit of the frontier soldiers in garrison regalia. Examples of a bandsman's uniform and a cavalry saber.

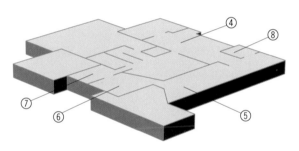

Silver-mounted California spurs with multipointed decorative rowels, late 19th century

ioux woman's dress, about 1890

Extensive collection of Colt firearms

Stockton Terminal & Eastern Railroad No. 1 (4-4-0). Built by Norris-Lancaster in 1864.

passenger cars and memorabilia. Its collection of 16 steam locomotives is the largest in the western United States.

Among the highlights are Stockton Terminal & Eastern No. 1 (1864); Atchison, Topeka & Santa Fe Railway No. 664, built by Baldwin Locomotive Works in 1899; Southern Pacific No. 3025, built by the Schenectady Locomotive Works in 1904; and California Western No. 26, an RS-12 diesel built by the Baldwin-Lima-Hamilton Corporation in 1955. The rolling stock collection features Los Angeles Railway trolleys (ca. 1890), "The Little Nugget" club-dormitory No. 701 from the Union Pacific Streamliner City of Los Angeles (1937),

㉔

Travel Town Transportation Museum

5200 Zoo Dr, Los Angeles, 90027. ✉ 3900 Chevy Chase Dr, Los Angeles, 90039. ☎ (213) 662-5874. **Fax:** (818) 247-4740. **Thomas Guide:** 563 H4. **Hours:** Mon-Fri 10am-5pm, Sat-Sun 10am-5pm. **Closed:** Christmas Day. $ free. **Reservations:** necessary for groups. P free. 📷 allowed for personal use. **Year founded/opened:** 1952. **Primary focus:** railroad history in southern California, 1860-1950. The museum also houses a substantial collection of southern California firefighting vehicles and apparatus. **Research fields:** American history, railroad technology, history of Los Angeles/southern California 1880s-

1940s. **Major exhibitions:** "Firefighting in Los Angeles: 1869-1940." **Publications:** *Green Eye*, newsletter. **Governing authority:** municipal. **Category:** specialized museum. **Activities/programs:** docent programs, educational programs, guided tours, school programs, volunteer programs. **Facilities:** cafeteria/restaurant, exhibit space/gallery, gift shop, research library, picnic area, rides on full-size railroad equipment. ♿ parking, strollers permitted. **Collection focus:** firefighting, local American history, machines and machinery, railways, transportation, vehicles.

Atchison, Topeka & Santa Fe No. 664. Built by Baldwin in 1899

Travel Town covers 7 acres on the northwest corner of Griffith Park and exhibits railroad equipment from California and the Southwest, representing both short-line and main-line railroading with an emphasis on the steam era. This open-air museum concentrates on the history of southern California and Los Angeles, showing the impact of railroads on the development of the area. The collection is comprised of locomotives, freight and

Atchison, Topeka & Santa Fe M.177 Motorcar. Built by GE/Pullman in 1929

sleeping cars "Rose Bowl" and "Hunters Point," both from Union Pacific's City of San Francisco Streamliner. Other exhibits include Los Angeles Metro Transit Authority #1543 (1902), Western Pacific caboose #754 (1910) and Richfield Oil tanker #670 (1911).

Heisler locomotive. Used for hauling timber from forest to mill in the Mother Lode

Pacific Electric No. 1544, called "Electra." This one-of-a-kind electric steeple-cab was built in 1902 by the North Shore Railroad in a progressive step toward an electrified standard-gauge railroad

Combination Fire Engine and Chemical Truck, American-La France Company (1921)

Ladder Wagons

The museum's collection of automobiles, horse-drawn vehicles and fire trucks is housed in the 1910 Southern Pacific Arcadia Freight Depot. Among the exhibits of wagons and carriages are a circus animal wagon built in 1850, a Carnation milk wagon, an oil delivery wagon and a platform spring wagon. Through photographs, maps and artifacts, the historical exhibit tells the story of firefighting in Los Angeles from the creation of the fire department in 1869 till 1940. Notable

Oil Tank Wagon

Three-wheeled Railroad Handcar. Used in railroad track maintenance.

Hose Wagons, Seagrave Company (1929)

Among the displayed documents are the journals of station activities, which every station was required to keep beginning in 1905. The exhibit illustrates other significant events, such as the establishment of Fire College in 1925. An impressive collection of turn-of-the-century fire engines includes pumpers, hose wagons, hook and ladder wagons and other ancillary equipment.

1910 Cadillac

SOUTH CENTRAL

1. Museum of Jurassic
   Technology (MJT)
2. Kaizuka Meditation Garden
3. Western Museum of Flight
4. Museum of African
   American Art (MAAA)
5. Museum in Black
6. William Andrews Clark
   Memorial Library— UCLA

7. Amateur Athletic
   Foundation of Los Angeles
   — Paul Ziffren Sports
   Resource Center
8. Golden State Mutual Life
   Art Collection
9. California Afro-American
   Museum (CAAM)
10. California Museum of
    Science and Industry

11. Natural History Museum of
    Los Angeles County
12. Exposition Park Rose Garden
13. USC — Doheny Library:
    Special Collections
14. Hancock Memorial Museum
15. USC — Fisher Gallery

Horn of Mary Davis of Saughall

❶ Museum of Jurassic Technology

9341 Venice Blvd, Culver City, 90232-2621. ☎ (310) 836-6131. Fax: (310) 287-2267. **Thomas Guide:** 672 G1. 🚌 bus. **Hours:** Thu 2-8pm, Fri-Sun noon-6pm. 💲 $3 general, $2 students and seniors, children under 12 free. 🅿 street. 📷 allowed. **Membership:** available. **Year founded:** 1984. **Year opened:** 1988. **Special collections:** foundation collection donated by Mary Rose Cannon, collected by Owen Thums (father and son). **Major exhibitions:** "Tell the Bees... Belief, Knowledge and Hypersymbolic Cognition" (1994); "Antiquities from the Foundation Collection of the MJT" (annex of the MJT in Hagen, Germany, opened 9/94; "No One May Ever Have the Same Knowledge Again" 1993). **Publications:** *No One May Ever Have the Same Knowledge Again* (1993); guide leaflets. **Governing authority:** nonprofit. **Category:** specialized museum. **Activities/programs:** audio guides, changing exhibitions, concerts, educational programs, internships, lectures, slide presentations. **Facilities:** bookstore, gift shop, 1,200-volume research library. ♿ strollers permitted. **Collection focus:** astronomy, bees, curiosities, folk art, folklore, funeral rites and ceremonies, modern history, miniature painting, miniatures, optics, waxworks.

At the same time a museum and a work of art, this most unusual cultural institution eludes categorization. It is "dedicated to the advancement of knowledge and the public appreciation of the Lower Jurassic" (the Lower Jurassic being defined on the museum's pamphlet map as the Nile delta). Even the museum's name seems contradictory: the Jurassic era was a period when dinosaurs were the predominant creatures on earth, and no hominids were in sight; therefore, there could not have been technology in its usual sense. But this is not the only riddle visitors face here. The museum's strange exhibits appear scientific at first sight, but their blend of fact and fiction creates paradox that leaves those unprepared to face the provocation confused.

head"; an exhibit describing the eccentric behavior of the peculiar stink ant of the Cameroon; and a brass apparatus used to produce synthetic gems.

There is an astonishing display of *deprong mori*, or piercing devil, discovered on the Tripsicum Plateau in the circum-Caribbean region of northern South America. As believed by local Dozo people, the tiny white bat, *Myotis lucifugus*, is capable of flying through solid objects by means of its highly elaborate echolocation system based on x-rays. Another exhibit, illustrating the theory developed by researcher Geoffrey Sonnabend that all memory is only illusion, presents an enigmatic model of obliscence, showing how past experiences are irrecoverably lost. From a diorama of the desert, featuring a head of an American gray fox,

Animated model of Noah's ark (scale 1 inch:1.25 cubits)

On display are both permanent and temporary exhibits. They include dioramas, models and diagrams, stuffed animals and slide shows. Some exhibits employ a three-dimensional viewing system, and most of them are visitor activated: pressing the button begins a sophisticated presentation that consists of visual images, music and taped narrations. Among the museum's highlights are a small rectangular model of Noah's ark, "the most complete museum of natural history the world has ever seen"; the horn of Mary Davis of Saughall: according to legend, it is "an extraordinarily curious horn that grew on the back of a woman's

apparently comes a howling sound. Taking a closer look, visitors find themselves peering into the skull of the fox, discovering a fat man on a chair who is barking.

An exhibition inspired by folk beliefs and superstitions features 28 exhibits, including a pair of mice on a slice of toast, with an explanation that "bed-wetting or general incontinence of urine can be controlled by eating mice on toast, fur and all.... Mouse pie when eaten with regularity serves as a remedy for children who stammer." Another display shows a child holding a duck's beak in his mouth. According to one belief, children with throat disorders could be cured by inhaling duck's breath. The text beneath an exhibit of slightly open scissors says that if scissors are snapped behind a bridegroom, he would become incapable of consummating his marriage.

Mice on toast, a remedy for bed-wetting

Stone lantern and water wheel in
the Kaizuka Meditation Garden

② Kaizuka Meditation Garden

4975 Overland Ave, Culver City,
90230. ☎ (310) 559-0882, 559-
1676. Fax: (310) 559-2994.
Thomas Guide: 672 G3. 🚌 bus.
Hours: daily. Closed: never. 💲 free.
P at rear of Culver City Library,
free. 📷 allowed. Year founded/
opened: 1974. Governing authority:
county. Category: botanical gar-
den/arboretum. ♿ parking. Garden
features: Japanese garden. Collection focus: botany.

This small Japanese garden in
front of the Culver City Library
was a gift from the people of
Kaizuka City, Japan, Culver
City's sister city. The garden was
fully constructed by Kaizuka engineers in Japan, dismantled and
reassembled here in 1974. It features stone lanterns, a water basin
comprised of an old coin, bamboo
water pipes and a water wheel.

③ Western Museum of Flight

12016 S Prairie Ave, Hawthorne,
90250. ☎ (310) 332-6228.
Thomas Guide: 733 D1. 🚌 bus,
metro. Hours: Tue-Sat 10am-3pm.
Closed: holidays. 💲 free, donations
accepted. Reservations: recommended. P free. 📷 allowed.
Membership: available. Year
founded: 1983. Year opened: 1984.

Primary focus: all aspects of aviation
and restoration. Publications: Tail-
dragger, quarterly newsletter. Governing authority: nonprofit. Parent
institution: Southern California Historical Aviation Foundation. Category: specialized museum. Activi-
ties/programs: events, films, guided
tours, inter-museum loans, lectures,
outreach programs, slide presentations. Facilities: audiovisual holdings,
exhibit space/gallery, research
library, micro holdings, visitors' center. ♿ parking, strollers permitted,
wheelchair accessible. Collection
focus: aerospace.

The Western Museum of Flight
is dedicated to restoring vintage
aircraft, preserving aviation history and promoting interest in
Southern California's aviation
heritage. The museum focuses on
the evolution of the local aircraft
industry, covering the enormous
contribution to the growth of aviation by various organization and
individuals, including the Lockheed brothers, Donald Douglas,
Howard Hughes and Jack
Northrop, among others.

The present facility (a 1950
Quonset hangar) is more oriented
toward airplane restoration,
although it has some of the historic aircraft in the collection on
display. Included are a Northrop
YF-17 Cobra (the McDonnell
Douglas/Northrop FA-18 Hornet
prototype), one of only two manufactured; a Douglas A-4A Skyhawk; a Lockheed YO-3A Quiet-
star, one of 14 made, this one
served in Vietnam; and a DeHav-
illand Tiger Moth, a WWII
British trainer being restored to
flying condition. The collection
highlight is a JB-1 Buzz Bomb, a
one-of-a kind manned glider,
nicknamed "the Bat" because of
its unusual shape. In addition to
aircraft, the museum contains
models, pho-
tographs and
aviation memo-
rabilia.

④ Museum of African American Art

4005 Crenshaw Blvd, 3rd floor, Los
Angeles, 90008-2534. ☎ (213)
294-7071. Fax: (213) 294-7084.
Thomas Guide: 673 E2. 🚌 bus.
Hours: Wed-Sat 11am-6pm, Sun
noon-5pm. Closed: Christmas,
Easter, Thanksgiving, New Year's
Day. 💲 free. P free at Robinson's
May Co parking lot. 📷 allowed.
Membership: available. Year
founded: 1976. Primary focus:
interpret, promote and preserve art
by or about people of African
descent and their contributions to
world culture. Special collections: th
Palmer Hayden Collection. Major
exhibitions: "Shades of LA" (1995).
Governing authority: private, nonprofit. Category: art museum. Activi-
ties/programs: changing exhibitions,
educational programs, lectures.
Facilities: exhibit space/gallery, gift
shop. ♿ elevator, wheelchair accessible. Collection focus: African art,
Afro-American art.

This museum was founded by
noted artist and art historian Dr.
Pamela Lewis and a group of
enthusiasts, in the interest of
increasing public awareness and
supporting the artistic expression
of African American art. It is
housed on the 3rd level of the
Robinson's-May department store
building, featuring several changing exhibitions of artworks and
artifacts every year. The
museum's permanent collection
includes art objects from Africa,
the Caribbean, South America
and the United States. It also
houses the collection and
archives of Palmer Hayden, one
of the leading artists of the
Harlem Renaissance.

Western Museum of Flight. JB-1 Buzz Bomb, a WWII secret project incorporating the famous flying-wing design of Jack Northrop.

eremonial wine container, Fang,
ameroon. Monkey skulls, shells,
lastic fibers, gourd.

Museum in Black

331 Degnan Blvd, Los Angeles,
0008. ☎ (213) 292-9528.
homas Guide: 673 F3. 🚌 bus,
etro. Hours: Tue-Sat noon-6pm.
losed: holidays. 💲 free. P free.
allowed. Year founded: 1974.
imary focus: cultural education.
overning authority: private. Cate-
ory: art museum. Activities/pro-
rams: art rental gallery, artist talks,
nanging exhibitions, classes/
ourses. ♿ strollers permitted,
heelchair accessible. Collection
cus: African art.

This museum/sales gallery
ouses more than 1,000 objects
f traditional African art, includ-
g religious items, figurines, tex-
es, pottery and jewelry. The
ollection comprises masks and
atues 200 to 300 years old, cere-
onial knives, weapons, house-
old items, farming and cooking
nplements, and drums and other
usical instruments. Among the
ghlights are shackles used to
ring slaves from Africa, a lie
etector used for questioning by
ne Pende tribe in Zaire and a
eremonial wine container used
funerals by the elders of the
ang people in Cameroon. A spe-
al collection of black memora-
lia includes dolls, signs, adver-
sing, photographs and docu-
ents.

⑥ William Andrews Clark Memorial Library — UCLA

2520 Cimarron St, Los Angeles,
90018-2098. ☎ (213) 731-8529.
Fax: (213) 731-8617. Thomas
Guide: 633 G6. Hours: Mon-Fri
9am-4:45pm. 💲 free; a reader's
card may be obtained by application
in person. Reservations: by appointment only. P on site. 📷 permitted.
Year founded: 1926. Year opened:
1934. Primary focus: English literature and history, 1640-1800.
Research fields: same. Major exhibitions: four small exhibits every year.
Publications: *Center/Clark Series,
Consumption and Culture Series,
Augustan Reprint Society Publications
(ARS), Clark Library Seminar Papers,
Clark Professor Series*, biannual
newsletter. Governing authority: col-
lege/university. Category: library with
collections other than books. Activi-
ties/programs: changing exhibitions,
concerts, educational programs,
guided tours, lectures, scholarships
and fellowships. Facilities: 90,000-
volume research library. ♿ parking,
wheelchair accessible. Collection
focus: book arts, books, calligraphy,
graphic arts, language and literature, modern history, printing.

The Clark library's holdings
consist of about 90,000 books and
21,000 letters and other manuscripts. It is housed in a 1926
building designed by Robert Farquhar, standing on the 4-acre
grounds of the old Clark estate.
The core of the collection represents 18,000 volumes bequeathed
to UCLA in 1934 by William
Andrews Clark, Jr. His library was
particularly strong in 17th- and
18th-century rare British books
and boasted an extensive Oscar
Wilde collection. It contained all
four Shakespeare folios and fine
editions of Chaucer, Byron, Dick-
ens and Robert Louis Stevenson.
French literature, examples of
fine printing, Western Americana, and letters and manuscripts
by authors, musicians and statesmen were also included.
The Clark library specializes in
British works of the period 1641-
1750. Some of its remarkable collections focus on Milton, Defoe,
Fielding, Swift and Pope. The
Dryden collection is unique, com-

paring only with that of the
British Library. The Clark
library's particular strength lies in
its background materials in the
fields of anthropology, criminology, mercantile practice, psychol-
ogy and social history. The collection of Oscar Wilde materials
is almost unparalleled in the
world, consisting of numerous
editions, Wilde's original drafts
and letters, and books and materials related to Wilde or to the
decadent and modernist movement of the 1890s.
The library owns a complete
run of the books printed by the
two most renowned and influen-
tial presses in 19th-century England, the Kelmscott and the
Doves. Other holdings of fine
printing include modern California presses.

Marie Antoinette Imprisoned in the
Conciergerie, pen-and-ink watercol-
or sketch dated October 1793 and
signed by Louis David

The Western American holdings include books, periodicals
and documents related to the settlement of Montana and the
development of its mining industry. This section also encompasses early editions of the *Book
of Mormon*; manuscripts referring
to the Louisiana Purchase; Spanish explorations in New Mexico
and California; and trade with
the Indian territories.

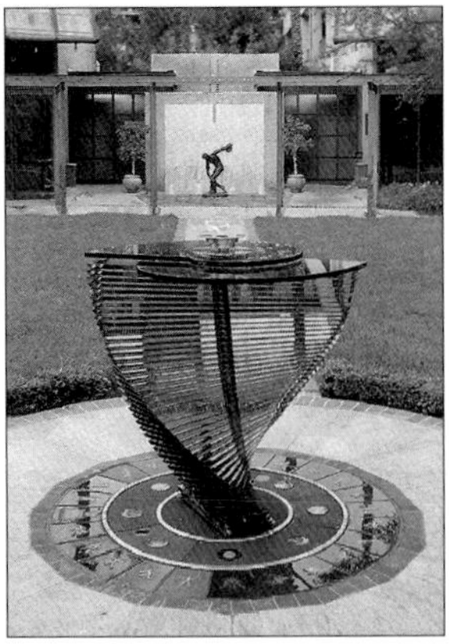

The Paul Ziffren Sports Resource Center

7

Amateur Athletic Foundation of Los Angeles — Paul Ziffren Sports Resource Center

2141 W Adams Blvd, Los Angeles, 90018. ☎ (213) 730-9696. **Fax:** (213) 730-9637. **Thomas Guide:** 633 H6. **Hours:** Mon-Tue, Thu-Fri 10am-5pm; Wed 10am-8:30pm; even-dated Sat 10am-3pm. [$] free. **Reservations:** recommended. [P] free on Gramercy Pl. 📷 permission required. **Year founded/opened:** 1988. **Primary focus:** sports, especially Olympic Games. **Research fields:** sports. **Special collections:** the Bill Schroeder Collection, the Fred Imhof Collection, the Avery Brundage Collection. **Publications:** sportsletter. **Governing authority:** private, nonprofit. **Category:** library with collections other than books. **Activities/programs:** awards, changing exhibitions, educational programs, inter-museum loans, school field trips. **Facilities:** audiovisual holdings, exhibit space/gallery, lecture hall, 30,000-volume research library, micro holdings, theater. ♿ strollers permitted, parking, wheelchair accessible. **Collection focus:** medals, postage stamps, posters, sports and recreation.

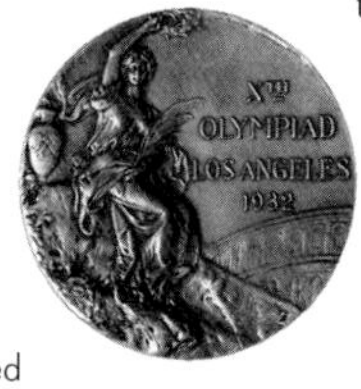

Games of the Xth Olympiad, Los Angeles 1932. Gold Olympic prize medal.

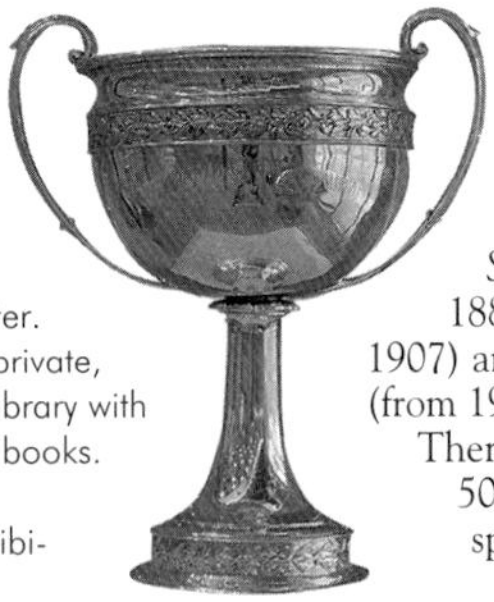

Boston Marathon Trophy, won by Michael J. Ryan, 1912. The Boston Marathon was begun in 1897 and is the oldest marathon run in the United States

The Amateur Athletic Foundation (AAF) of Los Angeles is a private, nonprofit institution created by the Los Angeles Olympic Organizing Committee (LAOOC) to manage southern California's endowment from the 1984 Olympic Games. The foundation operates the state-of-the-art Paul Ziffren Sports Resource Center, named after the chairman of the board of the LAOOC and the AAF's first chairman. It is the first and only facility of its kind in the US. Its modern building was completed in 1988 with proceeds from the 1984 Olympic Games, and it houses the nation's largest sports library, and sports art and artifacts collection.

The library features 30,000 printed volumes, game programs and media guides. Among the highlights are 5,000 Olympic publications, including Olympic official reports and proposals to host the Games. The periodicals collection includes *The Sporting News* (from 1886), *Yachting* (from 1907) and *Field and Stream* (from 1911), among others. There are more than 50,000 photographs, spanning the period from the turn of the century to the present, with a remarkable collection from the 1984 Olympics. Other library holdings include *The Los Angeles Times* sports section dating back to 1930, over 5,000 instructional and historical sports videos, together with oral histories of more than 100 southern California Olympians. The Avery Brundage Collection is contained on 149 reels of microfilm, representing a compilation of his papers and correspondence over more than 60 years.

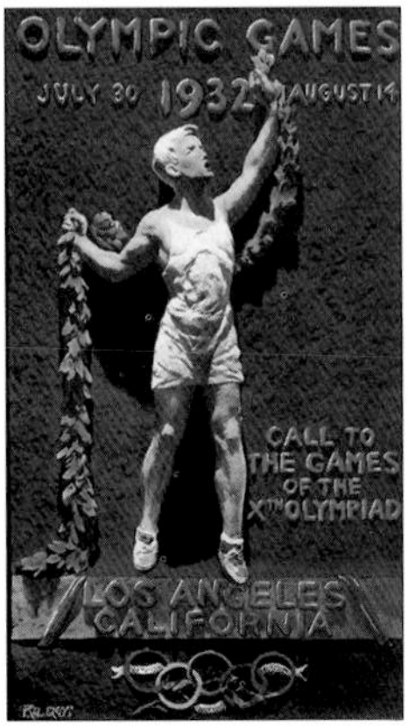

Games of the Xth Olympiad, Los Angeles 1932. Official poster.

The sports art and artifacts collection consists of 10,000 items, and its largest section is Olympic related. It includes 400 works of art on paper, mainly posters of the Olympic Games, Olympic torches and a philatelic collection of Olympic stamps from around the world. The general sports collection includes uniforms, equipment and artifacts such as baseball gloves, tennis rackets and golf clubs. Among the famous pieces are Joe Louis's glove, Babe Ruth's bats, a Peggy Fleming costume, Jesse Owens' shoe, Lillian Copland's shoe and discus, and one of Bill Tilden's tennis rackets. The trophy collection features major awards and medals given out in amateur sports, including Olympic medals, the Heisman Trophy and many trophies won by renowned athletes.

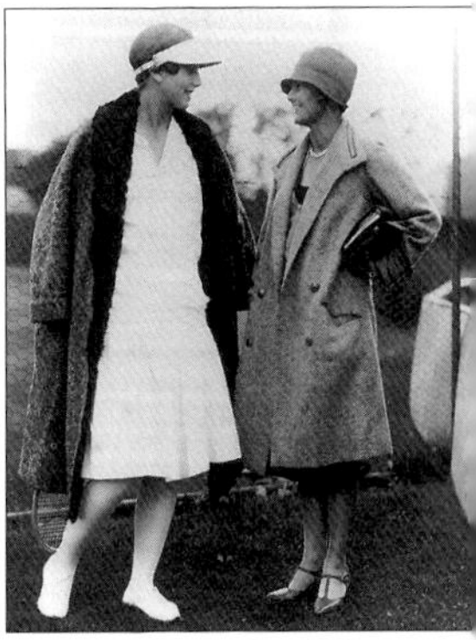

Helen Wills and Mary K. Browne, winners of women's doubles, US Lawn Tennis Championship, 1925

8

Golden State Mutual Life Art Collection

999 W Adams Blvd, Los Angeles, 90018. ☎ (213) 731-1131. **Fax:** (213) 732-2193. **Thomas Guide:** 633 H6. 🚌 bus. **Hours:** Mon-Thu 8am-4:45pm. $ free. **Reservations:** by appointment only. [P] free behind building. **Year founded:** 1925. **Year opened:** 1965. **Primary focus:** to perpetuate a true image of black forefathers and create pride in young black citizens in their splendid heritage. **Governing authority:** company. **Category:** art museum. **Collection focus:** Afro-American art.

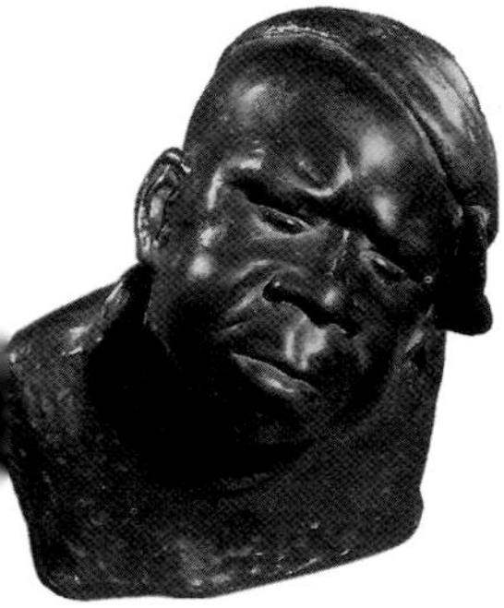

Bad Boy by Beulah Woodard

One of the leading minority-owned financial institutions in the United States today, the Golden State Mutual Life Insurance Company was founded in 1925. The present home office building was dedicated in 1949, when two large murals depicting the history of black settlers in California were unveiled. The first one, *Exploration and Colonization*, painted by Charles Alston, covers the period between 1527 to 1850. The second, *Settlement and Development*, by Hale Woodruff, illustrates the period between 1850 and 1949.

The company's Afro-American art collection features over 200 paintings, sculptures, drawings, prints and photographs. Among the major works are *Queen* by Herman Kofi Bailey, *Embrace* by Elizabeth Catlett, *Braids* by Rose Green, *Controlled Force* by John T. Riddle and *Bad Boy* by Beulah Woodard.

9

California Afro-American Museum (CAAM)

600 State Dr, Los Angeles, 90037. ☎ (213) 744-7432, education (213) 744-7537. **Fax:** (213) 744-2050. **Thomas Guide:** 674 B2. 🚌 bus. **Hours:** Tue-Sun 10am-5pm. **Closed:** Thanksgiving, Christmas, New Year's Day. $ free. [P] $3, parking lot. 📷 not allowed. **Membership:** available. **Year opened:** 1981. **Primary focus:** to collect and preserve artifacts documenting the Afro-American experience. **Major exhibitions:** "The Musical Renaissance of Black Los Angeles 1890-1950" (1995); "Environments: Extending the Artist's Realm" (1995). **Publications:** *Museum Notes*, newsletter; catalogs. **Governing authority:** state. **Category:** art museum. **Activities/programs:** changing exhibitions, classes/courses, concerts, docent programs, events, films, guided tours, lectures, multimedia presentations, performances, performing arts, storytelling, summer programs, traveling exhibitions, volunteer programs, workshops. **Facilities:** bookstore, exhibit space/gallery, gift shop, picnic area, research library, theater. ♿ wheelchair accessible. **Collection focus:** African art, Afro-American art.

The museum is housed in a one-level contemporary structure designed by Los Angeles architects Jack Haywood and Vincent Proby specifically for the 1984 Olympic Arts Festival. Dedicated to the achievements of people of African descent in art, history and culture, the museum organizes changing thematic exhibitions and displays selected pieces from its collections.

Its permanent collection comprises paintings, sculptures, works in mixed media, prints, photographs, decorative arts, various artifacts and documents and African wood sculptures. Among the works are paintings by Haitian artist F. Turenne de Pres and early American paintings by Ernie Barnes, Clementine Hunter and James Porter. There are sculptures by Richard Barthe, John Outerbridge and John Wilson, and assemblages by David Hammons and Noah Purifoy.

10

California Museum of Science and Industry

700 State Dr, Los Angeles, 90037. ☎ education (213) 744-7444, summer science workshops 744-7440, membership and volunteers 744-7504 or 744-7505, IMAX Theater show information 744-2014. **Recorded information:** (213) 744-7400. **Thomas Guide:** 674 B2. 🚌 bus. **Hours:** daily 10am-5pm. **Closed:** Thanksgiving, Christmas and New Year's Day. $ free, except IMAX Theater. [P] $3 parking lot. 📷 allowed. **Membership:** available. **Year opened:** 1950. **Publications:** newsletter. **Governing authority:** state, nonprofit. **Category:** science and technology museum. **Activities/programs:** changing exhibitions, educational programs, films, guided tours, multimedia presentations, school programs, summer programs, traveling exhibitions, volunteer programs, workshops. **Facilities:** cafeteria/restaurant, gift shop, theater. ♿ parking. **Collection focus:** aerospace, biology, chemistry, ecology, electricity, energy, food, geology, medicine, physics, technology.

The California Museum of Science and Industry is the most visited of all museums in Los Angeles, attracting more than 2.5 million visitors annually. The Exposition Building was constructed by the State of California as a place to display agricultural products grown in the area. It was transformed into a museum in 1950 and since then new edifices have been added. The museum's complex comprises the Armory Building, the Aerospace Building, the Kinsey Hall of Health, the Kinsey Auditorium, Technology Hall, Science Hall South and the spectacular IMAX Theater, showing films projected onto a 5-story-high screen with Surround-Sound.

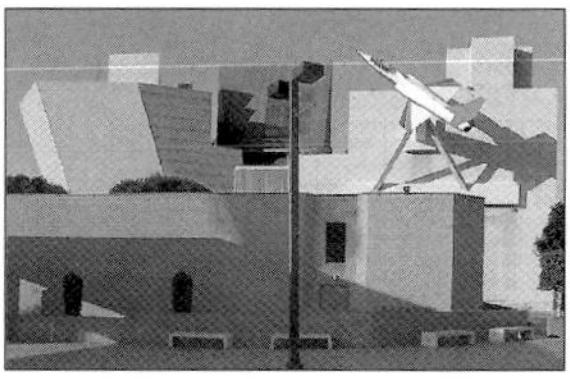

Aerospace Hall

The museum offers exhibits of science and technology, explaining the basics of mathematics, computer science, physics, biology and chemistry. Lively, hands-on displays enable visitors to actively engage in scientific inquiries.

Technology Hall presents many working model-exhibits, including demonstrations of how invisible forces, such as electricity and magnetism, work. There is a Mathematica display designed by Charles Eames, with bubbles, spirals and a Moebius strip. The earthquake exhibit features a simulated earthquake and many safety tips; computer presentations enable visitors to see how computer graphics and animation work. A bicycle company exhibit is presented as an example of the factory of the future.

Kinsey Hall houses exhibits concerning health and the body, showing how alcohol, tobacco, marijuana and cocaine affect life; the "What You Don't Know *Can* Hurt You" exhibit educates visitors about AIDS and the immune system. There is a display on food and nutrition, showing the value of different kinds of food; and workshops where visitors can explore the human body and test their vital signs.

Science Hall South is devoted to the urban environment, presenting ways of reducing, reusing and recycling waste. A giant trash can represents the 4,238 pounds of trash that the average Los Angeles resident threw out in 1988! The "EGGciting Beginnings" exhibit deals with animal development, showing how chicks hatch, tadpoles turn into frogs and human embryos develop. In addition, an exhibit on chemistry features rocket fuel and molecules in motion.

California Museum of Science and Industry

1. Science South
2. Technology Hall
3. Kinsey Hall of Health
4. Kinsey Auditorium
5. Aerospace Hall
6. IMAX Theater
7. Corwin D. Denney Air and Space Garden

Mathematica: a world of numbers and beyond

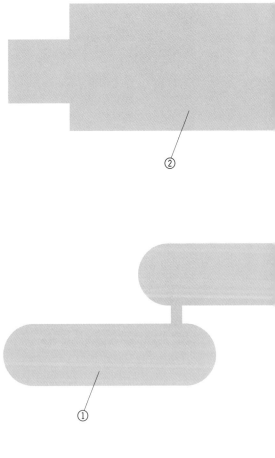

Invisible forces: electricity and magnetism

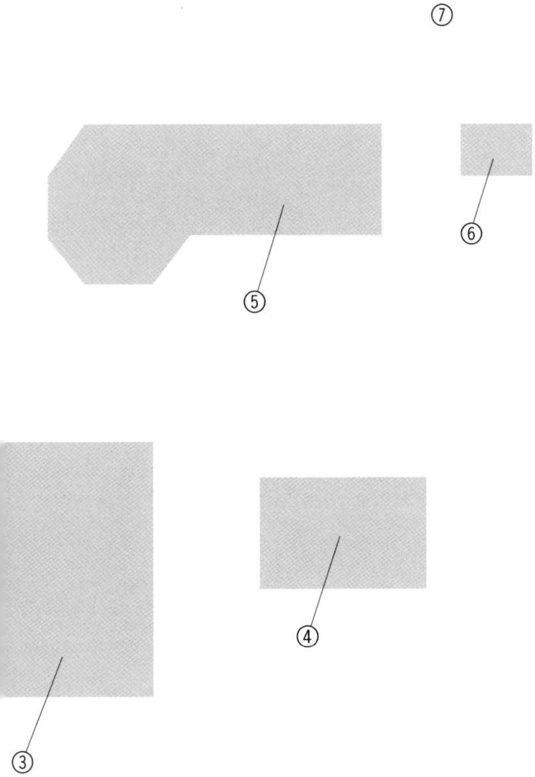

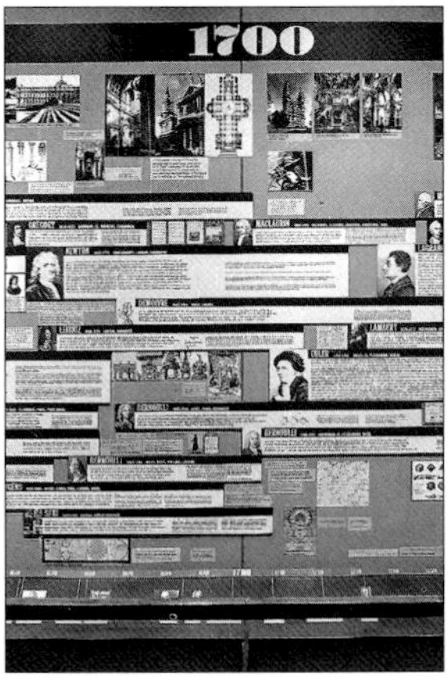

History wall: well known events in history

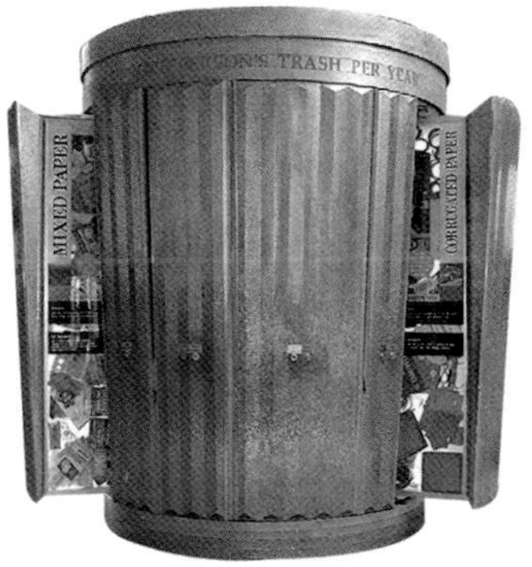

Trash can, representing the 4238 pounds (1920 kg) or nearly 22 cubic yards (17 m^3) of trash that the average LA County resident threw out in 1988.

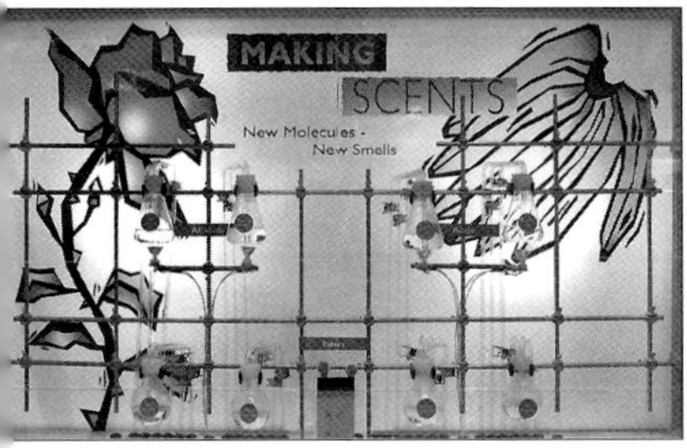

Making scents: new molecules — new smells

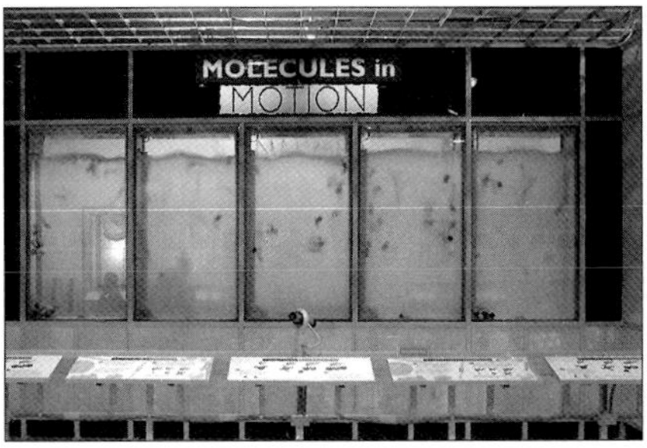

Molecules in motion

Aerospace Hall

The 3-story Aerospace Building, designed by Frank Gehry in 1984, houses real aircraft and spacecraft, as well as replicas and models of satellites. Among various exhibits are graphic presentations of the history of flight, hands-on displays demonstrating basic principles of flight and cross-section models of piston and jet engines. Scale-model aircraft highlight selected design changes in general aviation from the 1903 Wright Flyer onward.

Aircraft on display include a full-scale flying replica of the glider in which the Wright brothers made almost 1,000 flights in September and October of 1902; the Monocoupe, a two-seat, enclosed monoplane (1928); a P-51 Mustang (1940), one of the best fighters of WWII; a T-38, the nation's first twin-engine, high-altitude, supersonic jet trainer (1959); and a Northrop F-20 Tigershark (1986), which had the fastest scramble time of any fighter in the world.

The satellite area has replicas of Soviet Sputnik 1 (1957), the first artificial satellite to orbit the Earth; Pioneer 5 (1960), the first US deep-space probe; Intelsat 3 (1968), the world's first global commercial communications system; and Pioneer 10 (1972), whose original mission was to tra-

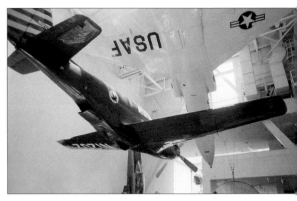

P-51 Mustang (1940) and T-38 (1959)

verse the asteroid belt and study Jupiter. There are real Mercury MR-2 (1961) and Gemini 11 (1966) space capsules, recovered by aircraft carrier from the Atlantic Ocean after splashdown.

The aerospace complex includes the Corwin D. Denney Air and Space Garden, featuring DC-3 and DC-8 aircraft.

Pioneer 10 (1972)

Gemini 11 (1966)

Spacesuit, worn during the Apollo 16 lunar mission by astronaut Thomas Mattingly

HS 376, advanced spin-stabilized communication satellite (1980)

1

Natural History Museum of Los Angeles County

00 Exposition Blvd, Los Angeles, 0007. ☎ (213) 744-3414. ecorded information: (213) 744-INO. **Thomas Guide:** 674 B2. 🚌 us. **Hours:** Tue-Sun 10am-5pm. losed: Thanksgiving, Christmas, ew Year's Day and Mon (except ationally celebrated Monday holi-ays). $ $6 general, $3.50 seniors nd students over 12, $2 children ges 5-12, children under 5 free. ree on first Tue of every month. [P] eters throughout Exposition Park. 📷 no tripods or lighting equipment; o photos for commercial purposes. **embership:** available. **Year unded:** 1913. **Primary focus:** the cquisition, conservation and dis-laying of objects and artifacts relat-g to natural and human history. ne museum is a center for exhibi-on, education, publication and ommunity outreach programs. **esearch fields:** history and life sci-nces (anthropology, archaeology, hnology, botany, entomology, her-etology, ichthyology, invertebrate ology, mammalogy, ornithology). **blications:** *Terra* magazine. **Gov-rning authority:** county. **Category:** atural history museum. **Activities/ ograms:** changing exhibitions, asses/courses, docent programs, ducational programs, guided tours, ctures, school programs, summer ograms, traveling exhibitions, vol-nteer programs. **Facilities:** book-ore, cafeteria/restaurant, exhibit ace/gallery, gift shop, lecture hall, search library. ♿ strollers permit-d, parking, wheelchair accessible. **ollection focus:** amber; anthropol-gy; Meso American, South Ameri-n and North American archaeol-gy and antiquities; arms and armor; dian American, Latin American and exican art; baskets; bees; biology; rds; bones; carriages and carts; othing and dress; dolls and pup-ets; domestic utensils; ecology; folk e and traditions; fossils; furniture nd interiors; gold; early, general nerican and local history; insects; de; jewelry; machines and machin-y; mammals; manuscripts; metals nd metallurgy; meteorites; mineral-gy; mollusks; oceanography; pre-ous stones; reptiles; transportation.

The Natural History Museum was established in 1913 as the Museum of History, Science and Art in Exposition Park. Its original Spanish Renaissance building, featuring a marble rotunda, was added to the National Register of Historic Places in 1975. Since its opening the museum has gradually been enlarged, so it now encompasses an area five times the size of its original structure. With over 16 million specimens and artifacts covering more than 600 million years of the earth's history in its collections, this is the third largest natural history museum in the US. The museum is divided into three departments: Life Sciences, Earth Sciences and History.

Natural History Museum

The museum's three habitat halls show African and North American mammals in their natural environments. Dinosaurs on display include the skeleton of a *Mamenchisaurus* — one of the largest dinosaurs ever discovered — and one of the finest *Tyrannosaurus rex* skulls on view anywhere. Examples of nearly half of the 25,000 known fish species comprise the ichthyology collection, recognized as an International Resource Center for fishes. It includes a Megamouth, the world's rarest shark, one of only five found since the species was first discovered in 1975. The museum boasts the second largest collection of marine mammals in the world, as well as the world's largest collection of southwestern moths and butterflies and North America's largest collection of ants. The museum's invertebrate zoology collection is the second largest in North America. The Schreiber Hall of Birds, opened in 1991, features 27 separate learning stations and three walk-through habitats, with an ornithological collection of 104,000 birds. The Insect Zoo opened in 1992; it includes rhinoceros beetles, red-kneed tarantulas, scorpions and giant walking sticks, among other exotic creatures.

The museum has the largest catalogued vertebrate fossil collection and the sixth largest invertebrate fossil collection in North America. The Hall of Gems and Minerals houses over 2,000 specimens, including a 212-carat emerald cabochon and the Ashberg Diamond, the second largest on exhibit in the US. In the Ralph M. Parson's Discovery Center, children can explore hands-on exhibits of fossil rubbings, shells, musical instruments, jewelry, live animals and historic costumes, among other activities.

The Times Mirror Hall of Native American Cultures, opened in 1993, features 16 different interpretive areas with 800 objects from the museum's permanent collection. Highlights include a 2-story replica of a Pueblo cliff dwelling, Navajo textiles, California and Great Basin baskets, Plains beadwork and Southwest pottery and jewelry. The Lando Hall of California and Southwest History is divided into four sections. The first one concentrates on California prehistory, featuring the area's earliest inhabitants, Indian dwellings, dioramas and artifacts. The second section covers Spanish exploration and the pueblos and missions of the Hispanic period, featuring navigation instruments, arms and armor, models of key events and other objects. The third and fourth sections serve the themes of American California and California the metropolis. Farm and industrial artifacts, movie memorabilia and a huge model of Los Angeles in the 1940s are some of the highlights displayed there. The Hall of American History spans the period from 1492 until 1914, presenting a variety of events and industries. Exhibits cover various topics, including architecture, astronomy, ironworking and weaponry. The museum's art collection consists of over 500 paintings, drawings and prints by American artists.

The Seaver Center for Western History Research contains a large collection of photographs, manuscripts, maps and posters particularly relating to the history of southern California.

Natural History Museum of Los Angeles County

Main Level

American History 1492-1815: gold scales

American History 1815-65: a walk through covered wagon filled with artifacts

American History 1815-65: Civil War, Union drum

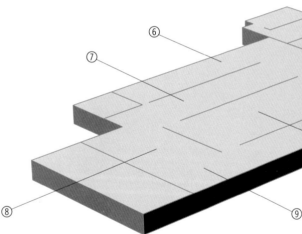

2-story replica of a Pueblo cliff dwelling

American History 1865-1914

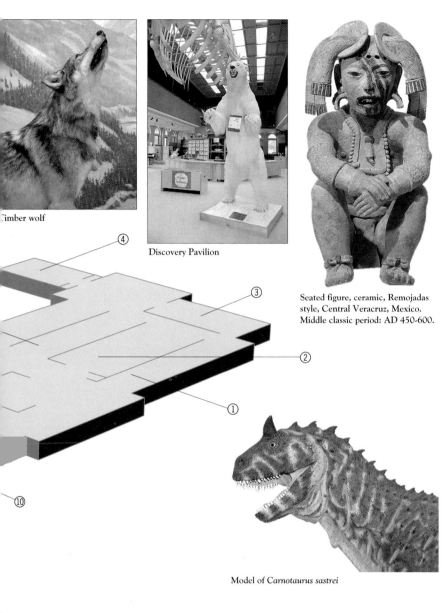

Timber wolf

Discovery Pavilion

Seated figure, ceramic, Remojadas
style, Central Veracruz, Mexico.
Middle classic period: AD 450-600.

Model of *Carnotaurus sastrei*

African elephants

American bison

Natural History Museum of Los Angeles County

Walrus

Lower Level

① California History, 1540-1940

Upper Level

② Bird Hall
③ Chaparral
④ Marine Life
⑤ North American Mammals

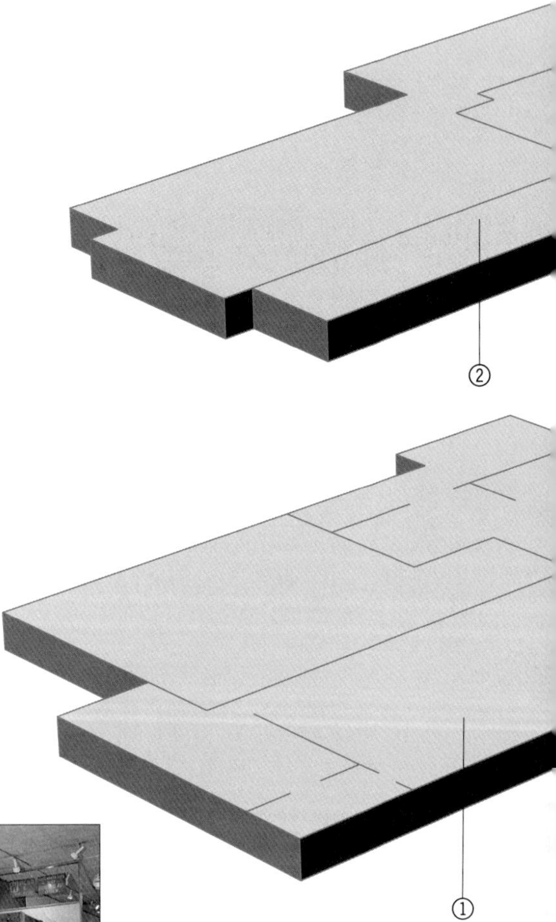

Walt Disney's first animation equipment

Oil well pump (1920s)

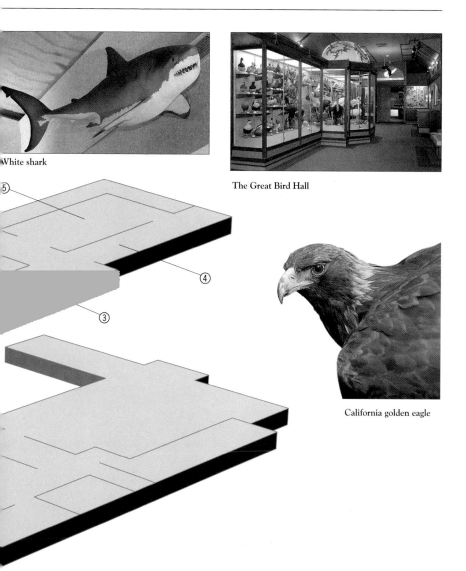

White shark

The Great Bird Hall

California golden eagle

Carreta from the Pueblo of Tesuque in New Mexico, probably built in the late 1700s

Life-size replica of a Chumash dwelling, built out of straw

Exposition Park Rose Garden

⑫

Exposition Park Rose Garden

701 State Dr, Los Angeles, 90037. ☎ (213) 748-4772. **Fax:** (213) 346-7396. **Thomas Guide:** 674 B2. 🚌 bus. **Hours:** daily 8:30am-sunset. 🅢 free. 🅟 $3. 📷 allowed. **Year opened:** 1927. **Primary focus:** to plant and maintain rosebushes. **Governing authority:** municipal. **Category:** botanical garden/arboretum. **Activities/programs:** docent programs, events, films, volunteer programs. **Facilities:** available

All-America Rose Selection, Hybrid Tea *Perfect Moment*

for rent. ♿ strollers permitted. **Garden features:** rose garden; peak time: Jun — Sep. **Collection focus:** agriculture, botany, horticulture.

Late in the 19th century the site now occupied by Exposition Park was used as a horse track and a place to exhibit agricultural products. By 1910 it had become the sunken garden in Agricultural Park. It was improved for the California Garden Show and Horticultural Exhibition in 1921 and gained its current appearance between 1926 and 1928 through the efforts of George C. Robinson and Fred F. Howard.

This is one of the largest and most significant public rose gardens in California. Covering 7.5 acres, it contains over 19,000 rosebushes representing about 200 cultivars. Highlights include grandifloras, hybrid teas, climbers and miniatures. As a display garden, it provides visitors the opportunity to see many rose varieties, and it offers various activities such as educational pruning demonstrations. The garden is the recipient of new hybrids, especially the annual All-America rose selections, many of them developed locally. Since the

1940s and particularly the 1950s, southern California has become one of the world's most important areas for rose hybridization.

The garden features a circular fountain and lily pond in the center and four wooden pergolas in each quadrant. Broad grass walkways enable visitors to closely view more than 200 rosebeds. The flowering period occurs from the end of April to early November, but the peak time is between June and September.

Pergola in Exposition Park Rose Garden

Rosebeds with the 1912 County Museum of History, Science and Art Building (now the Natural History Museum of Los Angeles County) in the background

13

USC — Doheny Library: Special Collections

USC, University Park, Los Angeles, 90089-0182. ☎ (213) 740-5946. Fax: (213) 749-1221. **Thomas Guide:** 674 B1. 🚌 bus: 81, 38, 200; metro: Grand with bus. **Hours:** daily 9am-4:30 (appointments preferred). **Closed:** national and academic holidays. $ free. [P] on-campus, $6 per entry; on Figueroa St, south of Jefferson Blvd. **Primary focus:** supporting the academic community and independent researchers. **Research fields:** literature, art, history. **Special collections:** the Richard J. Hoffman Collection, the Hamlin Garland Collection, the Willard S. Morse Collection, the *Los Angeles Examiner* Collection, the California Historical Society Collection, the Whittington Collection, the Lion Feuchtwanger Collection, the Lawrence Lipton Archive. **Major exhibitions:** book-related exhibitions rotate every 3-4 months. **Governing authority:** college/university. **Category:** library with collections other than books. **Activities/programs:** changing exhibitions, installations, lectures. **Facilities:** exhibit space/gallery, research library available to the public. ♿ wheelchair accessible. **Collection focus:** book arts, books, education, language and literature, photography, printing.

The Department of Special Collections is located on the second floor of Doheny Memorial Library, the 1930-2 building designed by architects Cram & Ferguson. Library materials are generally not on view and many of the department's holdings are stored off site, but they can be reviewed on request. The department contains more than 130,000 volumes, 1.4 million manuscripts and 1.7 million photographs.

The Printing Arts Collection includes books printed by some of the most famous presses of the western world. It has significant holdings of 20th century fine presses and is particularly rich in the works of California printers. The core of the collection is the Richard J. Hoffman Collection, consisting of 3,500 rare books and journals on all aspects of printing and typography.

The Rare Books and Manuscripts Collection is particularly strong in the fields of aeronautical history, American pamphlets 1745-1827, the British East India Company, Darwin and evolution, costume, philosophy, theology, and Western Americana and Californiana. Among the major works are first editions of Audubon's *Birds of America*, Diderot's *Encyclopédie* and Columbus' 1493 account of his discovery of the New World.

The Regional History Collection comprises the Hearst Collection (the *Herald*, the *Examiner* and the *Herald Examiner*), consisting of 1.2 million photographs (1904-61) and negatives (1950-61); the State Politicians Collection; and the California Historical Society Collection of Photographs.

The Feuchtwanger Memorial Library consists of 30,000 volumes and extensive archives bequeathed to the USC Libraries by the German-Jewish novelist Lion Feuchtwanger (1891-1987). It is rich in volumes exploring German literature and culture, French Revolution, philosophy, Judaica and art history.

Entrance to Doheny Memorial Library

The American Literature Collection was assembled from several private holdings. Emphasis is placed on first editions, manuscripts and documents of American writers since 1850, including Herman Melville, Jack London, Henry James, Bret Harte and Mark Twain. The collection contains modern and contemporary poetry, and newly developed holdings of works and manuscripts by Charles Bukowski, Paul Bowles and Lawrence Ferlinghetti.

***Biblia Germanica*, Nuremberg, 1483, from the Doheny Memorial Library. The Israelites celebrate their deliverance after the parting of the Red Sea.**

14

Hancock Memorial Museum

USC, University Park, Hancock Bldg, #251, Los Angeles, 90089-0371. ☎ (213) 740-0433. **Thomas Guide:** 674 B1. 🚌 bus. **Hours:** by appointment only. $ free. [P] on-campus, $6 per entry; on Figueroa St, south of Jefferson Blvd. 📷 not allowed. **Year opened:** 1936. **Governing authority:** college/university. **Category:** specialized museum. **Activities/programs:** guided tours. **Collection focus:** furniture and interiors.

The museum is located on the second floor of the Hancock Building on the USC campus. It includes the reception hall, dining room, music salon, library and foyer salvaged from a 23-room Palladian-style mansion. Built for oil magnate G. Allan Hancock in 1907, the structure stood at the corner of Wilshire Blvd and Vermont Ave. In 1936, it was demolished except for the five rooms, which were transferred to the campus and rebuilt. The rooms contain original mansion furniture, featuring examples from the High Italian Renaissance, Rococo, Louis XV and Georgian periods.

Up the Hudson to West Point (1858) by David Johnson

⑮
USC — Fisher Gallery

823 Exposition Blvd, Los Angeles, 90089-0292. ✉ University Park, Los Angeles, 90089-0292. ☎ (213) 740-4561. **Fax:** (213) 740-7676. **Thomas Guide:** 674 B1. 🚌 bus. **Hours:** Tue-Fri noon-5pm, Sat 11am-3pm. **Closed:** between exhibitions. ⓢ free. Ⓟ $6 on USC campus (enter gate 1), metered parking on Exposition Blvd and/or Vermont Ave. Parking lots also available on Menlo Ave at Exposition and in Exposition Park. 📷 not allowed. **Year founded/opened:** 1939. **Primary focus:** collection, preservation, exhibition and interpretation of

Isabella Hunter (ca. 1776-90) by Angelica Kauffmann

objects. **Research fields:** related to collections. **Special collections:** the Elizabeth Holmes Fisher Collection, the Armand Hammer Collection. **Major exhibitions:** "In Search of... USC's Baroque Masterworks From the Armand Hammer Collection" (1994-5), "Romance With Nature — 19th-Century American Landscapes" (1989), "A Selection of British Paintings From the Fisher Gallery Collec-

tion" (1988), "Masterworks From the 16th and 17th Centuries" (1987). **Publications:** exhibition catalogues. **Governing authority:** college/university, nonprofit. **Category:** art museum. **Activities/programs:** artist talks, changing exhibitions, educational programs, inter-museum loans, lectures. **Facilities:** exhibit space/gallery. ♿ strollers permitted, parking, wheelchair accessible. **Collection focus:** European art; modern and contemporary art; Dutch, Flemish, English, European, French and North American painting; 17th- — 20th-century painting.

As a branch of University of Southern California, the Fisher Gallery formed its permanent collection in 1939 from the bequest of Elizabeth Holmes Fisher. It was later enlarged by gifts from the Armand Hammer Foundation (1964/5) and other donors.

The collection of 16th- and 17th-century Dutch, Flemish and French masterworks include *View of Dordrecht* (1637) by Jan van Goyen and *Portrait of a Lady* and *Portrait of a Gentleman* (1675-85) by Nicholaes Maes. The 15th- to 19th-century British paintings are highlighted by Mrs. *Burroughs* (1769) by Thomas Gainsborough, *Arthur Maister* (ca. 1764) by Frances Cotes, *Sir Patrick Blake* (ca. 1765) by Sir Joshua Reynolds and *John Utterson of Fareham* (1769) by Benjamin West.

The collection of 19th-century American landscapes contains *Along the Mohawk* (1828) by Thomas Doughty, the first Native American artist to declare

himself a "landscape painter," later referred to as "the father of American landscape painting"; *The Woodchopper, Lake Featherstonhaugh* (1896) by the father of the Hudson River school, Thomas Cole; and *A Stream in the Rocky Mountains* (1882) by Albert Bierstadt.

The 19th-century French Barbizon school of landscape painting is represented by approximately a dozen paintings, including *The Lake in the Forest* by Theodore Rousseau, *Borde de Rivière* by Charles François Daubigny and *Le Lac* (ca. 1872) by Jean-Baptiste-Camille Corot. The col-

Vessels in a Calm (ca. 1674) by Willem van de Velde the Younger

lection also contains one pastel drawing: *Femme Etendent du Linge* (1858) by Jean François Millet.

The 20th-century collection is varied in style and media, comprising 125 ivory miniatures by Martha Wheeler Baxter and Gertrude Little, serigraph prints by Yaacov Agam, embossed lithographs by Rufino Tamayo and photographs by Robert Rauschenberg.

Classical Landscape (ca. 1651) by Claude Lorraine

SOUTH BAY

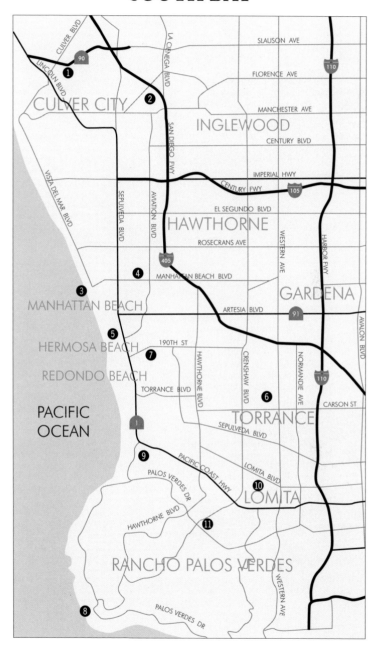

1 Lannan Foundation
2 Centinela Adobe
3 Roundhouse Marine Studies
  Lab and Aquarium/
  Museum
4 Manhattan Beach Historical
  Museum

5 Hermosa Beach Historical
  Museum
6 Torrance Historical Museum
7 Redondo Beach Historical
  Museum
8 Point Vicente Interpretive
  Center

9 Salvation Army Western
  Territorial Headquarters
10 Lomita Railroad Museum
11 South Coast Botanic Garden

The Poetry Garden (1992) by Siah Armajani, a permanent environmental work that incorporates Wallace Stevens's poem *Anecdote in the Jar* into the design of the garden

❶

Lannan Foundation

5401 McConnell Ave, Los Angeles, 90066-7027. ☎ (310) 306-1004. **Fax:** (310) 578-6445. **Thomas Guide:** 672 D7. 🚌 bus. **Hours:** Tue-Sun 11am-5pm. **Closed:** holidays. 💲 free. **Reservations:** recommended for groups. **P** free. 📷 not allowed in galleries, allowed in garden. **Year founded:** 1960. **Year opened:** 1990. **Primary focus:** dedicated to the support and presentation of contemporary visual art and literature. **Research fields:** permanent

Frau, die Treppe herabgehend (1965) by Gerhard Richter

collection archives. **Special collections:** the J. Patrick Lannan Collection. **Major exhibitions:** "Miroslaw Balka: 37.1" (1994), "Siah Armajani: The Poetry Garden and Recent Works" (1992), "Nicholas Africano:

Innocence and Experience" (1991). **Publications:** *Nicholas Africano: Innocence and Experience.* **Governing authority:** nonprofit. **Category:** art museum. **Activities/programs:** artist talks, awards, changing exhibitions, installations, inter-museum loans, multimedia presentations, retrospectives. **Facilities:** exhibit space/gallery, 2,000-volume research library, sculpture garden. ♿ parking, wheelchair accessible. **Collection focus:** modern and contemporary art.

The Lannan Foundation was established in 1960 by the entrepreneur and financier J. Patrick Lannan. Its aim is to support the creation and acceptance of high-quality, innovative and sometimes controversial forms of art through charitable programs. Lannan was a dedicated patron of the arts and literature, serving as chairman of the board of the Modern Poetry Association for more than 30 years. The foundation's literary programs include the annual Lannan Literary Awards and Fellowships and the production of Lannan Literary Videos. It also produces a series of literary events, *readings & conversations*, and a summer reading series.

The Lannan Foundation occupies a renovated industrial building designed in 1968 by William Krisel for Feuer Corp. It houses art exhibition and storage and study spaces, administrative offices and a literary library.

Through its grant program the foundation supports emerging and under-recognized artists and promotes controversial or experimental works of art. The foundation's permanent collection began as the private collection of Lannan, who actively acquired contemporary American and European works of art from the late 1950s until his death in 1983. It numbers about 1,800 pieces in a full spectrum of media and includes some important early works by emerging artists who

Lannan Foundations headquarters

later in their careers developed international reputations.

The collection features masterworks of abstraction such as *Abstract Painting* (1960-5) by Ad Reinhardt, *Nunca Pasa Nada* (1964) by Frank Stella and *Untitled* (1958) by Clyfford Still. Sculpture is represented with funk assemblages by Bruce Conner and Ed Kienholz, and with geometric floor pieces by Jackie Ferrara, Donald Judd and Jackie Winsor.

Among the photographers whose works are included are Thomas Ruff, Cindy Sherman and Mitchel Syrop. The collection also has works on paper by David Hammons, Jim Shaw and Lucas Samaras, and the video works *Tall Ships* (1992) by Gary Hill and *Clown Torture* (1987) by Bruce Nauman. The

Walter Hopps, Hopps, Hopps (1959) by Ed Kienholz

work of some artists is represented in depth, including Chris Burden, Chuck Close, Robert Irwin, Mike Kelley, Charles Ray and Kiki Smith.

Alex (1991) by Chuck Close

Centinela Adobe

[2]

Centinela Adobe

7634 Midfield Ave, Los Angeles, 90045. ☎ (310) 676-4363. **Recorded information:** (310) 649-6272. **Thomas Guide:** 703 A1. **Hours:** Wed, Sun 2-4pm. $ free, donations welcome. **Reservations:** (310) 677-7916 (recommended). [P] free on grounds and street. 📷 allowed on grounds, not in buildings. **Membership:** available. **Year founded:** 1965. **Primary focus:** to preserve, protect and maintain historic buildings in the Centinela Valley and to acquaint and educate the youth. **Research fields:** history of Inglewood, Westchester and the Centinela Valley. **Special collections:** the Bernard M. Guy Collection. **Publications:** *History of Schools in Inglewood* and *History of Inglewood.* **Governing authority:** private, nonprofit. **Category:** historic building/site open to the public. **Activities/programs:** changing exhibitions, docent programs, educational programs, films, guided tours, lectures, slide presentations, volunteer programs. **Facilities:** audiovisual holdings, research library, picnic area. ♿ strollers permitted, parking, wheelchair accessible. **Collection focus:** architecture, clothing and dress, furniture and interiors, local history, personal history, photography.

The Centinela Adobe Complex consists of three buildings, Centinela Adobe, the Freeman Land Office and the Centinela Valley Heritage and Research Center. Centinela Adobe was built before 1834 as the main house of the Rancho Aguaje del Centinela and is considered to be one of the best-preserved adobe structures in Los Angeles. It was built by Ignacio Machado, son of Jose Manuel Machado, a *soldado de cuero* (leather jacket soldier), who escorted the group of settlers from Mexico who founded Los Angeles in 1781. The Adobe is furnished with Victorian furniture, and the bedroom displays Machado family memorabilia.

The Land Office was built in 1887 by Daniel Freeman, the third owner of the ranch and the founder of Inglewood. The building was used as his office until 1918 and changed locations several times before it was moved to its present site in 1975. It now serves as a showplace for early Inglewood businesses.

The Heritage and Research Center was dedicated in 1980. It houses the materials saved from the 1888 Freeman Mansion, demolished in 1972, as well as over 10,000 negatives, prints, slides and tape recordings from the Bernard M. Guy Collection, documents and books on California and Inglewood history, a collection of historic clothing and various artifacts.

[3]

Roundhouse Marine Studies Lab and Aquarium/Museum

Manhattan Beach Pier, Manhattan Beach, 90266. ✉ PO Box 1, Manhattan Beach 90266. ☎ (310) 379-8117. **Thomas Guide:** 732 E6. **Hours:** Wed-Fri 3pm-sunset, Sat-Sun 10am-sunset. $ $2 donation. **Reservations:** (310) 922-6330 (recommended for classes). [P] on street, metered. 📷 not allowed. **Year founded:** 1982. **Year opened:** 1993. **Primary focus:** to teach conservation. **Research fields:** plankton, water chemistry (bacteria counts). **Governing authority:** nonprofit. **Category:** aquarium. **Activities/programs:** classes/courses, docent programs, educational programs, events, films, lectures, outreach programs, school programs, storytelling, summer programs, volunteer programs, workshops. **Facilities:** cafeteria/restaurant, research library, research lab. ♿ wheelchair accessible. **Aquarium features:** endangered species. **Collection focus:** biology, ecology, mollusks, oceanography, shells, water, zoology.

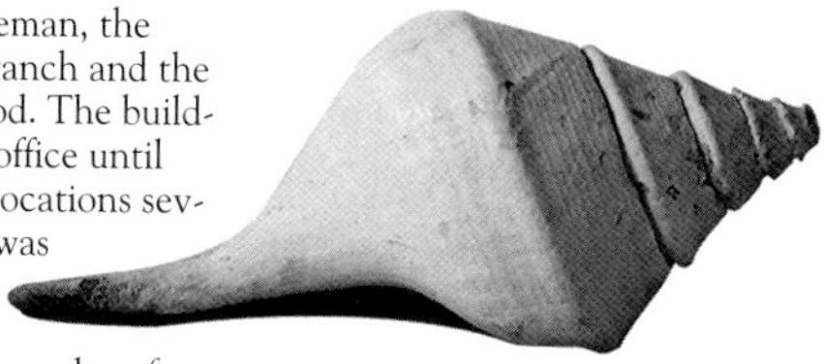
Syrinx, world's largest snail

The aquarium is operated by Oceanographic Teaching Stations, a nonprofit educational organization, and features eight different aquariums and the marine research lab. Visitors can experience a variety of marine life, including live sharks, moray eels and local fish in a shark tank; tide pool animals common to southern California in a touch tank; a 50-year-old, 17-lb spiny rock lobster in a lobster tank; a re-creation of the intertidal environment in a surge tank; schooling fish in a cylinder tank; many local invertebrates in a reef tank; a baby octopus in a bioluminescent tank; and brightly colored, nonnative fish and invertebrates in a tropical aquarium. Exhibits on view include whale bones, mounted fish, shells and other animals. An interesting display features shark adaptation in jaws, teeth, skin and shape.

Shark adaptation in jaws, teeth, skin and shape

4

Manhattan Beach Historical Museum

1601 Manhattan Beach Blvd, Manhattan Beach, 90266. ✉ PO Box 3355, Manhattan Beach 90266. ☎ (310) 374-7575. **Thomas Guide:** 732 J6. **Hours:** Sat noon-3pm, Sun noon-5pm, or by appointment. $ free. [P] street. 📷 allowed. **Membership:** available. **Year opened:** 1990. **Primary focus:** to educate about the history of Manhattan Beach. **Publications:** monthly newsletter. **Governing authority:** private, nonprofit. **Category:** history museum. **Activities/programs:** docent programs, educational programs, guided tours, school programs, volunteer programs. **Facilities:** bookstore, gift shop, picnic area, theater. **Collection focus:** local history, porcelain and ceramics.

Manhattan Beach Historical Museum

The museum is a restored beach cottage, built between 1905 and 1907, when settlement of Manhattan Beach began. The museum features photo displays, a time line of the Manhattan Beach Pier, memorabilia and various household items from the early 20th century. An exhibit of Gabrielino Indian artifacts includes seashell beads used both as jewelry and money, mortar and pestles, and cutting stones. The museum contains a small exhibition of dinnerware, ceramic items and Disney ceramic figurines made by the local Metlox Potteries between 1927 and 1989.

5

Hermosa Beach Historical Museum

710 Pier Ave, Hermosa Beach, 90254. ☎ (310) 318-9421. **Thomas Guide:** 762 H2. **Hours:** Sat-Sun 2-4pm. **Closed:** major holidays, Memorial Day, Labor Day. $ free. [P] free, at Community Center. 📷 permitted. **Membership:** available. **Year founded:** 1987. **Year opened:** 1992. **Primary focus:** to preserve and chronicle the history of Hermosa Beach. **Publications:** quarterly newsletter. **Governing authority:** municipal. **Category:** history museum. **Activities/programs:** changing exhibitions, docent programs, events. **Facilities:** exhibit space/gallery. ♿ parking, wheelchair accessible. **Collection focus:** local history.

Located in the Hermosa Beach Community Center (formerly the Pier Avenue School, where the girls' locker room was used for the film *Carrie* in 1973), this small museum houses a collection of photographs and artifacts illustrating the history of Hermosa Beach. Its displays provide a picture of the development of local industries and businesses, including the Hermosa Tile Factory, the Hermosa Glass Factory, silk mills and California Hand Prints. There is a large collection of early photographs of the city, memorabilia from the Hermosa Theater, pictures and various artifacts from schools, and vintage clothing from the early 1920s. Other exhibits include early surfboards and photos about surfing, which started in Hermosa in the 1920s.

Hermosa Beach, the Strand (1932)

Torrance Historical Museum

6

Torrance Historical Museum

1345 Post Ave, Torrance, 90501. ☎ (310) 328-5392. **Thomas Guide:** 763 H6. **Hours:** Tue-Thu, Sun 1-4pm. $ free. [P] street. 📷 allowed. **Membership:** available. **Year founded:** 1979. **Year opened:** 1980. **Primary focus:** history of Torrance and Rancho San Pedro. **Publications:** newsletter. **Governing authority:** nonprofit. **Category:** history museum. **Activities/programs:** changing exhibitions, docent programs, events, guided tours, lectures, volunteer programs. **Facilities:** exhibit space/gallery. **Collection focus:** local history.

The City of Torrance was founded in 1912 by industrialist and developer Jared Sidney Torrance, who planned it as a model city where industry and working-class residences could exist side by side. The museum is located in the former Torrance City Library, designed by the architectural firm of Walker and Eisen and built in 1936 using Federal Works Project Administration (WPA) funds. The building is considered the finest example of WPA Moderne-style architecture remaining in Torrance.

The museum houses a collection of over 1,000 photos and numerous documents, books, artifacts and other materials related to local history. There is an exhibit celebrating the role of women in the history of Torrance and the South Bay. The museum has a collection of more than 1,000 dolls, period furniture, as well as old fire-fighting equipment, including a well-preserved 1912 cart.

Redondo Beach Historical Museum

7

Redondo Beach Historical Museum

302 Flagler Ln, Redondo Beach, 90277. ✉ 302 Knob Hill Ave, Redondo Beach, 90277. ☎ (310) 318-0684, 318-0610 x3252. **Fax:** (310) 316-6467. **Thomas Guide:** 762 A7. **Hours:** Fri 1-4pm, Sun 2-5pm. $ free. [P] free. 📷 not allowed. **Membership:** available. **Year opened:** 1995. **Primary focus:** to investigate, maintain and catalog historical information, records, pictures and artifacts relating to Redondo Beach. **Governing authority:** municipal. **Category:** history museum. **Activities/programs:** changing exhibitions. **Facilities:** exhibit space/gallery, gift shop, picnic area. ♿ wheelchair accessible. **Collection focus:** local history.

The museum is situated in a Queen Anne-style Victorian house that was restored and moved to its present location in 1989. The exhibits aim to re-create the history and atmosphere of old Redondo Beach with displays related to Native Americans, Redondo schools and the fire and police departments. One hall concentrates on wharves and piers, water and the oceanfront playground. On display are wooden surfboards used in the early days of the sport. Photo exhibits illustrate the life of George Freeth (1883-1919), the man credited with reviving the lost Polynesian art of surfing. Advertised as "the man who can walk on water," he used a solid-wood, 8-foot, 200-lb surfboard.

8

Point Vicente Interpretive Center

31501 Palos Verdes Dr W, Rancho Palos Verdes, 90275. ☎ (310) 377-5370. **Fax:** (310) 377-9868. **Thomas Guide:** 822 F4. **Hours:** daily 10am-5pm in winter, 10am-7pm in summer. **Closed:** Thanksgiving, Christmas Eve and Christmas Day, New Year's Day. $ $2 adult, $1 children and seniors. **Reservations:** recommended for school tours. [P] free. 📷 allowed. **Membership:** available. **Year founded:** 1984. **Year opened:** 1984. **Primary focus:** the cultural and natural history of Palos Verdes Peninsula, marine mammals, whale watching. **Research fields:** history of the Gabrielino Indians, marine mammals. **Special collections:** the Thomas P. Tower Collection. **Governing authority:** municipal. **Category:** natural history museum. **Activities/programs:** changing exhibitions, docent programs, events (annual "Whale of a Day," 1st Sat in March), films, guided tours, school programs, volunteer programs. **Facilities:** bookstore, exhibit space/gallery, gift shop, research library, picnic area, visitors' center. ♿ strollers permitted, parking, wheelchair accessible. **Garden features:** native plant garden, restrooms; dogs allowed in park on leash; peak times: Jan-May. **Collection focus:** North American archeology and antiquities, bones, ecology, fossils, geology, local history, mammals, shells.

Whales exhibit in the Point Vicente Interpretive Center with replicas of toggle harpoon, flensing knife and blubber hook

Situated on a bluff overlooking the ocean at the tip of the Palos Verdes Peninsula, the center is a perfect spot for watching the Pacific gray whales. From December to April visitors can spot the whales on their annual, two-way migration from the Arctic to Baja California. Well-organized exhibits on whales and other coastal life include mounted animals, video shows and whale sound recordings. The museum focuses on the geology and natural and cultural evolution of Palos Verdes, with displays that explore land erosion, rocks, shells and fossils. The Gabrielino Indians exhibit illustrates the history of the area's earliest residents through weapons, tools and other artifacts.

9

Salvation Army Western Territorial Headquarters

30840 Hawthorne Blvd, Rancho Palos Verdes, 90274; annex: 2780 Lomita Blvd, Torrance, 90505. ☎ (310) 534-6097. **Fax:** (310) 534-7157. **Thomas Guide:** 793 E2. 🚌 bus. **Hours:** by appointment only. [P] free. **Year opened:** 1979. **Primary focus:** history of the Salvation Army. **Governing authority:** church, non-profit. **Category:** history museum. **Collection focus:** personal history, religious history and traditions, social conditions.

Although the Salvation Army does not have a museum at present (a new conference center is under construction), there are four built-in display windows in an upstairs hall at the main campus, and the annex houses the collection as well as a few display cases with rotating exhibits. The collection consists of more than 15,000 items dealing with the history of the Salvation Army, primarily in 13 western states. Highlights include a turn-of-the-century tea set used by General William Booth, founder of the Salvation Army; the lecture notes of Evangeline Booth (ca. 1896); a historic Alaska drum (1900) and the uniform of the "Doughnut Girl" (WWI, 1918).

Lomita Railroad Museum

⑩
Lomita Railroad Museum

2137 W 250th St, Lomita, 90717.
☎ (310) 326-6255. **Thomas Guide:** 793 H4. 🚌 bus, metro. **Hours:** Wed-Sun 10am-5pm. **Closed:** Thanksgiving and Christmas. 💲 $1 adults, $0.50 children. **Reservations:** recommended for groups. 🅿 free. 📷 personal allowed, charge for commercial use. **Membership:** available. **Year founded:** 1966. **Year opened:** 1967. **Primary focus:** to develop interest in steam railroading. **Governing authority:** municipal. **Category:** specialized museum. **Activities/programs:** guided tours. **Facilities:** gift shop, picnic area. **Collection focus:** railways.

Southern Pacific "Mogul" steam locomotive (1902)

The museum was built in 1966 by Irene Lewis and given to the City of Lomita. Mrs. Lewis was a dedicated railroader whose Little Engines Company developed and manufactured kits for miniature steam locomotives marketed all over the world. The passenger depot structure was designed and constructed by John W. Gallareto as a re-creation of Boston & Maine's Greenwood station at Wakefield, Massachusetts, built before the turn of the century. The depot's ticket office is furnished as a typical old-time station agent's office, and it is authentic in every detail.

Adjacent to the museum is a Southern Pacific #1765, "Mogul" steam locomotive, built in 1902 by the Baldwin Locomotive Works in Philadelphia, and a huge Southern Pacific tender. The locomotive served the route between Los Angeles and San Bernardino and on several local routes until 1958. Exhibited on tracks is a caboose (the office and home-on-wheels for the train crew) built in 1910 by Bettendorf and assigned to O.W.R. & N. in Washington, a subsidiary of Union Pacific. It was intended for long road service and equipped with bunks for the train crew, a stove for cooking and heating, an icebox for food storage, and water containers. The museum's velocipede, a three-wheeled handcar used by track inspectors,

was built in 1881 for the Maine-Central Railroad. On view in the park annex across the street are a 1923 oil-tank car and a 1913 box-car.

The museum exhibits equipment used in the era of steam engines and authentic railroad memorabilia. Among the objects on display are mileposts, switch-stand lights, semaphores, whistle posts, torpedoes used as warning devices, locomotive whistles and bells used by engineers to send messages, and link and pin couplers used by switchmen and brakemen. There are collections of kerosene hand lanterns used for signaling purposes, marker lights that were displayed at the rear of a train, locomotive builder plates and button-type number plates, locomotive classification lights and trainmen's uniform buttons.

Three scale models of steam locomotives on display represent

Union Pacific caboose interior (1910)

three distinct eras of steam railroading. The museum houses a fine collection of photographs, drawings, lithographs and posters of various types of locomotives, famous trains and railroads from all over the world. There is a painting on glass of the Golden State Limited, one of only two in existence of the original fifty made in 1904 by Chinese artists for the St. Louis Exposition.

Museum interior

⑪ South Coast Botanic Garden

26300 Crenshaw Blvd, Palos Verdes Peninsula, 90274. ☎ (310) 544-6815. **Fax:** (310) 544-6820. **Thomas Guide:** 793 C6. **Hours:** daily 9am-4:30pm. **Closed:** Christmas Day. Ⓢ $5 aduts, $3 seniors and students, $1 children 5-12, children under 5 free. Free admission 3rd Tue of every month. Ⓟ free. 📷 permit required for commercial use. **Membership:** available. **Year founded/opened:** 1961. **Primary focus:** to support horticultural education and a natural wildlife habitat. **Major exhibitions:** rose, dahlia, cactus, bromeliad, bonsai, orchid and violet shows. **Publications:** *Compost*, newsletter. **Governing authority:** county, nonprofit. **Division of:** Dept of Parks and Recreation. **Category:** botanical garden/arboretum. **Activities/programs:** classes/courses, concerts, docent programs, educational programs, guided tours, outreach programs, summer programs, volunteer programs, workshops. **Facilities:** gift shop, lecture hall, picnic area. ♿ activities for visually impaired, parking, wheelchair accessible. **Garden features:** desert garden, herb garden, rose garden, labels/descriptions, restrooms. **Collection focus:** botany, ecology.

The present site of South Coast Botanic Garden was formerly an open pit mine, producing diatomite until 1956. From 1957 until 1965 it was used as a sanitary landfill by Los Angeles County, which dumped over 3.5 million tons of trash there. The garden was created in 1959 when 87 acres were designated for the

Volunteer Garden

Rose Garden

garden; planting began in 1961. The plants grow in a 3-foot layer of soil over 100 feet of garbage. This is one of the first experimental gardens to be developed in such a way and now represents an important model in land reclamation. The garden developers still face several problems, such as ground settling and heat caused by decaying vegetation. The methane and other landfill gasses formed underground are now collected and burned to provide electricity.

The garden contains over 200,000 plants with approximately 140 families, 700 genera and more than 2,000 species from all over the world. The plant collection was designed to present a variety of textures, shapes and colors. The garden is particularly strong in plants from Australia, southern Africa and the Mediterranean, whose climates are similar to that of southern California. The plantings are divided into sections according to major plant families or similar habitats. There are over 200 species of birds in the garden.

Under screened awnings, the Fuchsia Garden grows begonias, camellias, ferns, impatiens, cycads, clivias and other shade-loving plants, along with many different species and cultivars of fuchsias. The Herb Garden displays herbs used for fragrance, medicinal and culinary purposes, including scented geranium, lavender, rosemary, lamb's ear, chamomile, sorrel, marjoram and thyme. The Children's Garden features several themes from fairy tales, with figures, plants and structures. The Flower Garden blooms all year, containing plants for each season: spring bulbs include irises, tulips and freesias; spring/summer flowers include California poppies, cosmos, zinnias and marigolds; fall/winter plantings consist of chrysanthemums, dahlias and calendula. Examples of bromeliads, a species native only to the Americas, include pineapple and Spanish moss.

The Rose Garden, which is still in the process of development, will contain more than 1,600 plants when completed. It displays floribundas, grandifloras, hybrid teas and miniatures, including the top picks of the All-American Rose Selection for each year since 1945. The Garden For the Senses allows visitors to appreciate plantings through the senses of sight, touch and smell. The Water-Wise Garden displays trees, shrubs and ground covers, including acacias, toyons, junipers, pampas grass, ice plant and African daisies. The Succulent and Cactus Garden features hundreds of specimens including cacti, euphorbias, aloes and haworthias. The coral tree (*Erythrina*) has been selected as the tree of the City of Los Angeles. The flowering fruit trees bloom in early spring and include apricot, cherry, plum and peach.

Duck swimming in the garden lake

The lake and stream provide habitats for the study of the interaction between various environmental components. The Redwoods Area features coast redwood (*Sequoia sempervirens*), and the white flowering plants section contains magnolias and some fruit trees. There is a small formal French Garden and a weather station. The Eucalyptus Area grows over 50 different species imported from Australia, its native habitat. The broad-leaf maidenhair tree, a living fossil, is found in *Ginkgo* section. The Woodland Walk features many pine trees, including the Monterey, Canary Island and Japanese black, as well as junipers, cedars and other conifers. The Palm Section grows king and queen palms, the Canary Island date palm, the pigmy palm and California native Washingtonia fan palm. Over 20 species of ficus and fig plants are exhibited in the Ficus Section, while the pittosporum area is planted with large shrubs and small trees, including mock orange and willow pittosporum.

South Coast Botanic Garden

1. Fuchsia Garden
2. Herb Garden
3. Children's Garden
4. Flower Garden
5. Bromeliad Section
6. Rose Garden
7. Garden For the Senses
8. Water-Wise Garden
9. Succulent Garden
10. Coral Tree Section
11. Flowering Fruit Trees
12. Lake
13. Stream
14. Redwood Section
15. White Flowering Plants
16. Formal French Garden and Asia Gate
17. Eucaliptus Section
18. Ginkgo Section
19. Woodland Walk
20. Palm Section
21. Ficus Section
22. Pittosporum Section

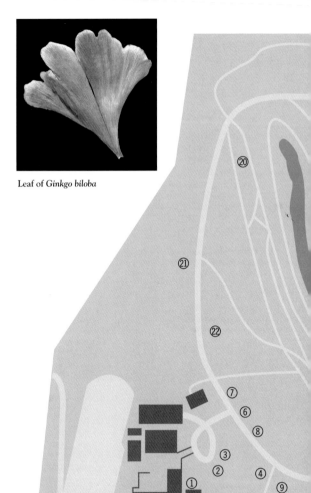

Leaf of *Ginkgo biloba*

Garden Lake

Cactus Garden

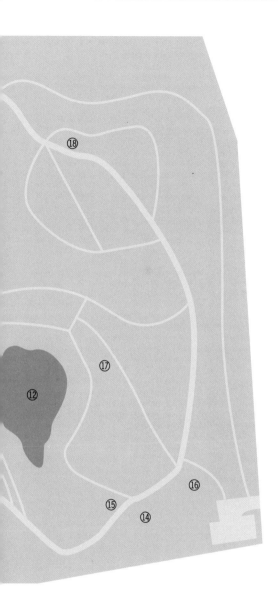

Garden For the Senses

Palm Section

Children's Garden

Woodland Walks, Juniper Trail

HARBOR DISTRICT AND LONG BEACH

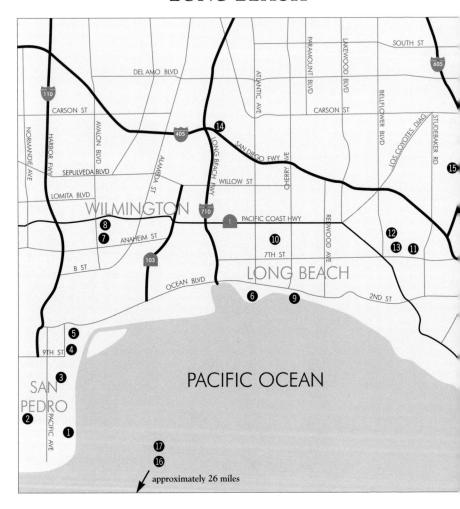

approximately 26 miles

1. Cabrillo Marine Aquarium
2. Fort MacArthur Military Museum
3. Muller House
4. Los Angeles Maritime Museum
5. SS Lane Victory
6. Queen Mary
7. Drum Barracks Civil War Museum
8. Banning Residence Museum
9. Long Beach Museum of Art
10. Long Beach Firefighters Museum
11. Rancho Los Alamitos
12. Earl Burns Miller Japanese Garden — CSULB
13. University Art Museum (UAM) — CSULB
14. Rancho Los Cerritos
15. El Dorado Nature Center
16. Catalina Island Museum
17. Wrigley Memorial Garden Foundation

Gray whale yearling, 28 feet long

1

Cabrillo Marine Aquarium

3720 Stephen White Dr, San Pedro, 90731. ☎ (310) 548-7562/3. **Fax:** (310) 548-2649. **Thomas Guide:** 854 C2. 🚌 bus. **Hours:** Tue-Fri noon-5pm, Sat-Sun 10am-5pm. **Closed:** Thanksgiving, Christmas. $ free. **Reservations:** recommended for groups. [P] beach; $6.50 Mar-Nov, $5.50 Dec-Feb. 📷 allowed. **Membership:** available. **Year founded/opened:** 1935. **Primary focus:** marine life of southern California. **Research fields:** coastal ecology, shore biology, tide pools, moon jelly rearing. **Governing authority:** municipal, nonprofit. **Parent institution:** Dept of Parks and Recreation. **Category:** aquarium. **Activities/programs:** changing exhibitions, classes/courses, docent programs, educational programs, events (Whale Fiesta — Jun, Sea Fair — Oct, Earth Day — Apr), guided tours, lectures, multimedia presentations, outreach programs, school programs, workshops. **Facilities:** audiovisual holdings, bookstore, classroom, exhibit space/gallery, gift shop, lecture hall, 2,500-volume research library, picnic area, theater. ♿ strollers permitted, parking, wheelchair accessible. **Aquarium features:** labels/descriptions. **Collection focus:** biology, birds, bones, botany, ecology, fishing and fisheries, fossils, geology, marine mammals, mollusks, oceanography, shells.

Shark!

Cabrillo Marine Aquarium was originally located in a 1930s Spanish-style bathhouse on Cabrillo Beach. Since 1981 it has occupied a multibuilding complex designed by architect Frank O. Gehry. Enveloped by chain-link fencing, the complex includes an exhibit hall, an auditorium, a classroom, offices and a laboratory. The aquarium aims to promote awareness and knowledge of the rich sea life in southern California through exhibits, programs and research.

Suspended in the courtyard are life-size models of a killer whale (orca), hammerhead sharks, dolphins and a leatherback turtle.

The aquarium's exhibits are organized around three major environments: rocky shores, sandy beaches and mud flats, and open ocean. They emphasize the diversity, adaptations and ecological relationships of local marine life. Each section shows common animals and plants, most of them live and displayed in 35 large aquariums.

California sealion (*Zalophus californicus*)

The rocky shores area illustrates various adaptations to the low- and high-tide environments, with house builders such as tube snails and piddock clams; plantlike animals such as anemones, which look like flowers, and corallike gorgonians; and grazers and browsers such as sea urchins, sea hares and keyhole limpets. Among the rocky seashore hunters are starfish (examples are both predatory and nonpredatory), hermit crabs and mantis shrimp. Other predators on view include octopus and moray eel. How fish protect their offspring is demonstrated in the shark-egg tank, and the many different ways in which marine animals hide from predators or lurk in ambush for their prey can be seen in the camouflage and color-change tanks. In the outdoor touch tank visitors can pet tide pool animals.

The sandy beach wave tank shows how waves shape the shore and features camouflaged flatfishes (the turbot and halibut), sand dollars and sand stars. Two mud-flat tanks present common animals and plants found in this habitat, and the large display case exhibits a variety of shorebirds.

Tanks in the open ocean section feature deep-sea and bioluminescent (light-producing) animals such as the solitary midshipman fish and the colonial sea pansy. The fish-diversity and schooling-fish tanks illustrate how different habitats affect the shapes, colors and behavior of fish. Leopard sharks, nocturnal horn sharks and swell sharks represent the family of 370 known species of sharks.

On display in the whale room are a 28-foot whale baby, the jaw bone of a blue whale (the largest mammal in the world), and the skeleton of a one-year-old Pacific gray whale.

Courtyard with life-sized models of sharks, dolphins, orca (killer whale) and gray whale

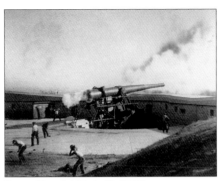

Battery Osgood, 14-inch rifle (1927)

❷ Fort MacArthur Military Museum

3601 Gaffey St, San Pedro, 90731. ✉ Fort MacArthur Station Box 2777, San Pedro, 90731. ☎ (310) 548-7705 (Mon-Fri), 548-2631 (Sat-Sun). **Fax:** (310) 832-5373. **Thomas Guide:** 854 A2. **Hours:** Sat-Sun noon-5pm. Ⓢ free. P free. ◙ allowed. **Membership:** available. **Year founded/opened:** 1985. **Primary focus:** harbor defenses of Los Angeles 1917-75, coast artillery, US Army in southern California. **Research fields:** Fort MacArthur. **Publications:** Alert, quarterly newsletter. **Governing authority:** municipal. **Parent institution:** Dept. of Parks and Recreation. **Category:** historic building/site open to the public. **Activities/programs:** guided tours. **Facilities:** bookstore, research library, picnic area. ♿ strollers permitted, parking. **Collection focus:** forts and fortifications, local history, military and naval history, military uniforms.

The construction of fortifications to guard the new Los Angeles Harbor facilities began in 1914 under a program outlined by the Taft Board Report of 1906. The fortification was named in honor of Lt Gen Arthur MacArthur, a Civil War Medal of Honor winner.

The Fort MacArthur Museum is housed in the Battery Osgood, which was built between 1916 and 1919 as part of the harbor defense system. It was named after Brig Gen Henry B. Osgood, a Civil War veteran. The Battery Osgood and three adjoining batteries were equipped with 14-inch rifled guns mounted on disappearing carriages. They could fire a 1,560-lb. shell 17 miles, which outranged any gun carried on battleships at that time. By 1941, however, improvements in naval armaments and the airplane made these guns obsolete, and in 1944 they were dismantled and the batteries were deactivated. Fort MacArthur was used again between 1954 and 1974, when it was a part of the Nike surface-to-air missile defense system. Battery Osgood-Farley was placed on the National Register of Historic Places in 1974.

While the guns and some electrical equipment were removed, much of the hardware has been left intact. Battery Osgood is probably the best-preserved example of modern (post-1890) coastal defense and the only Taft-era gun emplacement in the continental United States. Visitors can tour the plotting room, where all target information was gathered; the commander's station, which offers still-functioning speaking tubes that allowed communication throughout the battery; the decontamination room; and the gun pit.

The museum outlines the history of Fort MacArthur through its exhibits of historical photos, plans and documents from 1917 to 1975. Among the items on display are 1910 power-generating equipment; various types of US Army uniforms (dating from 1917 to 1945); Pearl Harbor attack photos and ship models; and Coast Artillery Corps artifacts, including regimental flags, medals and pins. There are several displays in the battery parade area, including 16-inch shells, mines, a Japanese 105mm howitzer and a Nike-Ajax missile.

❸ Muller House

1542 S Beacon St, San Pedro, 90733. ✉ PO Box 1568, San Pedro, 90733. ☎ (310) 548-3208. **Thomas Guide:** 824 C6. 🚌 bus. **Hours:** 1st, 2nd, 3rd Sun 1-4pm. **Closed:** major holidays. Ⓢ $2. **Reservations:** required for special groups. P street, free. ◙ not allowed in the interior. **Membership:** available. **Year opened:** 1990. **Primary focus:** to research, record and preserve the history, historical sites and artifacts of San Pedro. **Research fields:** history, people, port buildings, businesses. **Major exhibitions:** bimonthly changing exhibitions of local interest. **Publications:** San Pedro: A Pictorial History. **Governing authority:** nonprofit. **Category:** historic building/site open to the public. **Activities/programs:** changing exhibitions, educational programs, events, guided tours, school programs, slide presentations, quilt shows. **Facilities:** bookstore, exhibit space/gallery, gift shop, research library. ♿ parking, wheelchair accessible (downstairs). **Collection focus:** architecture, local history, period rooms, woodcarvings.

The Muller House

The museum is a restored Colonial Revival-style house built in 1899 by William Muller, a respected shipbuilder in Wilmington. The house was occupied continuously by members of the family until 1983, when it was donated to the San Pedro Bay Historical Society. The museum houses original furniture, decorative items and the memorabilia of community families from 1900 to 1930, recreating the lifestyle and atmosphere of the period.

Nike-Ajax MIM-3A at the Fort MacArthur Military Museum

Wood model ship *Tradition*

❹ Los Angeles Maritime Museum

Berth 84 (near the corner of Harbor Blvd and 6th St), San Pedro, 90731. ☎ (310) 548-7618. **Fax:** (310) 832-6537. **Thomas Guide:** 824 C5. **Hours:** Tue-Sun 10am-5pm. **Closed:** City of Los Angeles holidays. ⑧ free, donation requested. **Reservations:** necessary for groups. Ⓟ free. ◙ allowed, no tripods or lights. **Membership:** available. **Year founded/opened:** 1980. **Primary focus:** maritime history of California and the Pacific, US naval history, transportation and fishing industries. **Research fields:** photography of West Coast ports, marine archaeology of southern California. **Publications:** newsletter *Compass Rose;* research reports. **Governing authority:** municipal. **Category:** specialized museum. **Activities/programs:** changing exhibitions, classes/courses, competitions, docent programs, educational programs, events (regatta), films, foreign language tours, gallery talks, guided tours, inter-museum loan, internship program, lectures, outreach programs, youth sail training, retrospectives, school programs, slide presentations, traveling exhibitions, volunteer pro-

Sea chest (ca. 1855)

grams, workshops. **Facilities:** audio-visual holdings, bookstore, exhibit space/gallery, gift shop, lecture hall, 5,000-volume research library, picnic area. ♿ parking, wheelchair accessible. **Collection focus:** expeditions and explorations, fishing and fisheries, general American history, marine archaeology, maritime history and trade, ivory, military and naval history, oceanography, North American painting, rescue equipment, scientific and precision instruments, ships and shipbuilding, transportation.

The sea has played an important role in the history of the region, and this museum celebrates southern California's nautical heritage from the era of Indian sea travel to modern superships. The museum is located at the Port of Los Angeles in San Pedro, in the former Municipal Ferry Building constructed in 1941. From the museum deck visitors can enjoy a view of one of the busiest seaports in the world. This is the largest maritime museum on the West Coast, and its collections represent all aspects of seafaring, including the history of the navy, the

Propellers of WWII torpedo

merchant marine, the whaling and fishing industries, commercial shipping, recreational sailing, nautical lore and maritime arts and crafts. The museum exhibits include the *Ralph J. Scott* fireboat (built in 1926), located next to the museum; a seagoing tug, *Angels Gate* (built in 1944); a topsail schooner, *Swift of Ipswich*, built in 1938 by William Robertson and owned by James Cagney; and an authentic Thai fishing boat. On display are a life-size mock-up of the flying bridge of the USS *Los Angeles* and artifacts that include navigational instruments, ship guns, propellers and torpedoes,

Figurehead of Queen Victoria

name boards and other navy memorabilia.

A time line of San Pedro depicts the harbor's development from 1840 through numerous photographs and other documents. There is an exhibit of 129 braids and knots, all named and numbered, displayed with rope so visitors can attempt to duplicate them. Additional attractions include fine examples of the ancient seaman's art of scrimshaw (ivory carving), ships in bottles, figureheads and other sailors' paraphernalia. The museum's noted collection of original maritime paintings by Arthur Beaumont, the navy's official painter, is the largest in existence. Other artworks include a collection of John Stobart prints and a 14-foot mural of the cruiser USS *Los Angeles* by California artist Duncan Gleason.

US Navy diving helmet, Mark V, Model-1

Gun captured at Santiago de Cuba on July, 17, 1898, by the Fifth Army Corps, US Army

The museum houses a celebrated collection of more than 700 ship and boat models. Highlights include an 18-foot scale model of the *Titanic*, featuring the only known cutaway of the ship's interior; President Teddy Roosevelt's Great White Fleet of battleships and the USS *Constitution* ("Old Ironsides"). Among the models from films on view are the 22-foot model used in *The Poseidon Adventure* (1972) and the real-life *Bounty*, displayed with photographs from the original *Mutiny on the Bounty* (1935), starring Clark Gable and Charles Laughton.

SS *Lane Victory*

❺

SS Lane Victory

Berth 94, San Pedro, 90733. ✉ PO Box 629, San Pedro, 90733-0629. ☎ (310) 519-9545. **Fax:** (310) 519-0265. **Thomas Guide:** 824 D3. **Hours:** daily 9:30am-4:30pm. **Closed:** never. Ⓢ $2 general, $5 family. Ⓟ free. 📷 allowed. **Membership:** available. **Year opened:** 1992. **Primary focus:** merchant marine during WWII. **Governing authority:** nonprofit. **Category:** specialized museum. **Activities/programs:** cruises, guided tours, volunteer programs, film location shooting. **Facilities:** gift shop, research library. **Collection focus:** maritime history and trade, military and naval history, ships and shipbuilding, transportation.

The SS *Lane Victory* is one of 534 Victory ships built during WWII to transport cargo and war material. She is the only Victory ship on display in the world. Built in 1945 at the California Shipbuilding Corporation, Terminal Island, she served during WWII and the Korean and Vietnam wars. By an act of Congress signed in 1988, the ship was diverted from the scrap heap and given to the Merchant Marine Veterans of WWII. This nonprofit organization owns and operates the *Lane Victory* as a museum and a living memorial to all sailors who lost their lives at sea. She is restored to near-original operating condition and was declared a National Historic Landmark in 1991.

The ship was named in honor of Isaac Lane, a self-educated ex-slave who founded a high school in Jackson, Tennessee, that eventually grew into a college named after him (Lane College). Among

the areas open to visitors are the decks, the engine room, the radio room, the galley, the chart room, the bridge, the flying bridge and crew's quarters. Visitors may inspect the *Lane Victory*'s antiaircraft guns mounted on the forecastle and poop decks. Exhibits in the museum are related to WWII and the merchant marines and include navy and military uniforms, war posters, model ships, navigational instruments, books, documents and photos. The ship was used as a set for many film and TV productions, including *Murder, She Wrote* and *Naked Gun 2½*.

❻

Queen Mary

1126 Queens Hwy, Long Beach, 90802-6390. ☎ (310) 435-3511, reservations (800) 437-2934. **Fax:** (310) 437-4531. **Thomas Guide:** 825 E3. 🚌 bus (shuttle), metro. **Hours:** daily 10am-6pm. **Closed:** never. Ⓢ $10 adults, $8 seniors and military, $6 ages 4-11, under 4 free. Ⓟ $5. 📷 allowed for personal use only. **Membership:** available. **Year founded:** 1967. **Year opened:** 1971. **Primary focus:** preservation of the RMS *Queen Mary*, her history, technology, architecture and art. **Major exhibitions:** "Fit for a Queen: The Adornment of the RMS *Queen Mary*" (1994). **Publications:** *The Art of the RMS Queen Mary* (1994). **Governing authority:** private, nonprofit. **Category:** specialized museum. **Activities/programs:** audio guides, educational programs, films, foreign language audio tours, guided tours, performing arts, school programs, slide presentations. **Facilities:** bookstore, cafeteria/restaurant, exhibit space/ gallery, 200-volume research library, theater, hotel — banquet facilities. ♿ strollers permitted, wheelchair accessible (limited). **Collection focus:** modern and contemporary art, decorative and

SS *Lane Victory:* Compass and azimuth circle

applied art, furniture and interiors, maritime history and trade, military and naval history, English painting, 20th-century painting, ships and shipbuilding.

Spanning more than 1,000 feet (327 m) in length, weighing more than 81,000 gross tons and boasting 12 decks, the *Queen Mary* is the largest, fastest and most luxurious ocean liner ever built. During WWII she was transformed into a troopship, camouflaged with gray paint and nicknamed "The Gray Ghost." Hitler offered the equivalent of $250,000 and Germany's highest military honor to the U-boat captain who could sink her. By the end of the war, the *Queen Mary* had carried more than 800,000 servicemen and set a standing record for the most passengers carried in one crossing — over 16,000!

After completing 1,001 Atlantic crossings, the *Queen Mary* was retired from regular passenger service in 1967. She was purchased by the City of Long Beach and, after a three-year renovation, converted into a major tourist attraction and luxury hotel in 1971. The *Queen Mary* was included on the National Register of Historic Places in 1993.

Visitors may tour the ship from stem to stern, examining the engine room, the power train and the wheelhouse and enjoying the style and elegance of her Art Deco suites and facilities. Exhibits depict the history of trans-Atlantic travel and the *Queen Mary* as she was used during WWII. Artworks on permanent exhibition include paintings, bronzes, extraordinary decorative glass panels, ornamental woodwork, textiles and furnishings.

Queen Mary

Drum Barracks Civil War Museum

❼

Drum Barracks Civil War Museum

1052 Banning Blvd, Wilmington, 90744. ☎ (310) 548-7509. **Fax:** (310) 548-2946. **Thomas Guide:** 794 F6. 🚌 bus. **Hours:** tours: Tue-Thu 10, 11am, noon; Sat 12:30, 1:30, 2:30 pm. 💲 $2.50 donation. **Reservations:** recommended for groups. 🅿 free. 📷 not allowed in

Bedroom (ca. 1850)

building. **Membership:** available. **Year founded:** 1966. **Year opened:** 1986. **Primary focus:** California, 1861-71. **Research fields:** Civil War, history of LA Harbor. **Governing authority:** municipal. **Parent institution:** Dept. of Recreation and Parks. **Category:** historic building/site open to the public. **Activities/programs:** changing exhibitions, concerts, docent programs, educational programs, events (Civil War Christmas) guided tours, lectures, outreach programs, school programs,

slide presentations, volunteer programs. **Facilities:** bookstore, exhibit space/gallery, gift shop, 2,000-volume research library. ♿ strollers permitted, parking, wheelchair accessible (limited).
Collection focus: architecture, arms and armor, forts and fortifications, local history, period rooms.

The museum building is the last remaining major structure of Camp Drum, later renamed Drum Barracks, which was headquarters for the US Army in southern California and the Arizona Territory between 1862 and 1871. This is the only intact army building located in southern California from the Civil War period and one of the few remaining in the western United States. A 2-story, 16-room structure served as the junior officers' headquarters.

The camp occupied 60 acres of land donated by two Union supporters, Phineas Banning, founder of Los Angeles Harbor, and B. D. Wilson, who was the first mayor of Los Angeles and the grandfather of Gen George S. Patton. Camp Drum was named after Adj Gen Richard Coulter Drum, the head of the army's Department of the Pacific at the time. It consisted of 19 permanent buildings, including senior and junior officers' quarters, troop barracks, stables

and a hospital. The camp served as the main military training and supply base in the Southwest until its deactivation in 1871. At its peak, there were up to 8,000 men stationed here.

The museum's displays illustrate the history of the Civil War and California troops during the period, as well as development of the Los Angeles World Port. The

34-star flag found on the Vicksburg battlefield on May 22, 1863

restored bedroom and parlor feature period furniture dating from the 1850s. In the armory room visitors can see rifles, muskets and carbines from the Civil War era, along with many artifacts accompanying the weapons. One

Civil War rifles

of the more fascinating exhibits is a Gatling gun. These early machine guns, patented in 1861, could fire up to 350 rounds a minute. The collection highlight is a 34-star Union flag. Private William G. Stephens found it on the Vicksburg battlefield on May 22, 1863, and carried it with him until his discharge in 1865. Stephens won a Congressional Medal of Honor at Vicksburg, one of only 1,504 medals awarded during the war.

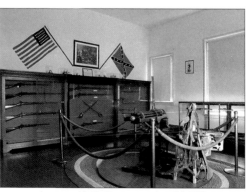

Armory, with Gatling gun naval model 1872

Banning Residence Museum, south façade — front entrance

8

Banning Residence Museum

401 E "M" St, Wilmington, 90744. ✉ PO Box 397, Wilmington, 90748. ☎ (310) 548-7777. **Fax:** (310) 548-2644. **Thomas Guide:** 794 F5. **Hours:** tours: Tue-Thu 12:30, 1:30, 2:30pm; Sat-Sun 12:30, 1:30, 2:30, 3:30pm. **Closed:** national holidays. $ $2 general, children under 12 free. **Reservations:** recommended for groups. [P] free on street. 📷 not allowed in house. **Membership:** available. **Year founded:** 1864. **Year opened:** 1927. **Research fields:** transportation, commerce, decorative arts. **Governing authority:** municipal. **Parent institution:** Dept of Recreation and Parks. **Category:** historic building/site open to the public. **Activities/programs:** artist talks, docent programs, educational programs, events (Victorian Christmas, Floriade, Summer Sociable), guided tours, lectures, school programs.

Stagecoach barn, wagon repair and blacksmith shop

Facilities: research library. ♿ wheelchair accessible (limited), special tours for handicapped. **Garden features:** rose garden. **Collection focus:** architecture, carriages and carts, clothing and dress, decorative and applied arts, dolls and puppets, education, glass and glassware, local history, maritime history and trade, period rooms, railways, transportation.

When 21-year-old Phineas Banning arrived virtually penniless at San Pedro Bay in 1851, Los Angeles was a small pueblo of 1,600 people, incorporated as a city only one year before. Born in Wilmington, Delaware, Banning left his parents' home at the age of 13 to work in his brother's law office in Philadelphia. Adventurous and energetic, he sailed to Panama, crossed the jungles and sailed 3,000 miles north. Upon his arrival, Banning entered the

Stagecoach barn, collection of horse-drawn vehicles

staging and freighting business, transporting people and goods from the small port to Los Angeles 20 miles to the north and further east to San Bernardino and south to Fort Yuma. His well-organized network of routes made him a fortune and formed the pattern for future freeways.

Phineas Banning played a key role in the development of the city of Los Angeles. He was called "The Father of the Port of Los Angeles." He brought the Southern Pacific Railroad to the port and contributed to linking Los Angeles and San Francisco by telegraph. He created a comprehensive transportation network that, together with harbor and railroad development, caused an unprecedented population boom and growth for the city and southern California. During the Civil War, Banning supported the Union and was named Brigadier General of the state militia. He founded

Dining room

the city of Wilmington, named after his birthplace, and was elected to the state senate.

The house that Banning designed for himself and built in 1864 is considered the finest example of Greek Revival residential architecture in California. The 3-story mansion, topped with a cupola, was built with lumber from the Mendocino Coast, Belgian marble and European stained glass. The house has been carefully restored, and today 18 of its original 23 rooms are open to the public. They are decorated in Victorian period furniture, including 32 original pieces donated by the Banning family.

The restored stagecoach barn features a wagon repair and blacksmith shop and houses a fine collection of horse-drawn vehicles.

Parlor of the Banning Residence

Long Beach Museum of Art

Long Beach Museum of Art

2300 E Ocean Blvd, Long Beach, 90803. ☎ (310) 439-2119. **Fax:** (310) 439-3587. **Thomas Guide:** 825 G1. **Hours:** Wed-Thu & Sat-Sun 10am-5pm, Fri 10am-8pm. 💲 $2 general, $1 students and seniors, children under 12 free. P free. 📷 allowed for personal use only. **Membership:** available. **Year founded/**

Elongated Head A (1920) by Alexej Jawlensky

opened: 1950. **Primary focus:** modern and contemporary art. **Special collections:** the Milton Wichner Collection. **Publications:** Long Beach Museum of Art Quarterly. **Governing authority:** nonprofit. **Category:** art museum. **Activities/programs:** artist talks, changing exhibitions, classes/courses, concerts, docent programs, educational programs, gallery talks, installations, internship programs, lectures, multimedia presentations, outreach programs, school programs, volunteer programs, work-

shops. **Facilities:** exhibit space/ gallery, gift shop, picnic area, sculpture garden. ♿ wheelchair accessible. **Collection focus:** Afro-American art, Asian art, modern and contemporary art, book arts, 19th- and 20th-century painting, photography, video art.

The museum building was constructed in 1912 as a summer home for Elizabeth Milbank Anderson, a businesswoman, philanthropist and collector. In this 15-room, California Arts and Crafts-style mansion, she housed her notable collection of paintings and Chinese porcelain. The building changed ownership several times until 1950, when it was purchased by the City of Long Beach and remodeled as a Municipal Art Center. In 1957 it officially became a museum and its name was changed to the Long Beach Museum of Art.

Since its founding, the museum has been dedicated to collecting and exhibiting the work of contemporary artists based in southern California. It also features experimental work by media artists, and it has developed an international reputation for its multimedia programs. The museum's permanent collection consists mainly of 20th-century paintings, drawings, prints and sculpture. Its nucleus is comprised of 61 works from the Milton Wichner Collection of European abstract art, including a significant survey of work by Russian artist Alexej Jawlensky. The collection features paintings such as Dreaming Head (1916) by Alexej Jawlensky, An Arabesque (1938) by Vasily Kandinsky and Untitled (1940) by Oskar Fishinger. Other works

include watercolors by Lyonel Feininger, prints and watercolors by Kandinsky and lithographs by Laszlo Moholy-Nagy.

The museum also houses works by Pablo Picasso, Salvador Dalí and Joan Miró. Among the pieces on view in the museum's sculpture garden are Two Lines Up-Spread (1970) by George Rickey, The Point as a Set #16 (1965) by Claire Falkenstein and Flora Fauna (1966) by Peter Voulkon.

The Long Beach Museum of Art maintains the largest public collection of video art on the West Coast. With more than

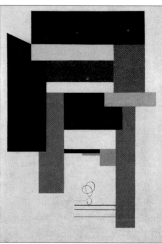

An Arabesque (1938) by Vasily Kandinsky

1,500 works, it is one of the most significant collections in the country. Among the major works are The Passing (1991) by Bill Viola, Height of Appetite (1992) by Paul Tossie and Selected Works (1975) by William Wegman.

A videotape still from From the Vaults of Memory (1991) by Anet Ris

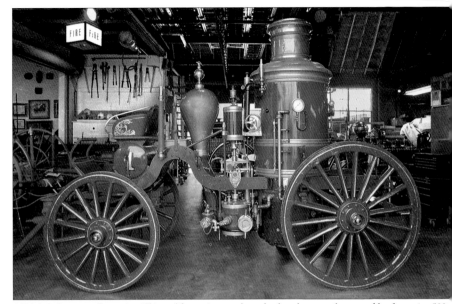

1894 Amoskeg steam fire engine. This coal fire engine was drawn by three horses and was capable of pumping 500 gallons of water per minute.

❿ Long Beach Firefighters Museum

1445 Peterson Ave, Long Beach, 90813. ✉ 2245 Argonne Ave, Long Beach, 90815. ☎ (310) 597-0351. **Fax**: (310) 597-0453. **Thomas Guide**: 795 F5. 🚌 bus. **Hours**: 2nd Sat of the month 10am-3pm. Ⓢ free. Ⓟ free. 📷 allowed. **Year opened**: 1982. **Primary focus**: fire equipment and history of Long Beach. **Governing authority**: non-profit. **Category**: specialized museum. **Activities/programs**: guided tours. ♿ parking, wheelchair accessible. **Collection focus**: firefighting, rescue equipment.

The building in which the museum is housed served as Station 10 and the fire department repair shop from 1925 until 1968. When a new fire station was built, the building was used for the storage and restoration of antique fire appliances and equipment. In order to preserve the structure, the City of Long Beach declared it a Building of Historical Significance.

The museum houses a range of firefighting apparatus and equipment, most of which was used by the Long Beach Fire Department. It contains many styles of ladders, a life net and a basket stretcher. There is a comprehensive collection of breathing equipment and even an original hitching post. The trophy room displays a large collection of trophies, badges, helmets and mementos. Photographs on display pertain to the history of Long Beach and the fire fepartment.

The museum contains firefighting apparatus dating from the late 19th century to the present. Among the equipment on display are an 1890 Rumsey

1935 General Motors squad wagon

hand-drawn ladder wagon, which was never restored and still has its original ladders and painted decorations; a 1894 Robinson hose wagon, one of very few in existence today; the hose cart "Howard Hughes," which was used to protect the *Spruce Goose* while it was in storage; and many other pumpers and ladder trucks.

Firefighter's helmet

1897 Hugo Maher hand pumper. It took up to 6 men to pump it at fires.

Rancho Los Alamitos, front lawn with two massive Moreton Bay figs

⑪ Rancho Los Alamitos

6400 Bixby Hill Rd, Long Beach, 90815. ☎ (310) 431-3541. Thomas Guide: 796 E6. **Hours:** Wed-Sun 1-5pm (last tour at 4pm). **Closed:** major holidays. Ⓢ free. **Reservations:** for groups only. Ⓟ free, on-site. Ⓞ exterior only. **Membership:** available. **Year opened:** 1970. **Primary focus:** primary interpretive period 1890-1940. **Research fields:** southern California history.

Cactus garden

Publications: Perspectives newsletter. **Governing authority:** municipal, non-profit. **Category:** historic building/site open to the public. **Activities/programs:** educational programs, events, guided tours, internship program, lectures, school programs, summer programs, volunteer programs, workshops. ♿ strollers permitted, wheelchair accessible. **Collection focus:** architecture, Western art, domestic utensils, farms and farming, glass and glassware, local history, horses, horticulture, period rooms.

The Gabrielino Indians were probably the first inhabitants of the site, establishing their village of Puvungna around 500 AD.

Rancho Los Alamitos (Ranch of the Little Cottonwoods) dates back to 1790, when Manuel Nieto, a Spanish foot soldier, received the area as part of a 300,000-acre land grant for his retirement. He was a member of the expedition of Don Gaspar de Portolá, which began the Spanish colonization of California. In 1806 the property was divided among Nieto's heirs into five ranchos. One of those, the Rancho Los Alamitos, was sold to Governor Jose Figueroa in 1834. Abel Stearns bought the rancho in 1842 as a summer home for himself and his bride, Arcadia Brandini. After losses due to the droughts of the 1860s forced foreclosure of the property, the rancho was acquired by John and Susan Bixby in 1881. The Bixbys lived at the house until 1961, and in 1968 the descendants gave the house, grounds and barns to the City of Long Beach as a gift.

The original adobe was built in 1806 as a shelter for vaqueros of the Nieto family. The earliest structure was changed by later additions and enlarged many times through its history to suit the needs of its numerous owners. It is considered the oldest domestic structure in the state and is listed on the National Register of Historic Places. With its historic building and 8-acre grounds, Rancho Los Alamitos recounts the history of the early days of ranching and farming in Southern California. Today the ranch house contains 21 rooms furnished with original Bixby furniture, including an extensive col-

lection of glassware. The grounds contain a working blacksmith shop, six early 20th-century barns featuring original farm tools and equipment. There are exhibits of old spurs, bridles, harnesses and veterinarian instruments, dating from the 18th to 19th centuries.

Susan Hathaway Bixby started the first developed garden on the site, planting the two Moreton Bay figs (Ficus macrophylla) around 1891. They are now the largest trees on the property. The present gardens were created between 1920 and 1936 by Florence Bixby, who greatly

Ranch equipment

expanded the existing garden and added most of the landscaping. She engaged several landscape designers, such as Paul Howard, Florence Yoch and William Hertrich, and created a series of gardens, including the cactus garden, native garden, herb garden, rose garden, secret garden and jacaranda walk.

Billiard room in the ranch house

Dry Garden

⑫

Earl Burns Miller Japanese Garden — CSULB

Earl Warren Dr, Long Beach, 90840.
✉ 1250 Bellflower Blvd, Long Beach, 90840. ☎ (310) 985-8885.
Fax: (310) 985-8884. **Thomas Guide:** 796 D5.
Hours: Tue-Fri 8am-3:30pm, Sun noon-4pm. **$**
free. **Reservations:** recommended for tours. **P** student lot "D", metered during weekdays.
📷 no professional photography or tripods. **Membership:** available.
Year founded/ opened: 1981.

Nure-sage lantern

Primary focus: to provide an aesthetic, educational, cultural and recreational resource to the community. **Governing authority:** college/university. **Category:** botanical garden/arboretum. **Activities/programs:** docent programs, educational programs, events (koi auction — Nov), guided tours, internship program, lectures, school programs, volunteer programs, horticulture workshops. **Facilities:** available for rent. ♿ strollers permitted, parking, sound augmentation systems, wheelchair accessible, restrooms. **Garden**

features: Japanese garden, pond, restrooms, rock garden, water garden, teahouse (demonstration only); peak times: Apr-Oct.
Collection focus: botany, horticulture.

The Japanese Garden was dedicated in 1981 and named in memory of local philanthropist Earl Burns Miller. It was designed by Long Beach landscape architect Edward R. Lovell, who traveled to Japan to study several Imperial gardens in preparation for this project.

The entry gate is designed after a gate in Kyoto, Japan, and guarded by mythical lion dogs. The garden features traditional Japanese elements, such as a three-tiered stone pagoda, an arched bridge, water-

Votive stone. It depicts Senju Kannon, or Kannon of the Thousand Hands, a symbol of infinite compassion

falls, an island and a lake, a teahouse, a stone water basin, a dry garden and traditional lanterns.

There is a zigzag bridge, designed to defy evil spirits, who, according to folklore, can travel only in straight lines. The 5-tiered pagoda symbolizes the five cardinal virtues of Zen — humanity, justice, politeness, wisdom and fidelity.

Traditional Japanese plantings include small pines, weeping willows, Japanese camellias and irises, azaleas, Japanese maples, heavenly bamboo and rare black-stemmed bamboo.

More than 200 colored koi inhabit the garden lake

❸
University Art Museum (UAM) — CSULB

250 Bellflower Blvd, Long Beach, 90840. ☎ (310) 985-5761. **Fax:** (310) 985-7602. **Thomas Guide:** 796 D5. 🚌 metro. **Hours:** Tue-Thu noon-8pm, Fri-Sun noon-5pm. 💲 free. P metered spaces. 📷 allowed, no flash or tripods. **Membership:** available. **Year founded:** 1973. **Primary focus:** contemporary art. **Major exhibitions:** James Rosenquist (1993), Jim Dine (1979), Frances Benjamin Johnston (1979), George Segal (1977), Roy Lichtenstein (1977), Lucas Samaras (1975), Tom Wesselman (1974). **Publications:** UAM, quarterly newsletter. **Governing authority:** state. **Category:** art museum. **Activities/programs:** artist talks, awards, changing exhibitions, classes/courses, docent programs, educational programs, events, gallery talks, guided tours, installations, internship program, lectures, multimedia presentations, outreach programs, retrospectives, summer programs, traveling exhibitions, volunteer programs. **Facilities:** audiovisual holdings, bookstore, exhibit space/gallery, gift shop, research library, sculpture garden, slide registry. ♿ strollers permitted, parking, wheelchair accessible. **Collection focus:** modern and contemporary art.

Since its founding as a museum program in 1973, the UAM has organized numerous exhibitions devoted to the work of some of

Installation of *Savoir, retenir, et fixer ce qui est sublime*

the world's most important contemporary artists. Through many of the museum's programs, artists are offered an opportunity to experiment and present their new

Now (1965) by Piotr Kowalski

and innovative works to West Coast audiences.

In 1965 the university (then college) organized the Long Beach International Sculpture Symposium. It was the first such event in the United States and the first in the world to be held on a college campus. Ten sculptors from seven countries were invited to attend the symposium and complete one sculpture each that would become the property of the college. These works became the core of the university's monumental sculpture collection. They include "U" as a Set (1965) by Claire Falkenstein, Mu 464 (1965) by Kengiro Azuma, Carlson/Bloc Tower (1965-72) by Andre Bloc, Long Beach Contract (1965) by Gabriel Kohn, Duet (Homage to David Smith) (1965)

by Robert Murray and wall mural *Sun Forces* (1965) by Rita Letendre. The collection was enlarged by later acquisitions, and today more than 20 works are installed throughout the campus.

The UAM's permanent collection includes contemporary works on paper by Frances Benjamin Johnston, Roy Lichtenstein, Robert Rauschenberg, Leland Rice, George Segal and Frank Stella, among others. The collection highlights include *Biarritz* (1987) by April Gornik, *Watercolor for Parade with Two D's An Evening of French Musical Theater* (1982) by David Hockney, *Horse Blinders* (1969-92) by James Rosenquist, *Tres Vestidos* (1983) by Perejaume, *Cherry Cakes* (1979) by Wayne Thiebaud and *Trap* (1985) by Nancy Graves.

Lovers Bench for a New Millennium (1994) by Eugenia Butler

Evening Shadows (1993) by Maren Hassinger

Courtyard view of 2-story portion of the adobe house

14

Rancho Los Cerritos

4600 Virginia Rd, Long Beach, 90807. ☎ (310) 570-1755. **Thomas Guide:** 765 C7. **Hours:** Wed-Sun 1-5pm. **Closed:** holidays. [$] free. **Reservations:** necessary for groups. [P] free, on site. **Membership:** available. **Year founded/opened:** 1955. **Primary focus:** restoration, preservation and interpretation of the historic adobe and grounds, focusing on the relationship of the rancho's diverse peoples with the development of the Long Beach area. **Research fields:** local and California history, ranching, the Temple and Bixby families, southern California landscaping/horticulture. **Major exhibitions:** "Piece by Piece: The Rancho Story" (1993); "More Than Just a Blanket" (1990); "Attic Finery: The Clothes We Saved" (1989). **Publications:** *Friends Footnotes*, quarterly newsletter, *The Branded Word* (occasional). **Governing authority:** municipal. **Category:** historic building/site open to the public. **Activities/programs:** changing exhibitions, classes/courses, docent programs, dramatic programs, educational programs, events (Stew Cook-Off, Mud Mania), guided tours, internship program, lectures, outreach programs, school programs, volunteer programs, workshops. **Facilities:** bookstore, exhibit space/gallery, gift shop, 4,000-volume research library, picnic area, visitors' center. ♿ parking, wheelchair accessible, Braille guides (by arrangement). **Garden features:** herb garden, labels/descriptions (limited), restrooms; peak times: late winter/early spring. **Collection focus:** architecturte, clothing and dress, decorative and applied art, farms and farming, furniture and interiors, local history, period rooms, textiles.

White eyelet Edwardian-style dress (ca. 1912)

Rancho Los Cerritos was once part of a 300,000-acre land grant that was awarded to foot soldier Manuel Nieto in 1790 by Governor Pedro Fages for his service to the Spanish Crown. After Nieto's death, this grant was divided among his heirs into five ranchos. One of these, Los Cerritos (Ranch of the Small Hills), became the property of Manuela Nieto de Cota and her husband, Guillermo. The rancho was purchased in 1843 by Los Angeles merchant Jonathan Temple, who built the adobe-and-redwood ranch house as headquarters for a cattle ranch. The house was located at its present site, and part of its original wall surface can still be viewed at the front entrance. When the cattle industry declined in the 1860s, Temple sold the ranch to Flint, Bixby and Co. in 1866. The adobe was abandoned between 1881 and 1931, when the new ranch owner, Llewellyn Bixby, started remodeling under architect Kenneth Wing, Sr. The City of Long Beach purchased the adobe in 1955. It was designated a National Historic Landmark in 1970.

The 2-story house is considered one of the finest examples of the Monterey-style adobe in southern California. The rooms are furnished with Victorian furniture belonging to the Bixby family and local residents. There is a large costume and textile collection dating from 1830 to 1930. Historical and archaeological materials, photographs and carpenter's and blacksmith's tools are on display in the visitors' center. The

An 1870 parlor exhibit

archives contain Sarah Bixby Smith's manuscripts, historic photos, diaries, maps and other documents.

Of the 27,000 acres that once comprised the ranch, only 4.9 acres remain today. The original Italian gardens were planted between 1840 and 1850 by Jonathan Temple. Today they contain Italian cypresses and fruit trees, as well as roses, heliconias, camellias, azaleas and flowering shrubs. Also in the garden are some very old and large trees, including the Brazilian cockspur coral tree (*Robinia pseudoacacia*), black locust (*Erythrina crista-galli*), *Ginkgo* and Moreton Bay fig.

Rancho Los Cerritos branding iron

Backyard view of the adobe

⓯

El Dorado Nature Center

7550 E Spring St, Long Beach, 90815. ☎ (310) 570-1745. **Fax:** (310) 570-1535. **Thomas Guide:** 796 G2. 🚌 bus. **Hours:** Tue-Fri 10am-4pm, Sat-sun 8:30am-4pm. **Closed:** Christmas. Ⓢ free. P $3 weekdays, $5 weekends and holidays. **Year founded/opened:** 1969. **Primary focus:** education. **Governing authority:** municipal. **Category:** nature center/wildlife refuge. **Activities/programs:** artist talks, changing exhibitions, classes/courses, docent programs, dramatic programs, educational programs, events, guided tours, lectures, outreach programs, performances, performing arts, storytelling, summer programs, volunteer programs, workshops. **Facilities:** bookstore, conservation center, gift shop, research library, picnic area, visitors' center. ♿ parking, sign-language interpretation, wheelchair accessible. **Garden features:** endangered species, labels/descriptions, ponds, restrooms. **Collection focus:** biology, birds.

El Dorado Nature Center Museum

The 85-acre El Dorado Nature Center is a wildlife area that is home to the gray fox, long-tailed weasel, garter snake, red-shouldered hawk, great blue heron, egret and a wide range of migratory birds. The museum displays changing art and photography exhibitions relating to natural history and the ecosystem of the Nature Center. There are exhibits of stuffed birds, bird's nests, animal skeletons and tracks. A small zoo features the harlequin bug, brown garden snails, crayfish, millipedes, tarantulas, snakes and other small animals. Over 40 species of plants that have adapted to the hot, dry climate of southern California grow in the native plant demonstration garden.

⓰

Catalina Island Museum

1 Casino Way, Avalon, 90704. ✉ PO Box 366, Avalon, 90704. ☎ (310) 510-2414. **Thomas Guide:** 5923 H3. **Hours:** daily 10:30am-4pm. **Closed:** never. Ⓢ $1 general, children under 12 free. **Reservations:** recommended for tours. 📷 not allowed. **Membership:** available. **Year founded:** 1953. **Primary focus:** history of Santa Catalina Island. **Governing authority:** nonprofit. **Category:** history museum. **Activities/programs:** films, guided tours, lectures. **Facilities:** bookstore. ♿ wheelchair accessible. **Collection focus:** local history.

The museum is located inside the circular Casino building, designed by Los Angeles Architects Webber & Spaulding. The building was constructed in 1929 by William Wrigley, Jr., the chewing gum magnate and owner of the Chicago Cubs, who bought the island in 1919. The 1,000-seat theater on the Casino's main floor was the first movie palace acoustically designed for the showing of motion pictures. It was used to preview new talkies by Cecil B. De Mille, Samuel Goldwyn and others.

The museum's permanent exhibits are devoted to the archeology and natural history of the island. They include specimens of flora and fauna, semiprecious stones and Channel Indian artifacts. There are models of the ships used to transport visitors from Los Angeles Harbor, as well as displays of tiles and pottery produced by the local tile industry. Exhibits of photographs document the island's history and natural history.

⓱

Wrigley Memorial Garden Foundation

1400 Avalon Canyon Rd, Avalon, 90704. ✉ PO Box 88, Avalon, 90704. ☎ (310) 510-2288. **Thomas Guide:** 5923 F6. **Hours:** daily 8am-5pm. **Closed:** never. Ⓢ $1 general, children under 12 free. P free. 📷 noncommercial only. **Membership:** available. **Year founded:** 1920. **Year opened:** 1970. **Primary focus:** to preserve endemic plants. **Governing authority:** nonprofit. **Category:** botanical garden/arboretum. **Activities/programs:** guided tours, internship program. **Facilities:** exhibit space/gallery, visitors' center. ♿ parking, wheelchair accessible. **Garden features:** greenhouse, labels/descriptions, rare species, restrooms, peak time: spring. **Collection focus:** botany, horticulture.

The Wrigley Botanical Garden was named after chewing gum magnate William Wrigley, Jr. It was founded in the 1920s, when Mrs. Ada Wrigley established a collection of cacti and succulents. Today, the 37-acre garden has expanded to include plants native to California, including toyon, Torrey pine, California laurel and mountain mahogany (*Cercocarpus betuloides*). Among the endemic species native only to California islands are Catalina mahogany (*Cercocarpus traskiae*), Catalina ironwood (*Lyonothamnus floribundus*) and Catalina manzanita (*Arctostaphylos catalinae*). Of particular interest are eight endemic plants that grow naturally only on Catalina Island, including St. Catherine's lace (*Eriogonmis giganteum*) and Catalina live-forever (*Dudleya hassei*). The visitors' center features display cases that depict the evolution of plants on Catalina Island.

SAN FERNANDO VALLEY —
WEST

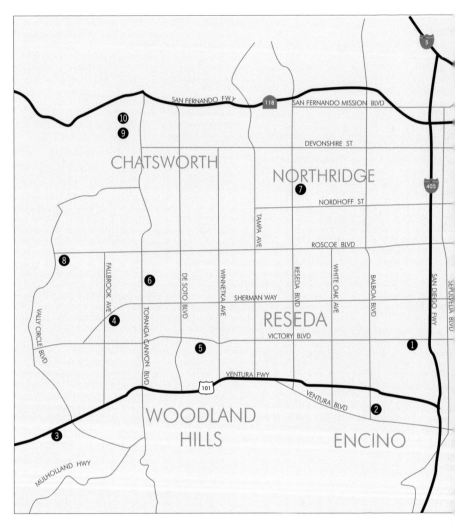

1. The Japanese Garden
2. Los Encinos State Historic Park
3. Leonis Adobe/Plummer House
4. Shadow Ranch
5. Life Science Museum and Nature Center — Los Angeles Pierce College
6. Canoga Owensmouth Historical Museum
7. Botanical Garden — CSU Northridge
8. Orcutt Ranch
9. Homestead Acre and the Hill-Palmer Cottage
10. Chatsworth Museum

Donald C. Tillman Water Reclamation Plant Japanese Garden

①

The Japanese Garden

6100 Woodley Ave, Van Nuys, 91406. ☎ (818) 756-8166. **Fax:** 818) 756-1648. **Thomas Guide:** 531 F7. **Hours:** Mon-Fri 9am-1pm by appointment only. $ free. P free on site. 📷 allowed. **Year founded/opened:** 1984. **Primary focus:** to present the design style of an authentic 6.5-acre showplace using reclaimed water, offering an overview of the water reclamation process by the Bureau of Sanitation. **Governing authority:** municipal. **Category:** botanical garden/arboretum. **Activities/programs:** docent programs, educational programs,

events, guided tours (special summer evening tours), outreach programs, slide presentations, volunteer programs. **Facilities:** available for rent, gift shop. ♿ parking, wheelchair

Shoin **building**

accessible. **Garden features:** Japanese garden, restrooms; peak time: spring. **Collection focus:** botany, horticulture.

The Japanese Garden is located at the City of Los Angeles Donald C. Tillman Water Reclamation Plant. Since the aim of the garden is to demonstrate how reclaimed water can be used, water is shown in three forms: a lake depicts its calm state, a waterfall presents vertical movement and a stream shows horizontal movement. The garden was designed by Dr. Koichi Kawana in the *Chisen-Kaiyushiki* (Wet Garden With Promenade) style, popular during the 18th and 19th centuries among Japanese feudal lords.

The garden contains traditional components, including the tile-roofed main gate, a shoin or residential dwelling, the teahouse, arbors, bridges and stone elements, such as a water basin and *kasuga* and *yukimi* lanterns. The dry garden, with its stone arrangements and gravel, symbolizes the ocean and the islands. Plantings include black pines, redwoods, coast bamboo, ferns, azaleas, wisteria, magnolias, iris and lotus, among others. The large lake and islands attract magnificent white herons and other waterfowl.

Roji **garden, with bamboo hedge, lantern and a teahouse**

The bridge

Los Encinos State Historic Park

❷

Los Encinos State Historic Park

16756 Moorpark St, Encino, 91436. ☎ (818) 784-4849. **Fax:** (818) 459-3031. **Thomas Guide:** 561 D3. **Public transportation:** bus. **Hours:** Wed-Sun 10am-5pm. **Closed:** Thanksgiving, Christmas, New Year's Day. Ⓢ free. **Reservations:** necessary for groups. Ⓟ street. ◙ by permit. **Year founded/opened:** 1949. **Primary focus:** home life at Rancho El Encino during the early American period and following. **Governing authority:** state. **Category:** historic building/site open to the public. **Activities/programs:** docent programs. **Facilities:** available for rent, picnic area. ♿ wheelchair accessible. **Collection focus:** architecture, clothing and dress, furniture and interiors, local history.

De la Ossa Adobe

The site of the present park was used as the Franciscan fathers' headquarters before they established San Fernando Mission in 1797. After the collapse of the mission system in 1833, ten years after Mexico won its independence from Spain, a group of San Fernando Mission Indians applied to Pio Pico, the last governor of Mexican California, for a land grant. In 1845 they received 4,460 acres in the part of the valley named Los Encinos (The Oaks) by early Spanish explorers. After only four years, the Indians sold the land to Vicente de la Ossa, a former tavern keeper and Los Angeles City Council member. De la Ossa and his family raised longhorn cattle and planted orchards and a vineyard. They built a 9-room adobe of sunbaked bricks made of mud and straw. During the 1860s and 1870s the rancho served as a stop on the El Camino Real, an important stagecoach route to the north. In 1869 the ranch was sold to the Garnier brothers, who created a reservoir, enclosed the spring and added wooden porches and a wooden roof to the adobe. They built a blacksmith storage building and constructed a 2-story limestone house, designed in the French Provincia style. The ranch changed hands several times before it came into the possession of the Amestoy family in 1891, who operated it until 1945. The remaining 5 acre and buildings were purchased in 1949 by the State Department of Parks and Recreation.

The park contains the Adobe de la Ossa (1849), the Garnier Building (1873), the blacksmith shop (early 1870s), the spring house (1870), the reservoir and food storage houses. The adobe rooms have been furnished to illustrate the 200-year history of ranching and the various owners' way of life. The collection includes period furniture, costumes, personal effects, saddles, antiques and artifacts. The museum in the Garnier Building has cases with photographs of the families, displays of glass, porcelain and pottery, educational panels, hands-on exhibits and archaeological material from the recent excavation of a nearby site and grounds. The blacksmith shop features agricultural tools, and there is a collection of farm equipment used in the early 1900s.

❸
Leonis Adobe

23537 Calabasas Rd, Calabasas, 91302. ☎ (818) 222-6511. **Fax:** (818) 222-0862. **Thomas Guide:** 559 F4. **Hours:** Wed-Sun 1-4pm. $ donation requested. **Reservations:** recommended for groups. P free on site. 📷 allowed. **Membership:** available. **Year founded:** 1964. **Primary focus:** to show ranch life during the 1880s. **Governing authority:** private, nonprofit. **Category:** historic building/site open to the public. **Activities/programs:** docent programs. **Facilities:** bookstore, picnic area. ♿ strollers permitted, parking, wheelchair accessible. **Collection focus:** architecture, carriages and carts, clothing and dress, domestic utensils, farms and farming, furniture and interiors, glass and glassware, local history, horses, machines and machinery, period rooms.

Leonis Adobe

Plummer House

The San Fernando Valley was discovered during a Spanish expedition headed by Don Gaspar de Portolá in 1769. This was the first campaign to explore California by land. At the time more than 200 Indian villages were scattered across the valley, given the name Valle de los Encinos Valley (of the Oaks) by Portola. Calabasas was the site of one of the Indian villages and later a stop on the coastal stage line operated by Flint, Bixby & Butterfield.

When young Basque immigrant Miguel Leonis arrived in Calabasas in the mid-1800s, the area was one of the wildest places in California. His marriage to an Indian widow, Espiritu Chijulla, brought him the El Escorpion rancho with 1,100 acres of land and considerable livestock holdings. He vastly enlarged his possessions through shrewd trading and gained a reputation as the most powerful local landholder, becoming known as the King of Calabasas.

The original Leonis Adobe was built in 1844. It was a simple adobe farmhouse at the time Leonis acquired it in the late 1850s. He extensively enlarged and remodeled the building as a Monterey-style house, adding more rooms, a balcony and other features in 1879. Other structures on the grounds include the barn, built in 1912, a well, a replica of the windmill and the tank house. The Leonis Adobe was designated as Historic Cultural Monument No. 1 by the Municipal Art Department of the City of Los Angeles in 1962 and placed on the National Register of Historical Places in 1975.

The house and grounds have been restored to depict rancho life during the 1880s. The collection consists of period furniture, rugs, Leonis family portraits and period costumes. Some photographs on display depict the house's history and various stages of its repair and restoration. The blacksmith shop in the barn features tools needed for the construction and repair of farm implements. A collection of agricultural equipment and restored horse-drawn carriages is also displayed.

Plummer House

The Plummer House, known as the "oldest house in Hollywood," stood in Plummer Park in West Hollywood until 1983, when it was relocated to the Leonis Adobe grounds. Plummer Park was a part of Rancho La Brea, granted by Governor Echandia to Antonio Rocha in 1826. The rancho was acquired by sailor John Plummer in 1874, and soon after, the house and a large barn were built. Los Angeles County bought the property in 1937, naming it Plummer Park. The house was used by the Audubon Society as a library and exhibit space until 1980. Almost destroyed by fire and vandalism, the house was bought by the Leonis Adobe Association in 1982. It has been repaired, restored and now serves as a visitors' center and orientation building, with displays of photographs, period costumes, personal items and other artifacts.

Horse-drawn carriage

❹

Shadow Ranch

22633 Vanowen St, West Hills, 91307. ☎ (818) 883-3637. **Thomas Guide:** 529 H6. **Public transportation:** bus. **Hours:** Mon-Fri 10am-5pm, Sat 9am-5pm, Sun noon-5pm. Ⓢ free. Ⓟ free, on site. 📷 allowed. **Year opened:** 1965. **Governing authority:** municipal. **Division of:** Dept of Recreation and Parks. **Category:** historic building/site open to the public. **Activities/programs:** classes/courses. **Facilities:** picnic area. ♿ strollers permitted, wheelchair accessible. **Collection focus:** architecture.

The ranch once belonged to the Los Angeles Farm and Milling Company, owned by Isaac Lankershim and I. N. Van Nuys. The house, made of adobe and redwood planking, was built between 1869 and 1872 by the ranch's superintendent, Albert Workman. He was an Englishman who made a fortune transporting lumber from the north. Workman planted a grove of eucalyptus trees brought from Australia in the early 1870s. They are said to be the parent trees for all the eucalyptus in southern California.

After several changes of ownership, the ranch was bought in 1932 by Florence and Colin Clemens. They restored and rebuilt the house using original materials and added the second floor. Because of its great eucalyptus trees, they renamed the property Shadow Ranch.

The City of Los Angeles purchased it in 1957 and remodeled the house's interior to create a community center.

Shadow Ranch House

Antrodemus valens in the Life Science Museum

❺

Life Science Museum and Nature Center — Los Angeles Pierce College

6201 Winnetka Ave, Woodland Hills, 91371. ☎ (818) 347-0551 x210. **Thomas Guide:** 530 D7. **Hours:** by appointment only. **Closed:** university holidays. Ⓢ free. Ⓟ free on site. 📷 allowed. **Governing authority:** college/university. **Category:** natural history museum. **Collection focus:** birds, bones, shells, zoology.

This small museum features exhibits on physical geography, local seashells, rocks, insects and California conifers (cone-bearing plants). Stuffed birds of the Santa Monica Mountains, including ducks, loons and birds of prey are also displayed. The most interesting exhibit is a skeleton of *Antrodemus valens*, a 150-million-year-old carnivorous dinosaur found in Utah.

❻

Canoga Owensmouth Historical Museum

7248 Owensmouth Ave, Canoga Park, 91303. ☎ (818) 884-4222. **Thomas Guide:** 530 B3. **Hours:** 2nd Sun of each month 1-4pm. Ⓢ free.

Ⓟ street or behind the building. 📷 not allowed. **Membership:** available. **Year founded/opened:** 1988. **Primary focus:** community history. **Research fields:** local community. **Publications:** *Historical Notes*, monthly newsletter. **Governing authority:** nonprofit. **Parent institution:** Canoga Owensmouth Historical Society. **Category:** history museum. **Activities/programs:** school programs, slide presentations. ♿ strollers permitted, wheelchair accessible. **Collection focus:** North American archaeology and antiquities, farms and farming, handicraft, local history.

The museum is located in the 1930s Community Center building, which served as Los Angeles City Fire Station #72. The museum's displays illustrate life in the San Fernando Valley from the days of the Chumash Indians, through the Mexican rancho and dry-farming era to the arrival of large aerospace industries (Rocketdyne, Litton and Hughes Aircraft) in the 1950s and 1960s. Exhibits include archeological artifacts, maps, photographs and other documents related to local history. There are special collections of the Canoga Park Women's Club and Canoga Park High School.

7

Botanical Garden — CSU Northridge

8111 Nordhoff St, Northridge, 91330-8303. ☎ (818) 885-3356, 3496. **Fax:** (818) 885-2034. **Thomas Guide:** 501 A7. **Hours:** Mon-Fri 8am-5pm. **Closed:** university holidays. ⓢ free. Ⓟ free on street. 📷 allowed. **Year founded:** 1968. **Primary focus:** collection of specimen material for biology dept, faculty and student research. **Research fields:** ecology, evolution, systematics of plants. **Governing authority:** college/university. **Category:** botanical garden/arboretum. **Activities/programs:** educational programs. **Facilities:** picnic area. ♿ wheelchair accessible. **Garden features:** greenhouses, water garden, desert garden. **Collection focus:** biology, botany.

Botanical Garden at the CSU Northridge

This one-acre botanical garden was established as part of the general educational collection at California State University, Northridge. It contains over 4,000 plants, featuring a redwood grove, water plants and small garden flower beds, as well as a fine collection of tropicals, cacti and succulents. Four greenhouses are open to the public.

Courtyard with fountain

8

Orcutt Ranch

23600 Roscoe Blvd, West Hills, 91304. ☎ (818) 883-6641. **Thomas Guide:** 529 F2. **Hours:** daily 8am-5pm. **Closed:** holidays. ⓢ free. Ⓟ free. 📷 allowed for personal use. **Year opened:** 1966. **Primary focus:** horticulture. **Governing authority:** municipal. **Division of:** Dept of Recreation and Parks. **Category:** historic building/site open to the public. **Facilities:** available for rent, picnic area. ♿ strollers permitted, parking, wheelchair accessible. **Garden features:** herb garden, rose garden, restrooms; dogs allowed. **Collection focus:** agriculture, local history, machines and machinery.

In 1917 the 200-acre estate, known as Rancho Sombra del Roble (Ranch of the Shaded Oak), was the country home of William and Mary Orcutt. William Orcutt was a geologist and engineer who organized the first petroleum geology department in the West. He discovered fossils in the La Brea tar pits while searching for oil, and he

later became a vice-president of the Union Oil Company. In 1920 the Orcutts commissioned C. G. Knipe, an architect from Arizona, to design their Spanish Revival-style house. The house contains a blend of Mexican and Indian elements, such as Mexican tile and Native American peace symbols and arrows applied to the bricks.

The grounds were planted with citrus and walnut groves, together with many varieties of trees and shrubs. These include Chinese wisteria, magnolia, dogwood, birch, incense cedar and many species of palm and pine. Besides old, large oaks (one is said to be 700 years old and measures almost 33 feet in circumference), there are bamboo groves, tropical plants and rose and herb gardens. In 1934 local artist Frank Knapp created the grotto, urns, stone walls and stone stat-

Farming equipment

ues, including one of Father Junipero Serra. There is a collection of farming equipment, and in the second wing of the house Orcutt family pictures are displayed along with a practicing piano, busts, memorabilia and photographs of Mario Lanza and Arturo Toscanini.

The City of Los Angeles purchased 24 acres of the Orcutt estate in 1966 and designated it Historical Monument No. 31.

Orcutt Ranch House with center garden area and sundial

Hill-Palmer Cottage

9

Homestead Acre and the Hill-Palmer Cottage

10385 Shadow Oak Dr, Chatsworth, 91311. ☎ (818) 882-5614. **Thomas Guide:** 499 J4. **Hours:** 1st Sun of each month 1-4pm. [$] free. [P] free on site. 📷 allowed. **Membership:** available. **Year founded:** 1963. **Year opened:** 1979. **Primary focus:** to preserve the historic sites and collect and preserve pictures, artifacts and archaeological items relating to local history. **Publications:** *Smoke Signal*, newsletter. **Governing authority:** municipal. **Division of:** Dept of Recreation and Parks. **Category:** historic building/site open to the public. **Activities/programs:** docent programs, guided tours, slide presentations. **Facilities:** available for rent, bookstore, library, picnic area. **Garden features:** herb garden, rose garden. **Collection focus:** architecture, local history.

This is the only homestead cottage with surrounding gardens and fruit trees remaining in the San Fernando Valley. Located on 1.3 acres within Chatsworth Park, it is all that is left of the original Hill ranch. Rhoda Jane and James David Hill homesteaded 110 acres in 1886, later purchasing 120 additional acres. The property was sold in 1950, but Minnie , the seventh of the Hill children (married Palmer), continued to live there, growing vegetables and canning fruit until 1976. Homestead Acre, with its original cottage, the Chatsworth Museum and the Frank H. Schepler, Jr. Memorial Library, is Los Angeles Historical Monument No. 133. It is included in the National Register of Historic Places.

The restored cottage house and its decorated rooms aim to re-create the history and lifestyle of the pioneers who homesteaded the valley in the late 19th century. The kitchen contains period equipment and shows the conditions under which women worked in the home at the turn of the century. On display are period furniture, household items (including the first sewing machine given to the Hoopa Indian reservation in Arcata, California) and other everyday objects.

Butter churn (1900s)

10

Chatsworth Museum

This small museum has been arranged to illustrate the history of the Chatsworth area. Exhibits include photographs of the community's historic landmarks and sites as well as its early residents. There are displays of Indian artifacts found in the San Fernando Valley, period costumes, documents and other artifacts.

SAN FERNANDO VALLEY —
EAST

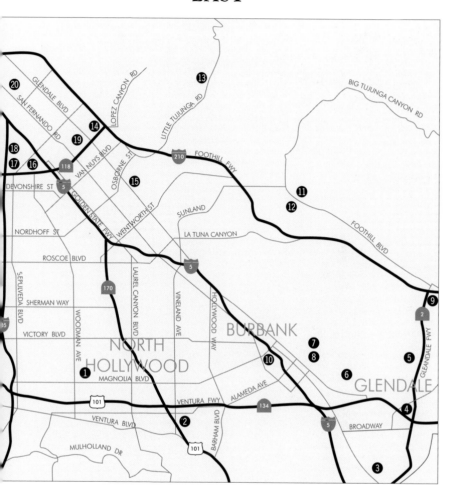

1. Los Angeles Valley College Historical Museum
2. Campo de Cahuenga
3. Forest Lawn — Glendale
4. Near East Institute and Archaeological Foundation
5. Verdugo Adobe
6. Casa Adobe de San Rafael
7. The Doctors' House
8. Friendship Garden
9. Descanso Gardens
10. Gordon R. Howard Museum/ Mentzer House
11. Bolton Hall Museum
12. McGroarty Arts Center
13. Wildlife Waystation
14. All Cadillacs of the Forties
15. World Wrestling Museum and Hall of Fame
16. Andres Pico Adobe
17. San Fernando Mission
18. Archival Center
19. Lopez Adobe
20. The Nethercutt Collection

1

Los Angeles Valley College Historical Museum

5800 Fulton Ave, Van Nuys, 91401. ☎ (818) 781-1200 x373. **Thomas Guide:** 562 D1. **Hours:** Mon-Fri 1-4pm. **Closed:** holidays. [$] free. [P] lot H. 📷 allowed. **Membership:** available. **Year founded:** 1974. **Year opened:** 1975. **Primary focus:** to collect documents, photographs and artifacts relating to the San Fernando Valley. **Research fields:** history of the San Fernando Valley. **Publications:** newsletter. **Governing authority:** college/university. **Category:** history museum. **Activities/programs:** guided tours, lectures. **Facilities:** exhibit space/gallery, 500-volume research library. ♿ parking. **Collection focus:** clothing and dress, farms and farming, local history, personal history.

The museum is housed in Bungalow 15, the first college administration building on the campus of Los Angeles Valley College. It recounts the history of the San Fernando Valley through collections of paintings, lithographs and photographs, geologic exhibits containing rocks and fossils, as well as artifacts used by early man. Plants native to the valley and used by Indians for food and medicine are also on display. Other exhibits include a collection of clothing dating from the late-19th through the early-20th centuries; archival material relating to William Paul Whitsett, the founder of Van Nuys; and tools and furnishings from the Lankershim ranch.

2

Campo de Cahuenga

3919 Lankershim Blvd, North Hollywood, 91602. ☎ (818) 763-7651. **Thomas Guide:** 563 B6. 🚌 bus. **Hours:** Mon-Fri 8am-2pm. **Closed:** holidays. [$] free. [P] street. 📷 allowed. **Year opened:** 1950. **Primary focus:** dedicated to the memory of the soldier-statesmen John C. Fremont and Andres Pico. **Governing authority:** municipal. **Division of:** Dept of Recreation and Parks. **Category:** historic building/site open to the public. **Activities/programs:** concerts, historic programs. **Facilities:** available for rent. **Collection focus:** local history.

Gate at Campo de Cahuenga

This is the site where the Treaty of Cahuenga was signed on January 13, 1847, by Lt. Col. John C. Fremont and General Andres Pico. The treaty ended the war between the United States and Mexico and signified the American acquisition of California and the vast territory now comprising Nevada, Utah, Arizona and parts of New Mexico, Colorado and Wyoming.

The existing building is a replica of the 6-room Feliz adobe on the Cahuenga rancho, built in 1845, where the signing took place. It features exhibits related to the history of the treaty, including copies of documents, historical artifacts and portraits of Fremont and Pico.

3

Forest Lawn — Glendale

1712 S Glendale Ave, Glendale, 91205. ☎ (800) 204-3131. **Fax:** (213) 344-9035. **Thomas Guide:** 564 F7. 🚌 bus, metro. **Hours:** daily 10am-5pm. **Closed:** never. [$] free. [P] free. 📷 outside only, no tripods. **Year founded:** 1951. **Year opened:** 1952. **Governing authority:** company. **Category:** art museum. **Activities/programs:** changing exhibitions, educational programs, school programs, slide presentations. **Facilities:** gift shop. ♿ strollers permitted, parking, wheelchair accessible. **Collection focus:** European art, Western art, ivory, jewelry, mosaics, numismatics, painted and stained glass, European painting, North American painting, precious stones, religious art, sculpture.

The museum is particularly rich in original marble and bronze statuary, including works by Jean-Antoine Houdon, Gladys Lewis-Bush, James Earle Fraser, Charles Russell and Frederic Remington. There are exhibits of medieval armor, rare jewels and 520 stained-glass windows dating from 1200 AD through modern times. The museum's extensive coin collection contains every coin mentioned in the Bible. The Hall of the Crucifixion-Resurrection houses the two largest oil paintings in the world, *The Crucifixion* (195 by 45 feet — 59,4 x 13,7 m) by Jan Stuka and *The Resurrection* (70 by 51 feet — 21,3 x 15,5 m) by Robert Clark.

The Crucifixion by Jan Stuka, the largest oil painting in the world (detail)

Fragments by Johannes Drucius (edition 1622)

❹ Near East Institute and Archaeological Foundation

500 E Chevy Chase Dr, Glendale, 91206. ✉ PO Box 1110, Glendale, 91209-1110. ☎ (818) 242-4441. **Thomas Guide:** 564 H4. **Hours:** by appointment only. Ⓢ free. Ⓟ free. 📷 not allowed. **Year founded/opened:** 1979. **Primary focus:** East Mediterranean — Bible lands. **Research fields:** daily life in biblical and ancient times. **Governing authority:** private, nonprofit. **Category:** specialized museum. **Activities/programs:** changing exhibitions, classes/courses, educational programs, lectures, multimedia presentations, scholarships and fellowships, slide presentations, volunteer programs. **Facilities:** audiovisual holdings, exhibit space/gallery, library, slide registry. **Collection focus:** Christian, Egyptian, Middle and Near Eastern archaeology and antiquities, prehistoric archaeology, books, numismatics, religious history and traditions.

The Near East Institute and Archaeological Foundation serves as a resource center for specialized materials relating to Bible study and teaching. The museum's displays on biblical subjects aim to create interest in the Bible, to share little-known information and to illustrate aspects of the biblical message. Exhibits include archaeological artifacts, small sculptures, coins, handicrafts, jewelry and other objects.

❺ Verdugo Adobe

2211 Bonita Dr, Glendale, 91208. ✉ Parks and Recreation, 613 E Broadway, Glendale, 91205. ☎ (818) 548-2000. **Thomas Guide:** 534 H7. 🚌 bus. **Hours:** daily 8am-4pm (grounds only). Ⓢ free. **Reservations:** necessary only for groups (818) 548-2147. Ⓟ street, free. 📷 allowed outside. **Year opened:** 1989. **Governing authority:** municipal. **Division of:** Parks, Recreation and Community Services. **Category:** historic building/site open to the public. **Facilities:** picnic area. ♿ wheelchair accessible (garden only). **Collection focus:** architecture, local history, dolls and puppets.

In 1784 Corporal Jose Verdugo, serving in the mission guard at San Gabriel, received a 36,000-acre land grant known as Rancho San Rafael. The Verdugo Adobe, the oldest house in Glendale, was built in 1828 for his blind daughter, Catalina. The well-preserved house is the last of the five adobes built on the rancho. It is listed on the National Register of Historic Places and declared State Historical Landmark No. 637. The adobe's collection includes Indian artifacts and over 800 foreign dolls. On the adobe grounds stood the 500-year-old Oak of Peace, the site where plans the for truce were made between Lt. Col. John C. Fremont's emissary and General Andres Pico in 1847.

Verdugo Adobe

❻ Casa Adobe de San Rafael

1330 Dorothy Dr, Glendale, 91202. ☎ (818) 244-4651, 548-2147. **Thomas Guide:** 564 D2. **Hours:** daily 8am-dusk (grounds only). Ⓢ free. Ⓟ street, free. 📷 allowed outside. **Membership:** available. **Year opened:** 1930. **Governing authority:** municipal. **Division of:** Parks, Recreation and Community Services. **Category:** historic building/site open to the public. **Activities/programs:** events, guided tours. **Facilities:** available for rent, picnic area. ♿ wheelchair accessible. **Collection focus:** architecture, furniture and interiors, local history.

Casa Adobe de San Rafael

In the 1860s, 100 acres of Jose Verdugo's Rancho San Rafael was deeded to Maria Sepulveda and her husband, Tomas A. Sanchez. He served as Los Angeles County sheriff from 1859 to 1867 and was one of the leaders in the area. In 1871 they built the one-story Sanchez Adobe, now known as Casa Adobe de San Rafael. After Maria sold the property in 1883, it was subdivided many times, until the last two acres were acquired by the City of Glendale in 1930. The adobe has furniture and artifacts of the period. The grounds feature magnolias, camellias, birds of paradise, as well as orange trees and huge eucalyptus said to be planted by Phineas Banning.

Doctor's office (ca. 1900)

7

The Doctors' House

1601 W Mountain St, Glendale, 91201. ✉ PO Box 4173, Glendale, 91202. ☎ (818) 243-8204. **Thomas Guide:** 534 B7. **Hours:** Sun 2-4pm. **Closed:** holidays. $ free. **Reservations:** necessary for groups. [P] free. 📷 allowed. **Membership:** available. **Year opened:** 1980. **Governing authority:** private, nonprofit. **Category:** historic building/site open to the public. **Activities/programs:** docent programs, guided tours, volunteer programs. **Facilities:** bookstore, exhibit space/gallery, gift shop, picnic area. ♿ wheelchair accessible. **Collection focus:** architecture, furniture and interiors, local history.

This 2-story house was constructed as a speculative venture during the Glendale boom times of the late 1880s. Built in the Queen Anne-Eastlake style, the house was the residence of four doctors between 1895 and 1914. Being notable figures in Glendale's social, cultural and economic life, they gave the house its name in the 1950s.

In 1979 the Glendale Historical Society and the City of Glendale saved the building from demolition and moved it to its present location. The house was extensively and authentically restored, the early exterior and interior paint was duplicated and wallpaper patterns werereplicated from a few surviving fragments. The lost or damaged elements were repaired and reproduced from early photographs. Some of the interior features, such as the speaking tube and plumbing and lighting fixtures, were recreated

Kitchen in the Doctors' House

in every detail. The rooms are furnished in the style of the time. The kitchen contains a period stove and utensils, and the doctor's office features medical equipment, furniture and fixtures from the turn of the century.

Doctors' House

Friendship Garden

8

Friendship Garden

1601 W Mountain St, Glendale, 91201. ✉ 613 E Broadway, #120, Glendale, 91201. ☎ (818) 956-2147. **Thomas Guide:** 534 B7. **Hours:** daily 10am-3pm. $ free. [P] free. 📷 allowed. **Governing authority:** municipal. **Category:** botanical garden/arboretum. **Facilities:** available for rent, picnic area. ♿ strollers permitted, wheelchair accessible. **Garden features:** Japanese garden, pond. **Collection focus:** botany.

Designed by landscape architect Eijiro Nunokawa, this Japanese garden is an expression of friendship between Glendale and its sister city in Japan, Higashiosaka. The garden contains a pond, stone lanterns and other traditional elements. A teahouse named *Sho-Shei-An* (Teahouse of the Whispering Pines) is open only with reservations.

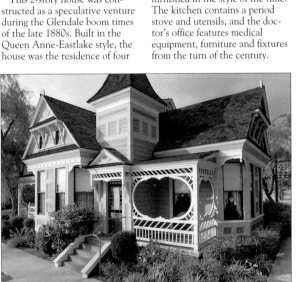

9

Descanso Gardens

1418 Descanso Dr, La Canada, 91011. ✉ PO Box 778, La Canada, 91012. ☎ (818) 952-4401. **Recorded information:** (818) 952-4392. **Thomas Guide:** 535 A4. **Hours:** daily 9am-5pm. **Closed:** Christmas. $ $5 general, $3 seniors, students and youth, $1 children, children under 5 free. [P] free. 📷 no commercial photography. **Membership:** available. **Year founded:** 1937. **Year opened:** 1957. **Primary focus:** botanical garden and nature preserve. **Governing authority:** county. **Parent institution:** Dept of Arboreta and Botanic Gardens. **Category:** botanical garden/arboretum. **Activities/programs:** changing exhibitions, classes/courses, concerts, docent programs, educational programs, events (flower shows, flower festivals), guided tours, lectures, performing arts, slide presentations, tram tours, volunteer programs, workshops. **Facilities:** cafeteria/restaurant, gift shop, lecture hall, library, picnic area. ♿ strollers permitted, wheelchair accessible. **Garden features:** Japanese garden, labels/descriptions, ponds, rose garden, water garden, restrooms; peak times: spring, fall. **Collection focus:** botany, horticulture.

***Kramer's Supreme* camellia**

The Descanso Gardens were part of the vast Rancho San Rafael, granted to Spanish soldier Jose Verdugo in 1784. Upon Verdugo's death the northern part of the rancho was inherited by his daughter Catalina, who named it Rancho La Canada. The land that forms the present garden changed hands many times and was undeveloped when E. Manchester Boddy bought 165 acres in 1937. Boddy, who was the owner and editor of the *Los Angeles Daily News*, built a 2-story mansion and renamed his estate Rancho del Descanso (Ranch of Rest). In 1953 the County of Los Angeles acquired the property and opened it to the public.

Descanso Gardens

The core of the Descanso Gardens is a 30-acre grove of California live oak (*Quercus agrifolia*). Realizing that oak forest provides a shady canopy perfect for cultivating camellias, Brody introduced this flower, which had gone out of fashion at the turn of the century.

Offering 100,000 bushes with more than 600 varieties, Descanso boasts the largest outdoor planting of camellias in the world. The collection features specimens from Japan, China, England and the American South, including varieties of *Camellia japonica*, *Camellia sasanqua* and *Camellia reticulata*. Some of the plants stand more than 20 feet tall.

The new 5-acre International Rosarium, dedicated in 1994, was designed as both an educational learning center and a tribute to the beauty of the rose. Uniquely, it is divided into 20 themed gardens, which present the world of roses from native species to modern hybrids. They include the Victorian Garden, the Mission Garden, Josephine's Garden, the Edwardian Tea Garden, the Butterfly Garden and the Tudor Herb Garden. Every All-American Rose Selection winner since 1939 is also on display.

Azaleas in the oak forest

The 7.5-acre California Native Plant Garden grows plants well adapted to California's hot, dry climate. Among the species represented are toyon, ironwood, mountain mahogany, manzanita and California sage. The Iris Garden features over 150 varieties, many of them award winners. The Lilac Garden exhibits over 100 varieties developed especially for southern California, including Sierra Blue, Mountain Haze and Descanso Giant.

Black swan

The Japanese Garden was inspired by the Oriental origins of the camellia. It features an authentic blue-tiled teahouse, the Minka (gift shop), waterfalls, pools and a Shinto bridge. The garden contains Japanese black palms, sago palms, heavenly bamboo, camellias, azaleas and mondo grass.

From the Bird Observation Station, more than 120 species of birds have been sighted. The Boddy mansion, now known as the Hospitality House, features rotating art exhibits.

Descanso Gardens

① Roses of Yesterday
② All-America Rose Selections
③ Iris Beds
④ Plant Propagation Area
⑤ Lake and Waterfall
⑥ Oak Woodland
⑦ California Native Plants
⑧ Fern Canyon
⑨ Nature Trail
⑩ Camelia Oak Forest
⑪ Lilac Garden
⑫ Special Education Garden
⑬ Bird Observation Station
⑭ Redwood Rest Overlook
⑮ Hospitality House
⑯ Japanese Tea House

Tulip

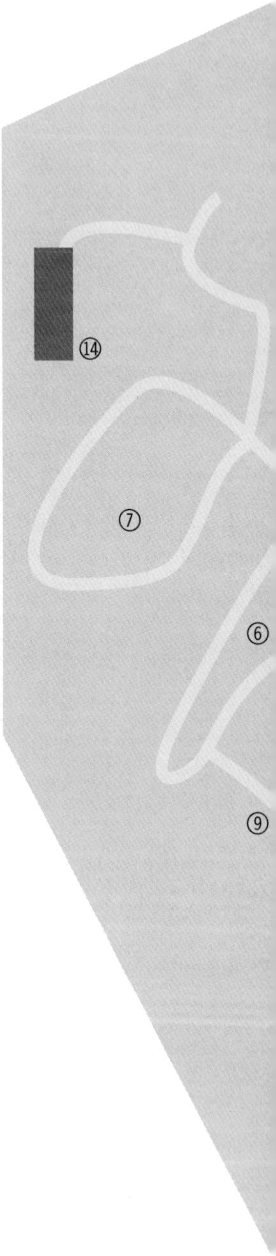

Hospitality House and Art Gallery

Red Shinto bridge, known as the Smiling Bridge

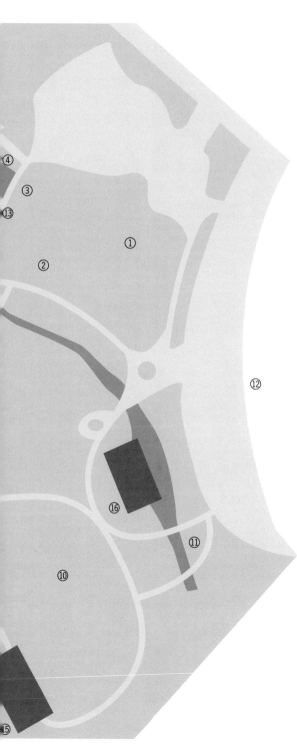

Lily pond

Japanese teahouse

International Rosarium

Lockheed exhibit

⑩
Gordon R. Howard Museum

115 N Lomita St, Burbank, 91506.
✉ 1015 W Olive Ave, Burbank,
91506. ☎ (818) 841-6333. **Fax:**
(818) 848-4739. **Thomas Guide:**
563 G1. 🚇 metro. **Hours:** Sun 1-
4pm. **Closed:** holidays. $ free,

Exhibit of James J. Jeffries, the 1899
World Heavyweight Champion

donations accepted. **Reservations:**
necessary for groups (818) 842-
7514. P street, free. 📷 no commercial photography. **Membership:**
available. **Year founded:** 1973.
Year opened: 1977. **Primary
focus:** collection and exhibition of
Burbank-related memorabilia and
artifacts. **Research fields:** 19th-
and 20th-century architecture and
costumes. **Major exhibitions:** "History of Route 66" (1994), "History
of St. Louis Browns" (1994). **Publications:** *About Times*, quarterly newsletter. **Governing authority:** private,

nonprofit. **Category:** history museum.
Activities/programs: changing exhibitions, docent programs, educational
programs, guided tours, volunteer
programs. **Facilities:** exhibit space/
gallery, picnic area. ⚮ wheelchair
accessible. **Collection focus:** aerospace, architecture, cameras, clothing and dress, curiosities, dentistry,
furniture and interiors, local history,
motion pictures, North American
painting, period rooms, transportation, vehicles.

Named after its founder,
dentist David Burbank, the
city of Burbank was developed during the California
land boom of the 1880s. The
Gordon R. Howard
Museum's collections illustrate the history of Burbank
from its early days to the present. The museum was
named after local businessman and its major benefactor,
Gordon R. Howard. All
aspects of Burbank's history are
covered, from the growth of
municipal services, schools,
churches, clubs, businesses and

farming to the history of famous
citizens and community leaders.
The museum also has an extensive collection of photographs
and other documents chronicling
the history of Los Angeles.

Memorabilia is displayed in a
series of vignettes replicating
offices, movie sets, living rooms,
bedrooms, etc., that highlight the
museum's collection of furniture
and antiques. Exhibits include a
large collection of antique costumes and dolls. There are displays of historic local businesses,
from the Moreland Motor Truck
Company, the first major business
in Burbank, through major studios including Walt Disney,
Warner Bros and NBC, to Lockheed. The museum houses more
than 200 cameras in its remarkable collection. Highlights
include the Kodak 4/Model C
Bullseye (1897), Kodak Brownie
No.2/Model C (1903) and Kodak
Brownie 2C/Model A (1916).

The museum's vehicle collection includes a 1949 Seagrave fire
engine, a 1904 Franklin, a 1912
Ford, a 1912 Buick Model 35

Mentzer House

Touring Car, a 1934 Packard
Town Car, a 1937 Jaguar SS 100
and a 1937 Rolls-Royce Razor
Edge Sedan, among others.

Mentzer House

Mentzer House, built in 1887
by the Providencia Land, Water
and Development Company, the
first Burbank land developer, is
part of the Gordon R. Howard
Museum complex. It is believed
that 30 houses were built by
this company and all were
Eastlake-style accented with
Queen Anne gingerbread.
The Mentzer House is com-
pletely restored and furnished
with period furniture, with all
original hardware and woodwork.

1912 Moreland bus, used in the
movie *Ron Ton Ton, The Dog That
Saved Hollywood*

Bolton Hall

11

Bolton Hall Museum

10110 Commerce Ave, Tujunga, 91042. ✉ PO Box 203, Tujunga, 91043. ☎ (818) 352-3420. **Thomas Guide:** 504 A4. 🚌 bus. **Hours:** Tue, Sun 1-4pm. **Closed:** holidays. $ free. **Reservations:** necessary for groups (818) 352-1545. [P] street, free. 📷 allowed. **Membership:** available. **Year founded/ opened:** 1980. **Primary focus:** history of Sunland-Tujunga area. **Major exhibitions:** "Schools of Sunland-Tujunga" (1994-95), "Historic Pharmacies of Sunland-Tujunga" (1994). **Publications:** *Green Verdugo Hills*. **Governing authority:** private, nonprofit. **Category:** history museum. **Activities/programs:** changing exhibitions, docent programs, educational programs, lectures, volunteer programs. **Facilities:** gift shop, library, picnic area. ♿ wheelchair accessible. **Collection focus:** architecture, local history.

This beautiful single-story building with a square tower was designed by George Harris, a local artist and craftsman. Constructed in 1913 of stones gathered from hillsides, it was originally a clubhouse for the Little Lands Colony, founded by William E. Smythe. The house was subsequently used as Tujunga City Hall, and it housed the city jail. In 1962 it was declared Historical Monument No. 2 by the City of Los Angeles. The museum displays artifacts, photographs, documents and mementos related to local history. On exhibit are two wagon wheels said to be from the last covered wagon to make the journey from Arizona to California.

12

McGroarty Arts Center

7570 McGroarty Terrace, Tujunga, 91042. ☎ (818) 352-5285. **Fax:** (818) 756-9997. **Thomas Guide:** 503 J4. **Hours:** Tue-Thu 9am-9pm, Fri 9am-6pm, Sat 9am-3pm. $ free. **Reservations:** recommended. [P] free. 📷 not allowed. **Membership:** available. **Year opened:** 1953. **Primary focus:** to preserve and promote the historical integrity of Rancho Chupa Rosa and the legacy of John Steven McGroarty. **Governing authority:** municipal, nonprofit. **Category:** historic building/site open to the public. **Activities/programs:** artist talks, classes/courses, educational programs, events, guided tours, installations. **Facilities:** exhibit space/ gallery, picnic area. ♿ strollers permitted, wheelchair accessible. **Collection focus:** books, local history, period rooms, personal history.

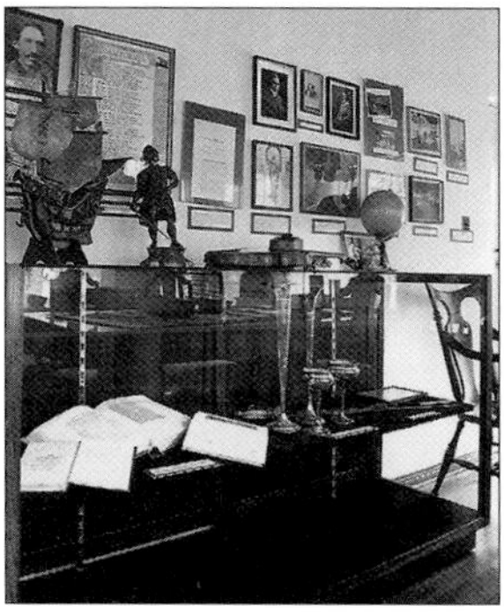

McGroarty's personal library

John Steven McGroarty (1862-1944), US Congressman, poet, journalist, dramatist and historian, was the author of eleven books and seven plays. He also worked as a journalist for over 40 years at the *Los Angeles Times*. His residence, built in 1923, was declared Historic Monument No. 63 by the City of Los Angeles and now serves as an arts center. The restored library contains books by McGroarty, photographs, correspondence and memorabilia. On display is the first prize silver cup that McGroarty's *Mission Play* won in the Pasadena Tournament of Roses in 1922 and his Hat and Sword of the Order of St. Gregory, awarded by Pope Pius XI.

13

Wildlife Waystation

14831 Little Tujunga Canyon Rd, Angeles National Forest, 91342-5999. ☎ (818) 899-5201. **Fax:** (818) 890-1107. **Thomas Guide:** 4723 C4. **Hours:** tours 1st and 3rd Sun each month. $ donation requested. **Reservations:** required. [P] free. 📷 allowed. **Membership:** available. **Year founded:** 1976. **Primary focus:** holding, rehabilitation, medical and problem-solving refuge for wild and exotic animals. **Publications:** quarterly newsletter. **Governing authority:** nonprofit. **Category:** nature center/wildlife refuge. **Activities/programs:** classes/courses, educational programs, events, guided tours, lectures, school programs, traveling exhibitions, volunteer programs. **Facilities:** gift shop, picnic area, visitors' center. **Zoo features:** rare species. **Collection focus:** birds, horses, mammals, reptiles, rescue equipment, zoology.

Located on 160 acres in the Angeles National Forest, the Wildlife Waystation is a safe haven for both native and exotic wildlife, dedicated to their rescue, rehabilitation and relocation. This is the only licensed facility of its kind in the country. It is home to 750 permanent residents and serves as a rehabilitation center for more than 2,000 animals each year. A 24-hour medical facility provides the animals with both routine and emergency care. The animals treated here include large cats (lions, tigers, leopards, jaguars, bobcats), primates, bears, wolves, foxes, deer, reptiles and birds.

Reesha the Tiger in the Wildlife Waystation

1948 Cadillac convertible that
belonged to actor Tyrone Power

⑭

All Cadillacs of the Forties

12811 Foothill Blvd, Sylmar, 91342.
☎ (818) 361-1147. **Fax:** (818)
361-9738. **Thomas Guide:** 482 E6.
Hours: Mon-Fri 8am-4:30pm.
Closed: holidays. Ⓢ free. **Reservations:** recommended. Ⓟ free. 📷
allowed on request. **Year founded:**
1979. **Year opened:** 1985. **Primary
focus:** Cadillacs of the 1940s and
1950s. **Governing authority:** private.
Category: specialized museum. **Facilities:** exhibit space/gallery. **Collection focus:** transportation, vehicles.

Some 150 vintage cars assembled by Ed Cholakian comprise
the largest privately owned Cadillac collection in the world. Displayed in a huge warehouse, it
features every Cadillac model
made in the 1940s and some
models of the 1950s. Nearly all of
the cars are in extraordinary
mechanical and cosmetic shape.

Highlights include the 1940
Model 62 four-door (1 of 2 still in
existence), the 1941 four-door
convertible (1 of 400 made), the
1942 convertible (1 of 308 made
and only 5 left). Also on display
are a fully outfitted 1948 ambulance with a gurney, oxygen bottle and Motorola radio, as well as
the 1948 convertible that
belonged to actor Tyrone Power.

⑮

World Wrestling Museum and Hall of Fame

12165 N Branford St, Sun Valley,
91352. ✉ PO Box 1602, Studio
City, 91614. ☎ (818) 897-6603.
Thomas Guide: 502 G4. **Hours:** 1st
Sun of each month. Ⓢ $5. **Reservations:** necessary. Ⓟ free. 📷 by
arrangement only. **Year founded:**
1989. **Primary focus:** pro wrestling
school/museum. **Research fields:** history of professional wrestling. **Governing authority:** private. **Category:**
specialized museum. **Activities/programs:** classes/courses, events.
Facilities: gift shop. **Collection focus:**
sports and recreation.

The museum is housed in Slammers Wrestling Gym, home to a
professional wrestling school
named Slam U. It can be seen
when attending the wrestling
matches that are held the first
Sunday of every month. This is
the only place of its kind in the
world. The museum's collection
consists of championship belts,
trophies, life masks, boots, jackets
and other memorabilia. Over 100
photographs, most of them
signed, and numerous posters line
the walls. One wing of the
museum is devoted entirely to the
legendary wrestler Gorgeous
George, nicknamed the "Human
Orchid." Other displays feature
the private collections of Intelligent Sensational Destroyer, Karl
von Hess, Count Billy Varga and
other notable pro wrestlers.

Pro wrestler Jay ("The Alaskan")
York points to vintage wrestling
poster listing him in competition

⑯

Andres Pico Adobe

10940 Sepulveda Blvd, Mission
Hills, 91345. ✉ PO Box 7039,
Mission Hills, 91346. ☎ (818) 365-
7810. **Thomas Guide:** 501 H2.
Hours: Wed-Sun 1-4pm. **Closed:**
holidays. Ⓢ free. Ⓟ free. 📷
allowed. **Membership:** available.
Year opened: 1967. **Research fields:**
San Fernando Valley. **Publications:**
The Valley, monthly newsletter. **Governing authority:** municipal, nonprofit. **Category:** historic building/site
open to the public. **Activities/programs:** lectures, volunteer programs.
Facilities: available for rent, 1,000-
plus-volume research library, picnic
area. ♿ parking. **Collection focus:**
architecture, clothing and dress,
farms and farming, local history.

Andres Pico Adobe (1932)

This is the second-oldest adobe
in the City of Los Angeles. The
main part of the building was
constructed in 1834 by Andres
Pico, general of the Mexican
forces in California. The house
changed hands several times, and
subsequent owners added rooms
at various intervals; the second
story was added in 1873. By 1925,
when Dr. M. R. Harrington,
archaeologist and curator of the
Southwest Museum, bought the
house and surrounding grounds,
the building was badly neglected
and nearly destroyed. He restored
it in 1932. The adobe is furnished
in late-Victorian style, with displays of fashion, toys and accessories. The exhibition hall features Indian artifacts, including
an arrowhead collection, rugs,
baskets and pottery.

San Fernando Mission *convento*

⑰
San Fernando Mission

15151 San Fernando Mission Blvd, Mission Hills, 91345. ☎ (818) 361-0186. **Fax:** (818) 361-3278. **Thomas Guide:** 501 H2. **Hours:** daily 9am-5pm. **Closed:** Thanksgiving and Christmas. Ⓢ $4 adults, $3 children 7-17, children 6 and under free. Ⓟ free. 📷 fee requested for commercial pictures. **Year founded:** 1797. **Primary focus:**

Two Spanish bells cast in 1686 and 1720

The East Garden with a flower-shaped fountain copied from an original in Cordoba

mission history and the Catholic church. **Special collections:** the Mark Harrington Collection. **Governing authority:** church. **Category:** history museum. **Activities/programs:** docent programs, educational programs, films, guided tours, school programs. **Facilities:** bookstore, exhibit space/gallery, gift shop, 5,000-volume research library. ♿ strollers permitted, parking, wheelchair accessible. **Garden features:** ponds. **Collection focus:** architecture, Christian archaeology and antiquities, Mexican art, basketsreligious art, religious history and traditions.

Mission San Fernando Rey de España was founded in 1797 by father Fermin Francisco De Lausen, who was president of all the California missions at the time. The mission was named after the canonized 13th-century king of Spain, Ferdinand III. It was the 17th in a chain of outposts along El Camino Real (the King's Road), between the Ventura and San Gabriel missions. The mission played a significant role in the economic life of Los Angeles, containing granaries, stables and workshops and supplying the growing community with large quantities of food.

During its history the mission suffered substantial damage from earthquakes, was periodically vandalized and fell into disrepair before it was extensively restored in 1923. The present church is the fourth on the grounds, rebuilt as an exact replica of the earlier structure erected in 1806 and demolished after the devastating

Sylmar earthquake in 1971. The most remarkable building on the mission complex is the 1822 *convento*, featuring 4-foot adobe walls and a corridor with 21 Roman arches.

The Historical Museum features a pictorial history of the mission, displaying vestments, altar settings, religious art, *santos* and pottery. There is an outstanding collection of Indian baskets from tribes scattered across the nation. It was gathered by Mark Harrington and presented to the mission in 1981. The *convento* rooms are authentically refurbished with Spanish period

Recreated blacksmith workshop

furniture. The Madonna Room is devoted to several hundred statues and paintings of the Blessed Mother. Visitors can view authentically recreated blacksmith, weaving and carpentry workshops as well as a saddlery.

Historical Museum

18

Archival Center

☎ (818) 365-1501. Fax: (818) 361-3276. **Hours:** Mon, Thu-Fri 1-3pm. **Closed:** holidays. **Year founded:** 1962. **Year opened:** 1980. **Primary focus:** history of the Catholic diocese of Los Angeles from 1840 to the present. **Research fields:** Catholic church, California, Los Angeles. **Special collections:** the Estelle Doheny Collection of Californiana. **Governing authority:** church. **Category:** library with collections other than books. **Activities/programs:** docent programs. **Facilities:** audiovisual holdings, micro holdings. ♿ strollers permitted, parking, wheelchair accessible. **Collection focus:** Christian archaeology and antiquities, postage stamps, religious history and traditions.

The San Fernando Mission Archival Center's museum preserves books, manuscripts, photographs, documents and other historical memorabilia related to the Catholic church. The center houses the Estelle Doheny Collection of Californiana consisting of rare books, manuscripts and works of art. On display are miters, zucchettos, reliquaries, medals and artwork. There is a stamp collection containing several hundred postage stamps issued by the Vatican since 1929. It is one of only a few complete collections in existence. The center also features six mosaic tablets designed by Isabel and Edith Piczek, depicting the geographical history of the Church of Los Angeles since 1840.

19

Lopez Adobe

1100 Pico St, San Fernando, 91340. ✉ 1303 Glenoaks Blvd, San Fernando, 91340. ☎ (818) 365-9990, 361-5050. **Thomas Guide:** 482 A7. Hours: Wed, Sat 11am-3pm, Sun 1-4pm. **Closed:** New Year's Day, Easter Sunday, July 4th, Thanksgiving, Christmas. [$] free. **Reservations:** necessary for groups. [P] free. **Year opened:** 1975. **Governing authority:** municipal. **Category:** historic building/site open to the public. **Activities/programs:** events, guided tours. **Facilities:** library with 500 books on California. ♿ wheelchair accessible (limited). **Collection focus:** architecture, clothing and dress, furniture and interiors.

The adobe was built in 1882 by Valentin Lopez for his sister and brother-in-law, Catalina and Geronimo Lopez. This was the first adobe structure in the San Fernando Valley planned and constructed as a 2-story building. The couple moved to the house from their previous home, known as Lopez Station, a stop on the Butterfield Stage Line route between Los Angeles and San Francisco. Lopez was a messenger for General Andres Pico, and he delivered the letter of truce to Lt. Col. John C. Fremont in 1847. Lopez established the first English-speaking school in the valley and opened the first post office in 1869. The adobe is furnished with authentic period furniture and displays fans, beads, dolls and authentic clothing worn by early residents of the valley. The adobe is registered as a National Historical Site.

Lopez Adobe

20

The Nethercutt Collection

15180 Bledsoe St, Sylmar, 91342. ☎ (818) 367-2251. **Fax:** (818) 367-8013. **Thomas Guide:** 481 H4. **Hours:** Tue-Sat tours at 10am and 1:30pm. [$] free (visitors must be 18 or older). **Reservations:** by appointment only. [P] street. 📷 allowed, but no flash or video cameras. **Year opened:** 1973. **Primary focus:** functional fine art. **Research fields:** antique and classic automobiles and mechanical musical instruments. **Publications:** *San Sylmar Book*. **Governing authority:** nonprofit. **Category:** specialized museum. **Activities/programs:** concerts, guided tours. **Facilities:** gift shop. ♿ parking, wheelchair accessible. **Collection focus:** carpets, clocks and watches, clothing and dress, decorative and applied arts, furniture and interiors, music and musical instruments, period rooms, silver, transportation, vehicles.

The Nethercutt Collection (formerly the Merle Norman Classic Beauty Collection) contains one of the world's most impressive exhibits of antique, classic and sport automobiles along with musical instruments and historical furnishings.

The collection highlights include a Duesenberg Torpedo Sedan, built for the 1933 Chicago World's Fair; a 1912 Premier Roadster; a 1932 Packard 12-cylinder convertible coupe; and Rudolph Valentino's 1923 Avions Voisin. There is a room filled with Rolls-Royces, dating from 1913 to the present, including all models of the Phantom series. On exhibit is one of the largest collections of hood ornaments in the world (more than 1,000 items), many of them designs in Lalique crystal. The world's largest and finest collection of restored mechanical musical instruments includes orchestrions, nickelodeons, grand pianos and the "Mighty Wurlitzer" theatre organ. The antique furnishings collection includes 18th-century French furnishings, such as classic timepieces and the oldest object in the collection — a 1680 crystal chandelier from Versailles.

ANTELOPE VALLEY

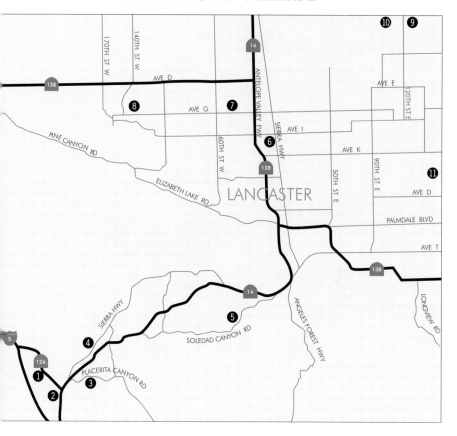

1. William S. Hart Museum
2. Heritage Junction Historic Park
3. Placerita Canyon Nature Center
4. Honey and Bee Museum/ Warmuth Honey House
5. Shambala Preserve
6. The Western Hotel/Museum
7. Milestones of Flight Air Museum
8. Antelope Valley California Poppy Reserve
9. NASA Dryden Flight Research Center
10. Air Force Flight Test Center Museum
11. Antelope Valley Indian Museum

Main entrance to the house

❶

William S. Hart Museum

24151 San Fernando Rd, Newhall, 91321. ☎ (805) 254-4584. **Fax:** (805) 253-2170. **Thomas Guide:** 4641 A2. **Hours:** Wed-Sun 11am-4pm (mid-Jun to mid-Sep); Sat-Sun 11am-4pm, Wed-Fri 10am-1pm (mid-Sep to mid-Jun). **Closed:** Thanksgiving, Christmas, New Year's Day. Ⓢ free. **Reservations:** necessary for groups. Ⓟ free. 📷 no flash inside the museum. **Membership:** available. **Year founded/opened:** 1958. **Primary focus:** to display, preserve and interpret the residence, furnishings and Western art collection of William S. Hart. **Special collections:** the William S. Hart Collection. **Governing authority:** county, nonprofit. **Parent institution:** Natural History Museum of Los Angeles County. **Category:** historic building/site open to the public. **Activities/programs:** classes/courses, concerts, docent programs, educational programs, events (Animal Fair, Dec Gala, Hart-of-the-West Sep Celebration), guided tours, outreach programs, school programs, slide presentations, storytelling, volunteer programs. **Facilities:** gift shop, picnic area. ♿ strollers permitted, parking, wheelchair accessible. **Garden features:** drought-tolerant garden, restrooms. **Collection focus:** North American archaeology and antiquities, architecture, arms and armor, American Indian art, North American art, baskets, bronzes, clothing and dress, decorative and applied arts, domestic utensils, motion pictures, North American painting, 19th- and 20th-century painting, period rooms, personal history, photography, sculpture, textiles, watercolors, woodcarvings.

William Surrey Hart was born in Newburgh, New York, in 1864, but spent most of his childhood traveling throughout the Midwest. His father was a miller, always in search of a job, and his work with Indians brought the family into contact with many native peoples. As a boy, Hart spent a great deal of time amid Indian friends; he learned the Sioux language and acquired deep esteem for Indians and their culture.

At the age of 24, Hart launched his acting career in New York, where he received critical acclaim for his work on the stage, both as an actor and producer. But his greatest success and international fame was in silent movies. When he moved to California in 1914 to make Westerns, he changed the way these films were made, correcting "the impossibilities or libels on the West." Hart introduced a new, original approach, based on his childhood frontier experience, using authentic costumes, locales and settings. "Two Gun Bill" became one of Hollywood's top filmmakers, working as an actor, screenwriter and direc-

Two Gun Bill **by Charles Cristadoro**

tor. When he retired in 1925 he left a legacy of 69 films, creating a unique style that influenced future generations of filmmakers.

In 1925, after the completion of his last film, *Tumbleweeds* (also considered one of his best), Hart purchased a ranch in Newhall. He commissioned Los Angeles architect Arthur Kelly to design and build a 13-room Spanish Colonial Revival-style house and named it La Loma de los Vientos (The Hill of the Winds). Grateful to the fans who supported him throughout his career, Hart deeded his estate to the County of Los Angeles.

The house is now a museum containing Western and Indian art and artifacts. It features Navajo textiles, Indian rugs, baskets, costumes and beaded articles. There is a collection of guns and antique firearms, as well as movie artifacts and memorabilia. Original artworks represented in the museum include paintings, bronzes, watercolors and drawings by Charles Russell; paintings by Frederic Remington, Joe de Yong and Charles Schreyvogel; bronzes by Charles Cristadoro; paintings and drawings by James Montgomery Flag; and wood carvings by Gene Hoback and Dee Flagg. On display in the original ranch house (1910) is a collection of saddles, lariats, spurs and bridles.

The William S. Hart Park includes an exhibit of farm machinery, live farm animals and a buffalo herd, a gift from Walt Disney in 1962; hiking and nature trails; a campground and a picnic area, as well as 110 acres of wilderness.

Living room

❷
Heritage Junction Historic Park

24101 San Fernando Rd, Newhall, 91321. ✉ PO Box 221925, Newhall 91322-1925. ☎ (805) 254-1275. **Thomas Guide:** 4641 A2. **Hours:** Sat-Sun 1-4pm. **Admission:** free. **Parking:** free on site. 📷 personal allowed. **Membership:** available. **Year founded:** 1976. **Year opened:** 1981. **Primary focus:** the collection and presentation of Santa Clarita Valley artifacts, education concerning local history. **Research fields:** Santa Clarita Valley history.

Cannon, known as "flying artillery" (1846)

Special collections: the Robert E. Callahan Collection, the Vierling Kersey Library of local history. **Publications:** *Santa Clarita Valley Historic Sites Map.* **Governing authority:** private, nonprofit. **Category:** historic building/site open to the public. **Activities/programs:** changing exhibitions, docent programs, educational programs, events (Olde Towne Days), guided tours, lectures, outreach programs, school programs, slide presentations, volunteer programs. **Facilities:** exhibit space/gallery, gift shop, research library, picnic area, visitors' center. ♿ parking, wheelchair accessible. **Garden features:** labels/descriptions, historic rose garden. **Collection focus:** architecture, general American history, local history, railways.

Heritage Junction Historic Park consists of eight buildings saved from demolition and moved from different locations to their present site. The park is operated by the Santa Clarita Valley Historical Society, founded in 1975 and dedicated to the rescue, restoration and conservation of important structures within the community. The largest building in the park is the Saugus Train Station, which opened in 1887. Since 1876, when the golden spike linking San Francisco and Los Angeles was driven at Lang, the railroad played an important part in the development of the valley. Several great train robberies took place near Saugus, the last of them in 1929, when "Buffalo" Tom Vernon derailed a locomotive and robbed its passengers. In 1971, however, all passenger service in Saugus was discontinued, and in 1978 Southern Pacific abandoned the facility. It was deeded to the Santa Clarita Valley Historical Society, which moved the structure to the park and restored it to its original condition.

Other buildings include the Mitchell Schoolhouse Adobe (1886), the second oldest school in Los Angeles; the Pardee House (1890s); the Newhall Ranch House (1860s); the Edison House and the Kingsburry House (1878). There is also a Little Red School House, built in 1898 for the education of the children of miners in the area southwest of Acton, and the tiny Ramona Chapel, constructed in 1925 for Callahan's Mission Village. The chapel was used as a movie set, and Gary Cooper was officially introduced into the Sioux nation there.

In 1982 the historical society acquired a Mogul Steam Engine, an oil-burning locomotive built in New York in 1900. This is one of 7 engines of its kind still in existence. The No. 1629 ran through the valley during its active service and was donated by Gene Autry.

Heritage Junction Historic Park, with Pardee House and Saugus Train Station

The Saugus Station now serves as headquarters for the historical society and as a museum of local history. Exhibits are devoted to the mining and petroleum industries (the longest-producing oil well and the oldest existing refinery in the world are located in the valley) and the first documented discovery of gold in California (which was in Placerita Canyon). There are also displays of silent movie memorabilia, Native American artifacts and items from the Mexican-American War, including a cannon, known as "flying artillery," invented by Major Sam Ringgold in 1846. The railroad exhibit includes the agent's office, signal lanterns, whistles, telephones, train timetables, old train tickets and railmen's uniforms. One of the star exhibits is a re-creation of the setting of "Wild Bill" Hickok's last poker game, consisting of the cards, table and chairs. "The Prince of the Pistoleers" was shot in the back while playing cards in Deadwood, South Dakota, in 1876. He fell holding two black eights and a pair of black aces, known ever since as "the Dead Man's Hand."

Locomotive steam whistle

Wild Bill Shot Dead!

Display of live snake at the Placerita Canyon Nature Center

3

Placerita Canyon Nature Center

19152 Placerita Canyon Rd, Newhall, 91321. ☎ (805) 259-7721. **Fax:** (805) 254-1426. **Thomas Guide:** 4641 G1. **Hours:** daily 9am-5pm. **Closed:** Christmas and New Year's Day. **Admission:** $3 per vehicle per day. **Reservations:** necessary for school groups. 📷 allowed. **Membership:** available. **Year founded/opened:** 1971. **Primary focus:** education of the general public on subjects of natural history. **Publications:** *The Placerita Rattler*. **Governing authority:** county. **Category:** nature center/wildlife refuge. **Activities/programs:** docent programs, educational programs, outreach programs, school programs, volunteer programs. **Facilities:** gift shop, picnic area. ♿ strollers permitted, parking, wheelchair accessible. **Collection focus:** North American archaeology and antiquities, biology, birds, bones, botany, ecology, geology, insects, mineralogy, reptiles, zoology.

Placerita Canyon Park comprises 350 acres of chaparral hillsides and oak woodlands, offering a hiking trail and several self-guided nature trails. The nature center features well-designed exhibits on biology, ecology, geology and history. It focuses on the local ecosystem, geological formations, microclimates and local plants and animals. Live animals and stuffed birds are also displayed. One display case contains authentic Native American artifacts, many of them from local Alliklik Indians.

Placerita Canyon was the site of the first discovery of gold in California. Legend has it that in 1842, Francisco Lopez, a local herdsman, was pulling up wild onions beneath an old oak tree when he saw small particles of gold clinging to the roots. The site, named Oak of the Golden Dream, is California Historical Landmark No. 168.

4

Honey and Bee Museum/Warmuth Honey House

17262 Sierra Hwy, Canyon Country, 91351. ☎ (805) 252-2350. **Thomas Guide:** 4552 A1. **Hours:** Tue-Sat 10am-4pm. **Closed:** holidays. **Admission:** varies. **Reservations:** recommended for groups. [P] free on site. **Year founded:** 1963. **Year opened:** 1985. **Primary focus:** to promote understanding of honeybees, beekeeping, pollination and the production of honey. **Governing authority:** private. **Category:** specialized museum. **Activities/programs:** educational programs, guided tours, videos. **Facilities:** gift shop, picnic area. **Collection focus:** bees, machines and machinery, waxworks.

This small museum offers exhibits on tools and equipment used in beekeeping, including honey extractors, smokers, steam knives and beekeepers' outfits. On view are honeybee products, models of straw beehives and a collection of various items and memorabilia relating to bees and honey. The Warmuth Honey House displays equipment used in the uncapping, extracting, wax melting, storing, bottling and packaging of honey and wax.

5

Shambala Preserve

6867 Soledad Canyon Rd, Acton, 93510. ✉ PO Box 189, Acton, 93510. ☎ (805) 268-0380. **Thomas Guide:** 4464 J6. **Hours:** one weekend each month or by arrangement (guests must be 18 or older). [$] donation requested. **Reservations:** by appointment only. [P] on site. 📷 allowed. **Membership:** available. **Year founded:** 1983 **Primary focus:** to increase public knowledge about wildlife. **Publications:** *The Cats of Shambala*. **Governing authority:** nonprofit. **Category:** nature center/wildlife refuge. **Activities/programs:** "adoption" programs, educational programs, guided tours, "safaris." **Facilities:** gift shop, picnic area. **Collection focus:** mammals, zoology.

Shambala is a unique wildlife refuge that provides protection, shelter, care and maintenance for exotic animals. The 60-acre preserve is home to over 70 animals, including African elephant, African lion, spotted and black leopard, Royal Bengal tiger, the endangered Siberian tiger, California native mountain lion, endangered cheetah, serval, snow leopard, rare Florida panther (only 30 to 50 remain in the world!) and American mountain lion.

IV Flying Service C-119 Argosy at the Milestones of Flight Museum

❻ The Western Hotel/Museum

557 W Lancaster Blvd, Lancaster, 93534. ☎ (805) 723-6250/6260. Thomas Guide: 4015 H5. **Hours:** Tri-Sun noon-4pm. **Closed:** holidays. $ free, donations accepted. P free. 📷 allowed. **Year founded:** 1888. **Year opened:** 1989. **Primary focus:** history of the Antelope Valley. **Governing authority:** municipal. **Category:** historic building/site open to the public. **Activities/programs:** guided tours, volunteer programs. **Facilities:** gift shop. **Collection focus:** North American archaeology and antiquities, clothing and dress, furniture and interiors, local history.

The Western Hotel is the oldest building in Lancaster and has been declared California Historical Landmark No. 658. Constructed in 1888 by Louis von Rockabrand, it played an important role in the commercial and social activity in the community in the late-19th and early-20th centuries. The museum's displays depict the history of the Antelope Valley and the people who built, worked at and lived in the hotel. Exhibits include Indian artifacts, period furniture, costumes dating from the 1880s to the 1920s, photographs and memorabilia.

❼ Milestones of Flight Air Museum

4549 William Barnes Ave, Lancaster, 93536. ✉ PO Box 2585, Lancaster, 93539. ☎ (805) 942-4022. Thomas Guide: 3924 J7. **Hours:** weekdays 10am-2pm, weekends noon-2pm. $ free. P free on site. 📷 allowed. **Membership:** available. **Year founded:** 1952. **Year opened:** 1967. **Primary focus:** aircraft and restoration. **Governing authority:** nonprofit. **Category:** specialized museum. **Activities/programs:** guided tours, volunteer programs. **Collection focus:** aerospace.

This museum's collection started with three airplanes donated by Howard Hughes: a Convair 220, a Martin A-20 and his personal North American B-25. Today, exhibits include a C-97 air-to-air refueler, a C-119 Argosy, a fighter TF-102 and a Sikorsky H-19 helicopter. On display are various jet and piston engines, including a Pratt & Whitney 4,300 hp, 28-cylinder, developed for Howard Hughes's *Flying Boat*. This is the largest piston engine ever built.

❽ Antelope Valley California Poppy Reserve

15101 W Lancaster Rd, Lancaster, 93536. ✉ PO Box 1408, Lancaster, 93584-9008. ☎ (805) 942-0662. Fax: (805) 940-7327. **Thomas Guide:** viii. **Hours:** Mar 15-May 15 daylight hours. $ $5 per vehicle. P on site. 📷 allowed. **Year founded:** 1976. **Year opened:** 1976. **Primary focus:** wildflower displays. **Special collections:** Jane S. Pinheiro paintings. **Governing authority:** state. **Category:** park museum/visitors' center. **Activities/programs:** docent programs, educational programs, school programs, slide presentations, volunteer programs. **Facilities:** bookstore, gift shop, picnic area, visitors' center. ♿ parking, wheelchair accessible. **Garden features:** labels/descriptions, restrooms; peak times: Mar-April. **Collection focus:** botany, energy, watercolors.

California poppy, the state flower

The reserve is one of the few remaining areas where California poppy (*Eschscholtzia californica*) flourishes in massive displays. This 1,800-acre natural habitat is spectacular in spring, when visitors can see staggering panoramas of orange wildflower fields. The Jane S. Pinheiro Interpretive Center displays a collection of over 160 original wildflower paintings. The building is also a state-of-the-art energy conservation facility. It features exhibits explaining the technology involved in space and water heating, cooling and electricity conservation.

Western Hotel/Museum

Boeing 747 jetliner used as the Space Shuttle Carrier Aircraft

9

NASA Dryden Flight Research Center

TR-42 Lakeshore Dr, Edwards AFB, 93523. ✉ TR-42, PO Box 273, Edwards AFB, 93523-0273. ☎ (805) 258-3449. **Recorded information:** (805) 258-3520. **Fax:** (805) 258-3566. **Thomas Guide:** ix. **Hours:** weekdays 7:30am-4pm (tours are at 10am and 1pm). **Closed:** federal holidays and shuttle landing days. $ free. **Reservations:** recommended (805) 258-3446. [P] free on site. 📷 allowed of NASA aircraft, not of Air Force facilities. **Year founded/opened:** 1946. **Primary focus:** aeronautic and flight research. **Governing authority:** federal. **Category:** specialized museum. **Activities/programs:** guided tours. **Facilities:** cafeteria/restaurant, exhibit space/gallery, gift shop. ♿ strollers permitted, parking, wheelchair accessible. **Collection focus:** aerospace.

Modified F-18 used in NASA's High Alpha Project

The Dryden Flight Research Center is NASA's premier installation for aeronautical flight research. It is also a primary and backup landing site for the space shuttle program, and a facility to test design concepts and systems used in the development and operation of the orbiters.

The Dryden complex dates back to 1946, when a group of five engineers arrived at what is now Edwards Air Force Base to begin preparation for X-I supersonic research flights. The center is named in honor of internationally known aeronautical scientist Dr. Hugh L. Dryden, who played a significant part in NASA history. Among the aircraft flown by pilots at Dryden are the original X-series, the research vehicles that pioneered flight at and beyond the speed of sound; a rocket-powered X-15, the most successful research aircraft to date; and a prototype supersonic bomber XB-70, the largest experimental aircraft. Some recent projects include testing of the mission adaptive wing, advanced propellers, the oblique wing and research on highly integrated digital electronic control systems. Flight-testing at Dryden contributed significantly to the development of the space shuttle thermal protection system, the solid rocket booster recovery system and flight control system computer software.

Perseus, remotely piloted aircraft

The museum's exhibits present the history of the center and describe its aeronautical research. On display are models of aircraft and spacecraft, pilot suits and space suits, including an Apollo suit worn on the moon.

A variety of aircraft representative of the fleet of research and support aircraft flown at NASA's Dryden Flight Research Center (front, left to right): F-18, X-29, F-15, F-16, three F/A-18s, T-38, F-104, SR-71, B-52 and 747

B-52 bomber displayed at Jimmy Doolittle Airpark

Air Force Flight Test Center Museum

Bldg 7211, 1100 Kincheloe, Edwards AFB, 93523. ✉ 1 S Rosa-

Sikorsky H-19D helicopter

mond Blvd, Edwards AFB, 93523-1032. ☎ (805) 277-8050. **Fax:** (805) 277-8051. **Thomas Guide:** ix. **Hours:** Tue-Sat 9am-5pm. **Closed:** Thanksgiving, Christmas and New Year's Day. Ⓢ free. **Reservations:** recommended. Ⓟ free on site. 📷 allowed except near flight line. **Year founded:** 1986. **Year opened:** 1994. **Primary focus:** history of Edwards AFB and USAF Flight Test Center. **Governing authority:** federal. **Category:** specialized museum. **Facilities:** gift shop, research library, theater.

♿ wheelchair accessible. **Collection focus:** aerospace.

Some of the most revolutionary advancements in aviation have occurred at the Air Force Flight Test Center at Edwards Air Force Base over the past 50 years. The number and magnitude of events that

have taken place there make Edwards's heritage of flight research and flight-testing unparalleled. The base was named in honor of Glen W. Edwards, whose name has become synonymous with the most challenging and visionary flight-testing in the world.

The museum's collection consists of over 60 aircraft, including some rarities such as the prototype Lockheed A-12 Blackbird; the only surviving NF-104A Starfighter rocket-assisted aerospace trainer; the first production McDonnell-Douglas F-4C Phantom II and the prototype

SR-71 Blackbird

F-4E; an unusual Douglas TB-26B Invader; the PA-48 Enforcer; the P-59B Airacomet; and the X-1E, X-21 and X-25B.

Additional attractions include various aircraft propulsion systems, such as the XLR-99 rocket engine, the most powerful aircraft engine ever used. Its thrust rating of 57,850 pounds is equal to 600,000 hp. There are also Atlas and Titan missile engines. Other

General Dynamics F-111A, the world's first production variable-sweep wing fighter. This aircraft was the first F-111A built and flown (Dec 12, 1964).

items in the collection include life-support equipment, hardware, technical drawings and test reports, as well as photographs and aviation memorabilia.

The Blackbird Airpark, located at Air Force Plant 42 in Palmdale, features a Lockheed SR-71A and the Blackbird prototype, the Lockheed A-12.

Gloster Meteor NF11

Antelope Valley Indian Museum

⓫

Antelope Valley Indian Museum

15710 E Ave M, Lancaster, 93535. ✉ 1051 W Ave M, Suite 201, Lancaster, 93534. ☎ (805) 942-0662. **Recorded information:** (805) 946-3055. **Fax:** (805) 940-7327. **Thomas Guide:** 4109 E4. **Hours:** Sat-Sun 11am-4pm. **Closed:** mid-Jun to mid-Sep. Ⓢ $2 adults, $1 children 6-12, children under 6 free. **Reservations:** (805) 942-0662 for arranged tours, weekdays only. Ⓟ free on site. 📷 not allowed. **Membership:** available. **Year founded:** 1940. **Year opened:** 1982. **Primary focus:** cultural, historical and anthropological collections housed in a folk art structure. **Research fields:** American Indian cultures; history of Euramerican interpretation of Native American material culture from late 1920s to 1960s, compared with contemporary

Anasazi pottery (1100-1200 AD)

anthropological interpretation. **Special collections:** the Howard Arden Edwards Collection, the Grace Wilcox Oliver Collection. **Publications:** *Bulletin*, quarterly. **Governing authority:** state, nonprofit. **Division of:** Dept of Parks and Recreation. **Category:** specialized museum.

Activities/programs: artist talks, docent programs, educational programs, events (annual American Indian Celebration — 3rd week of Sep), guided tours, intermuseum loans, outreach programs, school programs, slide presentations, volunteer programs. **Facilities:** gift shop, 4,000-volume research library, picnic area. ♿ strollers permitted, parking, wheelchair accessible. **Collection focus:** anthropology, North American, Meso American and South American archaeology and antiquities, prehistoric archaeology, architecture, African art, American Indian art, Eskimo art, Latin American art, Pre-Columbian art, baskets, decorative and applied arts, folk art, horticulture, hunting, jewelry, masks, mural painting and decoration, prehistory, shells, woodcarvings.

Apache cradle board

The museum building is a Swiss chalet-style structure constructed by artist and collector Howard Arden Edwards in 1932. The lower level is embedded in a natural rock formation, whose top serves as the floor of the upper room, built for Edward's collection of Indian art and artifacts. The house was sold in 1939 to Grace Wilcox Oliver, who converted all the living rooms into exhibit areas, added her own collections to those already existing and opened it as a museum. She operated it until 1979, when the property was purchased by the State of California.

Collections on view represent prehistoric and ethnographic groups from various regions. Exhibits in Kachina Hall and the Southwest Room on the lower level are devoted to the Indians of the Southwest. They include large painted Kachina panels, fine examples of Indian textiles, baskets, pottery and other artifacts. The Great Basin and Antelope Valley rooms contain regional

Athabaskan cooking basket

exhibits presenting the way of life of the Indians of the western Great Basin.

On the upper level, in the California Hall, visitors can find prehistoric artifacts from the southern California coast and Channel Islands, dating from 6000 BC to 1000 AD. Particularly interesting are the 2,500-year-old woven sea grass specimens, fishing equipment, jewelry and animal effigies. There are exhibits of cooking baskets, woven so tightly that they hold water without leaking.

Other attractions include a self-guided half-mile nature trail and the "touch table" which offers hands-on experiences in the fire starting and food preparation techniques practiced traditionally by Native Americans.

Ho'ote Kachina, Hopi

California Hall

PASADENA

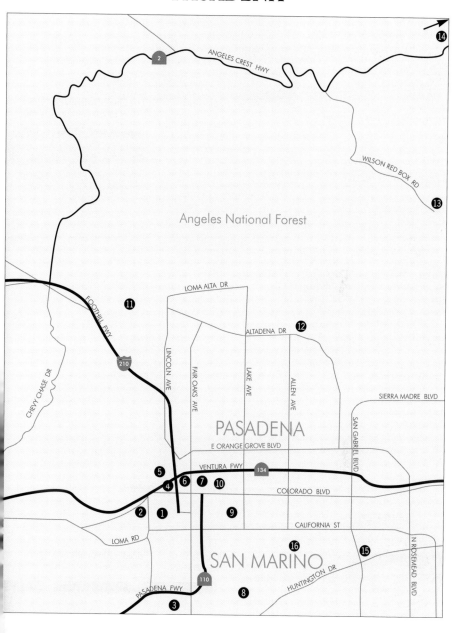

1. Tournament House and Wrigley Gardens
2. La Casita del Arroyo Garden
3. South Pasadena Preservation Foundation (Meridian Iron Works)
4. Norton Simon Museum of Art
5. Gamble House — USC
6. Pasadena Historical Museum (Fenyes Mansion)
7. Finnish Folk Art Museum
8. El Molino Viejo (The Old Mill)
9. Kidspace Museum
10. Pacific Asia Museum
11. Jet Propulsion Laboratory (JPL)
12. Henninger Flats Visitor Center
13. Mount Wilson Observatory
14. Chilao Visitor Center
15. Sunny Slope Water Co.
16. Huntington Library, Art Collections and Botanical Gardens

1

Tournament House and Wrigley Gardens

391 S Orange Grove Blvd, Pasadena, 91184. ☎ (818) 449-4100. **Fax:** (818) 449-9066. **Thomas Guide:** 565 G6. **Hours:** grounds open daily; house tours Thu 2-4pm, Feb through Aug. **Closed:** Dec 31-Jan 2. $ free. **Reservations:** necessary for groups. [P] free on street. 📷 allowed in gardens. **Year opened:** 1959. **Primary focus:** the Tournament of Roses. **Governing authority:** company. **Category:** historic building/site open to the public. **Activities/programs:** facilities for rent, guided tours. **Garden features:** rose garden. **Collection focus:** architecture, botany, sports and recreation.

Tournament House

The house was originally built by real estate tycoon George W. Stimson and designed by his architect son, G. Lawrence Stimson. The 3-story Italian Renaissance-style building was completed in 1914, when it was sold to chewing gum magnate William Wrigley, Jr. In 1958 the house was donated to the city of Pasadena to become the permanent base of operations for the Tournament of Roses. With its impressive woodwork and extensive use of marble, this remarkable house exemplifies the type of mansions once located on Pasadena's historic Millionaires' Row.

Today only the formal dining room is furnished with original furniture, and throughout the house are displays of Tournament of Roses artifacts, photographs and historical mementos. The Rose Bowl Room features a collection of memorabilia dating from the first game in 1902. On display is a permanent Player of the Game Trophy.

The original gardens have been redesigned and now only the

Wrigley Gardens

large Moreton Bay fig remains of Stimson's collection of trees from all over the world. Two rose gardens display more than 1,500 varieties of roses, among them many All-America Rose Selection winners. One of them, developed by the Jackson & Perkins Company, was named "Tournament of Roses" in honor of the Tournament Centennial celebration. It was one of four roses to win that award in 1989.

2

La Casita del Arroyo Garden

177 S Arroyo Blvd, Pasadena, 91105. **Thomas Guide:** 565 F5. **Hours:** always open. **Closed:** never. $ free. [P] free. 📷 allowed. **Year founded:** 1932. **Primary focus:** drought-tolerant garden. **Governing authority:** private. **Category:** botanical garden/arboretum. **Facilities:** available for rent. ♿ parking, wheelchair accessible. **Collection focus:** botany.

Sponsored by the Pasadena Garden Club, La Casita del Arroyo was designed by landscape architect Isabelle Greene as a small water-conserving garden. Requiring little maintenance, it demonstrates the effects of careful plant selection appropriate to southern California's dry climate. Situated on the grounds is a stone building designed by Myron Hunt and constructed of readily available materials. It was built in 1932 as a project that would help the unemployed in the community during the Great Depression.

3

South Pasadena Preservation Foundation Museum (Meridian Iron Works)

913 Meridian Ave, South Pasadena, 91030. **Mailing address:** PO Box 1095, South Pasadena, 91031-1095. ☎ (818) 799-9089. **Thomas Guide:** 595 G2. **Hours:** Sat 1-4pm. $ free. [P] free on street. 📷 allowed. **Membership:** available. **Year founded:** 1983. **Year opened:** 1986. **Primary focus:** South Pasadena history. **Research fields:** San Gabriel Valley history. **Publications:** *Preservation Press* newsletter. **Governing authority:** private. **Category:** historic building/site open to the public. **Activities/programs:** docent programs, guided tours. **Facilities:** gift shop, picnic area. ♿ strollers permitted, wheelchair accessible. **Collection focus:** architecture, local history.

The 2-story Meridian Iron Works, a wooden structure that now houses the South Pasadena Preservation Foundation Museum, was originally built in 1886 as a general store. It later served as a hotel, bicycle shop, ironworks and blacksmith shop and antiques store. The museum displays artifacts from the region's Spanish and Mexican periods and items from local Indian tribes, such as the Hahamogua. Other exhibits include old photographs of the Raymond Hotel and items from the Cawston Ostrich Farm, the Raab Dairy and local schools and businesses.

Meridian Iron Works

Iorton Simon Museum with Rodin's *Burghers of Calais*

Norton Simon Museum of Art

11 W Colorado Blvd, Pasadena, 1105. ☎ (818) 449-6840. **Fax:** 318) 796-4978. **Thomas Guide:** 65 G4. **Hours:** Thu-Sun noon-6pm. $ $4 adults, $2 students and eniors, children under 12 free. [P] ee. 📷 allowed with instamatic ash only, no other flash or tripods. **Membership:** available. **Year ounded/opened:** 1924. **Primary ocus:** European art from the Renaisance to the 20th century, as well as large collection of Asian sculpture. **Major exhibitions:** "The Spirit of Modernism: Galka Scheyer in the New World" (1995). **Publications:** *Masterpieces from the Norton Simon Museum*. **Governing authority:** nonrofit. **Category:** art museum. **Activities/programs:** changing exhibitions, uided tours (by reservation), school rograms. **Facilities:** bookstore, xhibit space/gallery, sculpture garen, slide registry. ♿ wheelchair ccessible. **Collection focus:** Asian rt; European art; Indian art; modern nd contemporary art; bronzes; andscapes; Dutch and Flemish, uropean, French, German, Italian, atin American, Renaissance, Spansh and 17th—20th-century painting; ortraits; sculpture.

This is one of America's most emarkable art collections and ne of the largest in the world massed by an individual. Over he course of 25 years, Norton Simon created an outstanding ollection of European art from he Renaissance to the 20th century and impressive examples of Asian sculpture spanning a period of 2,000 years. Simon was a 24-ear-old businessman when he bought a bankrupt orange juice bottling plant in Fullerton. The plant later become the giant Hunt Foods and Industries empire. The multinational corporation, Norton Simon Inc., was ultimately formed through mergers with McCall Publishing, the *Saturday Review of Literature* and Canada Dry Corp. The museum was founded in 1924 as the Pasadena Art Institute. The present building was constructed in 1969 by Ladd & Kelsey and dedicated as the Pasadena Art Museum. In 1974 the museum was reorganized, renamed and established as the home for Norton Simon's collection.

The earliest works from the European collection include Pre-Renaissance and Renaissance masterpieces, such as the 24-panel altarpiece *Coronation of the Virgin* (1344) by Guariento di Arpo, Giovanni di Paolo's *Branchini Madonna* (1427), Giovanni Bellini's *Portrait of Joerg Fugger* (1474) and Raphael's *Madonna and Child with Book* (ca. 1504). Other important works from this period include *The Blessing Christ* (1478) by Hans Memling and *Susanna and the Elders* (1564) by Jan Metsys. An extremely rare, complete series of six Romanelli tapestry cartoons (ca. 1630), depicting the story of Dido and Aeneasis also on display. 17th-century painting is represented by *Saint Cecilia* (1606) by Guido Reni; *Lemons, Oranges and a Rose* (1633) by Francisco de Zurbarán, which is his only signed and dated still life; *The Holy Women at the Sepulchre* (ca. 1611) by Peter Paul Rubens; and Rembrandt's *Self-Portrait* (ca. 1636). Works from the 18th century include *The Piazzetta, Venice, Looking North* (before 1755) by Canaletto, *A Pair of Still Lives* (ca. 1728) by Jean-Baptiste-Siméon Chardin, a tiny *Reclining Nude* (ca. 1713) by Antoine Watteau and *Vertumnus and Pomona* by François Boucher.

Impressionism is splendidly represented by Edouard Manet's *The Ragpicker* (ca. 1865), a canvas inspired by Velázquez; *Rouen Cathedral, Tour d'Albane, Morning* (1894) by Claude Monet; *Portrait of a Young Woman in Black* (ca. 1875) by Pierre Auguste Renoir; and *The Poultry Market at Pontoise* (1882) by Camille Pissarro. The Post-Impressionist collection includes *Farmhouse and Chestnut Trees at Jas-de-Bouffan* (ca. 1885) by Paul Cézanne, *Portrait of the Artist's Mother* (1888) by Vincent van Gogh, *Tahitian Woman and Boy* (1899) by Paul Gauguin and *Red-Headed Woman in the Garden* (1889) by Henri de Toulouse-Lautrec. There is a permanent exhibit of over 100 paintings, pastels, drawings and prints by Edgar Degas, including the renowned painting *The Ironers* (ca. 1884). A highlight of the collection is a group of 71 bronze modeles cast from the artist's wax originals.

Masterpieces of the 20th-century include *Nude Combing Her Hair* (1906) by Pablo Picasso, *Artist and Model* (1913) by Georges Braque, *Street in Murnau with Women* (1908) by Vasily Kandinsky, *The Black Shawl (Lorette VII)* (1918) by Henri Matisse and *Two Heads* (1932) by Paul Klee.

The museum's splendid Asian collection consists of religious sculpture from all parts of India and Southeast Asia. It is particularly rich in works from the Gandaran period (2nd-5th centuries BC), Gupta dynasty (4th-6th centuries AD) and Chola dynasty (10-12th centuries AD). Another section features Buddhist, Hindu and Jain bronze and stone sculpture from the Himalayas, Cambodia, Thailand and Pakistan.

View of one of the museum's galleries

Norton Simon
Museum of Art

Main Level

Triumph of Virtue and Nobility over Ignorance (ca. 1740) by Giovanni Battista Tiepolo

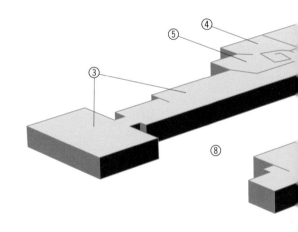

Parvati, South India: Chola period (ca. 990 AD)

The Ragpicker (ca. 1865) by Edouard Manet

Open Green (1923) by Vasily Kandinsky

Adam and Eve (ca. 1530) by Lucas
Cranach the Elder

Madonna and Child with Book (ca.
1502) by Raphael

Woman with a Book (1932) by
Pablo Picasso

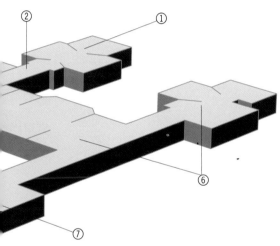

Tulips in a Vase (ca. 1890) by
Paul Cézanne

The Mulberry Tree (1889) by Vincent van Gogh

Norton Simon
Museum of Art

Lower Level

Three Old Beech Trees (ca. 1665) by Jacob van Ruisdael

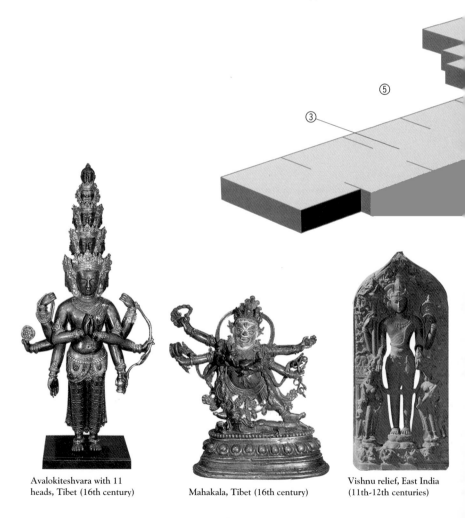

Avalokiteshvara with 11
heads, Tibet (16th century)

Mahakala, Tibet (16th century)

Vishnu relief, East India
(11th-12th centuries)

Portrait of the Artist's Son Titus (ca. 1645) by Rembrandt

Female Figure by Aristide Maillol

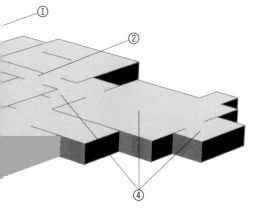

The Star: Dancer on a Point (ca. 1877) by Edgar Degas

The Little Fourteen Year Old Dancer by Edgar Degas

Gamble House, front elevation

Gamble House — USC

4 Westmoreland Pl, Pasadena, 91103. ☎ (818) 793-3334, (213) 681-6427. **Fax:** (818) 577-7547. **Thomas Guide:** 565 G4. **Hours:** Thu-Sun noon-3pm. **Closed:** holidays. Ⓢ $4 adults, $3 seniors, $2 students, children under 12 free. **Reservations:** necessary for groups.

Rear of the house with stepping stones

Ⓟ free. 📷 not allowed. **Membership:** available. **Year founded/opened:** 1966. **Primary focus:** to interpret the architecture and deco-

rative arts of Greene and Greene. **Research fields:** American domestic architecture, decorative arts. **Publications:** *Images of the Gamble House.* **Governing authority:** municipal, college/university. **Category:** historic building/site open to the public. **Activities/programs:** docent programs, educational programs, guided tours, intermuseum loan, school programs, slide presentations, volunteer programs. **Facilities:** bookstore, research library. ♿ parking, wheelchair accessible. **Garden features:** ponds. **Collection focus:** architecture, furniture and interiors.

The Gamble House was constructed in 1908 for David and Mary Gamble of the Procter and Gamble Company, as their retreat from the cold Midwestern winters. The house is considered a

masterpiece of the Arts and Crafts movement in America. It was designed by the famous architectural firm of Charles and Henry Greene of Pasadena and represents the finest and best-preserved example of their work.

They created a 2-story California bungalow, a structure strikingly different from many other residences on Millionaire's Row. Its style was influenced by Japanese and Swiss wood-building traditions and adapted to southern California's unique climate. The house features large terraces and open-air sleeping porches, while covering of redwood shingles and overhanging eaves protect it from the sun. Numerous doors and

The teakwood staircase in the entry hall

windows provide excellent cross-ventilation.

The interior decor is all custom-designed by the Greenes and includes furniture, paneling, wood carvings, built-in cabinets and fixtures. It was built with over 20 types of wood, including teak, mahogany, Port Orford cedar, maple and oak, **Lamp** and hand polished to a glossy finish. Numerous stained-glass windows were executed by Emile Lange of the Tiffany Studios.

The house was donated by the Gambles' heirs to the City of Pasadena in 1966 in a joint agreement with the University of Southern California. It was designated a National Historic Landmark in 1978.

Dining room. The furniture, stained-glass window and lamp fixtures were all custom-designed

enyes Mansion

Pasadena Historical Museum (Fenyes Mansion)

70 W Walnut St, Pasadena,
1103. ☎ (818) 577-1660. **Fax:**
318) 577-1662. **Thomas Guide:**
55 G4. 🚌 bus. **Hours:** Thu-Sun 1-
pm. **Closed:** holidays. 💲 $4
dults, $3 students and seniors, chil-
ren under 12 free. P free. 📷 call
r info. **Membership:** available.
ear founded: 1924. **Year opened:**
974. **Primary focus:** to preserve,
ollect and display artifacts from
asadena and the surrounding San
Gabriel Valley. **Special collections:**
ie Fenyes Collection, the Vroman
ollection, the Sheats Collection.
Major exhibitions: "Fenyes Watercol-
rs" (1994), "Colorado St. Bridge"
1993). **Publications:** *Pasadena's*
oneer Photographers. **Governing**
uthority: private, nonprofit. **Cate-**
ory: historic building/site open to
ie public. **Activities/programs:**
hanging exhibitions, classes/
ourses, concerts, docent programs,
ducational programs, events
Annual Gala), guided tours, inter-
iuseum loans, internship program,
ctures, outreach programs, perfor-
iances, school programs, slide pre-
entations, traveling exhibitions, vol-
nteer programs. **Facilities:** book-
ore, exhibit space/gallery, gift
hop, research library, picnic area.

iving room, used for formal recep-
ions and official gatherings

ﺪ parking, wheel-
chair accessible (lim-
ited). **Garden fea-**
tures: ponds. **Collec-**
tion focus: architec-
ture; North American
art; books; clothing
and dress; decorative
and applied arts; folk
art; furniture and
interiors; genealogy;
local history; manu-
scripts; English, Euro-
pean, North Ameri-
can, 19th-20th cen-
tury painting; period rooms; personal
history; photography; portraits;
watercolors.

The Beaux Arts Fenyes Mansion was designed in 1905 by
architect Robert D. Farquhar,
who also built the William
Andrews Clark Library and Beverly Hills High School. The 18-

Solarium, used by the family as a
greenhouse

room structure is one of the few
remaining examples of the grand
residences that represent a particular lifestyle prevalent at the turn
of the century when Orange
Grove Ave was known as Millionaires' Row. It was commissioned by Pasadena's leading citizens, Dr. Adalbert and Eva S.
Fenyes. In 1946 their granddaughter, Leonora, married Con-
sul Y. A. Paloheimo, and they
established the Finnish Consulate
in the house. During the next 18
years their home was a center for
frequent social gatherings and
diplomatic functions. The family
donated the mansion to the
Pasadena Historical Society in
1965, and it was placed on the

National Register of Historic
Places in 1985.

The house is furnished with
original antique furniture from all
over the world, Oriental rugs,
tapestries and decorative arts
gathered across four generations.
There is a fine collection of
American Impressionist paintings, portraits of the family and a
12-volume bound set of Eva
Fenyes's amateur watercolors.The
beautiful gardens are planted
with redwoods, fruit trees, camellias, ferns and bamboo and feature formal terraces, ponds and a
stream.

In the new History Center
building there is a research library
with more than 750,000 old photographs, manuscripts, books,
periodicals, maps and ephemera
relating to Pasadena and the surrounding San Gabriel Valley. The
center con-
tains the A. C. Vroman Collection of photographs and the
Sheats Collection, the newest
addition to the Black History
Archive.

❼ Finnish Folk Art Museum

This museum is a replica of a
19th-century Finnish farmhouse
and the only one of its kind outside Finland. The Finnish folk art
exhibits are displayed in three
rooms. The first room is a re-cre-
ated living room, or smoke cabin,
which contains an open hearth,
handmade furniture, utensils and
decorative objects. The second
room features farmhouse furnishings, *ryijy* rugs (produced in Finland for centuries) and folk costumes. The third room is a traditional Finnish sauna.

19th-century smoke cabin in the
Finnish Folk Art Museum, charac-
teristic of Ostrobothnia province

El Molino Viejo (The Old Mill)

8

El Molino Viejo (The Old Mill)

1120 Old Mill Rd, San Marino, 91108-1840. ☎ (818) 449-5450. **Thomas Guide:** 596 A1. **Hours:** daily 1-4pm. **Closed:** holidays. $ free. **Reservations:** recommended for groups. [P] free. 📷 not allowed. **Membership:** available. **Year opened:** 1962. **Primary focus:** southern California history. **Research fields:** same. **Publications:** *The Grinding Wheel*, quarterly newsletter. **Governing authority:** municipal. **Category:** historic building/site open to the public. **Activities/programs:** changing exhibitions, guided tours, school programs, volunteer programs. **Facilities:** bookstore, library. ♿ wheelchair accessible (limited). **Collection focus:** architecture, local history, mills.

The present entrance room served as the mill's grinding room

This well-preserved building is one of the last examples of Spanish Mission-style architecture in southern California. Built about 1816 by converted Gabrielino Indians under the supervision of the Franciscan padres at Mission San Gabriel, it was the first water-powered gristmill in southern California. The lower walls of the 2-story building were constructed of oven-baked bricks and volcanic tuff, while the upper walls were built of adobe. Three corners of the structure were strengthened by buttresses. The whole exterior surface was covered with mortar and the roof was tiled.

In 1823 another mill was built adjacent to the mission and the old mill was gradually abandoned. Following the secularization of the missions, Pio Pico, the last Mexican Governor of California, sold 16,000 acres of the mission lands in 1846. Since then the Old Mill went through several different hands. Among its more prominent owners were James S. Waite, the editor of Los Angeles' first newspaper, *The Star*, and Henry E. Huntington, who used the building as a clubhouse for his hotel's golf course. The Old Mill is the southern California headquarters of the California Historical Society. It was designated as State Historic Landmark No. 302 and placed on National Register of Historic Places.

The museum features changing exhibitions covering the history of the state and displays the water wheel and several pieces of old Spanish furniture. The wheel chamber contains a cross-sectioned working model, which demonstrates how the building functioned as a grist mill.

The gardens grow mainly California native plants.

9

Kidspace Museum

390 S El Molino Ave, Pasadena, 91101. ☎ (818) 449-9144. **Recorded information:** (818) 449-9143. **Fax:** (818) 449-9985. **Thomas Guide:** 566 A5. **Hours:** Wed 2-5pm, Sat-Sun 12:30-5pm during the school year; summer hours: Tue-Fri 1-5pm, Sat-Sun 12:30-5pm. $ $5 adults and children 3 and older, $2.50 children ages 1-2, children under 1 free, seniors $3.50. [P] free on the street. 📷 not allowed. **Membership:** available. **Year founded/opened:** 1979. **Primary focus:** to engage children in hands-on learning. **Publications:** *Kaleidoscope*, quarterly newsletter. **Governing authority:** nonprofit. **Category:** children's museum. **Activities/programs:** educational programs, events (Rosebud Parade in Dec), guided tours, performances, scholarships and fellowships, school programs, summer programs, volunteer programs. **Facilities:** bookstore, gift shop, facilities for rent. ♿ strollers permitted, parking. **Collection focus:** education.

Kidspace is a "hands-on" museum, whose programs are designed for children 2 to 10 year old. The programs are based on the idea that children learn more successfully through a combination of physical and intellectual

Kidspace Fire Station, featuring the back portion of a 1955 fire truck

activities. Permanent exhibits and special themes explore arts and culture, environmental science and communication.

Exhibits include "Eco-Beach" with sand, sound of the surf and reef aquarium; "International Mask Gallery" which displays masks from around the world and offers mask-making and art activities; "KCBS Television Station" includes real cameras and monitors; "Backstage" features costumes, dressing tables and a stage; "Firestation Kidspace" displays the back portion of an old fire engine. In "Vons Mini-Market" children can shop for food, while in "Stargazed Planetarium" they can watch the night skies of southern California.

Pacific Asia Museum

46 N Los Robles Ave, Pasadena,
91101. ☎ (818) 449-2742. Fax:
(818) 449-2754. Thomas Guide:
565 J4. Hours: Wed-Sun 10am-
5pm. Closed: holidays. Ⓢ $4
adults, $2 students/seniors, children
under 12 free. Free admission on
3rd Sat of each month. P $3. 📷
not allowed in galleries. Membership: available. Year founded/
opened: 1971. Primary focus: to
present, preserve and promote the
art and culture of Asia and the
Pacific. Special collections: the
Harari Collection, the Lydman Collection, the Otto Collection, the Mar-
iot and Hans Ries Collection, the
Raper Collection, the Wilmont G.
Gordon Collection. Major exhibitions: "A Gathering Place" (1995);
The Evolving Dreamtime" (1994-5).
Publications: museum newsletter.
Governing authority: private, nonprofit. Category: art museum. Activi-
ties/programs: artist talks, changing
exhibitions, classes/courses, docent
programs, educational programs,
films, gallery talks, guided tours,
internship programs, lectures, outreach programs, performances,
school programs, slide presentations,
storytelling, volunteer programs,
workshops. Facilities: bookstore,
exhibit space/gallery, 5,000-volume
research library, sculpture garden,
theater. ♿ strollers permitted, parking, wheelchair accessible. Garden
features: Chinese garden, rock garden. Collection focus: Asian art, Chinese art, Indian art, Japanese art,
modern and contemporary art, primitive art, Tibetan art, bronzes, calligraphy, folk art, folk life and traditions, icons, jade, lacquerware, landscapes, porcelai and ceramics,
tapestries, textiles.

Pacific Asia Museum

The Pacific Asia Museum is
housed in a Chinese Imperial
Palace Courtyard-style building,
the only example of this kind of
architecture in southern California. The 2-story structure was
designed and built by architects
Marston, van Pelt and Maybury.
It was completed in 1929 for
noted art collector and dealer
Grace Nicholson. All the roof
tiles, stone carvings and ornaments were made in China and
assembled here by Chinese craftsmen. The building was deeded to
the City of Pasadena in 1943, and
the museum has occupied it since
1971. It has been designated a
California State Historic Landmark and listed in the National
Register of Historic Places.

This is the only museum in
southern California specializing in
the arts of Asia and the Pacific
Rim. Its permanent collection
consists of more than 17,000 art
and ethnographic objects spanning more than 5,000 years.
Museum holdings comprise the
world-class Harari collection of
Japanese paintings and drawings
which includes more than 200
works of Eisen, Hiroshige, Hokusai, Utamaro and other artists of
the Edo (1603-1868) and Meiji
(1868-1912) periods. There are
more than 1,000 objects in the
costumes and textiles collection,
including 30 imperial Chinese silk
robes and textiles from the Ming
(1368-1643) and Qing (1644-
1911) Dynasties. Buddhist art is
represented by paintings, sculptures and ritual objects from
India, China, Korea, Japan,

Chinese Courtyard Garden

Southeast Asia, Central Asia and
the Trans-Himalaya Region. The
ceramics collection contains
Southeast Asian ceramics, Japanese *satsuma* and *kutani* ware and
Chinese Imperial ware of the
Qing Dynasty, as well as more
than 100 ceramics from the Song
(960-1279), Yuan (1280-1368)
and Ming Dynasties. The Pacific
Islands collection includes objects
from the original cultures of Poly-
nesia, Micronesia and Melanesia,
such as spears, shields, drums and
over 200 *tapa* (bark cloth). The
museum owns a collection of
ethnographic material representing most of the major ethnic
groups of the Philippine Islands.

The photography archive contains more than 1,500 photographs and slides, including
early photos documenting the
Boxer Rebellion in China and
Sino-Tibetan art. The museum
possesses one of the few existing
complete sets of 166 woodblock
prints created in Japan by French
artist Paul Jacoulet.

The museum contains a Chinese courtyard garden, designed
by Erikson, Peters, Thomas and
Associates in 1979. It is one of
only two authentic Chinese
courtyard gardens in the US (the
other is at the Metropolitan
Museum in New York). Designed
in the ancient tradition of the
scholar's meditation garden, it
contains a koi pond, a zigzag
bridge, *tai-hu* style rocks and garden statues, including the pair of
18th-century Ching Dynasty marble lion dogs. The garden features
Ginkgo biloba, *Pittosporum tobira*
and the golden rain tree, along
with mondo grass, azaleas,
orchids, magnolias, wisterias and
Chinese roses.

Pacific Asia Museum

First Floor

Carved jade marriage bowl, China (18th century)

Short sword, Tanto, Japan (14th century)

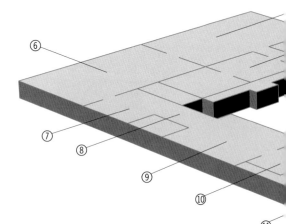

Roof gable sculpture, South Pacific

Vamana, Eastern Rajastan (10th century)

Female Hindu deity, India (12th century)

Vase, China

Folding horseshoe chair, China (ca. 1600)

Amoghasiddhi, Tibet (13th/14th century)

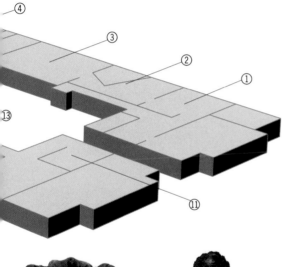

Netsuke, modeled after traditional character from Japanese drama

Seated Buddha, Korea, Yi Dynasty (ca. 1500)

Courtesan by Toyogawa Eishin, Japan, early 19th century (detail)

Full-scale model of *Voyager* (1977)

① **Jet Propulsion Laboratory (JPL)**

4800 Oak Grove Dr, Pasadena, 91109. ☎ (818) 354-9314. Fax: (818) 393-4641. **Thomas Guide:** 535 E4. **Hours:** vary, call for appointment. Ⓢ free. **Reservations:** by appointment only. Ⓟ free. ◉ allowed. **Year founded:** 1944. **Primary focus:** research, development and related activities under contract for the NASA. **Research fields:** basic and applied scientific and engineering research. **Governing authority:** federal, college/university. **Category:** specialized museum. **Activities/programs:** educational programs, guided tours, school programs. **Facilities:** exhibit space/gallery. ♿ wheelchair accessible. **Collection focus:** aerospace.

From its beginnings in 1944, JPL was engaged in aeronautics studies, rocket research, missile guidance, propulsion systems, satellite development, deep space communications, solar system exploration and Earth observation. It is an operating division of the California Institute of Technology (CALTEC) and one of nine NASA centers.

Guided tours start in an auditorium with a film *Outer Space*, which explains the history of the US space program and the laboratory's significant contribution to it. JPL conducts robotic planetary missions and operates the Deep Space Network for spacecraft communications, data acquisition, mission control and

radio-science space study. On exhibit is a full-scale model of *Voyager* (1977), a spacecraft that began exploration of the outer planets, capturing details of Jupiter and its moons, Saturn's ring system and Neptune's surface. Other prototypes and models of other space vehicles include *Explorer I* (1958), the first successful US satellite, a half-scale model of *Magellan* (1989), which mapped 97% of Venus' surface, *Galileo* (1994) and an experimental microrover used for Mars mission tests. Numerous panels display photographs taken from spacecraft of the planets of the Solar system, as well as pictures of Earth's surface.

Another building open for visitors is Space Flight Operations Facility. Through its network of computers housed in this build-

Model of *Explorer I* (1958), the first successful US satellite

ing, JPL communicates with spacecraft, relaying commands to them and processing and analyzing data received from them. The facility was designated a National Historic Landmark in 1986.

⑫ **Henninger Flats Visitor Center**

2260 Pinecrest Dr, Altadena, 91001. ☎ (818) 794-0675. Fax: (818) 794-9854. **Thomas Guide:** 536 D5. **Hours:** Sat-Sun 7am-5pm; during week opened on request. Ⓢ free. **Reservations:** recommended. Ⓟ free along Pinecrest Dr. ◉ allowed. **Year founded:** 1928. **Year opened:** 1993. **Primary focus:** public education of the San Gabriel Mountains and history of the Henninger Flats Facility. **Governing authority:** county. **Category:** nature center/ wildlife refuge. **Activities/programs:** educational programs, films, guided tours. **Facilities:** camping sites, visitors' center. ♿ wheelchair accessible. **Collection focus:** American Indian art, firefighting, foresting and logging, geology, glass and glassware, mammals.

Henninger Flats is located 3 miles up the Mt. Wilson Toll Rd. Since no private vehicles are allowed on the road, visitors should be prepared for a hike. The well-organized exhibits in the visitors' center provide information about the natural and social history of the Henninger Flats area. A display of the mammal skulls shows the difference in adaptation to different environments. Other exhibits feature these same mammals as they naturally appear. There are displays of birds, rattlesnakes and a cross-section of a giant California redwood, which was 750 years old when it was cut. Cones on display range in size from the tiny Hemlock to the enormous Coulter pine, the heaviest cone in the world. The Indian artifacts on display reflect the way of life of the early California inhabitants. Other exhibits include rocks and minerals, historic items, photographs and old glass bottles.

13

Mount Wilson Observatory

Mount Wilson Red Box Rd, Angeles National Forest. ☎ (818) 793-3100. **Thomas Guide:** 506 J7. **Hours:** weekends 10am-4pm (tour at 1pm). $ free. [P] free. 📷 allowed. **Membership:** available. **Year founded:** 1904. **Primary focus:** this is the world center for studying the Sun and stars of the Milky Way galaxy. **Category:** planetarium/observatory. **Activities/programs:** guided tours. **Facilities:** exhibit space/gallery, picnic area. **Collection focus:** astronomy.

Mount Wilson Observatory

The Mount Wilson Observatory was founded in 1904 by astronomer George Ellery Hale. He was known as a creator of important astronomical instruments, including four large telescopes. Each of them was regarded "the world's largest telescope" at the time it was completed. Hale is also famous for his discovery of magnetic fields in sunspots. Another world-renown Mount Wilson's astronomer is Edwin P. Hubble, who determined the existence of galaxies outside the Milky Way and proved that the universe is expanding. The observatory houses a 60-inch reflecting telescope, the 100-inch Hooker telescope, as well as other instruments. The small Astronomical Museum features pictorial exhibits devoted to Hale's and Hubble's achievements, along with photographs of the sun, moon, spiral nebulas and other heavenly bodies.

Chilao Visitor Center

14

Chilao Visitor Center

Angeles Crest Highway, La Canada, 91011. **Mailing address:** Star Route, La Canada, 91011. ☎ (818) 796-5541. **Thomas Guide:** 4647 F7. **Hours:** daily 9am-5pm. **Closed:** never. $ free. **Reservations:** necessary for groups. [P] free. 📷 allowed. **Year founded/opened:** 1982. **Primary focus:** ecosystem management. **Governing authority:** federal. **Category:** park museum/visitor center. **Activities/programs:** school programs, slide presentations, summer programs, volunteer programs. **Facilities:** bookstore, picnic area, visitors' center. ♿ activities for visually impaired, strollers permitted, parking, wheelchair accessible. **Garden features:** restrooms; dogs allowed. **Collection focus:** botany, zoology.

The Chilao Visitor Center was built in 1982 as a part of the Angeles National Forest High Country Plan. The structure imitates a wickiup, such as those built by the indigenous people. The center introduces visitors to the Forest through trails, nature walks and various activities, including children's programs and evening campfire programs. Over 20 indoor exhibits are devoted to themes such as national forest management, the history of the San Gabriel Mountains and forest wildlife.

15

Sunny Slope Water Co.

1040 El Campo Dr, Pasadena, 91107. ☎ (818) 795-4163, 287-5239. **Fax:** (818) 795-7061. **Thomas Guide:** 566 F7. **Hours:** weekdays 8am-5pm. $ free. **Reservations:** by appointment only. [P] free. 📷 allowed. **Year founded:** 1895. **Year opened:** 1994. **Primary focus:** water utility — major source of early California history from 1821 on to present. **Research fields:** local history — California history. **Publications:** *Ranches to Residences; L. J. Rose of Sunny Slope 1827-1899.* **Governing authority:** company. **Category:** specialized museum. **Activities/programs:** guided tours, retrospectives, school programs. **Facilities:** conservation center. ♿ parking. **Garden features:** labels/descriptions, ponds, rock garden, water garden, restrooms. **Collection focus:** agriculture, North American archaeology and antiquities, horticulture, water.

Founded in 1895, the Sunny Slope Water Co. is one of the few remaining early regional water systems still serving its customers. On the company grounds stands the historic San Gabriel Mission dam, La Presa (Spanish for the stone dam), built in 1821. It is the oldest surviving dam in the southwestern United States.

Beautifully maintained grounds feature palm and redwood groves, citrus and fruit orchards, many varieties of California oaks, Tasmanian blue gum trees, as well as wildflowers and plants adapted to dry climate. A small ranch museum displays items of daily use in the 1890s, water meters, farm tools and equipment.

The Sunny Slope Co. water wagon

Huntington Library

 16

Huntington Library, Art Collections and Botanical Gardens

1151 Oxford Rd, San Marino, 91108. ☎ (818) 405-2100. **Recorded information:** (818) 405-2141. **Fax:** (818) 405-0225. **Thomas Guide:** 566 C7. 🚌 bus. **Directions:** (818) 405-2274

Chaucer's *Canterbury Tales* (ca. 1410)

(recorded info). **Hours:** Tue-Fri 1-4:30pm, Sat-Sun 10:30am-4:30pm. **Closed:** holidays. Ⓢ suggested donation $7.50 adults, $6 seniors, $4 students and children 12 and over. Ⓟ free. 📷 no flash/tripods in the buildings. **Membership:** available. **Year founded:** 1919. **Year opened:** 1928. Primary focus: Anglo-American history, literature and art. **Research fields:** same. Spe-

cial collections: the Arabella Huntington Memorial Collection, the Adele S. Browning Memorial Collection, the Munro Collection. **Major exhibitions:** "The Traditional World of Medieval Manuscripts" (1995), "The Last Best Hope of Earth: Abraham Lincoln and the promise of America" (1994). **Publications:** *Calendar*, bimonthly; art catalogues. **Governing authority:** private, nonprofit. **Category:** art museum, botanical garden/arboretum, library with collections other than books. **Activities/programs:** artist talks, changing exhibitions, concerts, docent programs, dramatic programs, educational programs, guided tours, internship programs, lectures, scholarships and fellowships, school programs, slide presentations, volunteer programs, workshops. **Facilities:** bookstore, cafeteria/restaurant, conservation center, exhibit space/gallery, gift shop, lecture hall, research library with 700,000 books and over 3 million manuscripts, sculpture garden. ♿ strollers permitted, parking, wheelchair accessible. **Garden features:** cactus garden, endangered species, herb garden, Japanese garden, labels/descriptions, ponds, rare species, rock garden, rose garden, restrooms. **Collection focus:** European art; North American art; book arts; books; botany; decorative and applied art; drawing; furniture and interiors; graphic arts;

medieval, modern, general American and local history; landscapes; language and literature; manuscripts; English, French, North American and 18th—19th-centuries painting; photography, porcelain and ceramics; portraits; printing; sculpture; silver; tapestries; watercolors.

Created by Henry Edwards Huntington in 1919, this splendid estate is one of the greatest attractions in California and one of the nation's foremost cultural, research and educational centers, attracted by 500,000 visitors annually. It consists of a library, art collections and botanical gardens, with the emphasis on Anglo-American history, art and literature. Huntington was one of

Madonna and Child by Rogier van der Weyden

the most successful businessmen of his time, whose vast financial empire included railroad companies, real estate holdings and interests in water and power development. He greatly

Huntington Library, exhibition hall

Virginia Steele Scott Gallery of American Art

expanded the Los Angeles railway system, known as "Big Red Cars," creating an interurban network that made significant contribution to the population boom of the early 1900s. Huntington retired in 1910 and devoted all his time to art and book collecting and the landscaping of his 600-acre ranch. In 1913 he married Arabella Duval Huntington, the widow of his uncle and railroad magnate, Collis P. Huntington. She was a renowned art collector and had great influence

The Long Leg (1935) by Edward Hopper

over the development of the Huntington art collection.

The Huntington Library building was designed by Myron Hunt and H. C. Chambers and completed in 1920. This splendid Beaux-Arts structure houses one of the world's finest collections of rare books and one of the largest and most complete collections in the United States of British and American history and literature. Library holdings include 3 million manuscripts, over 350,000 rare books and almost as many reference works, along with numerous

prints, photographs, maps and other documents, ranging in date from 3500 BC to the present. Many rare books are rotated on display in the exhibit hall, including the Ellesmere manuscript of Chaucer's *Canterbury Tales* (ca. 1410), the Gutenberg Bible (ca. 1450), one of only three vellum copies in the US, and the double-elephant folio edition of Audubon's *Birds of America* (1827). The library possesses an unrivaled collection of Shakespeare's quartos and folios and the early editions of all the major British writers. The collection comprises the manuscript of Benjamin Franklin's *Autobiography* as well as the papers of the Founding Fathers, including George Washington, Thomas Jefferson and Abraham Lincoln.

The library's west wing houses the Arabella Huntington Memorial Collection, consisting of 18th-century Sèvres porcelain and French furniture, French sculpture and Renaissance paintings. The most important artworks include the sculpture *Portrait of the Lady* (1777), often called the Baroness de la Houze, by Jean-Antoine Houdon, the outstanding painting *Madonna and Child* by the Flemish 15th-century artist Rogier van der Weyden and two portraits attributed to Domenico Ghirlandajo.

The Virginia Steele Scott Gallery of American Art was designed by the architectural firm of Warner and Gray and opened in 1984. It displays American paintings, sculpture, drawings, prints, photographs and furniture from the 1730s to 1930s. Major works include portrait *Cornelis Wynkoop* (ca. 1743) by Pieter Vanderlyn, landscape *Rock Towers of the Rio Virgin* (1908) by Thomas Moran, *Sarah Jackson* (ca. 1765) by John Singleton Copley, and *The Top Man* (1931) by Walt Kuhn. The north wing is

devoted to the Arts and Crafts Movement, featuring decorative arts and furniture designed by Charles and Henry Greene.

The Huntington Art Gallery, formerly the Huntington residence, was designed in 1910 by Myron Hunt and Elmer Grey. It houses primarily British and French art of the 18th and early

Breakfast in Bed (1897) by Mary Cassatt

19th centuries. The Main Room displays the finest group of full-length British portraits anywhere in the world. Besides British and French paintings and sculpture, this fascinating collection contains tapestries, furniture, porcelain, silver, drawings and watercolors. Among the highlights are *Blue Boy* (ca. 1770) by Thomas Gainsborough, *Pinkie* (1794) by Sir Thomas Lawrence and *Jane, Countess of Harrington* (ca. 1777) by Sir Joshua Reynolds. The collection of 18th-century French furniture and decorative arts is one of the finest of its kind in the United States.

Robinson dining room by Greene & Greene (1905-7)

Huntington Art Gallery

Huntington Art Gallery

Main Floor

1. Large Library Room
2. Large Drawing Room
3. Small Drawing Room
4. Dining Room
5. North Passage
6. The Main Gallery
7. The Hall
8. The Small Library

Second Floor

9. Changing Exhibition Rooms
10. Quinn Room
11. The Southeast Room
12. Wedgwood Room
13. The Adele S. Browning Memorial Collection
14. The Moseley Collection
15. The Southwest Room

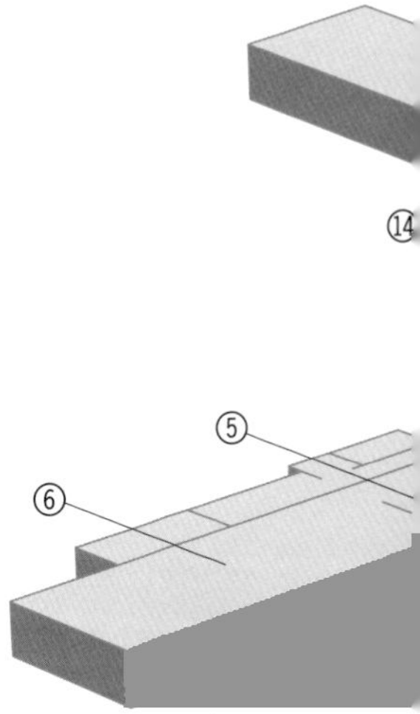

French furniture (ca. 1750) in the Large Library Room

Chair, designed by François Boucher and Jean-Baptiste Oudry (mid 18th century)

Young Knitter Asleep (1636) by
Jean-Baptiste Greuze

Portrait of a Lady (1635) by
Anthony van Dyck

Duke of Wellington by Sir Thomas
Lawrence

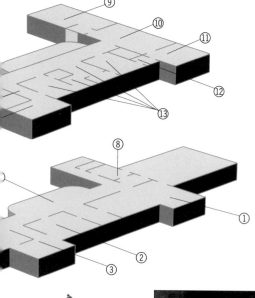

Vase, Chinese celadon and French
ormolu mounts

Blue Boy (ca. 1770) by Thomas
Gainsborough

Sarah Siddons as the Tragic Muse
(1784) by Sir Joshua Reynolds

Huntington Botanical Gardens

Before it was bought by Henry E. Huntington in 1903, the 600-acre property was a working ranch, sparsely covered with native plants. Development of the Botanical Gardens began in 1904, under the direction of German landscape designer, William Hertrich. Today, the majestically maintained gardens span 150 of the 207-acre estate, with almost 15,000 kinds of plants from all over the world, presented in fifteen specialized gardens. Two Camellia Gardens display one of the nation's largest collections of 1,700 camellia cultivars. The Shakespeare Garden features plants and flowers which were cultivated in English gardens during the 16th and 17th centuries. The Rose Garden contains 2,000 cultivars and traces the history of the rose over two thousand years. The Japanese Garden features a furnished 19th-century Japanese house, a drum bridge, a bonsai court, a zigzag bridge, water stones, stone lanterns and pagodas. A sand and rock arrangement in the Zen Garden represents a flowing stream. The most impressive is the Desert Garden, one of the largest research and display collections of cacti and other succulents in the world. It includes over 2,500 species of desert plants. The Palm Garden features 90 of about 140 palm species adapted to the dry climate of southern California. The Herb Garden is organized into sections according to the use of herbs: for medicines, teas, wines and liqueurs, cooking, cosmetics and dyes. The Subtropical Garden contains plants from all over the world, while the Jungle Garden features species from tropical forests. The Australian Garden grows more than 100 types of eucalyptus (of the over 600 types native to Australia).

(1) North Vista
(2) Shakespeare Garden
(3) Rose Garden
(4) Herb Garden
(5) Camellia Garden
(6) Japanese Garden
(7) Zen Garden
(8) Australian Garden
(9) Subtropical Garden
(10) Lily Ponds
(11) Jungle Garden
(12) Palm Garden
(13) Desert Garden
(14) Orange Grove
(15) Mausoleum
(16) Library
(17) Huntington Gallery
(18) Scott Gallery
(19) Japanese House
(20) Ikebana House
(21) Conservatory

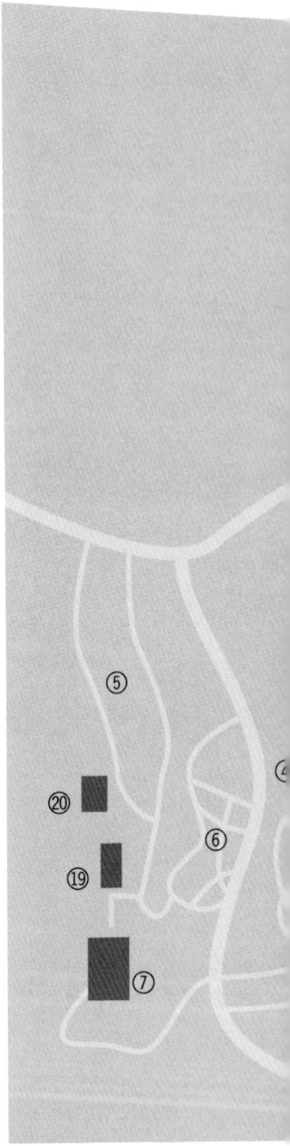

North Vista

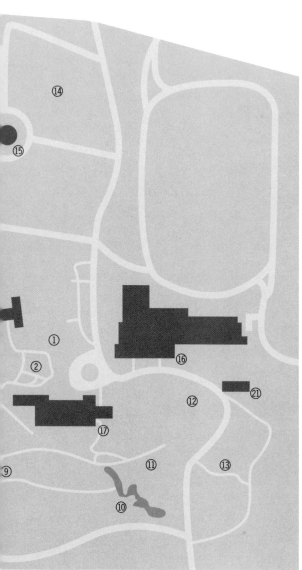

Desert Garden

Palm Garden

Japanese Garden

18th-century French stone temple

DOWNTOWN

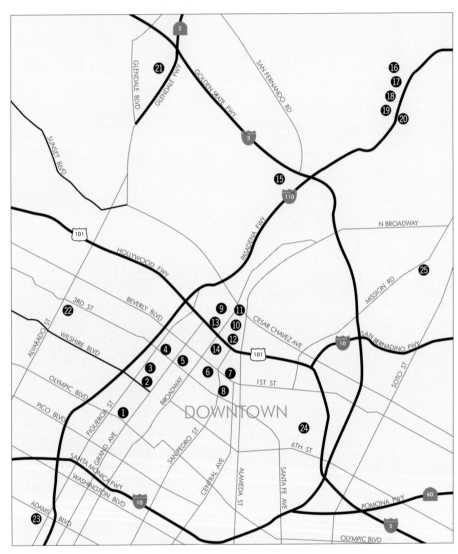

1. Museum of Neon Art (MONA)
2. Los Angeles Public Library — History Department/ Photographic Collections
3. Los Angeles Public Library — Art, Music and Rare Books Department
4. Wells Fargo History Museum
5. Museum of Contemporary Art (MOCA)
6. The New Otani Hotel Garden
7. Japanese American National Museum
8. James Irvine Garden
9. El Pueblo de Los Angeles Historical Monument
10. Avila Adobe
11. Sepulveda House
12. Old Plaza Firehouse
13. Old Masonic Hall
14. Los Angeles Children's Museum
15. Los Angeles Police Academy Rock Garden
16. Southwest Museum
17. Casa de Adobe
18. Ramona Museum of California History
19. El Alisal
20. Heritage Square Museum
21. Holyland Exhibition
22. Grier-Musser Museum
23. Automobile Club of Southern California
24. Los Angeles Poodle Museum
25. Plaza de la Raza

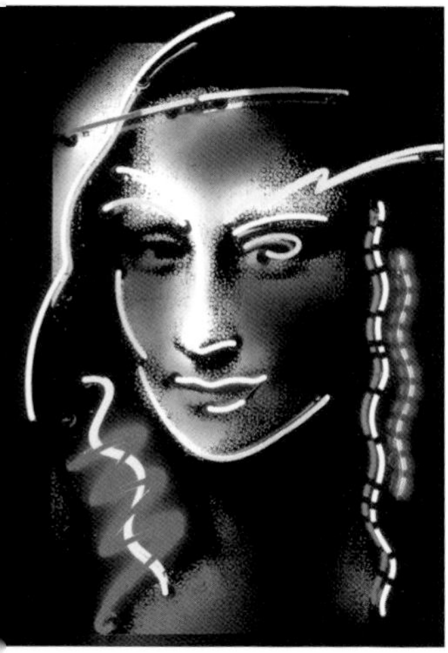

MONA (1981) by Lili Lakich

❶

Museum of Neon Art (MONA)

501 W Olympic Blvd, Los Angeles, 90015. ☎ (213) 489-9918. **Fax:** (213) 489-9932. **Thomas Guide:** 634 E5. 🚌 bus, metro. **Hours:** Wed-Sat 11am-5pm, Thu 11am-8pm, Sun noon-5pm. **Closed:** major holidays. $ $5 general; $3.50 seniors, students and teenagers; children under 12 free; no charge on Thu 5-8pm. [P] free underground, entrance on Grand Ave north of Olympic Blvd. 📷 not allowed. **Membership:** available. **Year founded/opened:** 1981. **Primary focus:** to exhibit, document and preserve works of neon, electric and kinetic art. **Research fields:** contemporary fine art in electric media, neon signs and movie marquees. **Major exhibitions:** "Mourning Becomes Electric," Lili Lakich retrospective (1993). **Governing authority:** nonprofit. **Category:** art museum. **Activities/programs:** artist talks, changing exhibitions, classes/courses, concerts, docent programs, educational programs, gallery talks, installations, lectures, retrospectives, school programs, slide presentations, traveling exhibitions, volunteer programs, workshops. **Facilities:** bookstore, exhibit space/gallery, gift shop, slide registry. ♿ strollers permitted, parking, wheelchair accessible. **Collection focus:** modern and contemporary art, electricity, sculpture.

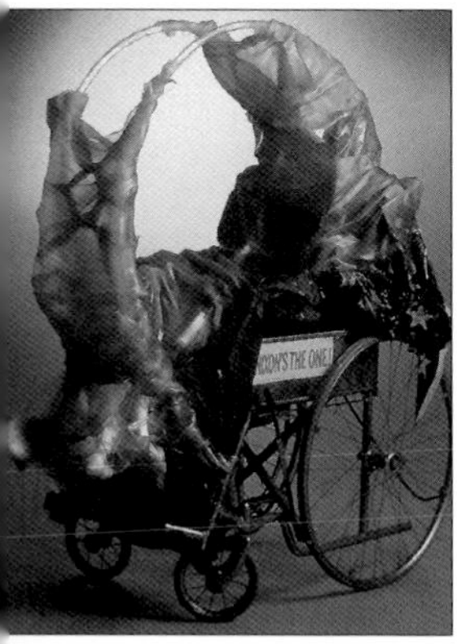

Nixon's the One (1988) by William Shipman

Looking for a cheap method to produce oxygen for medical use, Frenchman Georges Claude in 1910 accidentally developed the technology of injecting inert gases into glass tubes and striking them with electricity. He exhibited his device at Paris's Grand Palais, hoping to compete with Edison's light bulb. The first commercial use of neon was in 1912, when a barbershop advertising sign was installed on the Boulevard Montmartre. Neon was introduced to the United States in 1924, when Los Angeles car dealer Earle C. Anthony brought from Paris two neon Packard ads. Curious motorists lined up for miles to see the signs displayed on his showroom on Wilshire Blvd.

MONA was founded in 1981 by neon artist Lili Lakich and restorer Richard Jenkins. The museum aims to exhibit fine art in electric and kinetic media and to document and preserve outstanding examples of neon signs, billboards and marquees. It is the only permanent institution of its kind in the world. Visitors are encouraged to interact with exhibited pieces, take a close-up look, press buttons and activate artworks. MONA offers comprehensive introductory courses in neon design and techniques. It also conducts nighttime bus tours of neon signs and installations of contemporary electric fine art in the city.

MONA's permanent collection contains more than 50 vintage signs dating from the 1920s to the present, including the Art Deco light-bulb lady from the Melrose Theater (1923); a woman diver doing a pike into a swimming pool from Steele's Motel in the San Fernando Valley (1934); a unique animated Li Po, the Chinese philosopher riding a donkey (1937); and an RCA Victor double-sided banner sign (1940). Twenty neon signs from MONA's historic collection are on display at Universal Citywalk.

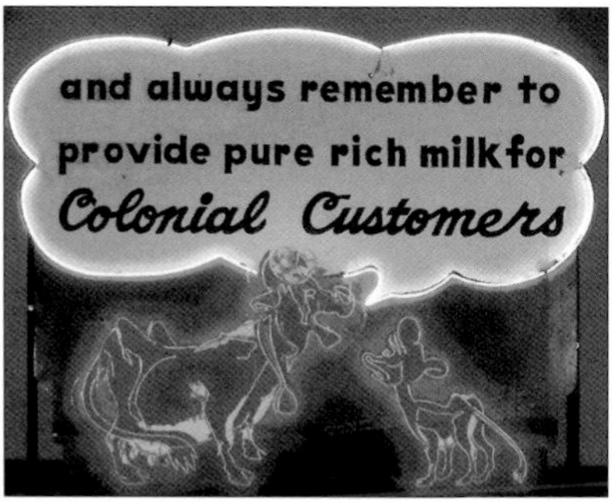

Colonial Dairy sign: animated neon cows (1953)

Contemporary neon art is represented by *The Ghost of John Coltrane* (1985) by Lili Lakich, *His Master's Voice* (1990) by Maurice Gray, *The Door* (1991) by Candice Gawne, *Speed of Life* (1992) by Korey Kline and *My Other Mother (Portrait of Frank Zappa)* (1993) by David Svenson.

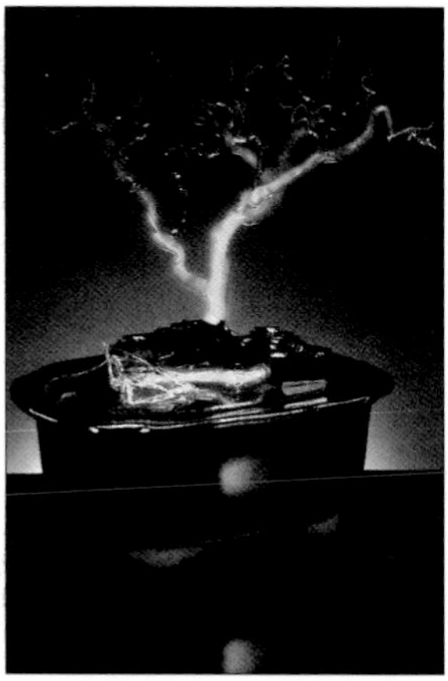

Bonsai (1986) by Peter David

Los Angeles Public Library

Los Angeles Public Library

❷

History Department/ Photographic Collections

630 W 5th St, Los Angeles, 90071.
☎ (213) 228-7400. **Fax:** (213)
227-7419. **Thomas Guide:** 634 E4.
🚌 bus, metro. **Hours:** Mon, Thu-Sat
10am-5:30pm; Sun 1-5pm. Ⓢ
free. **Reservations:** photo collection
by appointment only. Ⓟ in building.
📷 not allowed. **Year opened:**
1926. **Special collections:** Security
Pacific Collection, Ralph Morris
Archives, the *Los Angeles Herald
Examiner* Collection, the William
Reagh Collection. **Major exhibitions:**
"Then And Now/Los Angeles Photographs by William Reagh" (1993).
Governing authority: municipal. **Category:** library with collections other
than books. **Activities/programs:**
artist talks, changing exhibitions,
docent programs, educational pro-

grams, films, guided tours, internship
programs, lectures, multimedia presentations, performances, performing
arts, school programs, slide presentations, storytelling, traveling exhibitions, volunteer programs. **Facilities:**
audiovisual holdings, exhibit space/
gallery, gift shop, lecture hall, library,
theater. ♿ wheelchair accessible.
Garden features: garden with public
art. **Collection focus:** photography.

The Los Angeles Public
Library's Central Library is the
third largest central library in the
country. It contains more than
2.1 million books, 10,000 magazine subscriptions and over 2 million historic photographs. The
1926 Beaux-Arts historic landmark, designed by Bertram Good-
hue and placed on
the National Reg-
ister of Historic
Places in 1970,
was damaged in a
1986 arson fire,
when 400,000
books were
destroyed. The
newly renovated
building features a
multicolor-tiled
pyramidal tower,
historic murals,
sculptures and
inscriptions,
numerous chandeliers, lanterns
and other works of art created by
local artists. The Robert F.
Maguire III Gardens contain
waterways, pools and fountains,
along with works of art incorporated into the garden.

The History Department's
notable photographic collections
comprise the Central Library's
Historical California Collection,
which includes photographs of
general historic interest on California, Los Angeles
and the missions;
the Portrait Collec-
tion, containing
photos of promi-
nent early Califor-
nians; and the Fed-
eral Writers Pro-
ject, with pho-
tographs taken in
the late 1930s,
including Los
Angeles street
scenes, agricultural
views, the motion
picture industry and
architecture.

The Security Pacific Collection
includes three large collections
with over 250,000 photographs:
the Los Angeles Chamber of
Commerce Collection, the *Hollywood Citizen News/Valley Times*
newspaper collection; and turn-
of-the-century photographs that
document the growth of Los
Angeles.

The *Los Angeles Herald Examiner* Collection consists of 2.2 million photographs that document
southern California, the country
and the world. Other collections
include the Ralph Morris
Archives, with 25,000 advertising
and industrial photographs; the
William Reagh Collection of
images of Los Angeles; and the
"Shades of LA" Collection, with

Los Angeles in the 1870s

over 8,000 photographs representing 8 ethnic communities of
Los Angeles.

❸

Art, Music and Rare Books Department

☎ (213) 228-7225. **Fax:** (213)
228-7229. **Hours:** Mon 1-4pm, Sat
10am-2pm or by appointment. **Collection focus:** books, graphic arts,
Japanese art, language and literature.

This department of the Los
Angeles Central Library houses
some extremely rare and important items relating to the history
of California, including Picolo's
Informe, the first printed book
relating wholly to the Californias,
and Costanso's *Diario*, the first
account of the state of California.
There are a number of geographical works and atlases of particular
interest, such as Waghenear
Mariner's Mirror and several early

Business on the Beach, by the LA Chamber of
Commerce (1920s). Photographs like this one were
used to entice East Coast businesses to the West.

Courtesan with her Kamuro by Utamaro

Ptolemies, as well as a collection of works recounting voyages and travels to the New World and to the Pacific in the 17th and 18th centuries. The department contains important books on natural history, including Elliot's *Birds of North America* and Muybridge's *Animal Locomotion*. Other highlights include a number of incunabulas, rare early works on Mexican history (since the 16th century), and materials on architecture (since the 16th century) and costume (women's fashions and military uniforms since the 17th century).

The department also includes a collection of 270 Japanese prints, featuring works of notable 18th- and 19th-century artists such as Hiroshige, Hokusai and Utamaro.

4

Wells Fargo History Museum

333 S Grand Ave, Los Angeles, 90071. ☎ (213) 253-7166. **Fax:** (213) 620-9903. **Thomas Guide:** 634 F4. 🚌 bus, metro. **Hours:** Mon-Fri 9am-5pm. **Closed:** major holidays. 💲 free. **Reservations:** recommended for groups. P several garages nearby. 📷 personal photography allowed. **Year opened:** 1988. **Primary focus:** history of early California and Wells Fargo Bank. **Governing authority:** company. **Category:** history museum. **Activities/ programs:** educational programs,

guided tours, school programs. **Facilities:** audiovisual holdings, gift shop, theater. ♿ wheelchair accessible. **Collection focus:** banks and banking, carriages and carts, gold, local history, mining, weights and measures.

Four years after gold was discovered in January 1848 at Sutter's Mill, California, Henry Wells and William G. Fargo formed a new express and banking company in New York. These two eastern businessmen, founders of the American Express Company in 1850, recognized the almost unlimited potential of the Pacific Coast. Hundreds of thousands of fortune-seekers came from all over the world in the early years of the Gold Rush. Taking its name from its founders, Wells, Fargo & Co. opened its first office in San Francisco in 1852. The company operated the legendary Pony Express between Sacramento and Salt Lake City in 1861. During the late 1860s, Wells Fargo controlled all the major overland stage lines in the western US.

Located on the plaza level of the Wells Fargo Center, the Wells Fargo History Museum traces the history of the company, California and the American West. Beautifully designed exhibits display artifacts and memorabilia from Wells Fargo's stirring past, including money, postal envelopes, treasure boxes, original papers, early photographs and equipment. There is a recreated company office as it looked a

Massive safe decorated with pastoral southern California scenes

century ago, with an agent's desk, package scales and a complete display of the telegraph with code books, which visitors may use to send a message in code.

A museum highlight is an 1897 Concord coach, made by the Abbot-Downing Company of Concord, New Hampshire. It was made of the finest materials and craftsmanship and could transport 18 people. Drawn by six horses at the speed of 5 mph, the Concord took 3 weeks to travel from Tipton, Missouri, to San Francisco. Other displays present mining tools and equipment, maps of major mining areas and old photographs dating back to the California Gold Rush. A fascinating display of gold samples includes a 2-pound gold nugget unearthed in 1975 by a child during a casual attempt at panning near the town of Challenge.

1897 Concord stagecoach #599. Mark Twain called it "a cradle on wheels."

MOCA at California Plaza

Museum of Contemporary Art (MOCA)

MOCA at California Plaza: 250 S Grand Ave, Los Angeles, 90012; The Geffen Contemporary at MOCA: 152 N Central Ave, Los

The Reign of Narcissism (1988-89) by Barbara Bloom, mixed-media installation

Angeles, 90013. ☎ (213) 621-2766. **Recorded information:** (213) 626-6222. **TDD:** (213) 621-1651. **Fax:** (213) 620-8674. **Thomas Guide:** 634 F4. 🚌 bus, metro. **Hours:** Tue-Sun 11am-5pm, Thu 11am-8pm. **Closed:** Thanksgiving, Christmas, New Year's Day. Ⓢ $6 adults, $4 students and seniors, children under 12 free. Free to all every Thu 5-8pm. P California Plaza parking garage, the Music Center parking garage; rates vary. 📷 allowed for works in the museum's permanent collection. **Membership:** available. **Year founded:** 1979. **Year opened:** 1983. **Primary focus:** to collect, preserve, interpret and present contemporary art from 1940 to the present. **Special collections:** the Giuseppe Panza Collection, the

Barry Lowen Collection, the Rita and Taft Schreiber Collection, the Beatrice and Philip Gersh Collection, the Scott D. F. Spiegel Collection, the El Paso Natural Gas Company Fund for California Art. **Major exhibitions:** "Pure Beauty: Some Recent Works from Los Angeles" (1994), "Louis I. Kahn: In the Realm of Architecture" (1993), "Hand-Painted Pop: American Art in Transition" (1992), "Ad Reinhardt" (1991), "Blueprints for Modern Living: History and Legacy of the Case Study Houses" (1990). **Publications:** exhibition catalogues. **Governing authority:** private, nonprofit. **Category:** art museum. **Activities/programs:** artist talks, changing exhibitions, educational programs, guided tours, installations, lectures, multimedia presentations, performances, retrospectives, traveling exhibitions, volunteer programs. **Facilities:** available for rent; bookstore, cafeteria/restaurant, checkroom, exhibit space/gallery, gift shop, library, theater, visitors' center. ♿ strollers permitted, parking, sign-language interpretation, wheelchair accessible. **Collection focus:** modern and contemporary art, North American art, graphic arts, 20th-century painting, photography, sculpture, video art.

The Museum of Contemporary Art is the only museum in Los Angeles devoted exclusively to collecting and presenting art from 1940 to the present. It is also the only major museum in the US established with this charter in the last few decades. Founded in 1979, MOCA is the result of a partnership between the City of Los Angeles and major local collectors and artists. MOCA provides more than 20 exhibitions annually, featuring painting, sculpture, photography, drawings, prints, installations and environmental work, as well as architecture, video, film, music, dance, performance, design and new interdisciplinary forms. The museum is located in two internationally acclaimed facilities, The Geffen Contemporary and MOCA at California Plaza.

The Geffen Contemporary at MOCA (formerly MOCA at the Temporary Contemporary) opened in 1983 as a temporary exhibition space while the museum's permanent building was being constructed. Originally a hardware store and police garage in Little Tokyo, the building was transformed into a museum exhibition space by renowned Los Angeles architect Frank Gehry. He subtly converted a vast warehouse interior, retaining many of the building's original features both inside and outside. In 1986 the city extended MOCA's lease on the renovated structure for 50 years, thus providing LA with another extraordinary exhibiting facility.

Since its opening in 1986, MOCA's permanent facility at California Plaza received accolades from both critics and the general public. In 1991 the American Institute of Architects

Room for St. John of the Cross (1983) by Bill Viola, video installation

named the building one of the ten best works of American architecture completed since 1980. This was the first major building in the US by internationally renowned Japanese architect Arata Isozaki, who prepared 30 different designs before the final solution was accepted. Isozaki combined cube, pyramid and cylinder shapes with the textures of sandstone, granite, aluminum and crystallized glass to achieve this stunning blend of Western forms and Japanese tradition. From the street, visitors can see only the separate north and south wings; all galleries are on the entry level and surround a sunken courtyard.

MOCA's remarkable permanent collection comprises more than 1,600 works in all visual media created from 1940 to the present by established as well as emerging artists. Its core is made up of three outstanding private collections. The first one, the Giuseppe and Giovanna Panza di

The Geffen Contemporary at MOCA, interior

Untitled (Questions) (1989-90) by Barbara Kruger, mural on The Geffen Contemporary at MOCA

Biumo Collection, forms the foundation of the museum's permanent collection and contains 80 major works of Abstract Expressionism and Pop Art from the 1940s, `50s and `60s. Its particular strength lies in the in-depth representation of a number of artists and the selection of important works that define crucial periods in each artist's career. This purchase, valued in excess of $10 million, represents the largest and most significant single acquisition of post-World War II art. The collection includes works of Franz Kline (12), Mark Rothko (7), Robert Rauschenberg (11), Claes Oldenburg (16), James Rosenquist (8), Roy Lichtenstein (4), George Segal (2), Jean Fautrier (6) and Antonio Tàpies

(14). The 7 paintings by Mark Rothko represent the largest group of his works held by a public museum.

The Barry Lowen Collection is made up of 67 works, including paintings, sculpture, photographs and drawings from the 1960s, `70s and `80s. Featured are 40 Minimalist, Neo-Expressionist and Post-Modernist artists, such as Richard Artschwager, David Salle, Agnes Martin, Donald Judd, Julian Schnabel, Joel Shapiro and Frank Stella. Notable among the works are Untitled (1963) by Dan Flavin, Two Panels: Yellow with Large Blue (1970) by Ellsworth Kelly, Fass (1969-73) by Brice Marden and Untitled (1967) by Cy Twombly.

The Rita and Taft Schreiber Collection contains 18 paintings, sculptures and drawings created between 1939 and 1972 by 13 artists, including Alexander Calder, Jean Dubuffet, Alberto Giacometti, George Rickey,

Pierre Alechinsky, Nicolas de Staël and Joan Miró. Among the highlights are Number 1 (1949) by Jackson Pollock, Composition of Red, Blue and Yellow (1939) by Piet Mondrian and Arshile Gorky's Betrothal I (1947).

Other major collections include the Beatrice and Philip Gersh Collection, featuring Number 3 (1948) by Jackson Pollock, Black Dress (1982-3) by Susan Rothenberg and Stories from My Childhood (1977) by Alexis Smith; and the Scott D. F. Spiegel Collection, with 13 works donated in 1991. Artist Sam Francis's 1993 gift consisted of 10 major paintings created between 1951 and 1992. Other important works acquired through individual gifts and acquisitions include Andy Warhol's painting Telephone (1961), Jasper Johns' painting Map (1962) and Michael Heizer's earthwork Double Negative, located in Mormon Mesa, Nevada.

Aristotle — Plato — Socrates (1982) by Stephen Prina, mixed-media installation

Museum of Contemporary Art (MOCA) at California Plaza

Entrance Level

[1] J. Paul Getty Trust Gallery
[2] Richard & Geri Brawerman & The Firks Foundation Gallery
[3] South Gallery
[4] The Gordon F. Hampton Family Gallery & The Fred F. Fallek Gallery
[5] Collectors Gallery
[6] Northeast Gallery
[7] Douglas S. Cramer Family Gallery
[8] Shuwa Corporation Kobayashi Gallery
[9] Nicholas/Epstein Norton Gallery

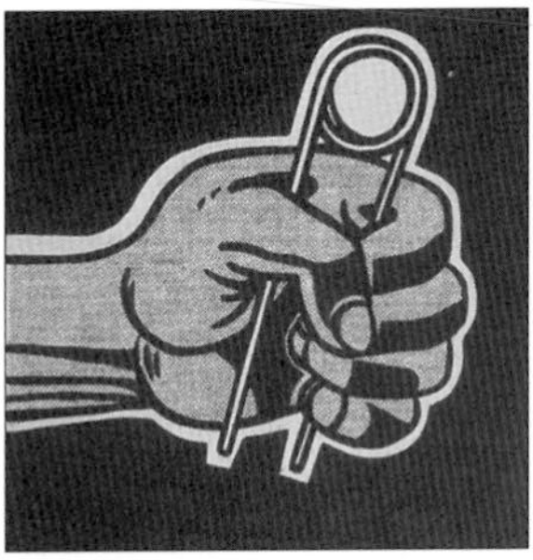

The Grip (1962) by Roy Lichtenstein

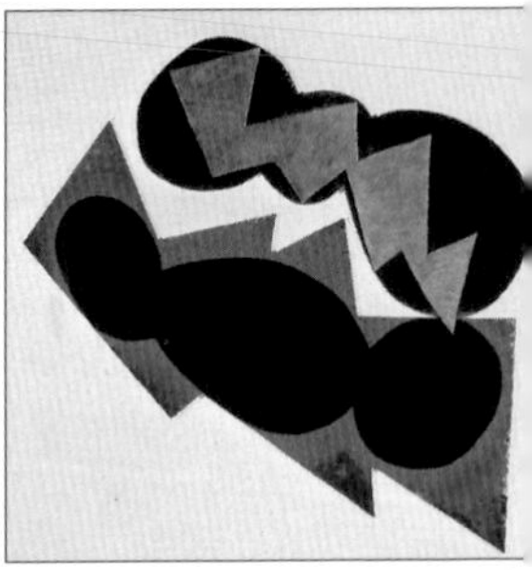

Heart and Mind (1981) by Elizabeth Murray

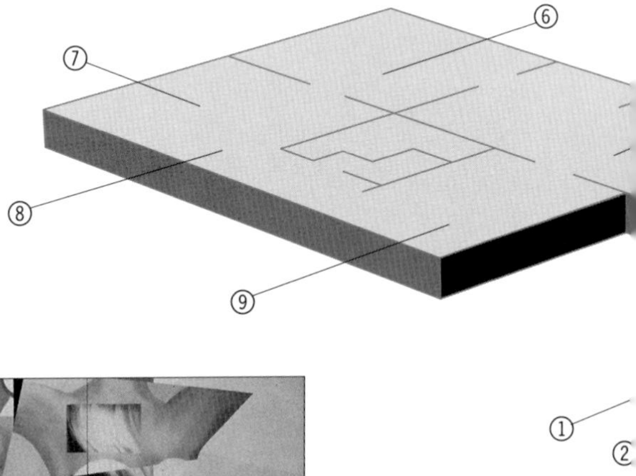

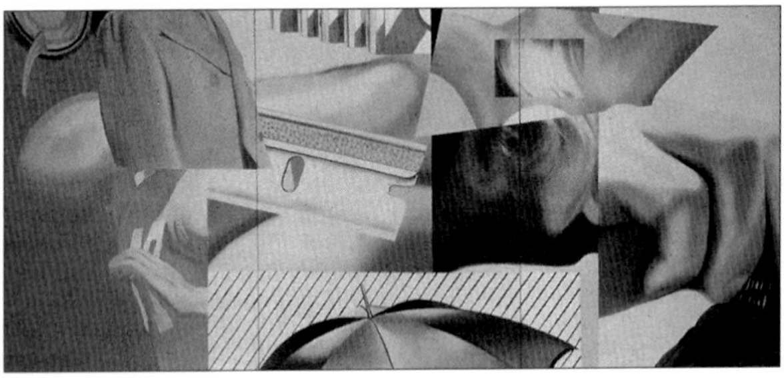

A Lot to Like (1962) by James Rosenquist

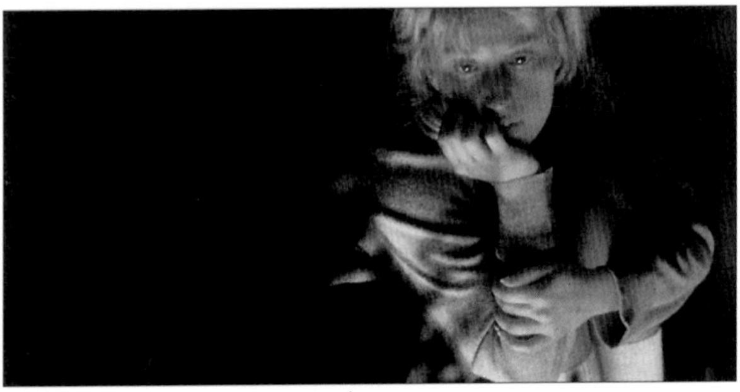

Untitled #88 (1981) by Cindy Sherman

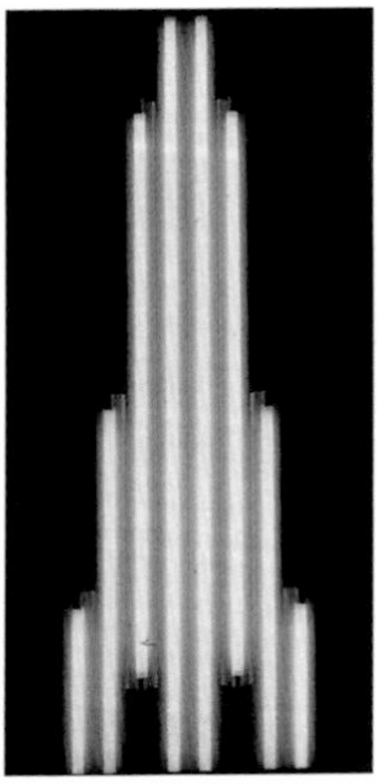

Monument for V Tatlin (1969) by Dan Flavin

Cigar (1991) by Robert Gober

Winter Garden (1975) by Louise Nevelson

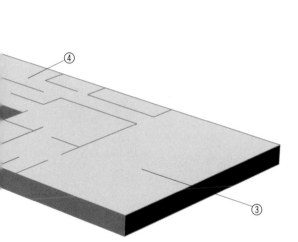

Telephone (1961) by Andy Warhol

Coca-Cola Plan (1958) by Robert
Rauschenberg

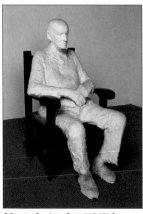

Man in the Armchair (1969) by
George Segal

White Shirt on a Chair (1962) by
Claes Oldenburg

6

The New Otani Hotel Garden

120 S Los Angeles St, Los Angeles, 90012. ☎ (213) 629-1200. **Thomas Guide:** 634 G4. **Hours:** daily; daytime viewing of garden suggested. **Closed:** never. $ free. [P] hotel parking or nearby lots on hourly basis. 📷 allowed. **Year opened:** 1977. **Governing authority:** private. **Category:** botanical garden/arboretum. **Facilities:** available for rent, cafeteria/restaurant. ♿ strollers permitted, parking, wheelchair accessible. **Garden features:** Japanese garden. **Collection focus:** botany.

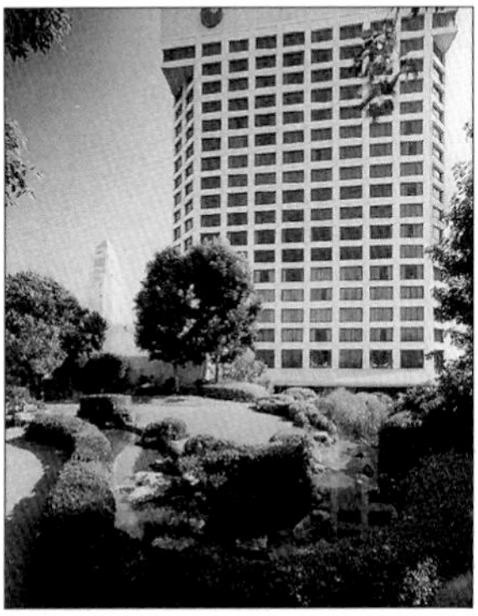

The New Otani Hotel and Garden

This half-acre authentic Japanese "Garden in the Sky" is located on the third floor of the New Otani Hotel in downtown Los Angeles. It is a miniature version of its 400-year-old, 10-acre sister garden at the New Otani in Tokyo. The garden was designed by renowned landscape architect Sentaru Iwaki, who employed the *shakkei* (borrowed scenery) technique, which incorporates distant landscapes into the garden panorama. The Zen-inspired strolling garden features tranquil pathways, ponds, waterfalls and unusual stone lanterns. It contains approximately 100 species of lush vegetation and a priceless Japanese red-rock collection. These precious rocks are found only on the island of Sado in central Japan.

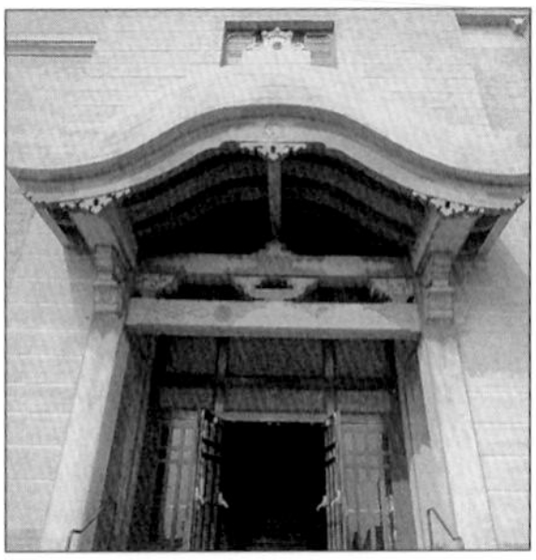

Japanese American National Museum, ceremonial entrance

7

Japanese American National Museum

369 E 1st St, Los Angeles, 90012. ☎ (213) 625-0414. **Fax:** (213) 625-1770. **Thomas Guide:** 634 G4. **Hours:** Tue-Sun 10am-5pm, Fri 11am-8pm. **Closed:** Thanksgiving, Christmas, New Year's Day. $ $4 general; $3 seniors, students; free 3rd Fri of each month. [P] $3 across the street. 📷 allowed, no flash. **Membership:** available. **Year founded:** 1985. **Year opened:** 1992. **Primary focus:** to preserve the history of Japanese Americans. **Research fields:** Japanese-American history and culture. **Major exhibitions:** "America's Concentration Camps: Remembering the Japanese-American Experience" (1994). **Governing authority:** private, nonprofit. **Category:** history museum. **Activities/programs:** changing exhibitions, classes/courses, performances, storytelling, traveling exhibitions, workshops. **Facilities:** bookstore, gift shop. ♿ wheelchair accessible. **Collection focus:** anthropology, folk art, general American history, motion pictures, personal history.

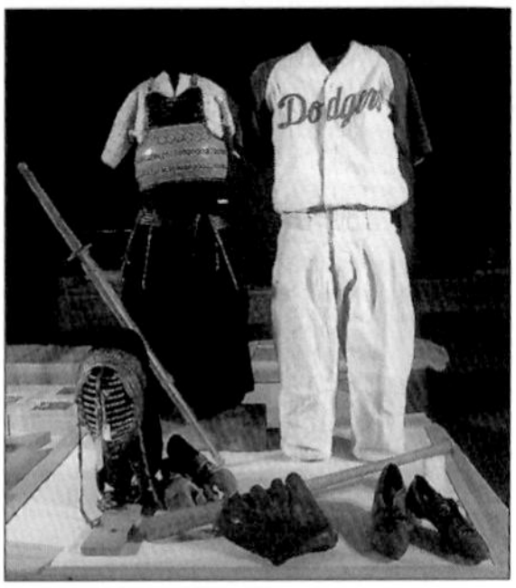

Sporting lives: exhibit of baseball and kendo outfits

This museum is housed in the former Nishi Hongwanji Buddhist Temple in the heart of the Little Tokyo historic district. The splendidly restored building was designed in 1925 by architect Edgar Cline in a mix of styles, including Buddhist, Italian and Near Eastern. This is the only museum in the country dedicated to the Japanese-American experience and the largest repository of Japanese-American materials in the world.

Its major exhibitions include "Issei Pioneers," featuring the experience of Issei, or first- generation Japanese immigrants, their family and community life, and the struggle for survival; "America's Concentration Camps," telling the story of more than 120,000 people of Japanese ancestry incarcerated in concentration camps during WWII; and "Japanese American Soldiers."

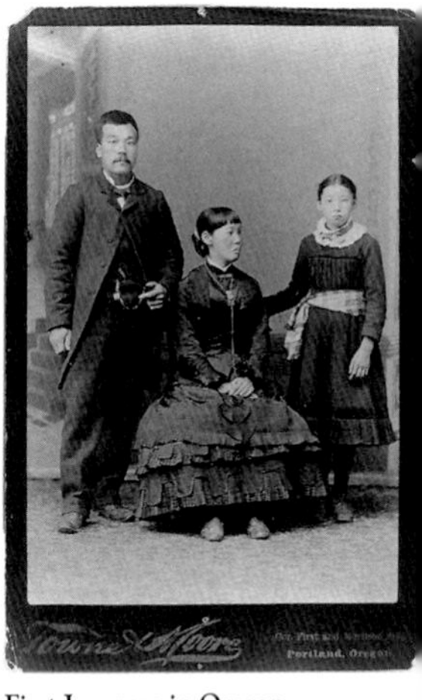

First Japanese in Oregon

The permanent Legacy Center features hands-on activities and interactive exhibits and programs, including a data base of concentration camp records, a historical timeline, family trees, replicas of photo albums and origami folding activities.

The museum's collection comprises 15,000 items, including 5,000 photographs and 100 reels of home movies depicting Japanese-American life, 100 linear feet of manuscripts, objects brought from Japan by early immigrants and arts and craft items made by interned Japanese Americans during WWII.

Winding stream

Tsukubai, stone water basin

den/arboretum. **Garden features:** Japanese garden, peak time: spring. **Collection focus:** botany.

The garden is adjacent to the Japanese American Cultural and Community Center in Little Tokyo and was named for the James Irvine Foundation, whose grant made it possible. It was designed by Dr. Takeo Uesugi and built in the Japanese tradition, though it is not a copy of a garden in Japan. Its design was inspired by the area near Mt. Baldy, and its 170-foot stream with small waterfalls symbolizes the experiences of several generations of Japanese in America. This winding stream gives the

8
James Irvine Garden

244 S San Pedro St, Los Angeles, 90012. ☎ (213) 628-2725. **Thomas Guide:** 634 G4. **Hours:** weekdays 8am-5pm, weekends 9am-5pm. **Closed:** holidays. Ⓢ free. Ⓟ nearby lots or on street. ◉ allowed. **Year opened:** 1980. **Primary focus:** to preserve and encourage an appreciation of Japanese heritage and to incorporate it into American culture. **Governing authority:** private. **Category:** botanical gar-

Bamboo glen with a well

garden its Japanese name, *Seiryuen* (Garden of the Clear Stream).

The garden features two kinds of bamboo fence, a waterfall, a wooden bridge, a well and a water

basin. It contains several bamboo species, including a grove of rare matake (*Bambusa matake*), Japanese black pine, Japanese maple and Japanese flowering cherry.

Other plants include Bermuda ground cover and dwarf mondo grass, azalea, pittosporum, wisteria and two species of camellia (*Japonica* and *sasanqua*).

In 1981 the garden received the distinguished National Landscape Award from the American Association of Nurserymen.

Wooden bridge in the James Irvine Garden

❾ El Pueblo de Los Angeles Historical Monument

Mailing address: 125 Paseo de la Plaza, Ste 400, Los Angeles, 90012. ☎ (213) 680-3800, 680-2525. **Fax:** (213) 485-8238. **Thomas Guide:** 634 G3. 🚌 bus, metro. Ⓢ free. **Reservations:** recommended, (213) 628-1274. Ⓟ 5 adjacent lots on both Los Angeles and Main streets; prices vary. 📷 for personal use only. **Year founded:** 1953. **Primary focus:** historic house museum reflecting the history of Los Angeles. **Major exhibitions:** "Spectrum 200 — Photos of Old Los Angeles." **Governing authority:** municipal. **Category:** historic building/site open to the public. **Activities/programs:** changing exhibitions, docent programs, traditional Mexican events, guided tours, workshops. **Facilities:** bookstore, cafeteria/restaurant, exhibit space/gallery, gift shop, visitors' center. ♿ strollers permitted, parking, wheelchair accessible (mostly). **Collection focus:** architecture, Hispanic art, Mexican art, firefighting, local history, religious history and tradition.

El Pueblo de Los Angeles Historical Monument is the oldest section of the city, comprising 27 historic buildings on a 44-acre state historic park. Although there are no remains of the original structures, this is the site where 44 *pobladores* (settlers), by order of King Carlos III of Spain,

founded the city of Los Angeles on September 4, 1781. With the growth of the town, its historic core was neglected and buildings steadily deteriorated until 1926, when Christine Sterling launched a campaign to save it. The symbol of the old pueblo, Olvera Street, named in honor of the first county judge, Agustin Olvera, was rebuilt and opened as a Mexican marketplace in 1930. Today it is a major tourist attraction with 2 million visitors per year.

❿ Avila Adobe

E-11 Olvera St, Los Angeles, 90012. **Hours:** daily 10am-5pm. **Year opened:** 1977.

The Avila Adobe is the oldest existing residence in Los Angeles, constructed in 1818 as a town house for the Avila ranching family. Its first owner, affluent cattle rancher Don Francisco Avila, became *alcade* (mayor) of the pueblo in 1810. During the Mexican-American War the house was briefly used as the headquarters of Commodore Robert F. Stockton, commander of the US Pacific Fleet. The building had several owners before it eventually became a boardinghouse and restaurant. Designated for demolition, the adobe was saved by Christine Sterling and now is part of El Pueblo de Los Angeles Historical Monument. It has been designated California Historical Landmark No. 145.

Originally built of adobe bricks, with walls three feet thick and floors of packed earth, the house was damaged by the 1870 and 1971 earthquakes and thoroughly restored in 1977. Today it is decorated to recall the atmosphere of the prosperous ranching family home in the late 1840s. Six rooms are furnished with period reproductions or antiques, including several pieces that belonged to the Avila family. An annex in the courtyard houses two permanent exhibitions: One is devoted to Christine Sterling and the other, the "History of Water in Los Angeles," outlines the development of the city's water supply system.

Kitchen in the Avila Adobe, used as a storeroom for food and cooking utensils as well as a family bathing room

⓫ Sepulveda House

W-12 Olvera St, Los Angeles, 90012. ☎ (213) 628-1274. **Hours:** Mon-Sat 10am-3pm. **Year opened:** 1986.

The 2-story combination business and residential building, called the Sepulveda Block, was constructed during the real estate boom of the 1880s, when the population in Los Angeles grew from 11,000 to over 50,000 in 10 years. The house was built in 1887 by architects George F. Costerisan and William O. Merithew in the Victorian Eastlake style and today is one of only a few such structures still existing in the city. Named for its owner, Señora Eloisa Martinez de Sepulveda, it contained 22 rooms and 2 commercial stores in front.

Sepulveda House

In 1972 the building was placed on the National Register of Historic Places. The exterior and some portions of the interior were restored in 1982. The visitors' center is located on the first floor, in a room decorated in Victorian style, and features exhibits on the history of the pueblo. An 18-minute film on the history of Los Angeles, *Pueblo of Promise*, is shown upon request. Two exhibits depict the lifestyle of the late 19th century: The kitchen has been restored to represent a boardinghouse kitchen of the 1890s and Señora Sepulveda's bedroom reflects the cultural changes in Los Angeles, from Mexican traditions to a more American style.

Champion chemical engine, made by Fire Extinguisher Mfg. Co., Chicago, Illinois (1891)

⑫ Old Plaza Firehouse

Paseo de la Plaza, Los Angeles, 90012. ☎ (213) 625-3741. **Hours:** Mon-Sat 10am-3pm. **Year opened:** 1960.

The beginnings of the Los Angeles Fire Department date back to 1869, when a meeting was held in Billy Buffum's saloon for individuals interested in creating a volunteer fire department to protect Los Angeles County. Plans were made to purchase a steam pumper and establish a volunteer fire department. In 1872 a company of volunteers was formed and an Amoskeag steam fire engine and hose cart were bought.

Walter S. Moore, the first paid fire chief in the city of Los Angeles (1886)

Plaza Firehouse's castellated brick building was the first structure erected in Los Angeles for the purpose of housing firefighting equipment and personnel. It was designed by architect William Boring and built by Dennis Hennessy in 1884. The firefighters on duty at the station were lodged on the second floor and horses were stabled on the ground floor. At the sound of the alarm men would slid down a pole, horses were moved forward to the harness hanging overhead, which was then secured to their backs. The Plaza Firehouse housed steam-engine companies until 1897, and after the station was relocated the building was used as a saloon, a lodging house, a drug store and a pool hall. In 1960 it was restored and opened as a museum of firefighting history. The building was designated California Historical Landmark No. 730.

The museum displays firefighting tools and equipment of the late 19th and early 20th centuries, including an original pumper and a chemical wagon, old photographs, maps, fire alarms, helmets and other memorabilia.

Fire alarm box 15, located at berth 90 in San Pedro, the first box to be pulled when the SS *Markay* exploded and burned in Los Angeles Harbor on June 22, 1947

⑬ Old Masonic Hall

416½ N Main St, Los Angeles, 90012. ☎ (213) 626-4933. **Hours:** Tue-Fri 10am-3pm. **Year opened:** 1962.

The city's first Masonic Hall was the 2-story brick and stucco structure constructed by the firm of Perry and Brady in 1858. Its second floor was used as a meeting hall for Los Angeles Lodge 42, the first American organization founded in the city. It was established in May 1854, when the Grand Lodge of Free and Accepted Masons of California granted permission to 16 local masons to organize a lodge. This was the first lodge in Los Angeles and the second oldest in southern California. The hall was used for meetings until 1868, when Lodge 42 relocated because of expanded membership.

Furnished with original furniture, the hall is still used for meetings of Los Angeles City Lodge 814. The anteroom of the building houses a museum that preserves the early history of Masonry in Los Angeles. The museum displays swords, fraternal pins, squares and compasses, 100-year-old officers' jewels, photos and other memorabilia. There is an 1890s gong used for rituals and a 45-star flag carried in Cuba during the Spanish-American War in 1898 by brother Moses B. Rosenthal of Utopia Lodge, Chicago, Illinois.

Apron and collar (early 20th century)

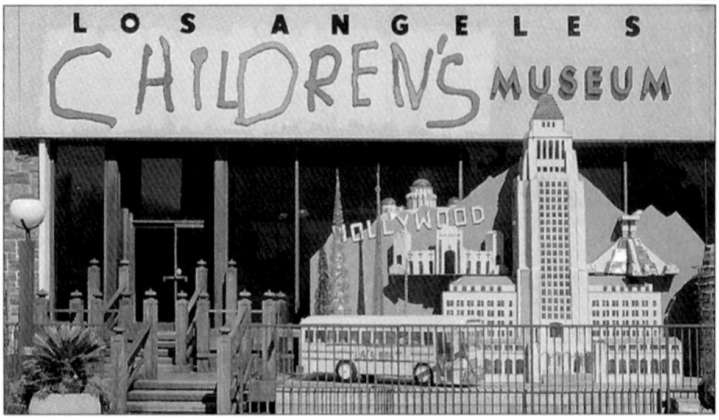

Los Angeles Children's Museum

[14]
Los Angeles Children's Museum

310 N Main St, Los Angeles, 90012. Phone: (213) 687-8801. **Recorded information:** (213) 687-8800. **Fax:** (213) 687-0319. **Thomas Guide:** 634 G3. 🚌 metro. **Hours:** Sat-Sun 10am-5pm; groups Tue-Fri 9:15am-1pm. $ $5. **Reservations:** recommended, (213) 687-8825. [P] Los Angeles Mall garage, underneath museum. 📷 allowed. **Membership:** available. **Year founded/opened:** 1979. **Primary focus:** hands-on children's exhibits. **Major exhibitions:** "Club ECO" (1995). **Publications:** quarterly newsletter. **Governing authority:** private, nonprofit. **Category:** children's museum. **Activities/programs:** changing exhibitions, docent programs, dramatic programs, educational programs, outreach programs, performances, school programs, storytelling, traveling exhibitions, workshops. **Facilities:** exhibit space/gallery, gift shop, theater. ♿ activities for visually impaired, strollers permitted, parking, wheelchair accessible. **Collection focus:** education.

The Los Angeles Children's Museum offers a hands-on, participatory environment, designed for kids from 2 to 12 years of age. Children learn by doing in an interactive, playlike ambiance. The museum's programs complement traditional classroom studies, integrating the arts and humanities with the sciences and technology. Fifteen permanent, life-size participatory exhibits and play areas encourage children to touch, create, explore and experience various objects. The museum's "discovery maze" ramp system was designed by renowned architect Frank Gehry.

The exhibits include "City Streets," with displays of an MTA bus, police motorcycles, street sweeper, gas pump, traffic signals and signs, all of which allow children to explore the workings of the street; in "H_2O: The Story of Water," children can play with water and discover how an Archimedes screw works, create a vortex with a bicycle and float a boat through locks and dams. In "MTA Station" visitors can explore the Metro subway system, complete with a real ticket machine, a crossing guard, video maps and the inside of a train. In "Recording Studio" guests can create their own music, radio dramas and sound stories, while "Videozone" offers full-color video recordings and playback of visitors' performances, such as singing, dancing and acting. "The Cave of the Dinosaurs" hides dinosaur footprints, bones and holograms. "Zoetrope," provided by Walt Disney Productions, enables visitors to watch their own drawings move on spinning discs. Other exhibits include "Lego Building Site," "Club ECO," "Shadow Box," "The Loft" and "Sticky City."

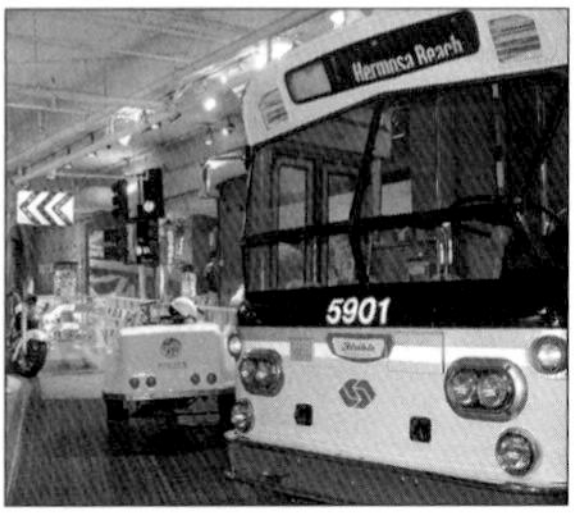

"City Streets" exhibit

[15]
Los Angeles Police Academy Rock Garden

1880 N Academy Rd, Los Angeles, 90012. ☎ (213) 222-9136. **Thomas Guide:** 594 G6. **Hours:** daily 9am-5pm or by appointment. $ free. [P] free. 📷 allowed. **Year opened:** 1937. **Governing authority:** municipal. **Category:** botanical garden/arboretum. **Facilities:** available for rent, cafeteria/restaurant. **Garden features:** rock garden. **Collection focus:** botany.

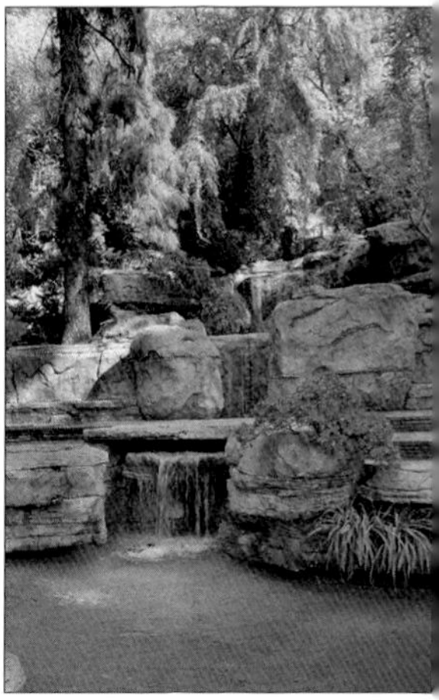
Los Angeles Police Academy Rock Garden

The construction of a pistol range in Elysian Park in 1925 marked the beginning of the Los Angeles Police Academy. During the Olympic Games in 1932 revolver and pistol matches were held at the facility. In 1935 an athletic center was developed that included an Olympic-size pool and a rock garden designed and built by landscape architect François Scotti. The delightful garden features a small amphitheater, pools, cascades and shade trees and is worth seeing at night, illuminated by multicolored lights.

Southwest Museum

16

Southwest Museum

234 Museum Dr, Los Angeles, 90065. ✉ PO Box 41558, Los Angeles, 90041-0558. ☎ (213) 221-2164. **Recorded information:** (213) 221-2163. **Fax:** (213) 224-8223. **Thomas Guide:** 595 B4. **Hours:** Tue-Sun 11am-5pm. **Closed:** major holidays. 💲 $5 adults, $3 students and seniors, $2 ages 7-18, children 6 and under free. P free on museum hillside. 📷 allowed (no flash or tripods). **Membership:** available. **Year founded:** 1907. **Primary focus:** the museum is a major educational center dedicated to the preservation and presentation of the history and culture of Native Americans, with particular emphasis on the peoples of North America. **Research fields:** anthropology and archaeology. **Special collections:** the Caroline Boeing Poole Collection of American Indian basketry. **Major exhibitions:** "Borderland/Dreamland: Decorative Arts of the Spanish-American Frontier" (1995). **Publications:** *Masterkey* magazine. **Governing authority:** private, nonprofit. **Category:** specialized museum. **Activities/programs:** artist talks, changing exhibitions, classes/courses, competitions, concerts, docent programs, educational programs, films, gallery talks, guided tours, lectures, multimedia presentations, outreach programs, performances, retrospectives, school programs, slide presentations, storytelling, summer programs, traveling exhibitions, volunteer programs. **Facilities:** audiovisual holdings, bookstore, exhibit space/gallery, gift shop, lecture hall, 50,000-volume

research library, micro holdings, picnic area. ♿ strollers permitted. **Collection focus:** anthropology, North American archaeology and antiquities, Meso and South American archaeology and antiquities, prehistoric archaeology, American Indian art, Western art, Eskimo art, Hispanic art, Latin American art, Mexican art, North American art, baskets, folk art, folklife and traditions, folklore, headdresses, masks, prehistory, sculpture, toys and games, weaving, woodcarvings.

The Southwest Museum is the oldest museum in Los Angeles, founded in 1907 by Charles F. Lummis and members of the Southwest Society, the Los Angeles branch of the Archaeological Institute of America. The society, formed by Lummis in 1903, assembled significant collections of Spanish Colonial and Indian art and artifacts amassed during expeditions it conducted in the Southwest and California. The museum was located in downtown Los Angeles until its present building was completed in 1914. Designed in the Mission Revival style by Sumner Hunt and Silas Burns, it is now a Los Angeles historic landmark.

The museum houses one of the most

important collections of Native American artworks and artifacts in the United States, ranging in date from prehistory to the present. Although it documents various cultures from Alaska to South America, the collection is particularly rich in holdings from western North America, especially the Southwest and California. The museum contains over 7,000 pottery vessels from the Southwest and one of the largest collections of baskets in the country, with more than 11,000 pieces. There are 6,600 Latin American colonial paintings, as well as examples of Hispanic folk and decorative arts. The museum houses an extensive collection of Meso and South American Pre-Columbian pottery and textiles. Other important holdings include Western Americana paintings and sculpture and documentary art related to the California missions.

Four permanent main exhibit halls concentrate on the native cultures of four major geographic areas: California, the Southwest, the Northwest Coast and the Great Plains. Each hall depicts cultural mores of Indian tribes, exploring daily life, social organization, art and religion, all of which reflect the considerable cultural diversity among Indian groups of North America.

The Braun Research Library contains 50,000 volumes, including 2,000 journals, 700 manuscript collections, over 100,000 photographs and 900 sound recordings. The library is a major information center in the areas of archaeology, anthropology, the art of the Americas and the history of the American West and Colonial Mexico.

Southwest Hall, Navajo blankets

Southwest Museum

Main Level

1. Northwest Coast
2. Plains
3. California
4. Temporary Exhibitions
5. Auditorium/Temporary Exhibitions

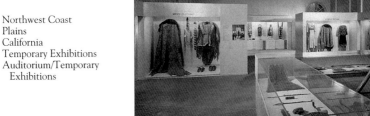

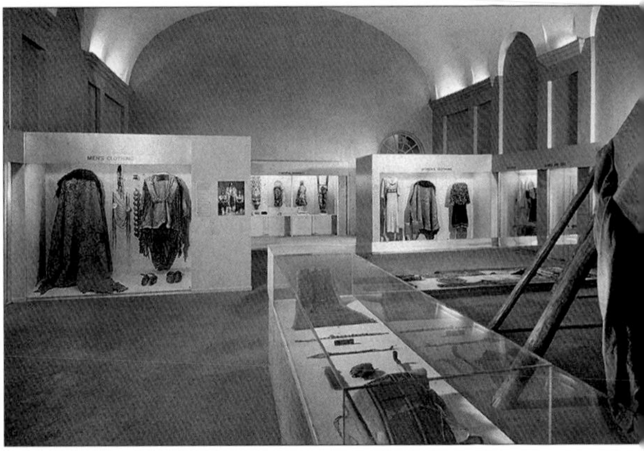
Southwest Museum, Plains Hall

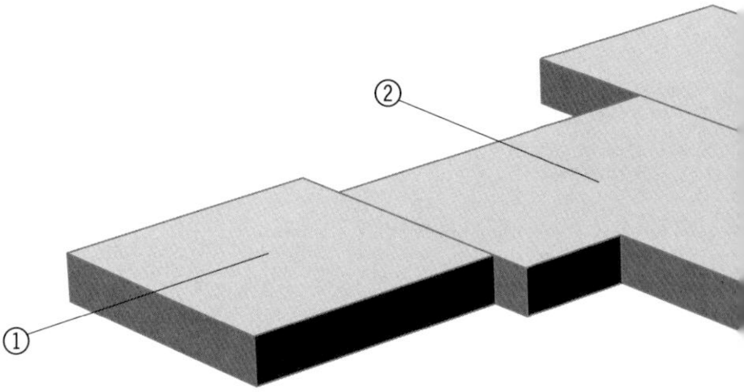

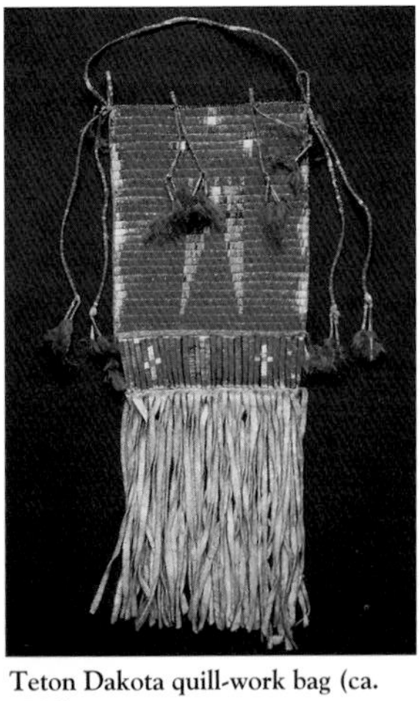
Teton Dakota quill-work bag (ca. 1890)

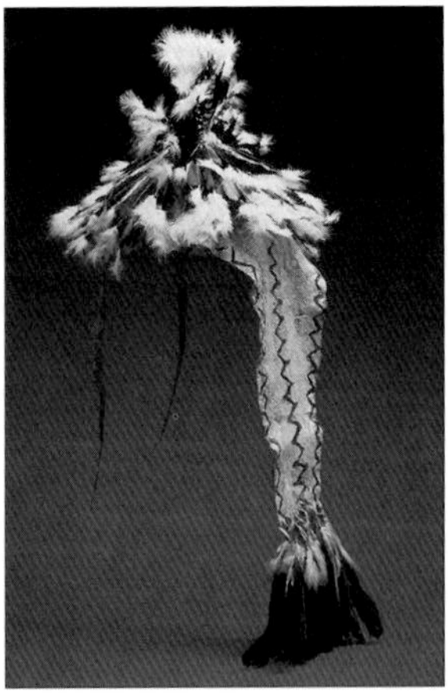
Hupa feathered headdress

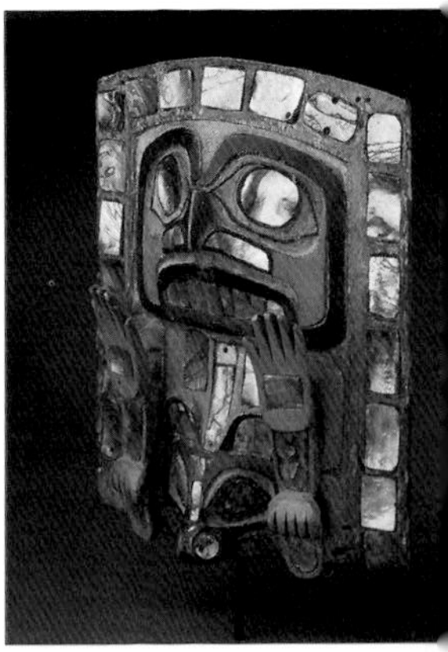
Tlingit frontlet (19th century)

Beaded vest, Plains or Plateau (ca. 1890)

Haida houseposts, Kasaan village, Prince of Wales Island (ca. 1860)

Shield, Southern Plains (mid 19th century)

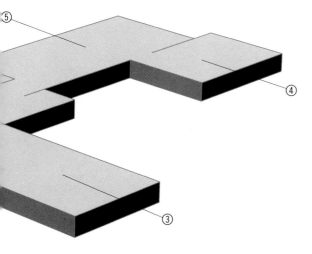

Karok Jump Dance basket

Tlingit raven rattle (19th century)

Southwest Museum

Lower Level

① Southwest
② Basketry Study

Anasazi stone figurines (ca. 1300)

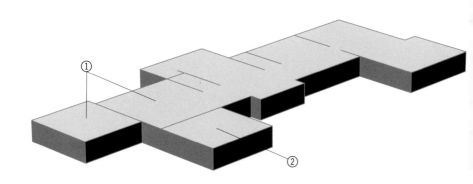

Ahole Kachina doll, Hopi, (ca. 1900)

Pueblo pottery: lower left, Hopi seed jar; upper right, Acoma jar

Navajo/Zuni painted hide (ca. 1930)

17

Casa de Adobe

4605 N Figueroa St, Los Angeles, 90065. ☎ (213) 221-2164, 225-8653.

Located at the foot of a hill just a few blocks below the Southwest Museum, the Casa de Adobe is a recreated upper-class home from California's rancho period. Modeled after Rancho Guajome in San Diego County, the adobe was intended to represent "the home of a young Californian of good family, of some means, who had just been married and was establishing a home of his own." It was designed in 1917 by architect Theodore Eisen and constructed in the traditional way, using adobe bricks made on site.

Kitchen, Casa de Adobe

The adobe boasts the Southwest Museum's Spanish Colonial collections, exhibited in 8 reconstructed period rooms. Its aim is to recreate the atmosphere of rancho life in California between 1800 and 1850. On display are original furnishings used by ranchers, including pieces from the Pico and Sepulveda families, religious articles, decorative arts, tools and the Caballeria collection of old paintings. Other exhibits include branding irons, riatas, household utensils, clothing, swords and firearms.

Ramona Museum of California History. Rockaway carriage used by Col. John C. Fremont on his historic return trip to Los Angeles in 1870.

18

Ramona Museum of California History

4580 N Figueroa St, Los Angeles, 90065. ☎ (213) 276-9359. **Fax:** (213) 276-9359. **Thomas Guide:** 595 B4. 🚌 bus. **Hours:** Sat 1-4pm. $ free. **Reservations:** by appointment for groups. [P] free. 📷 allowed, no flash. **Year founded:** 1972. **Year opened:** 1995. **Primary focus:** early California history. **Research fields:** early law enforcement in Los Angeles, Native Sons archives. **Publications:** *Ramona Roundup*, monthly newsletter. **Governing authority:** nonprofit. **Category:** history museum. **Activities/programs:** docent programs, guided tours, school programs, volunteer programs. **Facilities:** gift shop, picnic area. **Collection focus:** North American archaeology and antiquities, arms and armor, farms and farming, criminology, local history, personal history, politics and government.

Since Ramona Parlor #109 was chartered by the Native Sons of the Golden West on June 9, 1887, its members collected hundreds of artifacts, relics and memorabilia related to southern California history. Over the years the collection was divided and stored at several locations or loaned to various museums. In 1972 the museum's permanent building, Fletcher Hall, was dedicated and over 1,000 items were retrieved and displayed.

Among the collection highlights are a California Stage Company Concord Stagecoach, built in the 1850s, the first Bear Banner raised in Sonoma County in 1846, a Harwood pipe organ and a working Buffalo forge. The museum possesses a fine collection of Native American artifacts, mostly groundstone items, tools and arrowheads. Of particular interest is an arrow straightener from Santa Catalina Island. Items from the California rancho and mission periods include Pio Pico's personal notebooks, keys and bells from the San Fernando and San Gabriel missions, as well as spurs, harnesses, bridles and branding irons. An extensive collection of the personal memorabilia of Eugene Biscailuz, Los Angeles sheriff for over 50 years. includes his letters and personal papers, law enforcement records, firearms, awards and photographs. The museum's abundant arms assortment includes rifles, pistols, revolvers and swords.

Spur, California rancho period

A Native Sons archive contains past rosters, minutes, financial information, personal letters, scrapbooks and publications.

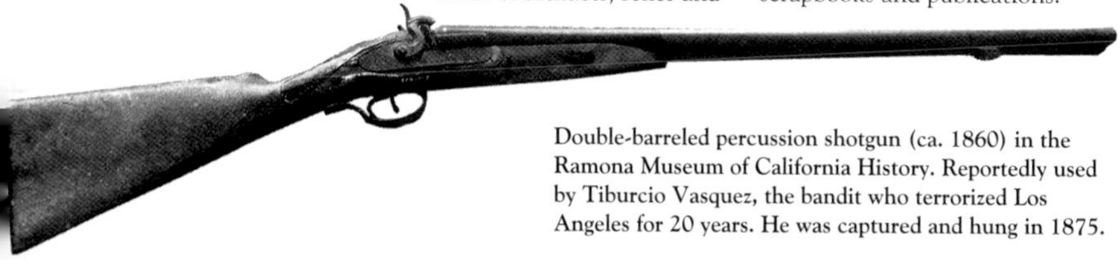

Double-barreled percussion shotgun (ca. 1860) in the Ramona Museum of California History. Reportedly used by Tiburcio Vasquez, the bandit who terrorized Los Angeles for 20 years. He was captured and hung in 1875.

El Alisal

19

El Alisal

200 E Ave 43, Los Angeles, 90031. ☎ (213) 222-0546. **Fax:** (213) 222-0771. **Thomas Guide:** 595 B5. 🚌 bus. **Hours:** Fri-Sun noon-4pm. **Closed:** major holidays. $ free. [P] free on street. 📷 with permission. **Membership:** available. **Year opened:** 1965. **Primary focus:** maintenance and continued development of El Alisal historic setting. **Governing authority:** private. **Category:** historic building/site open to the public. **Activities/programs:** docent programs, events (Open House — Apr), guided tours, volunteer programs. **Facilities:** bookstore, gift shop. ♿ wheelchair accessible. **Garden features:** water-wise garden, restrooms. **Collection focus:** architecture, personal history.

Water-wise garden

Charles Fletcher Lummis was known in Los Angeles before he even set foot in the city. On September 12, 1884, he started his 3,507-mile trek to California from Cincinnati, Ohio. The *Los Angeles Daily Times* published his weekly reports on his cross-country walk, making him a kind of local hero. After 143 days of traveling through 7 states and 2 territories, Lummis reached Los Angeles on February 1, 1885. Harrison Gray Otis, the *Times*'s publisher, hired him the next day as a city editor. During General George Crook's 1886 campaign against the Chiricahua Apaches' leader Geronimo in the Arizona Territory, Lummis was special correspondent for the *Times*. His interest in Indian cultures led him on numerous trips to New Mexico and Central and South America, where he joined several expeditions in Guatemala, Peru and Bolivia.

Lummis was a noted author, editor, photographer, historian and archaeologist. As the city's librarian, he built a Department of Western History Material. He founded several preservation, relief and historical organizations and helped save 4 Franciscan missions. He established the Southwest Museum, to which he bequeathed his 5,000-volume library and extensive collections of photographs, paintings, Indian blankets and artifacts.

Decorative ironwork on the front door, a copy of the flourish used by Francisco Pizarro

In 1898 he began construction of his house on the east bank of the Arroyo Seco, a usually dry riverbed about 3 miles from downtown Los Angeles. The 2-story structure, built of concrete and faced with local granite boulders, was intended to "last for a thousand years." Lummis did most of the work himself, using hand-hewn timber, iron rails and telegraph poles obtained from the Santa Fe Railroad. The construction was essentially completed in 1904, although Lummis never expected to end the work on the house; he regarded physical activity as a kind of counterbalance to his desk work. The house was named El Alisal (Place of the Sycamore in Spanish). Today the Lummis home, which was declared California Historical Landmark No. 531, is the headquarters of the Historical Society of Southern California. On display are photographs, books, memorabilia, Indian baskets and other historical artifacts.

Dining room

In 1985 landscape architect Robert Perry designed a 2-acre water-conserving garden, using California native and other dry-climate plants. The low-maintenance garden is organized into a number of distinct zones, in which plants with similar water requirements are grouped together. The entry garden displays Mediterranean plants such as rosemary, lavenders and rockroses. The regional plant garden features plants from Australia, including acacias and eucalyptus. Native bay trees and western sycamores provide a cool resting space in the shade garden, while citrus, walnuts, pomegranates and other fruit trees grow in the citrus garden. The California native garden is planted with wild cherries, wild lilac, manzanita and other native species rich in colors, textures and sizes. A small desert garden grows cacti and succulents well adapted to the dry southern California climate.

20

Heritage Square Museum

3800 Homer St, Los Angeles, 90031. ✉ 225 S Lake Ave, Suite 1125, Pasadena, 91101. ☎ (818) 796-2898. **Recorded information:** (818) 449-0193. **Fax:** (818) 304-9652. **Thomas Guide:** 595 B5. **Hours:** Sat-Sun noon-4pm; tours at 15 past the hour, last tour departs at 3:15. $ $5 adults, $4 seniors and teens 12-17, $2 children 7-11, children 6 and under free. **Reservations:** recommended for groups. [P] free. 📷 not allowed. **Membership:** available. **Year founded:** 1968. **Year opened:** 1970. **Primary focus:** to preserve, restore and interpret southern California's rich cultural history. **Research fields:** Victorian era and Los Angeles at the turn of the century. **Publications:** *On the Square* newsletter. **Governing authority:** private, nonprofit. **Category:** historic building/site open to the public. **Activities/programs:** docent programs, events (Mother's Day Victorian fashion show), guided tours, school programs. **Facilities:** audiovisual holdings, bookstore, gift shop, slide registry. **Collection focus:** architecture, carpentry, decorative and applied art, furniture and interiors, local history, period rooms.

Hale House, entry hall with fireplace

Heritage Square Museum is actually a recreated Victorian village consisting of 8 structures built in the late 19th century. They were saved from destruction and relocated here from various parts of Pasadena and Los Angeles. This open-air museum aims to give a picture of everyday life in Los Angeles between the Civil War and WWI through its collections, programs and exhibits.

The most remarkable of the buildings is the fully restored

Heritage Square Museum

Hale House, a superb example of the Queen Anne-Eastlake style. Built in 1887, it changed owners several times before it was bought by the Hale family in 1906. Its exterior boasts intricate wood carvings and plaster ornaments, elaborate wrought iron, ornate chimneys and stained-glass panels. The interior is decorated in the style of the 1900s, with pieces that belonged to the Hale family and other period furnishings.

Among the other structures are the Valley Knudsen Garden Residence, which was built between 1877 and 1885. It is one of only a few existing examples of 19th-century Mansard-style "Petite Chateau" architecture — a reminder of French influence in Los Angeles. The house was moved to the site together with a rare coral tree, the official tree of Los Angeles. Mount Pleasant House is the largest at the museum. It was built in 1876 in the Greek Revival-Italianate style. One of its owners was Judge Stephen J. Hubbell, a founder of the University of Southern California. Lincoln Avenue Methodist Church was designed in 1897 in the Carpenter Gothic and Queen Anne styles by architect George W. Cramer, famous for designing more than 2,000 Methodist churches around the world. Octagon House, built in 1893, is the last unaltered example in California of a style popular in New England in the 19th century. Built in 1887 in the Eastlake style, the Palms Depot stood along the Southern Pacific Railroad and was in use until 1953. The John J. Ford House was built in 1887 as a combination of styles and named after its owner, a well-known wood carver. The carriage barn was built in 1899 and combines Queen Anne Cottage and Gothic styles.

Entrance to the Valley Knudsen Garden Residence

Palms Depot

Holyland Exhibition, Damascus Room

21

Holyland Exhibition

2215 Lake View Ave, Los Angeles, 90039. ☎ (213) 664-3162. **Thomas Guide:** 594 E4. **Hours:** daily 8am-8pm. **Closed:** never. $ $2.50 adults, $2 children 16 and under. **Reservations:** by appointment only. [P] free on street. 📷 allowed; no videos. **Year founded:** 1924. **Year opened:** 1928. **Primary focus:** to inspire and encourage people to visit the Bible countries and get acquainted with biblical history, geography and the Bible. **Governing authority:** nonprofit. **Category:** specialized museum. **Activities/programs:** guided tours, slide presentations. **Facilities:** gift shop. ♿ strollers permitted, wheelchair accessible. **Collection focus:** Egyptian archaeology and antiquities, Middle and Near Eastern archaeology and antiquities, geography, religious art, religious history and traditions.

The Holyland Bible Knowledge Society, an interdenominational, nonprofit organization, was founded in 1924 by explorer Antonio F. Futterer in order to help others acquire knowledge of the Bible. The Holyland Exhibition galleries display items from biblical lands and explain biblical customs and traditions. The first gallery, called the Damascus Room, features fine inlay work, including games tables, chairs, taborets and desks. The Pharaoh's Treasury contains a 2,600-year-old mummy case from Egypt and hundreds of art pieces, pottery and appliqué work. The Bible Art and Archaeology Room displays oil lamps, tear bottles, coins and other items from archaeological digs. The Jerusalem Bazaar displays tapestries, embroideries, lace and other handwork.

22

Grier-Musser Museum

403 S Bonnie Brae St, Los Angeles, 90057. ✉ 219 S Irving Blvd, Los Angeles, 90004. ☎ (213) 413-1814. **Thomas Guide:** 634 C2. **Hours:** Wed-Fri noon-4pm, Sat 11am-4pm. $ $5 adults, $3 seniors, $2.50 children. **Reservations:** recommended. [P] free in rear. **Year founded:** 1984. **Year opened:** 1987. **Primary focus:** Victorian life in Los Angeles. **Governing authority:** private. **Category:** historic building/site open to the public. **Activities/programs:** changing exhibitions, events, guided tours. **Facilities:** gift shop. ♿ parking. **Collection focus:** architecture, dolls and puppets, furniture and interiors, handicrafts, hobbies, miniatures, needlework, textiles, toys and games.

The museum is an 1898 Queen Anne Colonial Revival structure that served as a doctor's house at the turn of the century, a maternity hospital during the 1920s and a rooming house before it was finally turned into a privately owned museum. It features Eastlake-style, Victorian and other period furniture, together with household objects and memorabilia. On display are women's dresses from 1850 to 1890, including a wedding dress from 1865 and a WWI Red Cross uniform. There is a collection of medicine bottles, perfume bottles and shaving memorabilia. Other exhibits include French and Japanese antique dolls, dollhouses and furniture, and children's books and clothes.

Grier-Musser Museum, formal parlor

23

Automobile Club of Southern California

2601 S Figueroa St, Los Angeles, 90007. ☎ (213) 741-4486. **Fax:** (213) 741-4670. **Thomas Guide:** 634 C7. 🚌 bus. **Hours:** the collection is currently not on display; there is a traveling exhibition program. **Major exhibitions:** "Scenic View Ahead" (1994), traveling exhibition. **Publications:** *Westways*, monthly magazine. **Governing authority:** nonprofit. **Category:** company museum/corporate collection. **Activities/programs:** traveling exhibitions. **Collection focus:** Western art, cartography, local history, North American painting, 20th-century painting, photography, transportation.

***Windmill, Santa Ynez* (1971) by Merv Corning**

The Automobile Club of Southern California amassed a significant collection of almost 500 works of art in a variety of media, including oil on canvas, watercolor, gouache, pen and ink and mixed media. These works, diverse in theme and style as well as subject matter, have appeared on the cover of the magazine produced by the Auto Club since 1909. Originally called *Touring Topics*, it was renamed *Westways* in 1933. Among the artists whose work is represented in the collection are Ansel Adams, Neil Boyle, Maynard Dixon, Merv Corning, James Hansen and Edward Weston. The club also possesses over 15,000 historic photographs of southern California and a small collection of old road signs.

Poodle spaghetti figurine

Los Angeles Poodle Museum

700 E 4th St, Los Angeles, 90033. ☎ (213) 780-8664. **Thomas Guide:** 634 J5. **Hours:** by appointment only. Ⓢ free. Ⓟ street. 📷 allowed. **Year founded:** 1979. **Governing authority:** private. **Category:** specialized museum. **Collection focus:** decorative and applied arts, hobbies.

Artist Doren Garcia, owner and curator of this one-of-a-kind museum, started collecting poodle paraphernalia in 1979 after buying a plaster poodle sculpture at a garage sale. Housed in his apartment/studio, the museum now contains over 1,000 items, most of which date from the 1950s, when poodle mania flourished. The collection includes poodle boot trees, poodle liquor bottle covers, poodle paintings, poodle brooches, poodle ashtrays, poodle lamps, poodle purses, poodle ceramic figurines and other poodle-related objects.

Plaza de la Raza

3540 N Mission Rd, Los Angeles, 90031. ☎ (213) 233-2475. **Fax:** (213) 223-1804. **Thomas Guide:** 635 B2. **Hours:** Mon-Sat 9am-5pm. Ⓢ free. Ⓟ free, across the street. **Membership:** available. **Year founded:** 1970. **Primary focus:** to preserve, foster and present the artistic contributions and achievements of Mexicans, Chicanos and other Latinos. **Special collections:** the Vincent Price Mexican Folk Art Collection, the Jose Galvez Photographic Collection, the Anheuser-Busch Hispanic Art Collection. **Governing authority:** nonprofit. **Category:** art museum. **Activities/programs:** changing exhibitions, classes/courses, competitions, concerts, educational programs, events (Con Sabor Latino), films, installations, internship programs, multimedia presentations, outreach programs, performances, performing arts, school programs, storytelling, summer programs, traveling exhibitions. **Facilities:** bookstore, exhibit space/gallery, gift shop, lecture hall, picnic area, slide registry, theater. ♿ strollers permitted, wheelchair accessible. **Collection focus:** Hispanic art, Latin American art, Mexican art, modern and contemporary art, Pre-Columbian art, folk art, masks, photography.

Plaza de la Raza's complex is the center of Latino culture and education in Los Angeles. It houses three important art collections. The Hispanic Art Collection was donated by Anheuser-Busch and contains a total of 30 works by notable Latino artists such as Colunga and Luis Jimenez. The Jose Galvez Collection was donated by the artist and includes 50 documentary-style black-and-white photos of the local community. The Mexican Folk Art Collection was donated by Vincent Price and includes 40 items, such as ceramic objects, tapestries, ceremonial masks from several regions of Mexico, *hoja de lata* (punched and cut tin), decorative items, toys, papier-mâché and hand-painted functional items from Michoacan.

Plaza de la Raza

SAN GABRIEL VALLEY — WEST

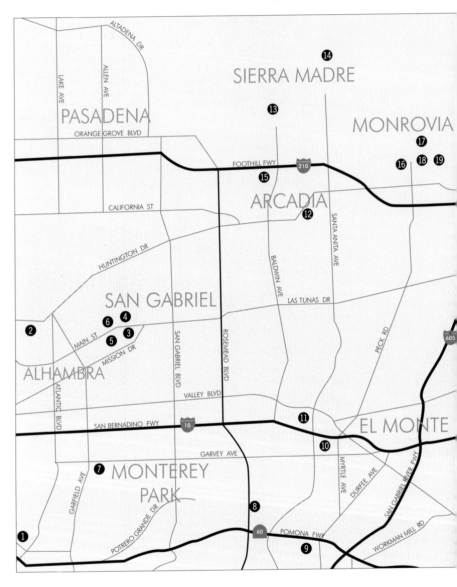

1. Vincent Price Gallery
2. Alhambra Historical Society Museum
3. San Gabriel Mission
4. Lopez de Lowther Adobe
5. San Gabriel Mission Museum
6. San Gabriel Historical Museum
7. Monterey Park Historical Museum
8. American Military Museum
9. Whittier Narrows Nature Center
10. El Monte Historical Museum
11. Santa Fe Trail Historical Park
12. Arcadia Historical Museum
13. Richardson House and Lizzie's Trail Inn
14. John Panatier Nature Center
15. The Arboretum of Los Angeles County
16. Little Learners Children's Museum
17. Olson See More Museum
18. George Anderson House
19. Monrovia Historical Museum

1

Vincent Price Gallery

301 Ave Cesar Chavez, Monterey Park, 91754-6099. ☎ (213) 265-3841. **Thomas Guide:** 635 J5. **Hours:** Mon-Fri noon-3pm (during exhibitions). Closed: Jun-Aug. Ⓢ free. **P** free on street. 🔾 allowed. **Year founded/opened:** 1951. **Primary focus:** to produce several art exhibitions each year, including one or more exhibits of its art collection. **Publications:** exhibition posters and catalogs. **Governing authority:** college/university. **Category:** art museum. **Activities/programs:** artist talks, changing exhibitions, gallery talks, guided tours, lectures. **Facilities:** exhibit space/gallery. & wheelchair accessible. **Collection focus:** North American archaeology and antiquities, Meso and South American archaeology and antiquities, African art, American Indian art, Hispanic art, Japanese art, Latin American art, Mexican art, modern and contemporary art, North American art, Pre-Columbian art, drawing, folk art, graphic arts, masks, European painting, sculpture.

Incense burner, Mexico, Veracruz (350-1000 AD)

Head of a Youth, **Etruria** (ca. 6th century BC)

The Vincent Price Gallery, on the campus of East Los Angeles College, houses the first "teaching art collection" owned by a community college in the United States. It was established in 1951 by noted actor and art collector Vincent Price, who donated artworks from his personal collection. Today, the gallery's holdings consist of over 2,000 pieces given by Price and other donors, ranging from antiquities to modern and contemporary art.

The gallery contains masks, sculpture and artifacts from New Guinea; vessels, masks and sculpture from Africa; Pre-Columbian pottery from Mexico, Peru (Nazca) and Bolivia (Tiahuanaco); North American ceramics; kachina; and baskets (Zuni, Hopi, Navajo and Anasazi). Highlights include a beautiful Egyptian torso from the 6th century BC, an impressive Etruscan head of a youth from the 6th century BC and Greek ceramics. European art from the Renaissance to the 20th century is represented by Albrecht Dürer's woodcut *Death of the Virgin* (1510), Edouard Manet's etching *Maja* and Pablo Picasso's etching *The Pauper's Family* (1905). Other works include etchings by Giovanni Piranesi and Francisco Goya, and lithographs by Eugène Delacroix, Honoré Daumier, Maurice Utrillo, Odilon Redon, Pierre Bonnard and Salvador Dalí. The collection of contemporary art includes an assemblage by Ed Kienholz and graphics by Richard Diebenkorn, Mark Rothko and David Hockney. The work of some artists is shown in depth, including Hans Burkhardt and Howard Warshaw.

2

Alhambra Historical Society Museum

1550 W Alhambra Rd, Alhambra, 91802. ✉ PO Box 6687, Alhambra, 91802-6687. ☎ (818) 300-8845. **Thomas Guide:** 595 J4. **Hours:** Thu 2-4pm; 2nd and 4th Sun of each month 2-4pm. Ⓢ free. **P** street. 🔾 allowed. **Membership:** available. **Year founded:** 1966. **Year opened:** 1990. **Primary focus:** history of Alhambra and the immediate surrounding area. **Governing authority:** nonprofit. **Category:** history museum. **Activities/programs:** docent programs, volunteer programs. **Facilities:** audiovisual holdings. & wheelchair accessible. **Collection focus:** local history.

Alhambra Police badge

Located in Dr. Gayle Thompson's former medical office building donated in 1987, the museum houses a collection of documents, photographs, artifacts and historical records of the City of Alhambra and its residents. The exhibits illustrate the development of local schools, businesses, police and fire departments. One interesting exhibit outlines the history of Veterans of WWI, San Gabriel Valley barracks No. 736. Other displays include furnishings, period clothing and memorabilia.

Vincent Price Gallery. 2-sided tapestry, Peru (Nazca), 5th century (detail).

San Gabriel Mission (1900s)

❸

San Gabriel Mission

537 W Mission Dr, San Gabriel,
91776. ☎ (818) 282-5191. **Fax:**
(818) 282-5308. **Thomas Guide:**
596 D4. 🚌 bus. **Hours:** daily 9am-
4:30pm. **Closed:** Thanksgiving,
Christmas, New Year's Day,
Easter. 💲 $3 adults, $1 children (free for school groups).
Reservations: recommended.
🅿 church lot. 📷 no
videos or cameras
allowed in the church.
Year founded: 1771.
Year opened: 1775. **Primary focus:** Catholic Church
and museum. **Governing**
authority: church. **Category:**
historic building/site open to the
public. **Activities/programs:** docent
programs, guided tours, traveling
exhibitions. **Facilities:** bookstore, gift
shop. ♿ strollers permitted, parking,
wheelchair accessible. **Collection**
focus: architecture, European art,
American Indian art, books, clothing
and dress, liturgical objects, Spanish
painting, religious art.

Mission bell

Named for the archangel
Gabriel, the 4th of 21 California
missions was founded in 1771 by
Franciscan fathers Pedro Cambon
and Angel Somera. It was originally established 4 miles to the
south, but floods forced it to
move to its present site 5 years
later. In 1779 a new church
was started, architec-
turally unlike any other
in the California mis-
sion chain. The
fortresslike structure
was designed by
Father Antonio
Cruzado, who was
influenced by the
cathedral in his native
Cordoba, Spain. Built
by local Indians of
stone, brick and mortar, it features Moorish elements such as
buttressed walls, narrow windows
and a vaulted roof. The roof was
damaged in the 1804 earthquake
and the original bell-wall on the
façade was toppled by another
earthquake in 1812. Today's *cam-
panario* has 6 bells that hang in
arched openings of graduated
size. It was con-
structed at the
other end of the
church in 1828.

The "Queen of
the missions," as
San Gabriel came
to be known, was
one of the most
prosperous in Cali-
fornia. Its holdings
once comprised
1.5 million acres,
encompassing all
of what today are
Los Angeles, San

Bernardino, Orange and River-
side counties. The fertile land
produced a bounty of corn and
beans, and 40,000 head of cattle,
sheep and horses grazed in its
pastures. The mission had the
oldest and largest winery in California and was famous for its
vineyards and fine wines. With it
significant soap-making and tal-
low-rendering industries, San
Gabriel supplied soap and candle
to most of the California missions.

The mission grounds feature a
water cistern, an aqueduct, soap
and tallow vats, tanks for tanning
hides, the winery and a replica of
the early mission kitchen. The

San Gabriel Mission façade with El
Camino Real (King's Road) mis-
sion-bell guidepost

Campo Santo is the oldest cemetery in Los Angeles County. It
was first consecrated in 1778 and
features a memorial to 6,000
Indians buried there.

Crucifix, a memorial to the 6,000
Indians buried on the mission
grounds

Wine cellar with wine-making equipment used in
the late 19th and early 20th centuries

Ceramic tiles on the Lopez Adobe

first orange grove in California was planted at the San Gabriel Mission in 1804 and consisted of 400 trees. The mission became a nucleus of California orange growing, supplying trees for home and commercial planting.

❹ Lopez de Lowther Adobe

333 S Santa Anita St.

Originally one of the buildings along the west wall of the mission, the adobe was constructed between 1792 and 1806. In 1849 it became the property of Don Juan Lopez and was occupied by his descendants until 1964. Redecorated in the 1920s by Maria Lopez de Lowther, it now contains family memorabilia.

❺ San Gabriel Mission Museum

537 W Mission Dr, San Gabriel, 91776.

The museum building was erected in 1812 and originally contained weaving rooms, carpentry shops, the granary and sleeping quarters. The museum houses a magnificent collection of embroidered and hand-painted vestments that were used by the mission fathers. Some of them date back to the 17th century and are older than the mission itself. There is a remarkable collection of books, the oldest one hand-printed from wooden blocks in 1489. On display are 14 paintings of the Stations of the Cross, probably the oldest Indian sacred pictorial art in California. It is believed that the colors in these paintings were derived from the crushed petals of native wildflowers and that olive oil was used as the base. Other artifacts include a Spanish bedroom set from 1623, a small French rosewood organ from around 1821, Indian baskets and various tools.

❻ San Gabriel Historical Museum

546 W Broadway, San Gabriel 91776. ☎ (818) 308-3223. **Thomas Guide:** 596 D4. 🚌 bus. **Hours:** Wed, Sat-Sun 1-4pm. **Closed:** major holidays, Aug. 🅢 free. **Reservations:** necessary for groups. 🅿 free on street. 📷 allowed, no flash. **Membership:** available. **Year founded:** 1976. **Year opened:** 1978. **Primary focus:** preservation of local history and artifacts. **Governing authority:** nonprofit. **Category:** history museum. **Activities/programs:** guided tours, lectures, slide presentations. **Facilities:** exhibit space/gallery. ♿ strollers permitted, wheelchair accessible. **Collection focus:** local history.

The museum's exhibits present the history of San Gabriel through photographs, artifacts and other materials documenting early businesses, schools and organizations. On display are Gabrielino Indian artifacts, and an exhibit of farming tools gives a picture of the development of local agricultural industry. The

❼ Monterey Park Historical Museum

781 S Orange Ave, Monterey Park, 91754. ✉ PO Box 272, Monterey Park, 91754. ☎ (818) 307-1267. **Thomas Guide:** 636 D3. **Hours:** Sat-Sun 2-4pm. 🅢 free. **Reservations:** necessary for groups. 🅿 free. 📷 allowed. **Membership:** available. **Primary focus:** history of the City of Monterey Park. **Governing authority:** nonprofit. **Category:** history museum. **Activities/programs:** docent programs, guided tours. **Facilities:** picnic area. **Collection focus:** local history.

This museum's highlight is a collection of 21 scale models of the California Franciscan missions, built and donated by Monterey Park resident Manuel Tovar. Other exhibits include Indian artifacts, three reconstructed rooms with household items, tools and period clothing, as well as photographs, documents and memorabilia reflecting the history of the city. The museum houses the archives of the local newspaper, the *Monterey Park Californian.*

Early store on San Marino Ave, San Gabriel. Photograph in the San Gabriel Historical Museum collection.

⑧ American Military Museum

1918 N Rosemead Blvd, El Monte, 91733. ☎ (818) 442-1776. **Fax:** (818) 443-1776. **Thomas Guide:** 636 J3. 🚌 bus, metro. **Hours:** Sat-Sun noon-4:30pm. 💲 $3 adults, $1.50 juniors, children under 5 free. **Reservations:** necessary for groups. 🅿 free. 📷 allowed. **Membership:** available. **Year founded:** 1962. **Year opened:** 1985. **Primary focus:** to collect, restore and preserve military equipment. **Governing authority:** nonprofit. **Category:** specialized museum, open-air museum. **Activities/programs:** volunteer

M1 combat car, made in 1934-38. This tank was used in the movie *Brisco County Jr.* (1993)

programs. **Facilities:** research library. **Collection focus:** arms and armor, military and naval history, vehicles.

This 7-acre outdoor museum has the largest collection of interservice military equipment on the West

Antitank self-propelled 90mm M56, used in airborne operations from 1958 to 1969. This one served in Vietnam.

M3A1 White Scout car 4x4, manufactured in 1941 and used in WWII

Coast, with more than 400 pieces that date from WWII, Korea and Vietnam to some modern armaments. On display are 120 mostly restored vehicles, including tanks, personnel carriers, cannons, trucks, jeeps and field pieces. The equipment is from the US Army, Navy, Marines and Air Force, although there are some German, French, Australian and other foreign exhibits. Highlights include the experimental M1 combat car (1934-38), the only one in existence; a German Schwimmwagen Type 166 (1943), an amphibious Volkswagen developed for river crossing in Russia; and guns from the USS *Missouri*.

⑨ Whittier Narrows Nature Center

1000 N Durfee Ave, South El Monte, 91733. ☎ (818) 444-1872. **Thomas Guide:** 637 C6. **Hours:** daily 9am-5pm. 💲 free. **Reservations:** necessary for groups. 🅿 free. 📷 allowed. **Membership:** available. **Year founded:** 1939. **Year opened:** 1970. **Primary focus:** to allow the wilderness area to continue to function under natural environmental influences. **Governing authority:** county. **Division of:** Dept of Parks and Recreation. **Category:** nature center/wildlife refuge. **Activities/programs:** docent programs, guided tours, lectures, workshops. ♿ wheelchair accessible. **Garden features:** ponds. **Collection focus:** biology, birds, botany, ecology, mammals, reptiles, zoology.

Mounted owl at the Whittier Narrows Nature Center

The 227-acre wildlife sanctuary is home to approximately 230 species of plants, about 260 species of birds and variety of fish, amphibians, reptiles and mammals. The Nature Center museum has exhibits focusing on the riparian (streamside) ecosystem, the geology of the region and the early cultural life of southern California. Live animal exhibits include turtles, tortoises, frogs, fish and snakes. Another interesting display shows stuffed birds matched with their nests and eggs.

Turn-of-the-century grocery store

⑪ Santa Fe Trail Historical Park

3537 Santa Anita Ave, El Monte, 91731. ☎ (818) 580-2200. **Fax:** (818) 580-2237. **Thomas Guide:** 597 C7. **Hours:** Mon-Thu 7:30am-3:30pm. $ free. P free. 📷 allowed. **Year opened:** 1987. **Primary focus:** local history. **Governing authority:** municipal. **Category:** historic building/site open to the public. **Activities/programs:** events. ♿ strollers permitted, wheelchair accessible. **Collection focus:** architecture, local history.

⑩ El Monte Historical Museum

3150 N Tyler Ave, El Monte, 91731. ☎ (818) 444-3813. **Fax:** (818) 580-2237. **Thomas Guide:** 637 C1. 🚌 bus. **Hours:** Mon-Fri 10am-4pm, Sun 1-3pm. $ free. P free in parking lot or on street. 📷 allowed with permission. **Membership:** available. **Year founded:** 1958. **Year opened:** 1961. **Primary focus:** history of El Monte. **Publications:** The Landmark, quarterly newsletter. **Governing authority:** municipal, nonprofit. **Category:** history museum. **Activities/programs:** docent programs, guided tours. **Facilities:** research library. ♿ strollers permitted, wheelchair accessible. **Collection focus:** local history.

El Monte Historical Museum

Established in 1851 on the bank of the San Gabriel River, El Monte is the oldest settlement in the San Gabriel Valley and the first American town to be incorporated in southern California. The migrants, who came from Lexington, Kentucky, built the first public school and the first Protestant church in the area. El Monte was so famous for its diverse agricultural activity that it was referred to as "The Garden of Los Angeles County." The city's greatest attraction was Gay's Lion Farm, which raised African lions for use in the film industry from 1924 to 1942. All moviegoers are familiar with the roar of the MGM lion, the most prominent of the farm's inhabitants.

The museum is located in a building constructed in 1936 by the Works Progress Administration as a library. Its archive includes letters and diaries of local pioneers, documents, newspapers, books, maps, films and photographs. The museum contains a varied collection of exhibits reflecting the history of the city, including memorabilia from the pioneer families, Indian, Spanish and Mexican artifacts, various tools, police firearms and firefighting equipment. On display are a 1911 Ford and a reconstructed interior of a local home in the late 1800s, with period furniture, dishes and glassware.

Other themes featured in the well-designed displays include a barbershop with chair, jars and druggist scales; a music shop with instruments, gramophones and records; a dress shop with period clothing, fabrics and laces; a grocery store with an old-fashioned calculating machine and cash register; and a classroom with wooden desks and a blackboard.

Covered wagon (early 1900s) in the Santa Fe Trail Historical Park

The first settlement established in southern California by US citizens, El Monte was called "The End of Santa Fe Trail" in the 1950s. Dedicated in 1987 as California Historical Landmark No. 975, the Santa Fe Trail Historical Park contains the Osmond farmhouse built in 1892 in El Monte, the original El Monte jail, built in 1880, and a covered wagon from the early 1900s.

El Monte Historical Museum. Reconstructed interior of an El Monte home in the late 1800s.

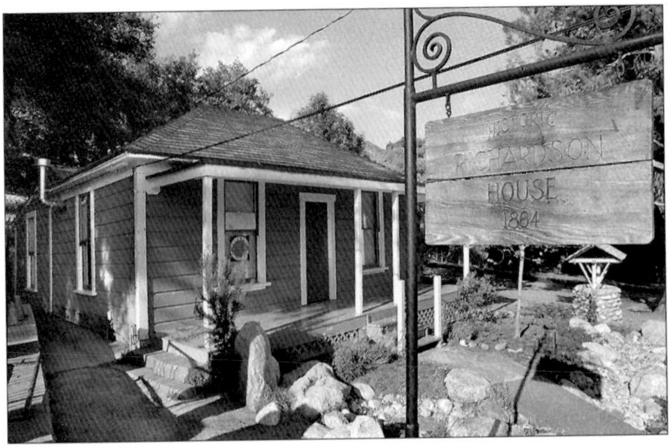

Richardson House

12

Arcadia Historical Museum

355 Campus Dr, Arcadia, 91007. ✉ PO Box 1804, Arcadia, 91077-1804. ☎ (818) 446-8512. **Thomas Guide:** 567 B6. **Hours:** Tue, Thu 12:30-3:30pm, Sat 10am-noon. **Closed:** legal holidays. [$] free. [P] free. 📷 with permission. **Membership:** available. **Year founded:** 1954. **Year opened:** 1988. **Primary focus:** preservation, collection and display of artifacts and materials related to the history of Arcadia. **Publications:** *Caminos*, quarterly newsletter. **Governing authority:** nonprofit. **Category:** history museum. **Activities/programs:** educational programs, lectures. **Facilities:** audiovisual holdings. ♿ wheelchair accessible. **Collection focus:** local history.

The museum's displays of artifacts, books and historic photographs illustrate the city's transition from ranch and farm life to a residential community. The exhibits include Gabrielino Indian stoneware, WWI and WWII artifacts, memorabilia, costumes, toys and dolls, and reflect the diverse natural and cultural heritage of Arcadia.

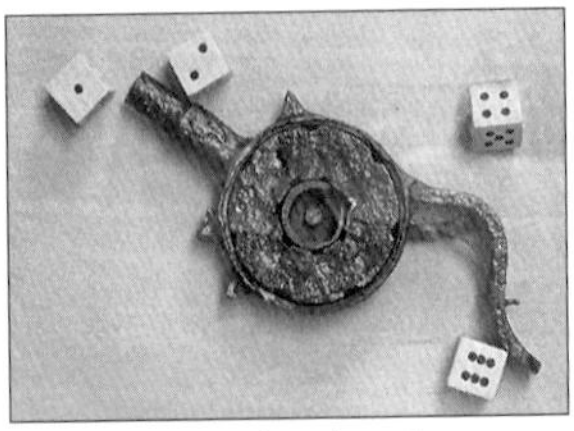
Gambler's gun, found on the Baldwin Ranch

13

Richardson House and Lizzie's Trail Inn

167 E Mira Monte, Sierra Madre, 91024. ✉ PO Box 202, Sierra Madre, 91025. ☎ (818) 355-3905. **Thomas Guide:** 567 A1. **Hours:** last Sun of each month 1-4pm. [$] free. [P] free on street. 📷 allowed. **Membership:** available. **Year opened:** 1964. **Primary focus:** history of Sierra Madre. **Governing authority:** municipal. **Category:** historic building/site open to the public. **Activities/programs:** changing exhibitions, docent programs, volunteer programs. **Collection focus:** architecture, furniture and interiors.

The Richardson House is the oldest in Sierra Madre, built in 1864 by an early pioneer. It has been restored and furnished with turn-of-the-century pieces. The house features changing exhibitions of local artifacts.

Adjacent to the Richardson House is Lizzie's Trail Inn, which was built in the early 1900s. Located at the base of the historic Mt. Wilson Trail, it served as a local restaurant. The floor of the house contains a trap door, probably used to hide liquor during Prohibition.

14

John Panatier Nature Center

2240 Highland Oaks Dr, Arcadia, 91006. ✉ PO Box 60021, Arcadia, 91066-6021. ☎ (818) 355-5309, -8419. **Fax:** (818) 821-4370. **Thomas Guide:** 537 E7. **Hours:** weekdays 8am-dusk, weekends 9am-dusk. **Closed:** July 4, Christmas, New Year's Day. [$] varies depending on group size and facility use; free on weekdays and for Arcadia residents. **Reservations:** recommended for large groups, necessary on weekends for all. [P] free. 📷 allowed. **Year founded:** 1958. **Year opened:** 1972. **Primary focus:** nature education and enjoyment for adults, children, organized groups and schools. **Governing authority:** municipal. **Category:** nature center/wildlife refuge. **Activities/programs:** changing exhibitions, classes/courses, docent programs, educational programs, guided tours, lectures, school programs, summer programs, volunteer programs. **Facilities:** research library, picnic area, visitors' center. ♿ strollers permitted, parking, wheelchair accessible. **Garden features:** dogs allowed, labels/descriptions, restrooms. **Collection focus:** birds, botany, ecology, mammals, reptiles, zoology.

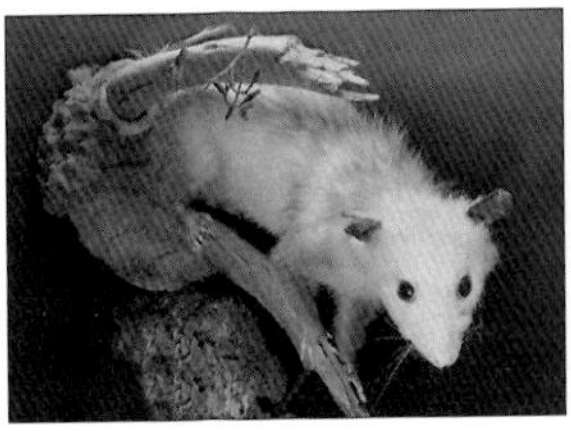
Mounted opossum

There are plenty of animals and plant life in Wilderness Park, a 120-acre wildlife sanctuary at the mouth of Big Santa Anita Canyon. The park is kept in its natural state, enabling visitors to see and learn more about its protected chaparral and riparian communities. The Nature Center features a live reptile exhibit and displays of local mammals, birds and insects, including a California black bear, a bobcat, a mountain lion, a raccoon, a red-tailed hawk, a bald eagle, a roadrunner and butterflies, dragonflies and damselflies.

⓯

The Arboretum of Los Angeles County

301 N Baldwin Ave, Arcadia, 91007. ☎ (818) 821-3222. **Fax:** (818) 445-1217. **Thomas Guide:** 567 A4. 🚌 bus. **Hours:** daily 9am-4:30pm. **Closed:** Christmas. Ⓢ $5 adults, $3 seniors and students, $1 ages 5-12. Free admission third Tue of each month. Ⓟ free. 📷 allowed for personal use only. **Membership:** available. **Year founded/opened:** 1948. **Primary focus:** to introduce as many plants, shrubs and trees from around the world to the southern California landscape. **Research fields:** botany. **Governing authority:** county. **Parent institution:** Dept of Parks and Recreation. **Category:** botanical garden/arboretum. **Activities/programs:** classes/courses, docent programs, educational programs, events (40 shows), guided tours, internship program, lectures, school programs, slide presentations, volunteer programs. **Facilities:** available for rent, bookstore, cafeteria/restaurant, gift shop, lecture hall, 25,000-volume research library, picnic area, tram tours. ♿ strollers permitted, parking, wheelchair accessible. **Garden features:** greenhouse, herb garden, labels/descriptions, ponds, rare species, water garden, restrooms; peak times: Mar-Sep. **Collection focus:** architecture, botany, carriages and carts, ecology, local history, horticulture, railways.

The earliest inhabitants of the land now occupied by the arboretum were the Gabrielino Indians, who settled around a spring-fed lake in the middle of the grounds. In the early 1800s the site became part of 13,319-acre Rancho Santa Anita, belonging to Mission San Gabriel. Hugo Reid, a Scottish immigrant, received title to the land from the Mexican government in 1841. He planted crops, raised cattle and built the adobe house on the property, which were conditions for ownership. Reid sold the ranch in 1847, and it changed hands many times before it was purchased by silver-mining magnate Elias Jackson "Lucky" Baldwin in 1875. The ranch was later the location for more than 100 films and TV programs, including *Tarzan and the Huntress* (1947),

The Arboretum of Los Angeles County

The African Queen (1952) and the recent *Fantasy Island*.

The Hugo Reid Adobe is the oldest of the arboretum's 4 historic buildings. The 3-room adobe, built in 1839 with the help of local Gabrielino Indians, was reconstructed of sun-dried blocks using original methods. Visitors are not allowed inside but can see the authentically furnished interior through the windows. The adobe was dedicated as California Historical Landmark No. 368.

The Queen Anne Cottage was constructed in 1885 by E. J. "Lucky" Baldwin as a honeymoon gift for his fourth wife, Lillie Bennett. The building was designed by the girl's father, architect Albert A. Bennett, who also designed the state capitol in Sacramento. The ornate wooden house, with four gabled roofs and a belltower, is named after the architectural style popular in the late Victorian era. Furnished with period pieces, it features the original stained-glass windows, marble fireplace mantels, mosaic floor and bathroom fixtures. The cottage was designated California Historical Landmark No. 367 and is listed in the National Register of Historic Places.

The Coach Barn, designed by Albert A. Bennett and built in 1879, houses Baldwin's carriage and buggies, an old firefighting wagon, saddles, harnesses and farm and blacksmith tools used in the late 1800s. The building is also listed in

the National Register of Historic Places.

The Santa Anita Depot was constructed in 1890 by the Atchison, Topeka and Santa Fe Railroad. The 2-story Gothic Revival-style building served as both a passenger and freight station, with living quarters upstairs for the agent. The depot was relocated from its original site and restored on the arboretum grounds in 1970. It is furnished with turn-of-the-century household items and period railroad equipment.

The 127-acre arboretum contains more than 30,000 plants adapted to the mild California climate, representing 4,000 species and varieties from all over the world. Among the major collections are 175 species of cycads, 27 species of coral trees, 79 species of ficus, 75 species of melaleuca and 17 varieties of magnolias. Arboretum highlights include the tropical greenhouse, which contains anthuriums, bromeliads, staghorn ferns, Spanish moss (*Tillandsia usneoides*) and one of the largest displays of orchids in the country, with over 1,500 species and varieties.

The Aquatic Garden is planted with water hyacinths, irises and water lilies. The North American/Asiatic Section grows mostly deciduous trees and shrubs, including Chinese tallow trees (*Sapium sebiferum*), empress trees (*Paulownia tomentosa*) and Indian cigar trees (*Catalpa speciosa*). The Grace Kallam Garden displays the blending of seasonal color in trees and shrubs. The Australian Section features 124 species of acacias, 24 species of bottlebrush trees (*Calistemon*) and the largest collection of eucalyptus outside Australia, consisting of more than half of the 500 known species and varieties.

Peacock in the Arboretum

The Arboretum of Los Angeles County

1. Redwood Grove
2. Tropical Forest
3. Cycad Collection
4. Palm & Bamboo Collection
5. Rose Garden
6. Southwestern Section
7. Engelmann Oak Grove
8. South American Section
9. Tallac Knoll
10. Herb Garden
11. Meyberg Waterfall
12. North American/Asiatic Section
13. Kallam Garden/ Meadowbrook
14. African Section
15. Australian Section
16. Water Conservation Garden
17. Garden for All Seasons
18. Juniper Collection
19. Groundcover Display
20. Home Gardens
21. Tropical Greenhouse
22. Begonia Greenhouse
23. Hugo Reid Adobe
24. Santa Anita Depot
25. Queen Anne Cottage
26. Coach Barn
27. Baldwin Lake
28. Tule Pond

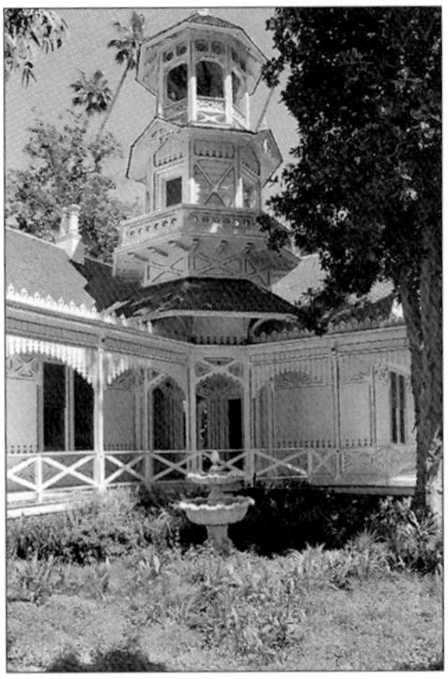
Queen Anne Cottage

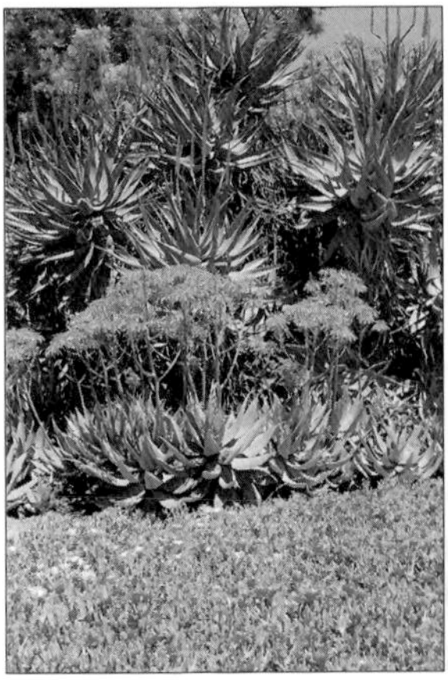
African Section, cape aloe

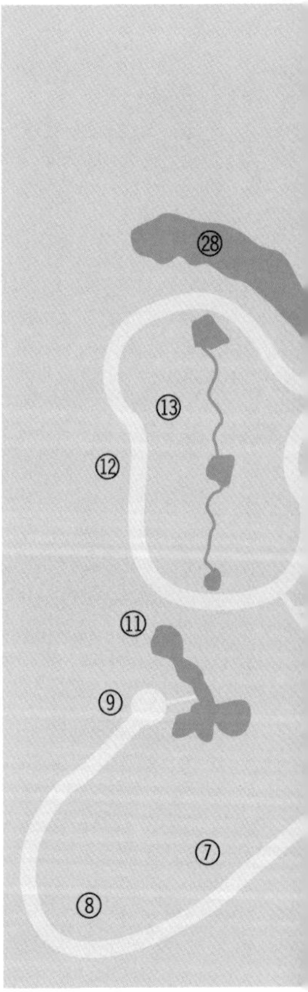

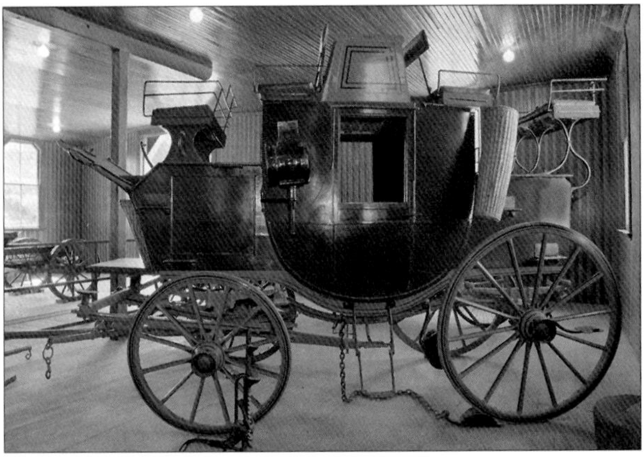
Gentleman's private coach (1876) in the Coach Barn

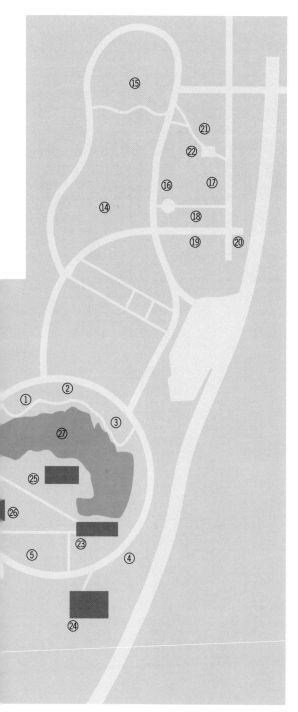

Tropical greenhouse

Southwestern Section

Aquatic Garden

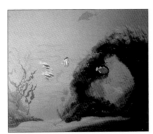

Underwater sea life mural at the Little Learners Children's Museum

⑯ Little Learners Children's Museum

601 S Myrtle Ave, Monrovia, 91016. ☎ (818) 359-1047, -3586. Thomas Guide: 567 G4. 🚌 bus. Hours: Mon-Thu 9am-6pm, Fri 9am-9pm, Sat 10am-5pm. Ⓢ $5.95 per child, adults free. Reservations: recommended. Ⓟ free. 📷 allowed. Membership: available. Year founded/opened: 1994. Primary focus: multicultural education and displays. Governing authority: private, nonprofit. Category: children's museum. Activities/programs: artists' talks, changing exhibitions, classes/courses, dramatic programs, educational programs, events, guided tours, lectures, school programs, slide presentations, storytelling, summer programs, volunteer programs, workshops. Facilities: bookstore, cafeteria/restaurant, gift shop, indoor picnic area. ♿ strollers permitted, parking, wheelchair accessible. Collection focus: education.

Designed for children ages 2 to 12, Little Learners Children's Museum and Learning Enrichment Center is a place where kids learn by exploration, discovery, guidance and fun. The museum features small sets resembling an Early American town designed by a Hollywood set builder. Children can review fire prevention with Smokey the Bear, study farm animals and food, practice stranger safety and dialing 911 in the Sheriff's Office, learn pedestrian rules and drive in little cars, watch stars and planets in the Space Center and learn math and reading in the Little Red Schoolhouse, among other things.

⑰ Olson See More Museum

205 E Hillcrest Blvd, Monrovia 91016. ☎ (818) 358-3897. Thomas Guide: 567 G2. Hours: by appointment only. Ⓢ $1 donation suggested. Ⓟ free on street. 📷 allowed. Year founded/opened: 1980. Primary focus: to share 50 years of collecting around the world. Governing authority: private. Category: specialized museum. Activities/programs: guided tours. Collection focus: clothing and dress, dolls and puppets, glass and glassware, hobbies, jewelry, miniatures, personal history.

This museum occupies the 16-room redwood Craftsman house built in 1905 and contains Fern Olson's collection of several thousand items she has assembled during 50 years of traveling around the world. On display are collections of porcelain dolls, teddy bears, costume jewelry and trinkets, old "beauty tips," needlework, Victoriana and antique dolls and toys. Additional attractions include traditional masks and ceremonial robes from Asia, an impressive collection of lace and numerous American Indian items.

The American Indian Room

⑱ George Anderson House

215 E Lime Ave, Monrovia, 91016. ☎ (818) 358-7822. Thomas Guide: 567 G4. Hours: 3rd Sun of each month 1-4pm. Ⓢ free. Ⓟ free on street. 📷 allowed. Membership: available. Primary focus: history of Monrovia. Governing authority: nonprofit. Category: historic building/site open to the public. Activities/programs: classes/courses, events, guided tours, lectures, school programs, slide presentations. Facilities: library. Collection focus: architecture, furniture and interiors.

George Anderson House

The 6-room, Queen Anne-style house was erected in 1886, the same year the City of Monrovia was founded. It was built by John Anderson, who constructed the first building in the city, the Monrovia Hotel. The house is decorated with period furniture, including an Eastlake parlor suite, a 5-piece bird's-eye maple bedroom suite and a 4-poster canopy bed. A settee and two chairs with stick-and-ball design in the dining room are the only remaining original pieces of furniture. An antique pump organ, an 1850 sewing machine and a collection of local memorabilia are also displayed.

Monrovia horse-drawn streetcar (ca. 1890)

⑲

Monrovia Historical Museum

742 E Lemon Ave, Monrovia, 91016. ✉ PO Box 2359, Monrovia, 91017. ☎ (818) 357-9537. **Thomas Guide:** 567 H4. **Hours:** Wed-Thu, Sun 1-4pm. $ free. P free. 📷 allowed. **Year founded:** 1986. **Year opened:** 1992. **Primary focus:** to promote, perpetuate and preserve the history of Monrovia and surrounding areas. **Special collections:** the Lucia Cromwell Collection, the Dr. Samuel E. Salsbury Collection. **Publications:** quarterly newsletter. **Governing authority:** nonprofit. **Category:** history museum. **Activities/programs:** artist talks, changing exhibitions, docent programs, educational programs, guided tours, lectures, performing arts, school programs, volunteer programs, workshops. **Facilities:** available for rent, gift shop. ♿ parking, wheelchair accessible. **Collection focus:** North American archaeology and antiquities, arms and armor, dolls and puppets, folklife and traditions, fossils, geology, local history, music and musical instruments, shells, telecommunications.

The 2-story structure that now houses the museum was once used as the municipal plunge building for the municipal pool. It was built in 1925 in Spanish Colonial Revival style and was in use for over 50 years. The building was completely renovated in 1992, and the collection of over 4,000 historical items is displayed in the transformed east and west wings.

The east wing features the founders' display, with items documenting the life of city founder William Monroe, pictures of early Monrovia, a kitchen display with a stove that once belonged to Gen George S. Patton, a school display that illustrates education over the past 100 years and a reconstructed parlor similar to those used for Woman's Club meetings at the turn of the century.

The west wing displays a collection of 800 dolls gathered by public school teacher Lucia Cromwell and a collection of dolls of all the American presidents from George Washington to John F. Kennedy. Dr. Samuel E. Salsbury's eclectic collection contains Indian musical instruments, pottery and one of the most varied collections of arrowheads in the country. A 12-foot-

GTE telephone exhibit

long canoe hewn from a cedar log from Fox Lake, Wisconsin was under water for more than 40 years before finally being salvaged, restored and placed on display. Other exhibits include prehistoric and modern idols, Chinese musical instruments and tobacco pipes as well as fossils, shells, minerals and crystals. The hands-on exhibit "GTE: History of the Telephone" depicts the development of GTE, which started in Monrovia as the California Water and Telephone Company in 1899. On display are numerous models, which show the changes the telephone has undergone through the years; workmen's equipment; a telephone pole top; and an early switchboard.

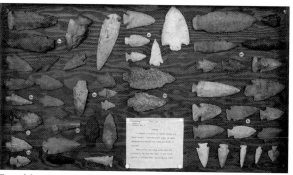

Part of the extensive collection of arrowheads. Many of the specimens shown here are claimed to be from the field of the Battle of Wounded Knee, South Dakota, 1891.

EAST LOS ANGELES AND
MID CITIES

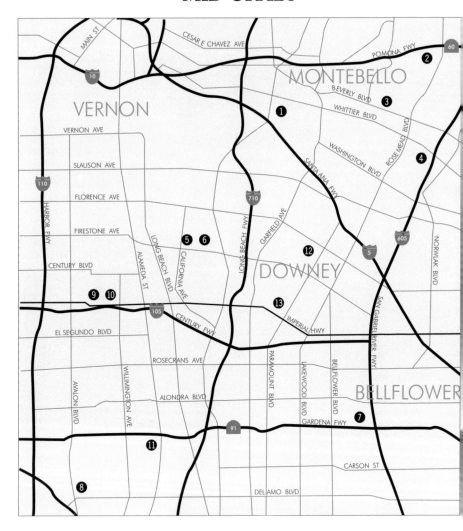

1 Goez Art Studio
2 Juan Matias Sanchez Adobe
   Museum
3 Montebello Barnyard Zoo
4 Pico Rivera Historical
   Display

5 South Gate Civic Center
   Museum
6 County of Los Angeles Fire
   Museum
7 Carpenter House Museum
8 Japanese Friendship Garden
9 Watts Towers Art Center

10 Watts Towers of Simon
    Rodia
11 Dominguez Ranch Adobe
12 Downey Museum of Art
13 Downey History Center

1

Goez Art Studio

5432 E Olympic Blvd, Los Angeles, 90022. ☎ (213) 721-2052. **Fax:** (213) 721-2445. **Thomas Guide:** 675 H1. **Hours:** Mon-Fri 10am-6pm. **Closed:** holidays. $ free. [P] free. 📷 by permission. **Year founded:** 1969. **Year opened:** 1971. **Primary focus:** to preserve the cultural and historical heritage of the Chicano. **Governing authority:** private. **Category:** art museum. **Activities/programs:** changing exhibitions, guided tours. **Facilities:** exhibit space/gallery. **Collection focus:** Hispanic art, Latin American art, Mexican art, folk art, graphic arts, 20th-century painting, sculpture.

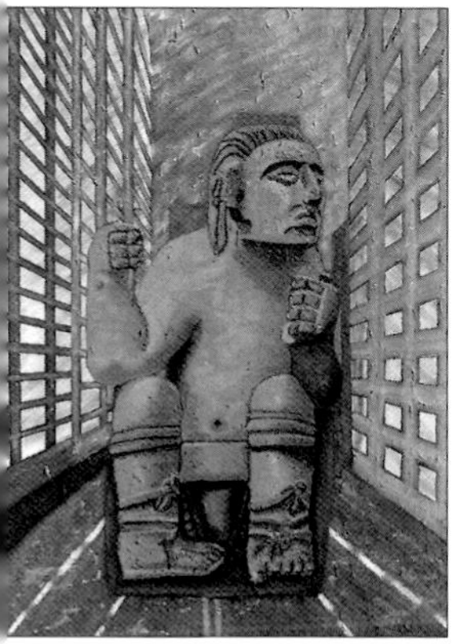

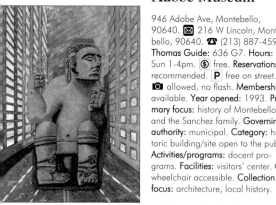

Donde Estoy (1992) by Jose Luis Gonzalez

This gallery/museum houses one of the largest collections of Chicano and Mexican art in the country, with more than 4,000 paintings, graphics, metal and wood sculptures, murals and photographs. Among the represented artists are Jose Luis Gonzalez, Rudy Escalera, Tony Ramirez, Javier Quijas and David Solomon. Goez Art Studio organized the first Chicano art exhibit ever held in Los Angeles and annually presents three exhibitions, including one-person retrospectives, group shows and works by young artists.

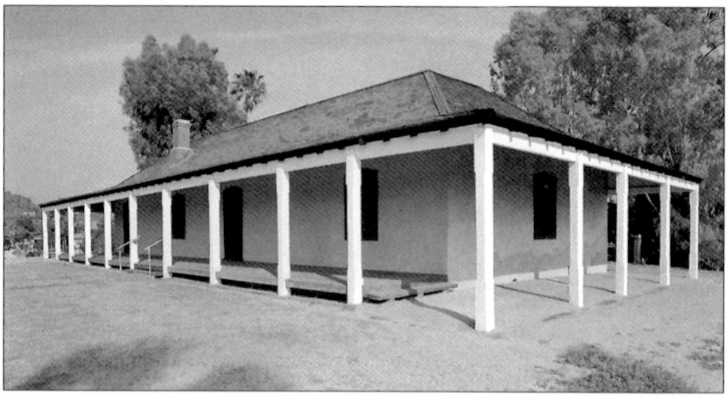

Juan Matias Sanchez Adobe

2

Juan Matias Sanchez Adobe Museum

946 Adobe Ave, Montebello, 90640. ✉ 216 W Lincoln, Montebello, 90640. ☎ (213) 887-4592. **Thomas Guide:** 636 G7. **Hours:** Sat-Sun 1-4pm. $ free. **Reservations:** recommended. [P] free on street. 📷 allowed, no flash. **Membership:** available. **Year opened:** 1993. **Primary focus:** history of Montebello and the Sanchez family. **Governing authority:** municipal. **Category:** historic building/site open to the public. **Activities/programs:** docent programs. **Facilities:** visitors' center. ♿ wheelchair accessible. **Collection focus:** architecture, local history.

Following the Secularization Act passed by the Mexican government in 1833, the Franciscan administration of missions came to an end and the California mission system disintegrated. In 1844 Mexican Governor Manuel Micheltorena granted the 2,363-acre Rancho La Merced to widow Dona Casilada Soto de Lobo. She built a small, 3-room adobe house with the help of her three sons in 1845. In 1851 the land was deeded to Juan Matias Sanchez, who lived in the adobe with his first and second wife and added a north wing to the house. With the collapse of Temple and Workman Bank in 1876, Sanchez lost most of his property, except the house and 200 acres of land. The adobe's last owners, the Scott family, restored the building in the late 1960s and donated it to the city of Montebello.

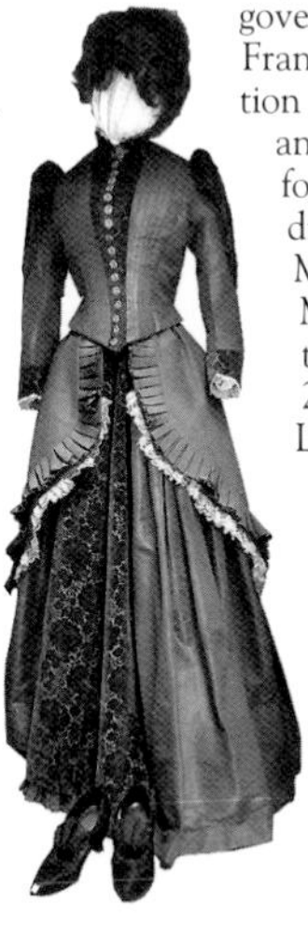

Wedding dress worn by Margarita Rowland Sanchez on March 5, 1885, at the San Gabriel Mission

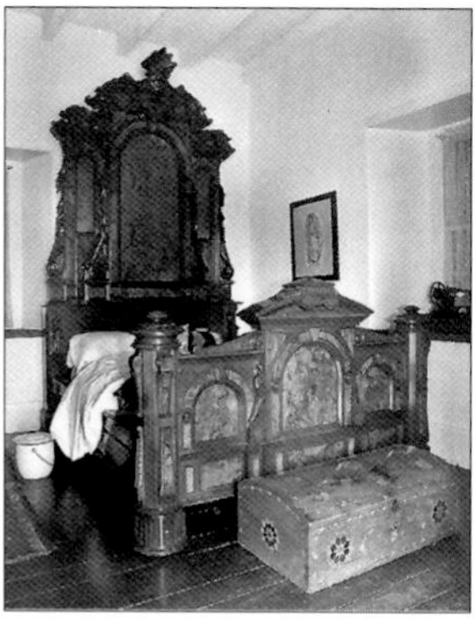

Bedroom (ca. 1880)

The museum houses a small collection of late 1800s costumes, old photos of the adobe and the Sanchez family, turn-of-the-century tools, some Indian artifacts and an 1906 dentist's drill that was operated by foot. A music book with old square notes, large enough for the choir to see from the pulpit, is also displayed. The kitchen, with its small cooking area and wine press, is a replica of one used in the 1850s. On display are dishes, utensils and handmade doilies and tablecloths. The bedroom contains 125-year-old, hand-carved furniture and the living room features a small 1840 piano with ivory keys. The flag room presents all 14 flags that flew over California before it became a state.

❸ Montebello Barnyard Zoo

600 Rea Dr, Montebello, 90640. ☎ (213) 887-4540, 727-0269. **Thomas Guide:** 676 F1. **Hours:** daily 9:30am-6pm. **Closed:** never. Ⓢ free. Ⓟ free. 📷 allowed. **Membership:** available. **Primary focus:** domestic animals. **Governing authority:** municipal. **Category:** zoo. **Activities/programs:** guided tours, school programs, pony rides, horseback riding. **Facilities:** animals available for rent, picnic area. ♿ strollers permitted, wheelchair accessible. **Zoo features:** dogs allowed (on leash), labels/descriptions. **Collection focus:** birds, mammals, zoology.

Pony in the Montebello Barnyard Zoo

This small zoo is a great attraction for children because they can not only see live animals, but they can also touch them. On display are horses, ponies, donkeys, cows, pigs, goats, sheep, llamas, chickens, peacocks and other barnyard animals. The zoo rents animals and brings them to parties and other events. Pony rides and horseback riding are also available.

❹ Pico Rivera Historical Display

9516 Whittier Blvd, Pico Rivera, 90660. ✉ PO Box 313, Pico Rivera, 90660. ☎ (310) 949-4026. **Thomas Guide:** 676 H4. 🚌 bus, metro. **Hours:** Tue, Thu 11am-2:30 pm. Ⓢ free. **Reservations:** by appointment only. Ⓟ free. 📷 allowed. **Year founded:** 1970. **Year opened:** 1992. **Primary focus:** history of Pico Rivera. **Publications:** *Pico Rivera: Where the World Began* by

T. B. Chapman House (1912). Pico Rivera Historical Display collection.

Martin Cole. **Governing authority:** private, nonprofit. **Category:** history museum. **Activities/programs:** educational programs, guided tours, lectures, outreach programs. **Facilities:** research library. ♿ wheelchair accessible. **Collection focus:** local history.

This small museum contains a collection of photographs from the 1850 to 1870s and the early 1900s, when the Pico Rivera area was a large supplier of walnuts. On display is farming equipment from the same time, original deeds, clothes, books and materials relating to local history. There are Native American artifacts from the 1700s as well as items that belonged to the early Anglo settlers, including pottery, dishes and English china and silver.

❺ South Gate Civic Center Museum

8680 California Ave, South Gate, 90280. ☎ (213) 569-4668. **Thomas Guide:** 705 B3. 🚌 bus. **Hours:** Tue 11am-3pm. Ⓢ free. Ⓟ free. 📷 allowed. **Membership:** available. **Year founded/opened:** 1980. **Primary focus:** to display historical items from South Gate's and America's past. **Governing authority:** municipal. **Category:** history museum. **Activities/programs:** school programs. ♿ parking, wheelchair accessible. **Collection focus:** local history.

Located in the old city library, which was built during the Depression in the 1930s, the museum features the 3-panel mural *History of Printing Through the Ages* painted by Suzanne Miller. Museum displays include household items such as an early example of a washing machine, typewriters, tools from the late 1800s and a small teapot collection. The museum has the first and last tires made at Firestone Tire and Rubber Co. in South Gate. There is a collection of the scientific papers of Dr. Glenn Seaborg, a Nobel Prize winner who spent his childhood in South Gate.

History of Writing, mural on the South Gate Civic Center Community Building

6

County of Los Angeles Fire Museum

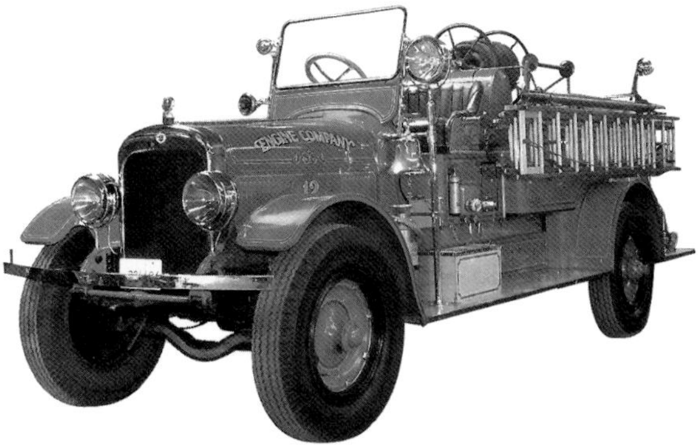

1928 Seagrave Triple Combination Pumper, the original Los Angeles County Fire Dept Engine 12 used in Altadena

8635 Otis St, South Gate, 90280; 1320 Eastern Ave, Los Angeles, 90063. ✉ PO Box 3325, Alhambra, 91803. ☎ (310) 634-6559, (805) 944-2123. **Thomas Guide:** 705 C3. **Hours:** by appointment only. [$] free. [P] free. 📷 allowed. **Membership:** available. **Year founded:** 1974. **Primary focus:** to preserve fire service history. **Publications:** *Fire Warden*, quarterly newsletter. **Governing authority:** nonprofit. **Category:** specialized museum. **Activities/programs:** volunteer programs. **Facilities:** gift shop. ♿ wheelchair accessible. **Collection focus:** firefighting, rescue equipment, vehicles.

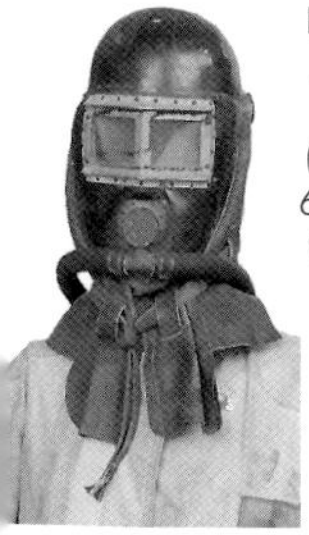

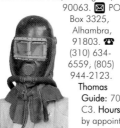

Draeger Helmet, an early example of a breathing apparatus (1880s)

Although the museum currently stores some of its antique apparatus at various locations throughout the county, the largest part of its collection is displayed at two locations: in South Gate and at the training center in Los Angeles.

The museum aims to provide a picture of the development of firefighting equipment from the "bucket brigade" tools and apparatus used 150 years ago to the advanced machines and fire engines in use today. Its collection consists of fire apparatus, equipment, rare artifacts, photographs and memorabilia. Among the items on display are helmets, firefighters' uniforms, badges, awards, communication equipment, antique bells and sirens, alarms, talking trumpets and fire extinguishers. There is an early example of a breathing apparatus with hand bellows, dating from the 1880s, used to pump air inside a helmet. Other items featured include a small collection of early American fire marks, used in the 18th and 19th centuries to identify buildings that were protected by fire insurance. The fire marks were first issued in 1752.

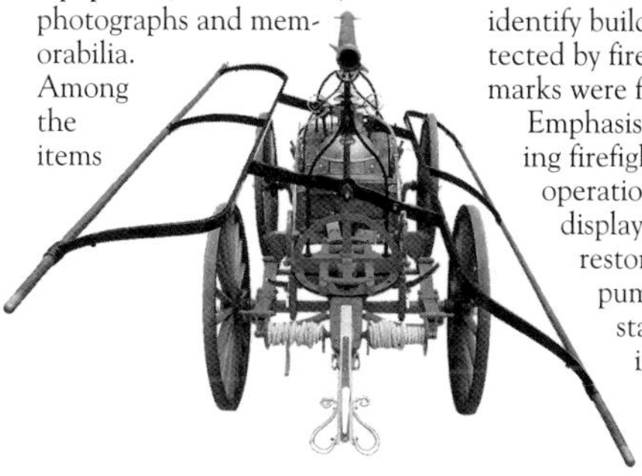

A hand-drawn 1853 Eagle hand pumper. It required 24 people to operate it, with 12 men on each side pumping in unison a stream of water to the fire.

Emphasis is placed on restoring firefighting vehicles to fully operational condition. On display are a beautifully restored 1853 Eagle hand pumper, which holds the state record for shooting a stream of water 190 feet; an 1853 Freedom hand-drawn ladder wagon; a 1903 Metropolitan steamer, which was owned by Fox Studios and appeared in *Gone with the Wind* (1939); a 1923 Ford TT chemical wagon; a 1928 Seagrave triple combination pumper, the original Engine 12 used in Altadena; and a 1965 Crown triple combination pumper, the first Engine 51 in the 1970s TV series *Emergency*.

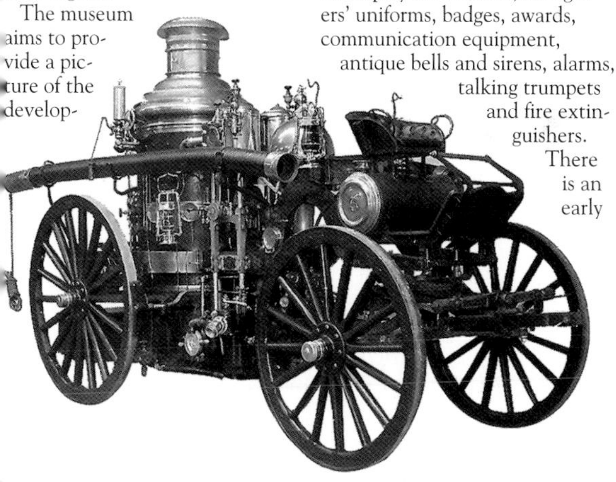

Fully operational 1903 American Fire Engine Co. Metro-politan steamer, used in the movie *Gone with the Wind*

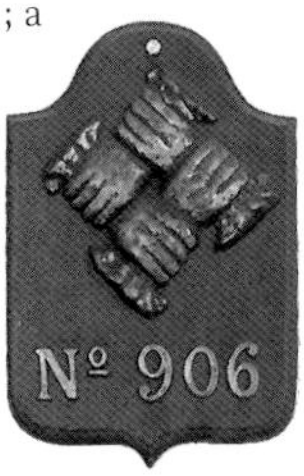

The Hand in Hand fire mark. It was the first to be issued in America by the Philadelphia contributorship to identify houses with fire insurance. The company was founded by Benjamin Franklin.

Japanese Friendship Garden at CSU Dominguez Hills

❼ Carpenter House Museum

10500 Flora Vista St, Bellflower, 90706. ✉ 16600 Civic Center Dr, Bellflower, 90706-5494. ☎ (310) 804-1424. **Fax:** (310) 925-8660. **Thomas Guide:** 736 D6. **Hours:** Sat 10:30am-2:30pm, Sun 12:30-3pm. $ free. **Reservations:** recommended. P free on street. 📷 allowed. **Primary focus:** history of Bellflower. **Governing authority:** municipal. **Category:** history museum. **Activities/programs:** guided tours. **Facilities:** picnic area. **Collection focus:** local history.

Carpenter House Museum

The 1928 house of the Fred B. Carpenter family has been preserved as a museum of local history, featuring old photographs of the farm and the family, period furniture, documents and artifacts. The Carpenters were pioneer dairy people who made the city the center of the dairy industry during the 1930s. The south bedroom outlines Bellflower's history. The dining room is a gift from Bellflower's sister city, Los Moches, Mexico.

❽ Japanese Friendship Garden

CSU Dominguez Hills, 1000 E Victoria Ave, Carson, 90747. ☎ (310) 516-3804, 516-3696. **Thomas Guide:** 764 F2. 🚌 bus. **Hours:** daily 8am-8pm. **Closed:** major holidays. $ free. P visitor parking. 📷 allowed. **Year opened:** 1978. **Governing authority:** college/university. **Category:** botanical garden/arboretum. **Activities/programs:** receptions. ♿ strollers permitted, parking, wheelchair accessible. **Garden features:** Japanese garden. **Collection focus:** botany.

Located in the atrium of the university's Social and Behavioral Sciences Building, this small tea garden, called *Shinwa-En* (An Island Dominated by Mountains and Forests), was designed in 1978 by Haruo Yamashiro. Among the evergreen trees, shrubs and groundcover are more than 60 tons of Malibu rock, representing the crane and tortoise, or male and female elements. The garden features a dry stream constructed of stones, a teahouse, a *tsukubai* or stone water basin, a *kakehi* or bamboo pipe, and *yukimi* and *kasuga* lanterns.

❾ Watts Towers Art Center

1727 E 107th St, Los Angeles, 90002. ☎ (213) 847-4646, 485-1795. **Fax:** (213) 564-7030. **Thomas Guide:** 704 G5. 🚇 metro. **Hours:** Tue-Sun 10am-4pm. $ free. **Reservations:** recommended. P free. 📷 not allowed. **Year founded/opened:** 1975. **Primary focus:** art education. **Special collections:** the Dr. Joseph Howard Collection of musical instruments, the Augustus Hawkins Collection of African masks. **Major exhibitions:** "A Classic African Art Exhibit" (1985). **Publications:** exhibition catalogs. **Governing authority:** municipal, nonprofit. **Division of:** Dept of Cultural Affairs. **Category:** specialized museum. **Activities/programs:** artist

Gourd vessel rattle, called sekere, used by the Yoruba of Nigeria. A loose-fitting net of beads hits against the gourd when shaken.

talks, changing exhibitions, classes/courses, concerts, films, gallery talks, guided tours, installations, internship program, performances, school programs, slide presentations, storytelling, workshops. **Facilities:** exhibit space/gallery, picnic area, slide registry. ♿ parking, wheelchair accessible. **Collection focus:** Afro-American art, Hispanic art, modern and contemporary art, drawings, folk art, masks, mural painting and decoration, music and musical instruments, postage stamps, watercolors, weaving, woodcarvings.

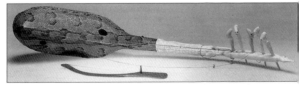

Harp from Uganda with a bow of 5 strings. The neck is carved from ivory in the shape of a woman and a bird. Rattlesnake skin covers the resonator.

The folk instrument collection on display at the Watts Towers Art Center comprises more than 100 percussion, wind and string instruments created by various cultures from all over the world. It is part of a large collection of over 600 ethnic musical instruments, postage stamps, dolls and

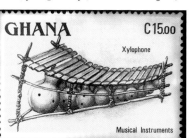
Postage stamp from Ghana depicting a xylophone

African art gathered by Dr. Joseph Howard over a 40-year period and donated to the City of Los Angeles in 1989.

The center also has a collection of classic African art objects (not on display) donated by Congress-

West African mask from the Augustus Hawkins Collection

man Augustus Hawkins. It contains 52 masks, figures, birds and animals from the Ivory Coast, Liberia, Mali and Upper Volta. The collection includes Senofu and Bobo wooden figures, Baule masks, Bambara headpieces and other objects used as fertility symbols, in rituals or for burial rites.

⑩ Watts Towers of Simon Rodia

1765 E 107th St, Los Angeles, 90002. ✉ 1727 E 107th St, Los Angeles, 90002. ☎ (213) 847-4646, 485-1795. TDD: (213) 847-3368. Fax: (213) 564-7030. Thomas Guide: 704 G5. 🚌 metro. Hours: Sat 10am-4pm, Sun noon-4pm. Ⓢ $1 adults, children 16 and under free. P free. 📷 for personal use only. Governing authority: municipal. Category: historic building/site open to the public. Activities/programs: educational programs, events (annual Simon Rodia Watts Towers Jazz Festival, Watts Towers Day of the Drum Festival), outreach programs, school programs. Facilities: picnic area. information center. ♿ wheelchair accessible (exterior). Collection focus: architecture, modern and contemporary art.

Los Angeles's most notable work of folk art, the Watts Towers, is the accomplishment of one man, Italian immigrant Simon Rodia. He erected the towers between 1921 and 1954 without any outside help, buying material out of his wages as a construction worker and using every moment of his free time during the 33-year period. Having no general plan and building without sketches or blueprints, Rodia improvised every stage of construction. He had no power equipment and used only a tile setter's tools and a window washer's belt and buckle.

The internationally acclaimed monument to the human spirit and imagination, which Rodia called Nuestro Pueblo (Spanish for Our Town), consists of nine major structures built of steel rods, pipes and

Watts Towers

wire mesh covered with cement. The tallest of his three towers is 99.5 feet (30,3 m) high and contains the longest slender reinforced concrete columns in the world. Every surface of his structures is embellished with broken glass, soda pop bottles, pottery, ceramic tile, colorful stones, over 25,000 seashells and other found objects, creating a colorful lacework of open structures. He made imprints into the fresh mortar using his hands and tools, horseshoes, gears and faucet handles.

After finishing his work in 1954, Simon Rodia deeded the property to a neighbor and moved to northern California, where he died in 1965, never seeing his life's work again. He was reluctant to talk about his masterpiece, but once said: "I had in mind to do something big and I did it."

The Watts Towers is listed in the National Register of Historic Places and dedicated as a State of California Historic Monument and a State of California Historic Park.

Watts Towers

Dominguez Ranch Adobe

⑪ Dominguez Ranch Adobe

18127 S Alameda, Rancho Dominguez, 90220. ☎ (310) 631-5981. **Fax:** (310) 631-3518. **Thomas Guide:** 765 A1. **Hours:** Tue-Wed, 2nd and 3rd Sat of each month 1-4pm. Ⓢ free. **Reservations:** recommended. Ⓟ free. ◙ allowed. **Year opened:** 1973. **Primary focus:** early California history. **Publications:** The Rancho San Pedro by R. C. Gillingham. **Governing authority:** church, nonprofit. **Category:** historic building/site open to the public. **Activities/programs:** guided tours. **Facilities:** picnic area. ♿ strollers permitted, parking, wheelchair accessible. **Garden features:** desert garden, rose garden. **Collection focus:** aerospace, architecture, dolls and puppets, folklife and traditions, furniture and interiors, local history, period rooms, railways, religious history and traditions.

Manuel Dominguez's bedroom

The first Spanish land grant in California was given to Juan José Dominguez, a leather-jacket soldier and member of the 1769 Portola expedition to Alta California. Dominguez served for 13 years as a guide and guard for

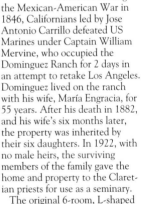
Dominguez Ranch brand

Junipero Serra and other Franciscan fathers during the establishment of the California mission chain. In 1784 King Carlos III of Spain granted him 75,000 acres of land, called Rancho San Pedro, as a reward for his service.

The ranch was inherited by Manuel Dominguez, grandnephew of Juan José, who built the first adobe house in 1826 and changed the name of the property to Dominguez Adobe. Manuel played an active role in local politics, was a member of the city council, a 2-term mayor of Los Angeles and one of the delegates from southern California who helped draft the state's first constitution. During the Mexican-American War in 1846, Californians led by Jose Antonio Carrillo defeated US Marines under Captain William Mervine, who occupied the Dominguez Ranch for 2 days in an attempt to retake Los Angeles. Dominguez lived on the ranch with his wife, María Engracia, for 55 years. After his death in 1882, and his wife's six months later, the property was inherited by their six daughters. In 1922, with no male heirs, the surviving members of the family gave the home and property to the Claretian priests for use as a seminary.

The original 6-room, L-shaped adobe has undergone several changes and extensions over the years. In 1907 it was remodeled in the Mission Revival style and turned into a U-shaped structure, with a new roof and arched porticos. The adobe's original 6 rooms were restored and furnished as they might have looked when the Dominguez family lived here. The furnishings include original family pieces, as well as period furniture, mementos, clothing, paintings and family photographs. Three other rooms are dedicated to the Carson, Del Amo and Watson families and decorated with family furniture and artifacts. One room contains photos, airplane models and a large diorama chronicling the 1910 Dominguez Air Meet, the first air show in the US. This event marked the beginning of

Fountain

the aviation and aerospace industry in California. The other room traces the role the ranch played in the development of the local railroads and houses 4 scaled live-steam locomotives.

Adjacent to the house is a small desert garden dedicated in 1976 and maintained by the Long Beach Cactus Club. The adobe is in the National Register of Historic Places and designated a California Historical Landmark.

Kitchen with the wood-burning recessed fire pits used for reheating food prepared outdoors

⑫ Downey Museum of Art

10419 Rives Ave, Downey, 90241. ☎ (310) 861-0419. **Fax:** (310) 928-8609. **Thomas Guide:** 706 A3. 🚌 bus. **Hours:** Wed-Sun noon-5pm. **Closed:** between exhibitions. 💲 free. P free. 📷 allowed. **Membership:** available. **Year founded:** 1957. **Primary focus:** 20th-century California art. **Governing authority:** nonprofit. **Category:** art museum. **Activities/programs:** artists' talks, changing exhibitions, classes/courses, competitions, gallery talks, installations, internship program, lectures, summer programs, volunteer programs. **Facilities:** audiovisual holdings, exhibit space/gallery, picnic area, sculpture garden, slide reg-

Woman with Cards (1940) by Boris Deutsch

istry. ♿ strollers permitted, parking, wheelchair accessible. **Collection focus:** African-American art, European art, Mexican art, North American art, modern and contemporary art, folk art, graphic arts, North American painting, 20th-century painting, photography, sculpture.

The Downey Museum of Art concentrates on exhibiting contemporary southern California artists and reintroducing artists and styles from the early 20th century. Its permanent collection comprises over 400 works in a wide range of media, spanning the period from the early 1920s to the present. The museum's highlights include works by Alfredo de Batuc, Gordon Wagner and

Failed Bluntslide (Skater #2) (1994) by Sandon Birk

over 200 works by Boris Deutsch, as well as contemporary southern California and Latino artists. The European master prints collection includes works by Marc Chagall, Joan Miró, Salvador Dalí and Pablo Picasso.

⑬ Downey History Center

12540 Rives Ave, Downey, 90241. ✉ PO Box 554, Downey, 90241. ☎ (310) 862-2777, 928-4006. **Thomas Guide:** 705 H7. 🚌 bus. **Hours:** Wed-Thu 9am-2pm, 3rd Sat of each month 10am-3pm. **Closed:** 1st and 3rd Wed in Jul and Aug; last two weeks of year. 💲 free, dona-

tions accepted. **Reservations:** recommended. P free. 📷 allowed. **Membership:** available. **Year founded:** 1965. **Year opened:** 1985. **Primary focus:** history of southeastern Los Angeles County, Governor John G. Downey. **Research fields:** local history, genealogy, local aircraft industry. **Major exhibitions:** "World War II: 50th Anniversary" (1991-95). **Publications:** *Photographers of 19th-Century Los Angeles County;* monthly newsletter. **Governing authority:** private. **Category:** history museum. **Activities/programs:** educational programs, events, films, guided tours, slide presentations. **Facilities:** audiovisual holdings, exhibit space/gallery, 800-volume research library. **Collection focus:** aerospace, architecture, genealogy, local history, law.

This museum contains artifacts documenting the city's past and includes an extensive collection of photographs from the 1870s to the present, records of arrest (1883-1919) from the Los Angeles County District Attorney's Office, a collection of documents and photos of the 7th California Governor John Gately Downey, Los Nietos Pioneer Register and original copies of local newspapers (1918-69). The museum tells the story of the aircraft industry in Downey, from the Edward Smith plant in 1929 through Vultee Aviation in 1936 to Rockwell International Space Division (the Apollo capsule was made in Downey). Adjacent to the center is the restored Dismukes Cottage, built in 1887 and furnished with turn-of-the-century furniture.

US Army basic trainer BT-13-VII Valiant. Some 16,000 were made at the Vultee Aviation plant in Downey. Photograph in the Downey History Center collection.

WHITTIER AND LA MIRADA

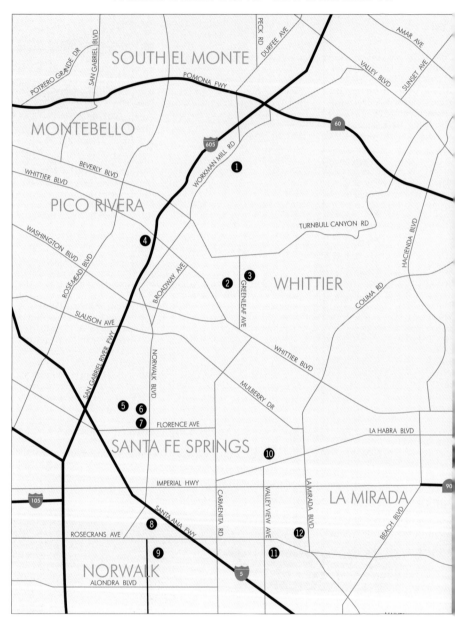

❶ Pageant of Roses Garden	❻ Heritage Park	❿ Los Angeles County Sheriffs'
❷ Whittier Museum	❼ Hathaway Ranch Museum	Museum
❸ The Bailey House	❽ Gilbert Sproul Museum	⓫ Neff Home
❹ Pio Pico Mansion	❾ Hargitt House	⓬ Biola University Art Gallery
❺ The Clarke Estate		

❶

Pageant of Roses Garden

3900 S Workman Mill Rd, Whittier, 90601. ✉ PO Box 110, Whittier, 90608. ☎ (310) 699-0921. **Fax:** (310) 699-6372. **Thomas Guide:** 677 C1. **Hours:** daily 8am-sunset. **Closed:** never. $ free. [P] inside Gate 1, free. 📷 for noncommercial use. **Year founded/opened:** 1959.

Bridal Pink rose

Primary focus: rose display and maintenance. **Governing authority:** private. **Category:** botanical garden/arboretum. **Activities/programs:** classes/courses, lectures, performances, school programs. **Facilities:** gift shop. **Garden features:** labels/descriptions, rose garden, Japanese garden, peak time: spring. **Collection focus:** botany, horticulture.

Located in the East Park section of the Rose Hills Memorial Park, this 3½-acre award-winning garden features more than 7,000 rosebushes including over 650 varieties. Designed by the landscape architecture firm of Cornell, Bridgers and Troller, it received recognition from the American Rose Society (ARS) and in 1984 was designated the most outstanding public rose garden in the country by the All-America Rose Selections (AARS).

Displayed in 85 beds, this remarkable collection includes a vast diversity of hybrid teas, grandifloras, floribundas and miniatures, such as *Little Fireball, Baby Ophelia* and *Rose Hills Red.* The garden exhibits some oldtime roses, the predecessors of modern cultivars, including the celebrated *Rose of Castille, Rouge Moss, La France* and *Rosa Mundi,* dating prior to 1400. Among the unusual varieties on display are roses that do not bloom, such as the Apple Rose from Central Europe and the Bamboo Rose from Japan. There are more than 500 climbing roses growing along the garden fences in the Miles of Roses display, representing one of the largest collections of climbers in the world. The garden also contains splendid weeping tree roses, including *Margo Koster* and *China Doll.*

Show Biz rose

As an official display garden for both the ARS and the AARS, the Pageant of Roses Garden receives the newest introductions, and it exhibits many of the AARS award-winning roses, such as *American Heritage* (1966), *Color Magic* (1978), *Olympiad* (1984) and *Voodoo* (1986).

Nearby West Park features a 5-acre Japanese garden with an *Azumaya*, or meditation house, an authentic Shogun monument, snow lanterns, rock formations, bridges and a lake inhabited with koi and mallards.

Pageant of Roses Garden

The early transportation exhibit includes a carriage made by Whittier Implement Co.

❷ Whittier Museum

6755 Newlin Ave, Whittier, 90601. ☎ (310) 945-3871. **Thomas Guide:** 677 C6. **Hours:** Sat-Sun 1-4pm. **Closed:** holidays. Ⓢ $2 adults, $1 seniors, $.50 children. Ⓟ free. 📷 allowed. **Membership:** available. **Year founded:** 1971. **Year opened:** 1982. **Primary focus:** collecting and preserving the history of Whittier. **Major exhibitions:** "Lariats and Lace" (1995), "Twentieth-Century Los Angeles Studio Photographers" (1994). **Publications:** *Gazette*, quarterly newsletter. **Governing authority:** nonprofit. **Category:** history museum. **Activities/programs:** artists' talks, changing exhibitions, docent programs, dramatic programs, educational programs, events (Design House, biannual), gallery talks, guided tours, internship program, lectures, performances, slide presentations, storytelling, volunteer programs, workshops. **Facilities:** bookstore, exhibit space/gallery, gift shop, lecture hall, 300-volume library. ♿ strollers permitted, parking, wheelchair accessible. **Collection focus:** local history.

The museum is housed in a converted telephone company building and presents interesting exhibits of life in early Whittier, a town founded in 1887 and named in honor of Quaker poet and humanitarian John Greenleaf Whittier. The Old Main Street exhibit features a reconstructed Queen Anne cottage with rooms decorated in turn-of-the-century style and arranged with period furniture and everyday items.

The agricultural center depicts orange packing and shipping as part of the important local citrus industry, while the old barn shows carts, saddles, farmers' tools and artifacts. Another exhibit traces the discovery of oil and the development of the oil industry in Whittier, displaying a working model of an early oil derrick. On view is a Bob Downey

Colt 38 owned by Pio Pico, the last Mexican governor of California (ca. 1875)

Formula 1 Racing Plane, flown in races and air shows in 1947. There is a reconstructed newspaper office of the Whittier *Register* and the Whittier History Trunk, a hands-on exhibit also available to local schools. Other displays feature Whittier's Quaker meeting house, early businesses, school days and medical life. The museum possesses an extensive textile collection, comprising antique, mostly Victorian clothes.

Memorabilia in the museum's collection include Governor Pio Pico's revolver, a traveling shaving box owned by Abraham Lincoln and the desk former President Nixon used in his first law office. The archives contain all issues of the local newspaper, over 6,500 vintage photographs, documents and other archival materials.

❸ The Bailey House

13421 E Camilla St, Whittier, 90601. ☎ (310) 698-3534. **Thomas Guide:** 677 D5. **Hours:** Wed 1-3pm, Sun 1-4pm. **Closed:** Sep; Wed in Jul and Aug. Ⓢ $.50 adults, $.25 children. **Reservations:** necessary for groups, (310) 945-3871. Ⓟ free on street. 📷 allowed. **Membership:** available. **Primary focus:** Whittier history. **Governing authority:** nonprofit. **Category:** historic building/site open to the public. **Activities/programs:** docent programs, events (Christmas tea), guided tours, school programs, volunteer programs. **Collection focus:** local history, personal history.

The Bailey House

One of the oldest homes in Whittier, this small ranch house was built in about 1868 by German immigrant farmer Jacob Gerkins. From 1887 it was the home of Jonathan and Rebecca Bailey and the center of local social and business activities. The town's first Quaker meetings were held on the front porch, attended by only 10 people. The restored house contains furnishings of the 1865-1904 period, including many Bailey family items, photographs, mementos and a Quaker library. On display in the converted barn is an old "gravel wagon" and a collection of antique tools. The house is in the National Register of Historic Places.

The agricultural center exhibit with a 1932 tractor

Pio Pico Mansion

4

Pio Pico Mansion

6003 Pioneer Blvd, Whittier, 90606. ☎ (310) 695-1217. **Fax:** (310) 699-6916. **Thomas Guide:** 676 J4. 🚌 bus. **Hours:** Wed-Sun 10am-5pm. $ free. **Reservations:** recommended. [P] free. 📷 for personal use only. **Primary focus:** to interpret the life and times of Pio Pico, the last Mexican governor of California. **Research fields:** California history — transition and early American periods; adobe. **Publications:** *Pio Pico State Historic Park*, booklet. **Governing authority:** state, nonprofit. **Parent institution:** Dept of Parks and Recreation. **Category:** historic building/site open to the public. **Activities/programs:** educational programs, events (Sat closest to May 5 celebration), guided tours, internship program, outreach programs, school programs, slide presentations, traveling exhibitions (Pico Exhibit), volunteer programs, special programs (junior ranger programs, ages 7-12; outdoor bread baking). **Facilities:** picnic area. **Collection focus:** architecture, baking and cookery, domestic utensils, furniture and interiors, local history, period rooms, politics and government, portraits.

Pio de Jesus Pico was one of the most prominent political figures in 19th-century California. He participated in some of the most important events in the state's history, was elected several times to the *diputación*, or legislature, served as interim governor and in 1845 became governor of California. Pico stayed in this position until 1846, when the American invasion forced him to flee to Mexico. In 1848, after the war was over, he returned to California and served on the Los Angeles City Council.

Pio Pico was one of the richest men of his time. He and his brother Andres owned 532,000 acres in 1850s, when Pio purchased the 9,000-acre Rancho Paso de Bartolo Viejo. In the same year he built a large, L-shaped adobe house on the rancho, which he called El Ranchito. The 10-room adobe was a typical country residence, and its size, lavishly furnished interior and beautiful gardens represent the lifestyle of the rich California dons of the time.

The house was destroyed in 1883 by the San Gabriel River flood, and the following year Pico began to rebuilt the house, adding a new section. The mansion as it is seen today is the result of this reconstruction. During the rebuilding Pico faced serious financial difficulties, and due to his passion for gambling and fraud he lost all his vast property, including El Ranchito. He was evicted from the ranch and moved to his daughter's home, where he died in 1894.

Pio Pico's cattle brand

The 13-room, 2-story, U-shaped adobe has undergone many changes since Pio Pico's time. Its collections include period furnishings, some having reportedly belonged to Pico, paintings, textiles, restoration plans and artifacts found during archaeological excavations. The archives contain Pico's letters and papers as well as photographs of Pico, his homes and businesses.

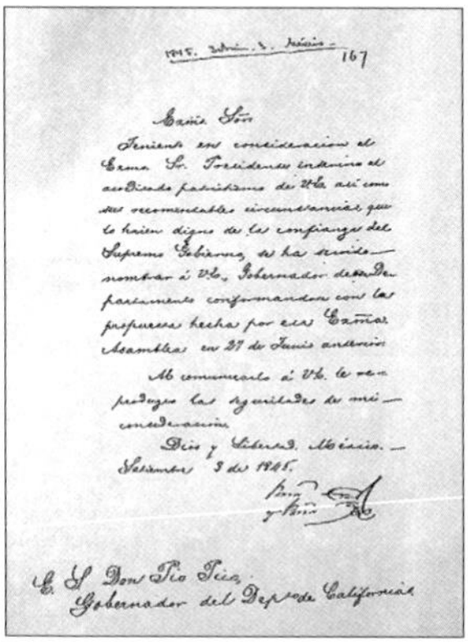
167

Dios y Libertad. Mexico

Sre. Don Pio Pico,
Gobernador del Dep.to de California

Letter of September 13, 1845, from the Supreme Governor of Mexico confirming Pio Pico's appointment as governor of California

5

The Clarke Estate

10211 S Pioneer Blvd, Santa Fe Springs, 90670. ✉ 11740 E Telegraph Rd, Santa Fe Springs, 90670. ☎ (310) 863-4896. **Recorded information:** (310) 868-3876. **Fax:** (310) 864-2431. **Thomas Guide:** 706 H4. **Hours:** Tue, Fri, 1st Sun of each month 11am-2pm. **Closed:** holidays and rainy days. $ free. **Reservations:** recommended. [P] free. 📷 allowed. **Year opened:** 1986. **Governing authority:** municipal. **Category:** historic building/site open to the public. **Activities/programs:** guided tours. **Facilities:** audiovisual holdings, picnic area, rental space for meetings, weddings, receptions. ♿ parking, wheelchair accessible. **Garden features:** restrooms; peak time; spring. **Collection focus:** architecture.

The Clarke House, central patio

This large, 2-story house was built on 60 acres of orange groves as a country retreat for Chauncey and Marie Rankin Clarke. When oil was discovered in the area in 1921, the Clarkes abandoned it as a country home and moved away. It was purchased by the City of Santa Fe Springs in 1986 and extensively restored. Designed by Irving Gill in 1919, the house features Tuscan columns, small Italian balconies overlooking the central patio and large exterior surfaces without ornamentation. It is the largest of Gill's houses still in existence and representative of his design axiom to "fling aside every device that distracts the eye from structural beauty."

Emerson surrey, built around 1900

6

Heritage Park

12100 Mora Dr, Santa Fe Springs, 90670. ☎ (310) 946-6476. **Fax:** (310) 946-8593. **Thomas Guide:** 706 H5. **Hours:** park: daily 7am-10pm; carriage barn: Tue, Fri-Sun noon-4pm, Wed-Thu 9am-4pm. **Closed:** never. [$] free. **Reservations:** necessary. [P] free. 📷 allowed. **Year opened:** 1988. **Primary focus:** history of Santa Fe Springs. **Governing authority:** municipal. **Category:** history museum. **Activities/programs:** concerts, docent programs, educational programs, events (fashion show and tea, car show, Las Posadas, Children's Day), school programs, summer programs, volunteer programs, workshops. **Facilities:** cafeteria/restaurant, picnic area; formal gardens and plaza available for rent. ♿ strollers permitted, parking, wheelchair accessible. **Garden features:** aviary, greenhouse, ponds, dogs allowed on leash. **Collection focus:** agriculture, architecture, carriages and carts, local history, railways.

English-style garden

Heritage Park is the restored ranch estate built by wealthy farmer Harvey Hawkins in 1880. The 100-acre ranch contained buildings erected in the popular Carpenter Gothic style. Hawkins spent $5,000 to build a carriage barn, making it the most expensive structure of its kind in Los Angeles County. His elegant estate included a formal English-style garden with rare plants, statuary and the first concrete fountains in southern California.

Tank house and windmill

The wooden buildings in the 6.5-acre park are copies of the ones built by Hawkins. The carriage barn, glass-roofed conservatory, tank house and windmill that supplied water to the estate were reconstructed using historic photographs. The original gardens have been replanted and a large aviary contains more than 150 birds. On the site are the remains of an older building, a large adobe constructed by Mexican Patricio Ontiveros about 1815. He was foreman of the cattle holdings of Mission San Juan Capistrano.

The local history museum, housed in the beautifully reconstructed carriage barn, contains well-designed theme exhibits. "Horse and Buggy Days" presents an Emerson surrey, a horse-drawn carriage built around 1900. "Keeping a Home" shows the role of the housewife running a turn-of-the-century household. "A Living From the Land" recreates daily life on the farm. "Inventing a Better Life" shows examples of Yankee ingenuity in the early 1900s, when America became the world's leading technological power. The museum displays many items uncovered during archaeological investigations on the property, including Gabrielino Indian artifacts.

The train exhibit site features a recreated Santa Fe Springs train depot, originally built in the 1880s. On display is an Atchison, Topeka & Santa Fe Railway steam locomotive, No. 870, built by Baldwin Locomotive Works in the 1920s, and a 1955 Santa Fe caboose.

7

Hathaway Ranch Museum

11901 E Florence Ave, Santa Fe Springs, 90670. ☎ (310) 944-6563. **Recorded information:** (310) 944-7372. **Fax:** (310) 946-0708. **Thomas Guide:** 706 H5. **Hours:** Mon-Tue, Thu-Fri 11am-4pm; 1st Sun of each month 2-4pm. **Closed:** holidays. [$] $1 suggested donation. **Reservations:** by appointment only for groups. [P] free. 📷 allowed. **Year founded/opened:** 1986. **Primary focus:** preserving local history and artifacts. **Publications:** museum newsletter. **Governing authority:** private, nonprofit. **Category:** historic building/site open to the public. **Activities/programs:** educational programs, guided tours, lectures, performances, school programs, slide presentations, volunteer programs. **Facilities:** gift shop, research library, picnic area, visitors' center. ♿ strollers permitted, parking, sound augmentation systems, wheelchair accessible. **Collection focus:** agriculture, carriages and carts, farms and farming, local history, machines and machinery, mills, oil industry and trade, period rooms, personal history.

Pre-1920s parlor

The gas station exhibit features a 1939 International D-30 series car with 1,250,000 miles on it, still in working condition

The Hathaway Ranch Museum is actually a remnant of a farm founded by Jesse E. and Lola Hathaway in the early 1900s. They raised cattle and hogs, grew vegetables and fruits, and did some experimental farming for a seed company. At one time the ranch had 400 head of cattle and the Hathaways won several awards for their steers. When oil was discovered in Santa Fe Springs in 1921, three Hathaway sons went into the oil business, forming the Hathaway Company.

Caterpillar & Holt half-truck (early 1920s)

The museum aims to give a picture of the daily life of local pioneers over the course of three generations. It is located in the 1935 Hathaway residence building and comprises rooms that follow a specific theme or period. The collection includes household items, period clothes, music, toys, military uniforms and items from WWI and WWII. There is a large photographic archive and a library devoted primarily to California history. The extensive collection of farming, cattle ranching and oil drilling equipment is displayed outdoors. Among the items on view are hay wagons, trucks, tractors, stationary engines and other equipment dating from the 1890s to the 1940s.

Visitors, schoolchildren in particular, can grind corn, feed chickens and see, hear and feel what it was like to live in that rural area during the first half of the 20th century.

⑧ Gilbert Sproul Museum

12237 E Sproul St, Norwalk, 90650. ☎ (310) 929-5625. Fax: (310) 929-5773. Thomas Guide: 736 J2. Hours: Tue-Sat 1-4pm. Closed: major holidays. $ free. Reservations: recommended. P free. 📷 allowed. Year opened: 1964. Primary focus: history of Norwalk. Governing authority: municipal. Category: historic building/site open to the public. Activities/programs: events (quilt shows), guided tours. Collection focus: architecture, furniture and interiors, local history.

The museum building was once the home of Gilbert Sproul, the founder of Norwalk. Built in 1870, his Eastlake cottage was one of the first homes in the Norwalk area, and town meetings were conducted there. Vida Sproul Hunter, Sproul's granddaughter, donated the house to the city, which moved the structure to its present location in Norwalk Park. The museum displays original furniture dating from the 1870s, as well as artifacts, maps, photographs and other materials pertaining to local history. Other exhibits include dolls, guns and Native American artifacts.

⑨ Hargitt House

12432 Mapledale St, Norwalk, 90650. ☎ (310) 929-5625. Fax: (310) 929-5773. Thomas Guide: 736 J3. Hours: Tue-Sat 1-4pm. Closed: major holidays. Admission: free. Reservations: recommended. P free. 📷 allowed. Primary focus: history of Norwalk. Governing authority: municipal. Category: historic building/site open to the public. Activities/programs: guided tours. Collection focus: architecture, local history.

Hargitt House

This 2-story Victorian house was built in 1891 by D. D. Johnson, organizer of the Norwalk school system. After the death of Charles Hargitt, Johnson's grandson, the house was donated to the City of Norwalk in 1975. The building is restored and furnished with period furniture, with displays of photographs and arts and crafts. Outside exhibits include an old tractor, a wagon and other farm equipment.

Gilbert Sproul Museum

⑩ Los Angeles County Sheriffs' Museum

11515 S Colima Rd "B," Whittier, 90604. ☎ (310) 946-7081. Fax: (310) 946-5302. Thomas Guide: 707 E6. Hours: Mon-Fri 9am-4pm. Closed: holidays. $ free. Reservations: recommended. P free. 📷 permission required. Year founded: 1987. Year opened: 1988. Primary focus: the Los Angeles County Sheriffs' Dept from 1850 to the present. Governing authority: county, nonprofit. Category: specialized museum. Activities/programs: changing exhibitions, volunteer programs. Facilities: cafeteria/restaurant, gift shop. ♿ parking, wheelchair accessible. Collection focus: criminology, local history.

1938 Studebaker patrol car

Sheriff's office and jail (1889)

The museum is housed in the Sheriffs' Training Academy Service Building. It offers a historical overview of the Los Angeles County Sheriffs' Dept from its early days in the 1850s, when the county was a lawless land without established government. Describing the Los Angeles of that era, Wyatt Earp, the pioneer US marshall, said: "Tombstone was but a Sunday school by comparison."

The Hall of Sheriffs traces the department's development and includes biographies, documents, mementos and photographs of all 25 county sheriffs, except the first one, George T. Burril. Another exhibit illustrates the history of women in law enforcement since 1912, when Margaret I. Adams, the first woman deputy in the US, was sworn in. One of the museum's highlights is a replica of Sheriff Aguirre's office and jail, restored as it might have looked in 1889.

Visitors can push a button and the exhibit comes to life, with a prisoner talking and a sheriff rocking in a chair.

The exhibit on street weapons presents a selection of con-

Deputy Sheriff's badge

fiscated legal and illegal weapons from 1850 to the present. They include machine guns and other assault weapons, as well as knives, ice picks, can openers and flying stars. The body armor test exhibit displays different types of vests made of Kevlar, showing bullet holes and what happened to bullets when they hit the material. There are also special exhibits

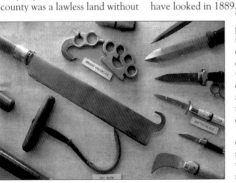

Guitar case with 3 banana clips and handheld semiautomatic

on identification systems, gambling, vice, narcotics, jails and famous criminals.

Additional attractions include a restored 1938 Studebaker patrol car, Harley-Davidson and Kawasaki motorcycles and a Hughes 300 "Super" B helicopter. Visitors are offered a look behind the scenes as divers, mountain climbers, paramedics and other members of the Emergency Services unit put their life-saving skills to work.

Street weapons

11

Neff Home

14300 San Cristobal Dr, La Mirada, 90638. ✉ 12900 Bluefield Ave, La Mirada, 90638. ☎ (310) 943-3739. **Fax:** (310) 947-5021. **Thomas Guide:** 737 E3. **Hours:** 2nd and 4th Sun of each month 2-4pm. [$] donations accepted. **Reservations:** by appointment only for groups. [P] free. 📷 allowed. **Membership:** available. **Year opened:** 1980. **Primary focus:** historic Neff site. **Special collections:** the Bob and Iris Camp Collection. **Publications:** *La Mirada: From Rancho to City* by C. W. Bob Camp. **Governing authority:** municipal. **Category:** historic building/site open to the public. **Activities/programs:** classes/courses, docent programs, events (historic fair in Oct), guided tours, lectures, volunteer programs. **Facilities:** available for rent; picnic area. ♿ strollers permitted, parking, wheelchair accessible. **Garden features:** dogs allowed on leash. **Collection focus:** agriculture, carriages and carts, domestic utensils, farms and farming, furniture and interiors, local history, period rooms, toys and games.

Neff Home

In 1888 Andrew McNally, president of the Chicago-based publisher Rand McNally & Co., purchased 2,378 acres of the former Les Coyotes Ranch in La Mirada. He planned to sell 20-acre parcels as "gentlemen's country estates," but due to the financial crisis of the 1890s, his plan was abandoned. On the remaining 1,500 acres, named Windermere Ranch, he planted olive and citrus groves. In the early 1900s the McNally Olive Co. had the largest olive groves in the US and produced the highest quality olive oil in the world.

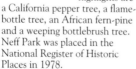

McNally's Pure Olive Oil can

McNally built the ranch's main residence as a wedding gift for his daughter Nannie and her husband, Edwin D. Neff, the first ranch manager. The wood-frame house was designed by Frederick Lewis Roehrig in 1893. Two other original buildings that still remain today are the carriage barn (1889) and the Queen Anne-style George House (1888). In the early 1900s more than 100 specimens of trees were planted, many of them rare and unusual. Among the highlights are a California pepper tree, a flame-bottle tree, an African fern-pine and a weeping bottlebrush tree. Neff Park was placed in the National Register of Historic Places in 1978.

The Neff home is furnished with original pieces from the families who lived in the house from 1894 to 1962. The barn displays the Bob and Iris Camp Collection of farm tools and implements used on the McNally Ranch. Other items include a station wagon from the late 1890s, an interesting collection of cast-iron toys, household appliances, flat irons and Indian artifacts, including Geronimo's grandson's ceremonial drum.

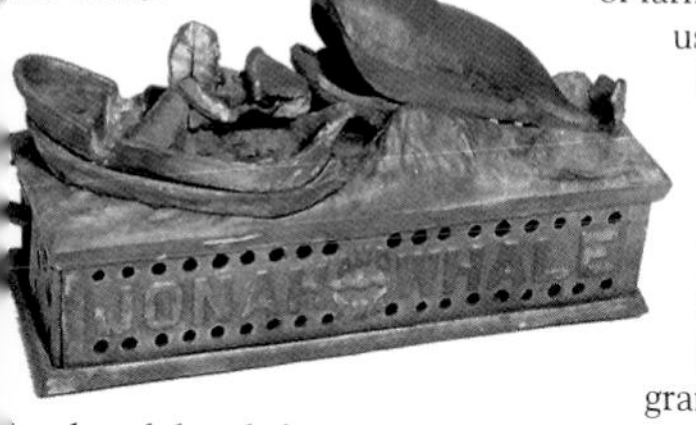

Jonah and the whale, cast-iron toy

12

Biola University Art Gallery

13800 Biola Ave, La Mirada, 90639. ☎ (310) 903-4807. **Fax:** (310) 903-4748. **Thomas Guide:** 707 F2. **Hours:** Mon-Fri 9am-9pm, Sat-Sun 1-5pm. [$] free. [P] free. 📷 allowed. **Year founded:** 1908. **Year opened:** 1971. **Governing authority:** college/university. **Category:** art museum. **Activities/programs:** artist talks, changing exhibitions, gallery talks, installations, lectures. **Facilities:** exhibit space/gallery. ♿ parking. **Collection focus:** drawing, graphic arts, icons, liturgical objects, photography, religious arts, sculpture.

Biola's small art collection is displayed throughout the university campus. Among the major works are *Logos* mural (1990) by Twitchell Kent and *The Talents* (1970) by Millard Sheets.

***Logos* (1990) by Twitchell Kent**

SAN GABRIEL VALLEY —
EAST

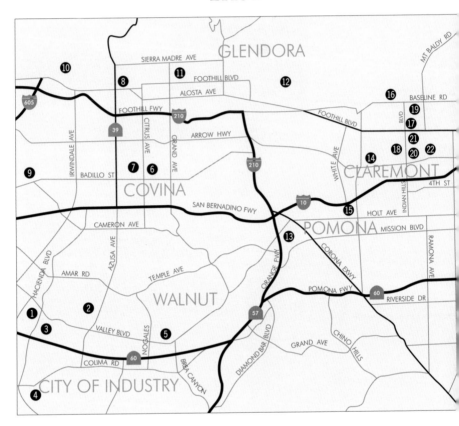

1. Workman and Temple
   Family Homestead
   Museum
2. Ralph W. Miller Golf
   Library/Museum
3. John Rowland Home and
   Dibble Museum
4. International Buddhist
   Progress Society
5. William R. Rowland Adobe
   Ranch House
6. Covina Valley Historical
   Society Museum
7. Heritage House
8. Azusa Historical Society
   Museum
9. Baldwin Park Museum
10. Duarte Historical Museum
11. Glendora Historical Society
    Museum
12. San Dimas Canyon Nature
    Center
13. Phillips Mansion
14. Adobe de Palomares
15. La Casa Primera
16. Raymond M. Alf Museum
17. The Ancient Biblical
    Manuscript Center
18. Petterson Museum of
    Intercultural Art
19. Rancho Santa Ana Botanic
    Garden
20. Montgomerry Gallery —
    Pomona College
21. Ruth Chandler Williamson
    Gallery
22. Kenneth G. Fiske Museum of
    Musical Instruments

La Casa Nueva, north façade

❶
Workman and Temple Family Homestead Museum

15415 E Don Julian Rd, City of Industry, 91745. ☎ (818) 968-8492. **Fax:** (818) 968-2048.

La Casa Nueva, main hall

Thomas Guide: 678 C1. 🚌 bus, metro. **Hours:** Tue-Fri 1-4pm, Sat-Sun 10am-4pm. **Closed:** 4th weekend of the month and major holidays. 💲 free. **Reservations:** necessary for groups. 🅿 free. 📷 allowed with permission. **Year founded:** 1963. **Year opened:** 1981. **Primary focus:** to interpret a century of California history from 1830 to 1930. **Publications:** *Homestead Quarterly.* **Governing authority:** municipal. **Category:** historic building/site open to the public. **Activities/programs:** changing exhibitions, concerts, docent programs, educational programs, events, for-

Brand iron

eign-language tours (Spanish and Chinese), guided tours, internship programs, lectures, performances, school programs, storytelling, volunteer programs, workshops. **Facilities:** research library, picnic area, visitors' center. ♿ activities for visually impaired, parking, sign-language interpretation, wheelchair accessible. **Collection focus:** architecture, books, clothing and dress, decorative and applied arts, domestic utensils, furniture and interiors, local history, painted and stained glass, personal history.

The Workman and Temple Homestead is a 6-acre historic site comprising 8 restored structures chronicling 100 years of California history. Besides the 2 family residences, it consists of a water tower, pump house, *tepee* (smokehouse), glorieta, visitors' center and mausoleum at El Campo Santo, LA County's oldest private cemetery. The homestead was once part of the 48,790-acre Rancho La Puente (Ranch of the Bridge), granted to William Workman and John Rowland in 1841 by Mexican governor Pio Pico. Those two men led the first organized overland expedition of American settlers into the Los Angeles area.

Agnes Temple, stained-glass window

Workman played a prominent role in the development of Los Angeles and founded the first bank in the city. In 1842 he built the original adobe with the help of San Gabriel Mission Indians. The building was later enlarged twice, and in 1872, it was remodeled into an English country manor house by architect Ezra F. Kysor. Following the discovery of oil on the property in 1917, Walter P. Temple, Workman's grandson, built a new residence between 1919 and 1925. It was designed by architects Walker and Ensen in the Spanish Colonial Revival style. The 16-room Temple mansion, called La Casa Nueva, is noted for its custom craftsmanship and decorative arts. It features carved wooden beams and entrance doors, glazed tiles and wrought-iron light fixtures. Among the many stained-glass windows are those depicting the Workman-Rowland wagon train, the family crest and famous authors and musicians. The house displays period furnishings from the 1840s to the 1920s and costumes of the 1920s.

The homestead was placed on the National Register of Historic Places and declared California Historic Landmark No. 874.

Workman House

[2]

Ralph W. Miller Golf Library/Museum

1 Industry Hills Pkwy, City of Industry, 91744. ☎ (818) 854-2354. **Fax:** (818) 854-2305. **Thomas Guide:** 638 G7. **Hours:** Tue-Fri 9am-6:30pm, Sat-Sun noon-4pm. **Closed:** major holidays. $ free. [P] free. 📷 permitted. **Year founded/opened:** 1979. **Primary focus:** golf research. **Research fields:** golf history, Scottish history. **Special collections:** photo archives from D. Scott Chisholm, Lester Nehamkin, Rich Bassett, Anne Miller. **Governing authority:** municipal. **Category:** library with collections other than books; specialized museum. **Activities/programs:** changing exhibitions, guided tours. **Facilities:** audiovisual holdings, cafeteria/restaurant, 6,500-volume research library. ♿ strollers permitted, parking, wheelchair accessible. **Collection focus:** sports and recreation.

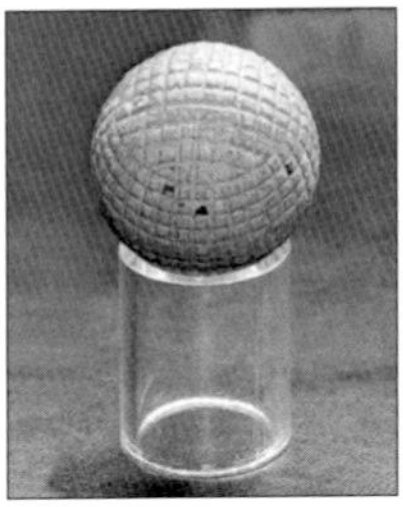

Gutta percha golf ball, machine-scored, mesh pattern (1845-1900)

This is one of only two significant public golf research libraries in the world (the other is the USGA museum and library in Far Hills, NJ). Neither Scotland nor any university can equal this collection for completeness and accessibility. The core of the library is made up of the golf book and memorabilia collection of Los Angeles attorney Ralph W. Miller. It has an automated catalog, indexed clippings and videos covering tournaments, instruction and golf history.

The book collection has more than 5,000 books, including rarities such as *Lawes and Actes* (1597) of the Scottish Parliament, in which the Scottish kings outlawed golf in the hope that their subjects would turn instead to archery, which would enhance national defense. Other highlights include Mathison's *The Golf* (1743), the first book devoted solely to the game, in verse; Adamson's *The Muses Threnodie* (ed. 1774), the first book to mention golf in 1668; *Rules of the Thistle Club* (1824) and *Laws of the Musselburgh Golf Club* (1829). Among the 1,500 bound periodicals from 1890 to the present is a complete run of *The Golfing Annual* from 1887 to 1910. The photo archives contain more than 20,000 golf-related images, while the art collection consists of numerous paintings and prints dating back to the late 1800s.

The museum's exhibits include hickory-shafted putters from 1865 to 1922, collectible golf clubs from 1890 to 1989 and historic irons and clubs used by Bobby Jones, Craig Woods, Walter Hagen and MacDonald Smith, among others. Of particular interest is an exhibition on the evolution of the golf ball, featuring a replica of a *featherie* (1600-1850), which was made from a tophat full of wet feathers stuffed into a stitched bullhide cover. One exhibit is dedicated to Babe Didrikson Zacharias, the first woman golf pro, showing her knickers, putters and scorecards. Additional attractions include General Eisenhower's olive-drab military golf bag and his clubs, as well as balls used and autographed by US presidents. Other displays feature historic tees and sand-tee molds, medals, trophies and other memorabilia.

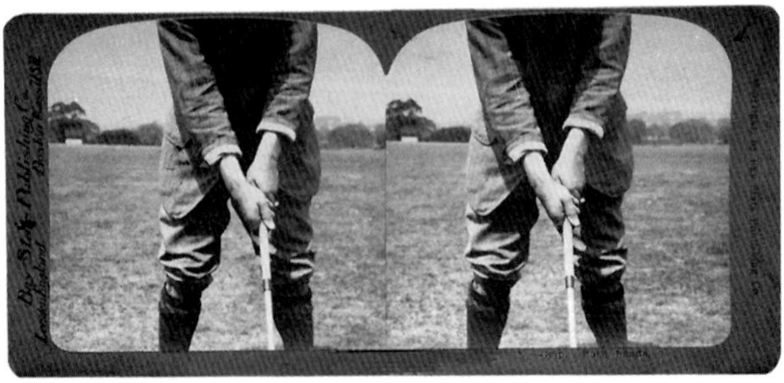

Stereoscopic card showing Harry Vardon demonstrating the famous "Vardon grip," which has influenced golfers to the present day. When viewed with a stereoscope, these cards produced a three-dimensional effect.

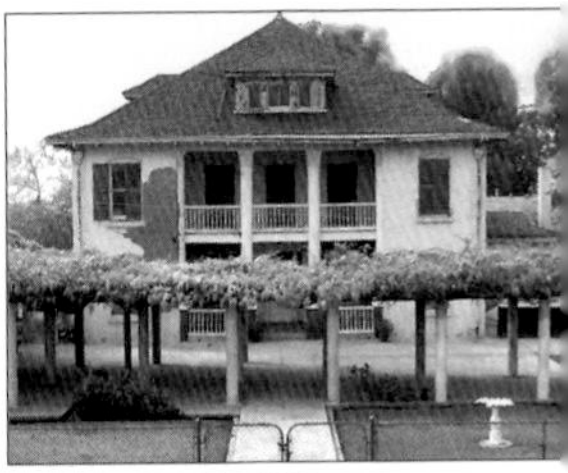

John A. Rowland Home

[3]

John Rowland Home and Dibble Museum

16021 Gale Ave, City of Industry, 91745. ☎ (818) 336-2382. **Thomas Guide:** 678 D2. **Hours:** 1st and 3rd Wed and Sun 1-4pm. **Closed:** Sept and holidays. $ free. [P] free. 📷 allowed. **Primary focus:** to depict the history of the local area. **Governing authority:** nonprofit. **Category:** historic building/site open to the public. **Activities/programs:** docent programs, educational programs, guided tours, school programs. **Facilities:** exhibit space/gallery. ♿ parking, wheelchair accessible. **Collection focus:** architecture, furniture and interiors, local history, period rooms.

The 2-story house was built in 1855 by John Albert Rowland, one of the leaders of the first wagon train of pioneers to arrive in southern California in 1841. It was the first fired-brick home in the San Gabriel Valley, and it is one of the oldest houses of its kind still remaining in this part of the state. Six of the rooms display original furniture, kitchen utensils and artifacts belonging to the 3 generations of the Rowland family who lived there. The Dibble Museum contains Indian artifacts and miscellaneous items recounting the history of the La Puente Valley during the rancho and the agricultural periods.

❹ International Buddhist Progress Society

456 S Glenmark Dr, Hacienda Heights, 91745. **Mailing address:** PO Box 5248, Hacienda Heights, 91745. ☎ (818) 961-9697. **Fax:** (818) 369-1944. **Thomas Guide:** 678 B6. **Hours:** daily 9am-5pm. **Closed:** never. Ⓢ $1 to museum. **Reservations:** necessary. P free. 🄾 no indoor photography. **Year founded:** 1984. **Year opened:** 1988. **Primary focus:** Buddhist monastery. **Research fields:** religious art. **Governing authority:** church. **Category:** art museum. **Activities/programs:** classes/courses, foreign-language tours, guided tours, volunteer programs. **Facilities:** audiovisual holdings, bookstore, cafeteria/restaurant, gift shop, lecture hall, 50,000-volume research library, sculpture garden, visitors' center. ♿ parking, sign-language interpretation, wheelchair accessible. **Garden features:** labels/descriptions, ponds, rock garden, water garden. **Collection focus:** Far Eastern archaeology and antiquities, Oriental archaeology and antiquities, Asian art, Chinese art, Japanese art, Tibetan art, books, calligraphy, ivory, jade, lacquerware, monasteries, religious art, religious history and traditions.

Mahavairocana Buddha, Sung Dynasty (960-1280)

Hsi Lai Temple

This imposing temple serves as an international Buddhist monastery and a spiritual and cultural center for Chinese Americans. Designed by a Chinese architect and financed with donations from devotees and patrons from around the world, the temple was completed in 1988. Hsi Lai is the largest Buddhist temple in the western hemisphere, built in the traditional architectural style of ancient Chinese monasteries of the Ming Dynasty.

On display in the Exhibition Hall are numerous sculptures and objects from China, Tibet, Nepal, Burma and Japan. There is a fine collection of statues of Buddha and bodhisattvas (divine beings), including Maitreya Buddha (the future Buddha), a giltwood carving from the Ming Dynasty; a 19th-century reclining Buddha made of white Burma jade that weighs 7 tons; and Avalokiteshvara Bodhisattva (representing great compassion), a bronze from the Sung Dynasty.

A collection of Buddhist stone sculptures is installed on either side of the main courtyard. Other highlights include ceramics, jade carvings, Buddhist paintings and Chinese scriptures and calligraphies.

Head of Avalokiteshvara Bodhisattva, Ming Dynasty (1368-1644)

Vajra, Tibet

❺ William R. Rowland Adobe Ranch House

Lemon Creek Park, 130 Avenida Alipaz, Walnut, 91789. ✉ City of Walnut, 21701 E Valley Blvd, Walnut, 91789. ☎ (909) 598-5605. **Fax:** (909) 598-2160. **Thomas Guide:** 679 E2. 🚌 bus. **Hours:** by appointment only. Ⓢ free. P free on street. 🄾 allowed. **Year founded/opened:** 1976. **Primary focus:** to preserve and display Spanish and Early American antiques. **Governing authority:** municipal. **Category:** historic building/site open to the public. **Activities/programs:** guided tours, school programs. **Facilities:** picnic area. **Collection focus:** architecture, local history.

William R. Rowland Adobe Ranch House is one of the last remaining original ranch structures in the area. The 3-room adobe was built about 1850 and contains furniture and artifacts documenting the Spanish lifestyle in the 1850s. Sheriff William R. Rowland added the redwood part of the building in 1883 as a home for his cattle ranch foreman. The 2-room redwood section is authentically restored and refurbished as an example of farm life in the 1880s.

William R. Rowland Adobe Ranch House

Orchard King orange box label

❻ Covina Valley Historical Society Museum

125 E College St, Covina, 91723.
☎ (818) 332-9523. **Thomas Guide:** 599 B5. **Hours:** Sun 1-3pm. **Closed:** most holidays. Ⓢ free. **Reservations:** (818) 966-3978. P free. 🔘 allowed. **Membership:** available. **Year founded:** 1969. **Year opened:** 1979. **Primary focus:** community history with an emphasis on the citrus industry of the east San Gabriel Valley. **Publications:** quarterly newsletter. **Governing authority:** municipal. **Category:** history museum. **Activities/programs:** docent programs, guided tours. **Facilities:** audiovisual holdings, gift shop. ♿ parking, wheelchair accessible. **Collection focus:** agriculture, farms and farming, local history.

The museum is a restored firehouse/jail, the first structure in the City of Covina, constructed in 1911. Exhibits are mainly devoted to the early citrus industry and include tools, packing house items, citrus labels and citrus records dating back to the 1890s. There are meteorological reports documenting the area's climate from the turn of the century. Biographies of early settlers are housed here, together with oral histories taken from pioneers and Covina citizens. Other items featured are early photographs, maps and police and fire memorabilia (visitors can see an authentic jail cell, used up to 1975). The museum possesses a small collection of WWI bond posters, uniforms and arms.

❼ Heritage House

300 N Valencia Pl, Covina, 91723.
☎ (818) 331-8615. **Thomas Guide:** 599 A5. **Hours:** 4th Sun of each month 1-3pm. **Closed:** holidays. Ⓢ free. P free on street. **Membership:** available. **Year opened:** 1989. **Governing authority:** private. **Category:** history museum. **Activities/programs:** docent programs, events, guided tours, school programs, volunteer programs. ♿ wheelchair accessible. **Collection focus:** local history.

This 13-room Craftsman-style house was built in 1908 for the family of one of the first pharmacists in Covina, the Nashes. It is restored and contains home furnishings of its first owners. Other items on display relate to the citrus industry and the city's history.

Heritage House

❽ Azusa Historical Society Museum

Civic Center Park, Alameda Ave, Azusa, 91702. ✉ PO Box 1131, Azusa, 91702. ☎ (818) 334-5125 x364. **Thomas Guide:** 568 J5. **Hours:** Tue 10am-noon, Thu 1:30-3:30pm, 1st Sun of each month 1-3pm. **Closed:** holidays. Ⓢ free. **Reservations:** recommended for groups. P free. **Year founded/opened:** 1960. **Primary focus:** history of Azusa. **Governing authority:** private. **Category:** history museum. **Activities/programs:** school programs. ♿ wheelchair accessible. **Collection focus:** local history.

The museum's collection documents the early history of Azusa and surrounding areas with exhibits of household and orchard equipment, period furniture and kitchen utensils. There is a collection of photographs and some old local papers.

❾ Baldwin Park Museum

14327 Ramona Blvd, Baldwin Park, 91706. ☎ (818) 337-3285. **Thomas Guide:** 598 C5. 🚇 metro. **Hours:** Tue 10am-noon and 2-4pm; Sat 10am-noon. **Closed:** holidays. Ⓢ free. **Reservations:** recommended. P on street. 🔘 allowed. **Membership:** available. **Year founded:** 1983. **Year opened:** 1987. **Primary focus:** Baldwin Park history. **Publications:** *The Heritage of Baldwin Park.* **Governing authority:** municipal, nonprofit. **Category:** history museum. **Activities/programs:** docent programs, educational programs, films, guided tours, school programs, slide presentations. **Collection focus:** local history.

The museum has exhibits relating to the history of Baldwin Park, including photographs, maps, old local newspapers, historic clothing and domestic items. Also displayed are reconstructions of a blacksmith shop, a kitchen from the 1890s, a parlor from the 1910s and a one-room schoolhouse. The veterans' display features Civil War, WWI "dough boy," WWII sailor and Korean War marine uniforms.

World War I "dough boy" uniform in the Baldwin Park Museum

⑩

Duarte Historical Museum

777 Encanto Pkwy, Duarte, 91010. ✉ PO Box 263, Duarte, 91009-0263. ☎ (818) 357-9419. **Thomas Guide:** 568 E4. 🚌 bus. **Hours:** Wed 1-3pm, Sat 1-4pm. **Closed:** holidays. 💲 free. P free. 📷 by permission only. **Membership:** available. **Year founded:** 1965. **Year opened:** 1989. **Primary focus:** local history. **Publications:** *Branding Iron*, bimonthly newsletter. **Governing authority:** nonprofit. **Category:** history museum. **Activities/programs:** awards, changing exhibitions, docent programs, events (Native Americans Art Fair), guided tours, lectures, scholarships and fellowships, school programs. **Facilities:** exhibit space/gallery, research library. ♿ **Parking,** wheelchair accessible. **Collection focus:** agriculture, farms and farming, local history.

The history of the famed Duarte citrus industry is presented here via a special exhibition featuring ranch equipment and various small tools and instruments used by orange growers.

Rancho de Duarte branding iron

On display are a ladder, a bag for picking, a smudge pot, packing boxes and pictures of the packing houses. Of particular interest is a fine collection of Duarte citrus box labels, used from 1890 until the 1950s, when the packers changed from wooden to cardboard boxes. Other sections are devoted to pioneer families, the history of the city, the early local church, period furniture and costumes, and tennis in southern California in the late 19th century.

Duarte citrus industry exhibit

Square grand piano (1875) in Glendora Historical Society Museum

⑪

Glendora Historical Society Museum

314 N Glendora Ave, Glendora, 91741. ✉ PO Box 532, Glendora, 91741. ☎ (818) 963-0419. **Thomas Guide:** 569 E5. **Hours:** Sun 1-4pm. 💲 free. **Reservations:** by appointment only for tours. P free on street. 📷 allowed. **Membership:** available. **Primary focus:** history of Glendora and other San Gabriel Valley areas. **Publications:** *Glorious Glendora.* **Governing authority:** private. **Category:** history museum. **Activities/programs:** changing exhibitions. **Facilities:** gift shop. ♿ strollers permitted, wheelchair accessible. **Collection focus:** local history.

This museum is located in the first City Hall building, constructed in 1913, which once housed the police department, jail, library and fire department. On display are Indian artifacts found in Glendora, household items and vintage women's clothing from the late 1890s to the early 1900s. There is also an exhibit devoted to the famous fan dancer and actress Sally Rand, who was a Glendora resident for many years. The citrus industry display features citrus field and shipping boxes, photographs and the packing house bookkeeper's desk (ca. 1895).

⑫

San Dimas Canyon Nature Center

1628 N Sycamore Canyon Rd, San Dimas, 91773. ☎ (909) 599-7512. **Thomas Guide:** 570 C5. **Hours:** Sat-Sun 9am-5pm. 💲 free. P free. 📷 allowed. **Year founded:** early 1950s. **Primary focus:** wildlife sanctuary. **Governing authority:** county. **Category:** nature center/wildlife refuge. **Activities/programs:** animal adoption/sponsorship program, docent programs, events (Nature's Child), volunteer programs. **Facilities:** camping, gift shop, picnic area. **Collection focus:** birds, mammals, zoology.

This nature center has an enclosed wildlife sanctuary containing birds and animals indigenous to southern California that can no longer live in the wilderness. Among the treated and rehabilitated animals are coyotes, deer, raccoons and birds of prey. A small museum has displays of plants, animals and minerals.

Phillips Mansion

⑬

Phillips Mansion

2640 Pomona Blvd, Pomona, 91768. ☎ (909) 623-2198. **Thomas Guide:** 640 D2. **Hours:** currently closed for restoration. **Governing authority:** municipal, nonprofit. **Category:** historic building/site open to the public. **Collection focus:** architecture, furniture and interiors.

In 1866 German immigrant Louis Phillips bought Rancho San Jose de Abajo and erected this 3-story mansion in 1875. The French Second Empire-style building was the first brick house in the vicinity, lighted with gas produced on the property. The house is furnished in the later Victorian style.

⑭ Adobe de Palomares

491 E Arrow Hwy, Pomona 91767.
☎ (909) 620-2300. **Thomas
Guide:** 601 A4. **Hours:** Sun 2-5pm.
Closed: holidays. ⑨ donations
accepted. **Reservations:** by appointment only for groups. ⓟ free on
street. ◉ permission required.
Membership: available. **Year
opened:** 1940. **Primary focus:**
preservation of Pomona Valley history. **Research fields:** archaeology,
pioneer biographies. **Governing
authority:** municipal, nonprofit. **Category:** historic building/site open to
the public. **Activities/programs:**
docent programs, dramatic pro-

Saddles and ranching tools

grams, educational programs, events
(Adobe Days in Mar), guided tours,
outreach programs, performances,
school programs, summer programs,
volunteer programs. **Facilities:** bookstore, gift shop, picnic area. ♿
strollers permitted, wheelchair accessible (limited). **Garden features:** herb
garden, labels/descriptions. **Collection focus:** North American archaeology and antiquities, architecture,

West bedroom with excellent examples of mid-19th
century furniture

carriages and carts,
clothing and dress,
domestic utensils,
farms and farming,
folklife and tradi-
tions, furniture and
interiors, local his-
tory, period rooms,
personal history.

Shortly before
the southern Cal-
ifornia gold rush,
two citizens of the
Pueblo de Los
Angeles, Ygnacio
Palomares and Ricardo Vejar,
were granted 15,000 acres of
vacant mission land by Mexican
Governor Juan Bautista
Alvarado. In 1854 Don Ygnacio
and his wife, Doña Concepción,
built this 13-room house on the
northern part of Rancho San
Jose. The one-story, T-shaped
adobe with a cloth ceiling and
shake roof was their second home
built on the rancho. The adobe,
known as the House of Hospitality, was a station on the once-
important stage route between
Los Angeles and San Bernardino.

The ranch, started by Ygnacio's
two brothers-in-law in the 1840s,
prospered during the gold rush
but later was abandoned and
gradually deteriorated into ruins.
The City of Pomona acquired the
site and completed reconstruction in 1940. The adobe is
authentically furnished in the
style of the period, with pieces
gathered from throughout southern California, including some
items from the original adobe. It
boasts a fine collection of early
California furniture, cooking
utensils, household items and
clothing. Adjacent to the house is
a blacksmith shop with old tools,
branding irons and a horse-drawn
carriage from the
1880s. Parts of the
courtyard and gar-
dens were recon-
structed as they
might have looked
when the Palo-
mares family lived
here and the herb
garden was
reestablished with
original plantings.
The adobe is des-
ignated California
Historical Land-
mark No. 372.

Adobe de Palomares

⑮ La Casa Primera

1569 N Park Ave, Pomona 91767.
☎ (909) 623-2198. **Thomas
Guide:** 600 J6. **Hours:** Sun 2-5pm.
Closed: holidays. ⑨ free. ⓟ free
on street. ◉ permission required.
Membership: available. **Year
opened:** 1972. **Primary focus:** preserving the heritage of the Pomona
Valley. **Governing authority:** municipal, nonprofit. **Category:** historic
building/site open to the public.
Activities/programs: docent programs, guided tours, school programs, volunteer programs. **Facilities:** patio available for rent. ♿
strollers permitted. **Collection focus:**
architecture, furniture and interiors,
local history.

La Casa Primera de Rancho San
Jose, the first home of Ygnacio
Palomares, restored to 1890 period

This is the oldest house in the
Pomona Valley, built in 1837 by
Ygnacio Palomares. The family
lived in a 5-room adobe for 17
years, when they moved a mile
farther north to their new adobe
home, now known as Adobe de
Palomares. The house has been
restored and contains authentic
19th-century furniture, clothing
and photographs. La Casa
Primera is on the National Register of Historic Places.

16

Raymond M. Alf Museum

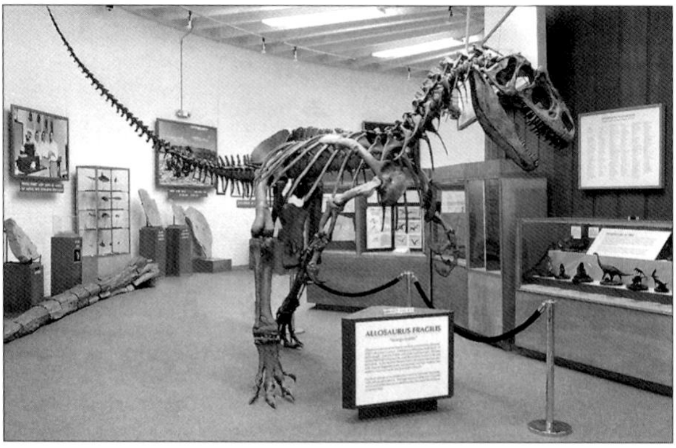

Allosaurus fragilis, **perhaps the largest predator of the late Jurassic period, lived in North America 150 million years ago**

1175 W Base Line Rd, Claremont, 91711. ☎ (909) 624-2798. **Fax:** (909) 621-4582. **Thomas Guide:** 571 A7. **Hours:** Mon-Thu 1-4pm; 1st Sun of each month (Sep-May). **Closed:** school holidays and Jun-Aug. [$] $1, children under 5 free. **Reservations:** necessary for morning school tours. [P] free. 📷 allowed. **Membership:** available. **Year founded/opened:** 1968. **Primary focus:** to present the history of life on earth. **Research fields:** paleontology. **Special collections:** the Thompson and Vivian Webb Indian Pottery Collection. **Publications:** *Environment West*, quarterly magazine; *Quest*, quarterly newsletter. **Governing authority:** nonprofit. **Category:** natural history museum. **Activities/programs:** classes/courses, docent programs, educational programs, guided tours, outreach programs, school programs, summer programs, volunteer programs. **Facilities:** gift shop. ♿ parking, wheelchair accessible. **Collection focus:** Egyptian archaeology and antiquities, North American archaeology and antiquities, fossils, mineralogy, zoology.

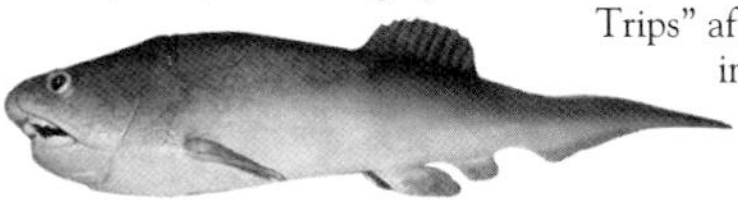

Model of *Coccosteus*, a fish that lived 200 to 500 million years ago

This museum was founded by Dr. Raymond Alf, a teacher at the Webb Schools in Claremont, to house a vast collection of fossils gathered on research and collecting trips he organized beginning in the 1930s. These expeditions became known as "Peccary Trips" after the discovery of an important fossil of a new genus of peccary, or ancient pig. The majority of the fossils on permanent display were collected and prepared by students of the Webb Schools. The building, designed by Millard Sheets, was completed in 1968.

The Hall of Life, the museum's main hall, traces the history of life on earth from the first living organisms 3.5 billion years ago. On display are the oldest known rocks, minerals, shells and other fossil invertebrates, paleobotany, insects, marine life and an extensive mammal collection. The museum contains a variety of dinosaur specimens, including complete and partial skeletons, skulls, footprints and eggs. Among the highlights are complete skeletons of *Allosaurus fragilis* and *Monoclonius* and a rare cast of a *Protoceratops* egg, found in Mongolia in the 1960s. Archaeological artifacts from around the world include Bronze Age pottery that is 3,500-4,500 years old, found at Ban Chiang in Thailand, Egyptian artifacts from 10,000 BC to 640 AD, Coptic textiles, Pre-Columbian art and American Indian pottery and baskets.

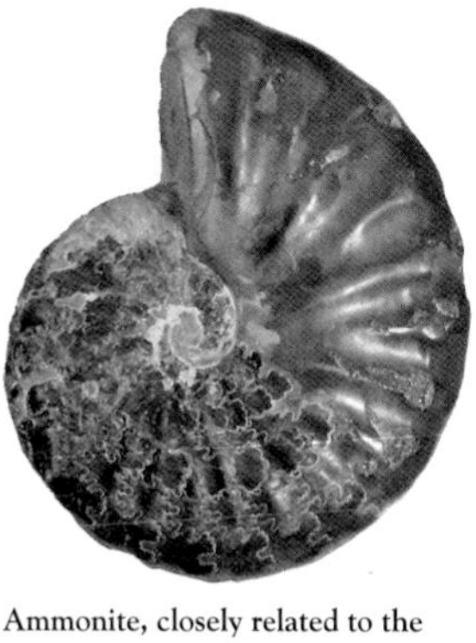

Ammonite, closely related to the chambered nautilus, which became extinct with the dinosaur

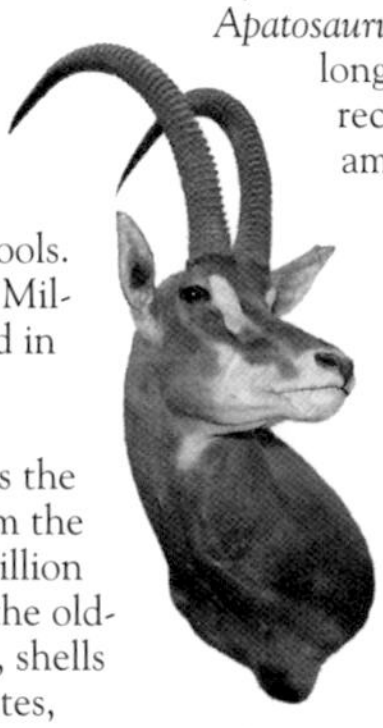

Giant sable antelope (*Hippotragus niger variani*)

The Hall of Fossil Footprints contains the largest and most diverse display of animal footprints in the US, dating from 4 million to 500 million years ago. They include a cast of an *Apatosaurus* footprint 2.5 feet long and numerous records of spiders, amphibians, reptiles, birds, camels, elephants and horses. Of particular interest is an *Amphicyon*, or bear-dog exhibit, one of only two of its kind in the world. It includes a skeleton of this large carnivorous mammal and tracks that were collected by the museum near Barstow and represent the oldest mammal footprints in North America.

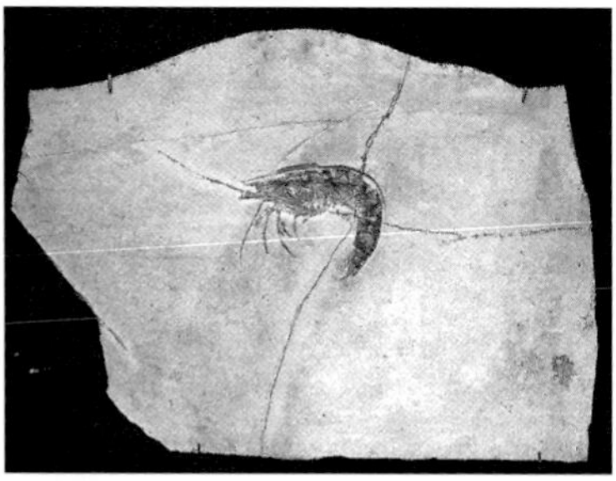

Solenhofen limestone from Germany, 150-160 million years old

17

The Ancient Biblical Manuscript Center

1325 N College Ave, Claremont, 91711. ✉ PO Box 670, Claremont, 91711. ☎ (909) 621-6451. **Fax:** (909) 621-1481. **Thomas Guide:** 601 D2. 🚌 bus. **Hours:** Mon-Fri 10am-5pm. **Closed:** holidays. $ free. **Reservations:** recommended. [P] free on street. 📷 permission needed. **Membership:** available. **Year founded:** 1978. **Primary focus:** to preserve and make available on film manuscripts of the Bible and related documents from antiquity. **Publications:** *Dead Sea Scrolls Catalogue*, book; *The Folio*, quarterly bulletin; *The Fragment*, semiannual newsletter. **Governing authority:** private. **Category:** specialized museum. **Activities/programs:** interlibrary loans, lectures. **Facilities:** micro holdings. **Collection focus:** books, Christian archaeology and antiquities, Judaica, manuscripts.

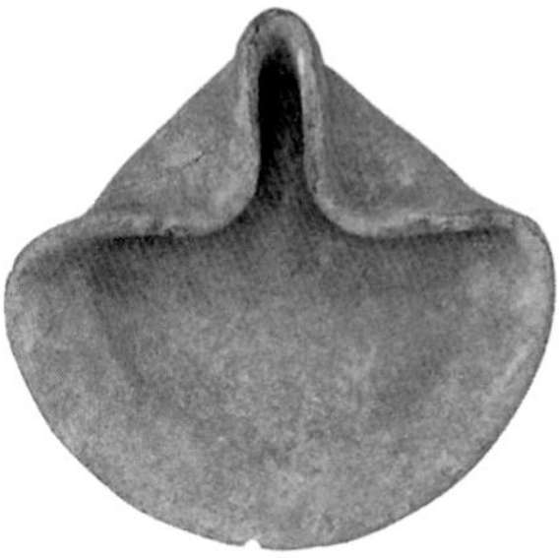

Oil lamp, late Bronze Age (ca. 1200 BC), from the Traver Collection

The Ancient Biblical Manuscript Center has one of the world's largest photographic archives of manuscripts of and related to the New and Old Testaments, including the largest single collection of Dead Sea Scroll images. The center offers photo exhibits on ancient manuscripts, the history of the writing, archaeology of the Holy Land, the Dead Sea Scrolls and excavations at Khirbet Qumran and Qumran caves. On display are artifacts ranging in date from 30,000 years ago to the Hellenistic period.

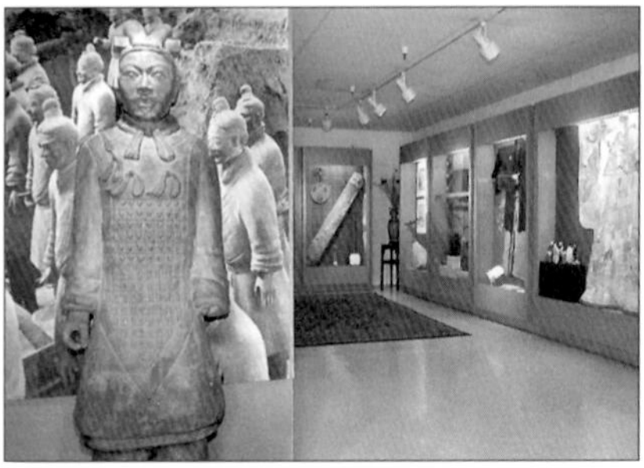

Main gallery with the cast figure of the commander from the clay army tomb of Chin Shih Huang Di

18

Petterson Museum of Intercultural Art

730 Plymouth Rd, Claremont, 91711. ✉ 660 Avery Rd, Claremont, 91711. ☎ (909) 626-0023, 621-9581. **Fax:** (909) 399-5508. **Thomas Guide:** 601 C3. **Hours:** Mon-Wed 9am-4pm; Fri-Sun 2-4pm. **Closed:** holidays. $ free. [P] free. 📷 not allowed. **Membership:** available. **Year founded:** 1968. **Year opened:** 1986. **Primary focus:** folk and fine art from all parts of the world. **Special collections:** the Richard Petterson Collection. **Governing authority:** private, nonprofit. **Category:** art museum. **Activities/programs:** concerts, changing exhibitions, docent programs, events (Celebration of the Arts — May), guided tours, lectures, school programs, shadow puppet shows, volunteer programs. **Facilities:** exhibit space/gallery, library. ♿ parking, wheelchair accessible. **Garden features:** Japanese garden. **Collection focus:** North American archaeology and antiquities, Far Eastern and Oriental archaeology and antiquities, American Indian art, Asian art, Chinese art, Japanese art, clothing and dress, shells.

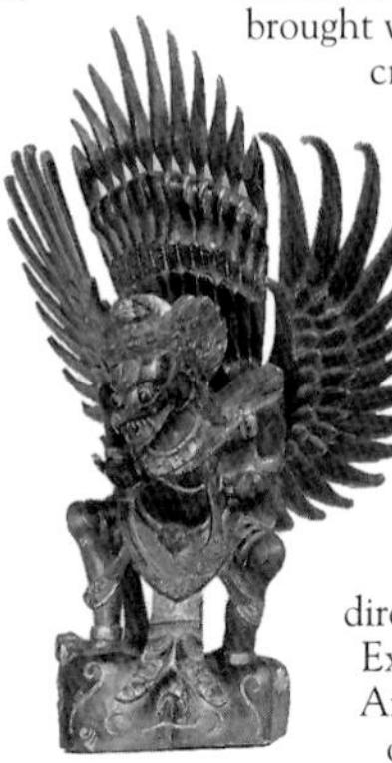

Garuda, Bali, 18th century

The museum is located in Pilgrim Place, a community founded in 1915 for retired pastors and missionaries. These "pilgrims" brought with them arts and crafts from various cultures around the world. The core of the museum's collection is comprised of items gathered by Richard Petterson, a ceramics professor at Scripps College during the 1950s and director of the Fine Arts Exhibitions at the Los Angeles County Fair for over 30 years.

Among the items on display are Japanese prints, lacquerware, toys and dolls, fans and musical instruments. There are masks from the *bigaku* and *gagaku*, ancient Japanese dance dramas, and marriage dresses, including a splendid wedding *furisode* from the late 1800s. The museum has ancient Chinese bronzes dating from 1400 BC and bronze mirrors from the Han and T'ang periods, Kuan-Yin figures, Ming porcelain and Imperial court robes from the Ming and Ching dynasties. Other exhibits include handwoven baskets and ebony figures from Africa, loomed *huipiles* from Guatemala, Native American textiles and pottery, European and American fashions from the 1880s, and shells and dolls from around the world.

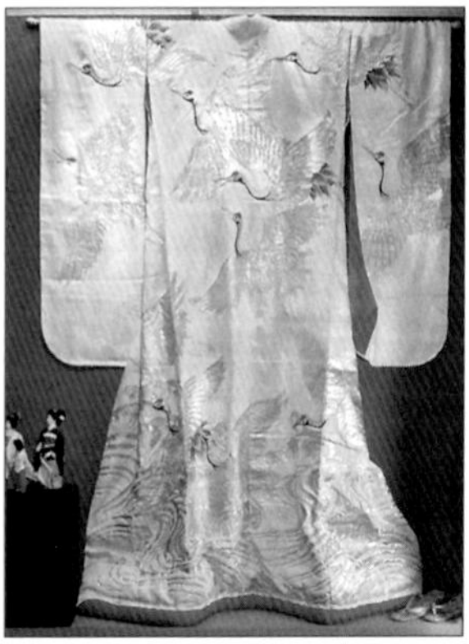

Japanese wedding kimono

⑲
Rancho Santa Ana Botanic Garden

1500 N College Ave, Claremont, 91711-3157. ☎ (909) 625-8767. **Fax:** (310) 626-7670. **Thomas Guide:** 601 D1. 🚌 bus. **Hours:** daily 8am-5pm. **Closed:** New Year's Day, 4th of July, Thanksgiving and Christmas. Ⓢ free. Ⓟ free. 📷 allowed with reservations. **Membership:** available. **Year founded:** 1934. **Primary focus:** dedicated to the conservation and cultivation of native California plants through research, education and horticultural programs. **Research fields:** systematic wood anatomy, monographic, molecular genetics biology. **Special collections:** herbarium. **Publications:** *Aliso*, scientific journal. **Governing authority:** private, nonprofit. **Category:** botanical garden/arboretum. **Activities/programs:** classes/courses,

Maguey (*Agave Desertii*)

docent programs, educational programs, events (annual plant sales in Nov, annual wildflower show in Apr), guided tours, internship programs, lectures, outreach programs, school programs, slide presentations, volunteer programs, workshops. **Facilities:** available for rent, bookstore, gift shop, greenhouse, 40,000-volume research library. ♿ strollers permitted, parking, wheelchair accessible. **Garden features:** Desert garden, endangered species, greenhouse, labels/descriptions, ponds, rare species, restrooms, seed store; peak time: Mar-May. **Collection focus:** biology, botany, horticulture, plant genealogy.

The garden was founded in 1927 by Susanna Bixby Bryant in memory of her father, California pioneer John W. Bixby. Originally established on her Rancho Santa Ana in Orange County,

the garden was moved to its present location in 1951. It is the largest botanic garden devoted exclusively to California native plants. With over 6,000 kinds of native flora, California has the richest native plant heritage in the continental US.

Among 1,500 different species on display are wild and cultivated forms, as well as close relatives of California native species. They were collected by field botanists and recorded with their original provenance as scientific specimens. Rancho Santa Ana Botanic Garden is an internationally recognized research and educational institution, comprising a herbarium with 1 million specimens (currently ranked 13th in the US), sophisticated laboratory facilities and a 40,000-volume research library. It offers a graduate program in botany with the Claremont Graduate School. The garden developed many cultivated forms of native flora for use in landscaping and organizes a broad variety of community education programs.

The 86-acre garden is organized into three distinct areas and grows many rare and endangered species. Indian Hill Mesa contains wild species and cultivars of native plants, including California wild lilacs, manzanitas and

Rancho Santa Ana Botanic Garden, lower pond

the only native California lily species, *Nuphar polysepala*. This area is divided into several communities, including the Southern Riparian Woodlands, the Oak Woodland Trail and the Home Demonstration Garden. There bigleaf maple, western ash, oak and walnut trees are grown, as well as native coast redwood (*Sequoia sempervirens*) and Sierra redwood (*Sequoiadendron giganteum*).

The East Alluvial Gardens features the Desert Garden with many cactus species, including beavertail (*Opuntia basilaris*) and desert willow (*Chilopsis linearis*), along with desert shrubs and succulents. The California Palm Oasis displays the state's only native palm, *Washingtonia filifera*.

The Plant Communities area contains specimens arranged in ecological associations, such as Island Chaparral or Coastal Chaparral. On display are a rare and endangered crucifixion thorn (*Castela emoryi*), the largest cultivated examples of big-berry manzanita (*Arctostaphylos glauca*), Joshua trees (*Yucca brevifolia*), Catalina crossosomas (*Crossosoma californicum*) and madrone trees (*Arbutus menziesii*).

A variety of wildflowers grows throughout the garden, including farewell-to-spring, meadowfoam, brodiaeas and California poppies.

Desert Garden, beavertail cactus

Rancho Santa Ana Botanic Garden

1. Desert Garden
2. Percy Everett Garden
3. Palm Oasis
4. Coastal and Island Collections
5. Oak Woodland Trail
6. California Plant Communities
7. California Cultivar Garden
8. Home Demonstration Garden
9. Upper Pond
10. Southern Riparian Woodland
11. Basketry Trail
12. Lower Pond
13. Research and Horticulture Complex
14. Maintenance Center

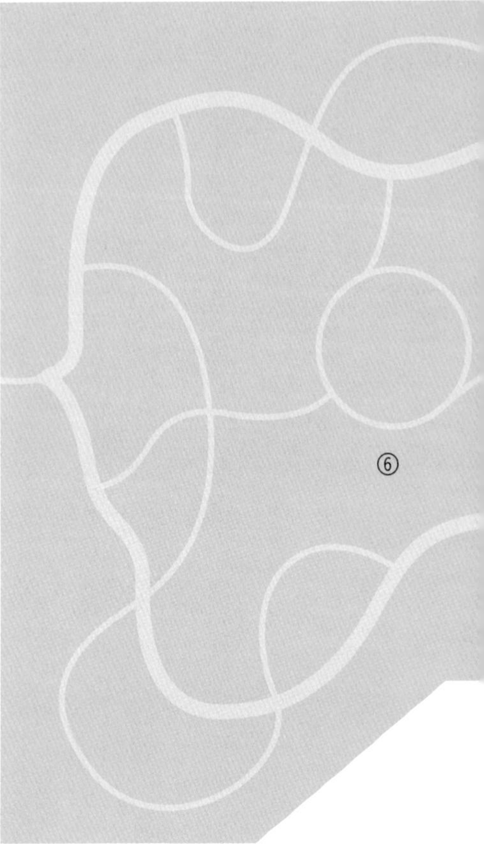

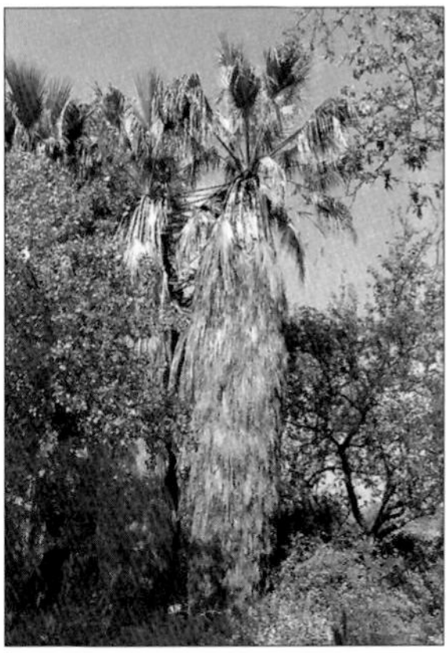

Palm Oasis, California fan palm

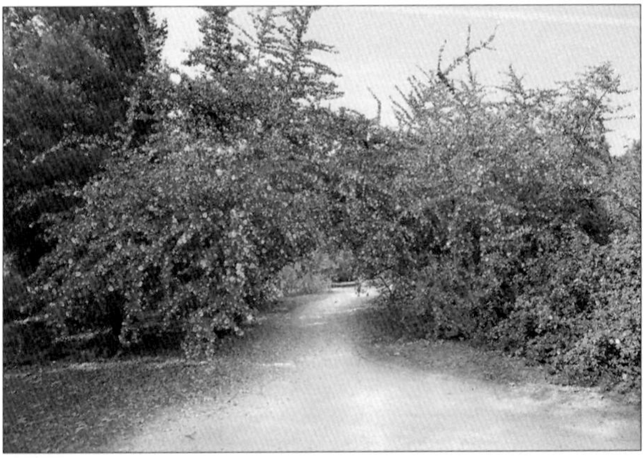

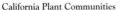

California Plant Communities

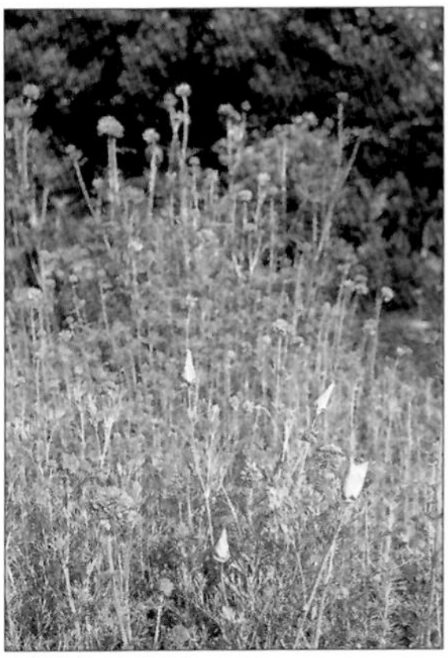

Wildflowers

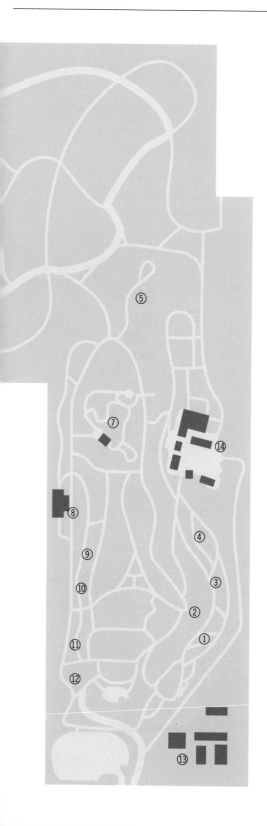

Southern Chaparral

Foothill Woodland

Oak Woodland Trail

Ecce Homo by Ferrarese Painter

[20]

Montgomery Gallery — Pomona College

330 N College Ave, Claremont, 91711-3948. ☎ (909) 621-8283. **Fax:** (909) 621-8989. **Thomas Guide:** 601 D3. 🚌 bus, metro.

Basket (1910), Western Apache, Arizona

Hours: Wed-Sun 1-5pm. $ free. [P] free on street. 📷 allowed (no flash). **Year opened:** 1958. **Primary focus:** educational institution dedicated to the collection and care of works of art and to their exhibition for the benefit of the public. **Special collections:** the Gerald R. Pomerat Collection, the S. H. Marcy Collection, the Norton Simon Collection, the Culley Collection, the June Wayne Collection, the Samuel H. Kress Foundation Collection. **Major exhibitions:** "Karl Benjamin: The Pomona Years 1979-1994" (1994); "Ways of Seeing/Exhibiting American Indian Art" (1994); "Masters from Three Collections, 1300-1800" (1993). **Publications:** catalogs for most exhibitions. **Governing authority:** college/university. **Category:** art museum. **Activities/programs:** artist talks, changing exhibitions, docent programs, gallery talks, guided tours, lectures, retrospectives. **Facilities:** exhibit space/gallery. ♿ strollers permitted, wheelchair accessible. **Collection focus:** North American archaeology and antiquities, American Indian art, Asian art, Chinese art, Japanese art, modern and contemporary art, baskets, bronzes, drawing, ivory, landscapes, mural painting and decoration, European painting, North American painting, Renaissance painting, 19th- and 20th-century painting, photography, portraits, sculpture, watercolors, woodcuts.

Founded in 1958, Montgomery Art Gallery started as an extension of Pomona College's art department, with the purpose of serving the studio and art history curricula. The gallery's art collection is particularly strong in prints, drawings and photography. Notable works are an Albrecht Dürer engraving, *St. Thomas* (1514), and *Negress Lying Down* (1658), an etching by Rembrandt van Rijn. There are exceptional woodcuts by a number of German Expressionists, including Emil Nolde, Ernst Ludwig Kirchner, Käthe Kollwitz, Max Pechstein and Karl Schmidt-Rotluff. The gallery has an important collection of late 19th-century French prints, mainly by Barbizon school masters, as well as early 20th-century German and English prints. Highlights of the collection include fine first editions of *Los Caprichos*, *Los Desastres de la guerra* and *Los Proverbios* by Francisco Goya. Also among the gallery's holdings is an important collection of contemporary graphic art.

The collection of photographs includes works by Ansel Adams, Imogen Cunningham and Walker Evans, as well as by younger American photographers. The collection of paintings contains significant examples of panel paintings, ranging in date from the 14th to the 18th century, including *Saint Claire* (ca. 1360) by an anonymous Sienese Master and *Crucifixion* (ca. 1470) attributed to Niccolo da Foligno. The gallery's collection of works on paper is represented by artists such as Andrea Mantegna, Luca Cambiaso and Jacques Callot.

Blonde Frau by Emil Nolde

American painting is represented by *Medfield Landscape* (ca. 1863) by George Inness, *Moonlit Lake* (1865) by Jasper Francis Cropsey and *Offshore Wind* (ca. 1905) by Elliott Daingerfield.

The extensive Native American art collection contains over 5,000 objects, ranging in date from Pre-Columbian times to the 20th century. It is particularly rich in the basketry and clothing of North America, Southwest ceramics and quillwork and beadwork of the Plains and Great Lakes.

Negress Lying Down (1658), an etching by Rembrandt van Rijn

Four Fishwives (1881) by Winslow Homer

㉑ Ruth Chandler Williamson Gallery

1030 Columbia Ave, Claremont, 91711. ☎ (909) 621-8000 x3517 or 3397. **Fax:** (909) 621-8323. **Thomas Guide:** 601 E2. 🚌 bus, metro. **Hours:** Wed-Sun 1-5pm. 💲 free. 🅿 free. 📷 allowed. **Year founded/opened:** 1939. **Primary focus:** to display works from the permanent collection and to present historical and contemporary exhibitions of important themes and ideas. **Special collections:** the Gen. Edward Young Collection, the Mrs. James Johnson Collection, the Dorothy Adler Routh Collection, the Marer Collection, the Wagner Collection. **Major exhibitions:** "Body, Mind and Spirit: Eight

Newfoundland Harbor (ca. 1914) by Rockwell Kent

Sculptors" (1995); "Earthly Delights: Landscapes from the Scripps College Permanent Collection" (1994); "Revolution in Clay: The Marer Collection

Mask, Bambara, West Africa

of Contemporary Ceramics" (1994). **Publications:** exhibition catalogs. **Governing authority:** private, nonprofit. **Category:** art museum. **Activities/programs:** artist talks, changing exhibitions, gallery talks, internships, retrospectives, traveling exhibitions. **Facilities:** exhibit space/gallery. ♿ parking, wheelchair accessible. **Collection focus:** Meso and South American archaeology and antiquities, African art, Japanese art, modern and contemporary art, Pre-Columbian art, bronzes, clothing and dress, decorative and applied art, mural painting and decoration, North American painting, 19th- and 20th-century painting, porcelain and ceramics.

Since 1974 the art collections and exhibition programs of Scripps and Pomona Colleges have been jointly administered as the Galleries of the Claremont Colleges. In 1993, after construction began on its new Ruth Chandler Williamson Gallery, Scripps College started its own independent gallery program.

The gallery's holdings include a significant collection of 19th- and 20th-century American Realist and Impressionist paintings spanning the period between 1870 and 1930. Among the major works are *On the Pequonic* (1877) by George Inness, *Pasture Hills* (ca. 1890) by Alexander Helwig Wyant, *Newfoundland Harbor* (ca. 1914) by Rockwell Kent and *Storm at Sea, Cornwall, England*

(ca. 1906) by the noted painter of the American West, Thomas Moran. Important Impressionists' works include *Smiling Sarah in a Hat Trimmed with a Pansy* (ca. 1901) by Mary Cassatt, *Street in Pont-Aven, Brittany* (1897) by Frederick Childe Hassam, *The Approaching Festival* (1922) by Willard Leroy Metcalf and *Snowbound* by John Henry Twachtman.

The gallery's extensive collection of more than 900 contemporary American and Japanese ceramics features works by Laura Andreson, Shoji Hamada, Beatrice Wood, Peter Voulkos, John Mason, Jun Kaneko and Ron Nagle, among others.

The Asian collection contains 250

F. M. Case (1981) by Marilyn Levine

Japanese prints by artists such as Chikanobu, Kunisada, Yoshitoshi and Hiroshige, as well as Chinese hand scrolls of the 19th and 20th century. Pre-Columbian art is represented by Mayan and Anasazi ceramics, while the collection of African art includes 50 masks and statues from West Africa.

Vessel (1966) by Paul Soldner

Kenneth G. Fiske Museum of Musical Instruments

22

Kenneth G. Fiske Museum of Musical Instruments

Bridges Auditorium, 450 N College Way, Claremont, 91711-4491. ☎ (909) 621-8307. **Fax:** (909) 621-8517. **Thomas Guide:** 601 D3. **Hours:** by appointment only. $ free, donations welcome. [P] free. 📷 allowed. **Year founded:** 1954. **Year opened:** 1986. **Primary focus:** to collect, catalog and preserve musical instruments, educate about instruments and their evolution and provide access to visitors. **Research fields:** organology (the study of musical instruments); performance practice. **Special collections:** the Curtiss Janssen Collection, the Eames Collection, the Leon Whitsell Collection, the Gordon L. Smith Collection. **Governing authority:** college/university. **Category:** specialized museum. **Activities/programs:** changing exhibitions, concerts, guided tours, intermuseum loans. ♿ parking, wheelchair accessible. **Collection focus:** music and musical instruments.

Serpent with ivory mouthpiece of French origin (ca. 1880)

The Fiske Museum contains one of the most comprehensive collections of musical instruments in the country and the largest such collection in the Western US. Over 1,100 American, European and ethnic musical instruments, dating from the 17th to the 20th century, are on permanent display on the lower level of Bridges Auditorium. The core of the collection is made up of 550 instruments gathered by Ohio University music professor Curtiss Janssen. He began his collection during World War I while serving in France as a navy musician.

The museum's particular strength lies in its collection of brass instruments. It includes a group of fine American and European instruments that depict this family's development during the 19th century, together with examples of innovative brass instruments. The collection's highlight is the only known complete set of seven over-the-shoulder saxhorns dating from 1872 designed by Hall and Quinby of Boston. Other items include a ca. 1810 slide trumpet by Ulyate, London, and the largest trumpet in the world — 7 feet of brass cast in Cleveland, Ohio, in the 1920s.

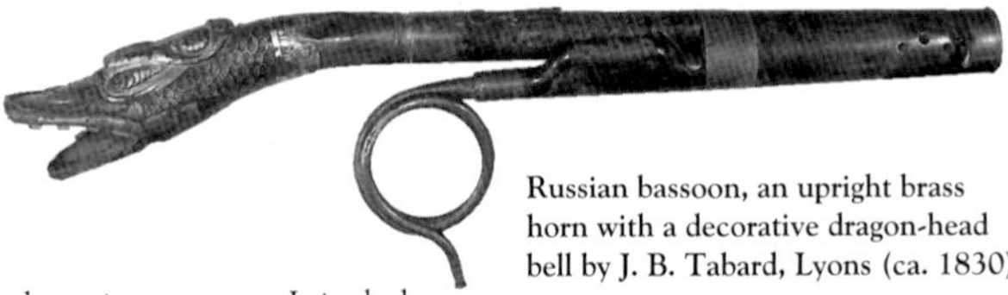

Russian bassoon, an upright brass horn with a decorative dragon-head bell by J. B. Tabard, Lyons (ca. 1830)

Among the important woodwind instruments are an outstanding ca. 1790 one-key flute by Friedrich Gabriel August Kirst of Potsdam, flute maker to Frederick the Great of Prussia; a ca. 1825 6-key bassoon of the Jeantet School of Lyon; a beautiful ca. 1850 oboe by Gehrs of Berlin; and a unique prototype saxello (ca. 1925) by the H. N. White Co., Cincinnati.

Keyboard instruments include a fine transverse spinet (ca. 1690) by Stephen Keene, London; a square piano by Erard Fréres (1799), Paris; one of the earliest documented pianos in the US in the 18th century; a grand piano by Jean Henri Pape (ca. 1835), Paris. Also on display are a rare lap organ (ca. 1850) by Nichols, Williams and Co., Barre, Vermont; and a three-manual reed organ by Mason and Hamlin, Boston (ca. 1890), the only known example in a museum in the United States.

Notable among string instruments are an important violin (1672) by distinguished maker Andrea Guarneri of Cremona; a viola d'amore (ca. 1750) by Johann Andreas Doerffel of Klingenthal, still in its original state of construction; a fine treble viol by Leandro Bisiach (ca. 1895), Milan, one of two known reproductions of a 16th century viol; and a mandora (late 18th century) of the Presbler School in Milan.

The ethnic collection covers the full range of traditional wind, string and percussion instruments from China, Tibet, Japan, Africa, Indonesia and South America.

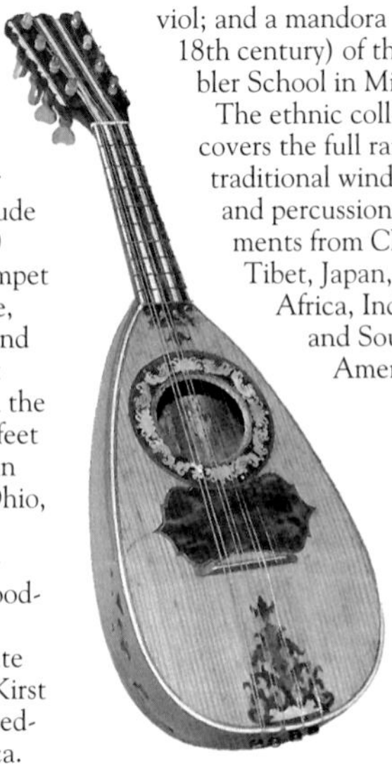

Mandolin (1763) by Joanies Vinnacia of Naples, one of two instruments known by this maker

NEW MUSEUMS

On the following pages are museums which
were opened or came to our attention
during the final stages of this book

The Museum of Television & Radio

The Museum of Television & Radio

465 N Beverly Dr, Beverly Hills, 90210-4654. ☎ (310) 786-1000. **Fax:** (310) 786-1086. **WWW site:** http://www.mtr.org. **Thomas Guide:** 632 F1. 🚌 bus. **Hours:** Wed-Sun noon-5pm; Thu noon-9pm. **Closed:** Mon-Tue, New Year's Day, Independence Day, Thanksgiving and Christmas. 💲 $6 adults; $4 students; $3 seniors and children under 13. **P** free on premises with 2 hour validation; $1 per each additional half hour. 📷 not allowed. **Membership:** available. **Year founded:** 1975. **Year opened:** 1996. **Primary focus:** to collect, preserve and interpret television and radio programming and to make these programs available to the public. **Major exhibitions:** "Stand-Up Comedians on Television"; "Witness to History"; "Rock 'n' Roll and Radio"; "Star Trek: Tradition Continues..."; "Hirschfeld: Radio and Television Drawings" (1996) **Publications:** MT&R Review (membership magazine). **Governing authority:** private. **Category:** specialized museum. **Activities/programs:** artist talks (seminars), changing exhibitions, educational programs, films, lectures, multimedia presentations. **Facilities:** gift shop, 75,000-volume research library, theater. ♿ wheelchair accessible. **Collection focus:** mass media.

The Museum of Television and Radio was founded by William S. Paley, former head of the CBS television network, in New York in 1975. Until then, much of the vast heritage of radio and television programs was preserved only by private collectors and was unavailable to the general public.

The museum aims to collect, preserve and interpret more than 70 years of radio and television history through its exhibitions and educational programs.

In the Console Center visitors can privately study their selections from the museum's program collection

The museum's entire 75,000-item collection was duplicated, with no loss of quality, to make it available to the public in California on a permanent basis. It is completely accessible through the museum's state-of-the-art, computerized retrieval and catalogue system. The museum also has sophisticated radio and television equipment, including a fully functioning radio broadcast studio. Satellite technology allows visitors in Los Angeles and New York to participate in the events presented in both cities concurrently.

The museum's collection includes news, public affairs programs and documentaries, performing arts programs, comedy and variety shows, sports, children's programming and commercial advertising.

Among the highlights are the Nixon-Kennedy Debate (1960); Epic Journey of Apollo 11: Moonwalk (1969); The Glass Menagerie with Katharine Hepburn and Sam Waterston (1973); ABC Wide World of Sports: Ali vs. Frazier (1974); Edward R. Murrow's interview with Marilyn Monroe (1955) and America's Civil Rights Years 1954-65.

The new $8.5-million museum facility in Beverly Hills, named The Leonard and Isabelle Goldenson Building, was designed by internationally renowned architect Richard Meier. The 23,000-square-foot, 3-story Modernist structure is the latest in a series of museum projects he completed in the United States and Europe.

Whoopi Goldberg

Skirball Cultural Center (aerial view)

Skirball Cultural Center and Museum

2701 N Sepulveda Blvd, Los Angeles, 90049. ☎ (310) 440-4600. **Fax:** (310) 440-4696. **Recorded information:** (310) 440-4500. **Reservations:** (310) 440-4666. **Thomas Guide:** 591 F1. **Hours:** Tue-Wed, Fri 10am-4pm; Thu 10am-9pm; Sat-Sun noon-5pm. **Closed:** Thanksgiving, Yom Kippur, Rosh Hashanah. [$] $6 adults, $4 seniors and students, children 13 and under free. [P] free on site. 📷 not allowed in galleries. **Membership:** available. **Year founded:** 1913. **Year opened:** 1972/1996. **Primary focus:** American Judaica, Jewish ceremonial art, fine art, works by Jewish artists on Jewish themes, Biblical archaeology. **Research fields:** American Judaica, contemporary art and artists. **Special**

Fragment of a Byzantine mosaic floor, Antioch, Syria (AD 324-640)

collections: the Hamburger Collection of coins and medals; the Solomons and Grossman Collection of etchings, medals and seals; the Kirschstein Collection of Jewish ceremonial art. **Major exhibitions:** "Henry Mosler Rediscovered"; "Becoming American Women"; "Converging Cultures"; "Blessings and Beginnings" (1996). **Publications:** *Henry Mosler Rediscovered: Nineteenth Century American-Jewish Artist; New Beginnings: The Skirball Museum Collections and Inaugural Exhibition.*

Governing authority: non-profit. **Category:** specialized museum. **Activities/programs:** artist talks, changing exhibitions, classes/courses, concerts, docent programs, dramatic programs, educational programs, events (Family Festival), films, gallery talks, guided tours, installations, inter-museum loan, internship program, lectures, multimedia presentations, outreach programs, performances, performing arts, retrospectives, school programs, slide presentations, storytelling, summer programs, traveling exhibitions, volunteer programs, workshops. **Facilities:** audiovisual holdings, auditorium, bookstore, cafeteria/restaurant, checkroom, conservation center, exhibit space/gallery, gift shop, lecture hall, research library, picnic area, sculpture garden, slide registry. ♿ strollers permitted, parking, wheelchair accessible. **Collection focus:** Middle and Near Eastern archaeology and antiquities, modern and contemporary art, book arts, decorative and applied art, folk life and traditions, Judaica, liturgical objects, European painting, religious art, religious history and traditions.

Hanukkah lamp, Moscow, Russia (1836)

Opened to the public in April 1996, the new Skirball Cultural Center presents Jewish culture and experience as part of American life as a whole. Located on a 15-acre site in the Santa Monica Mountains, the 65-million, 125,000-square-foot complex was designed by renowned architect Moshe Safdie.

The Skirball Museum was opened in 1972 on Hebrew Union College campus in Los Angeles. Its collection was moved from Cincinnati, Ohio, where the museum was founded in 1913. It has one of the world's largest collections of art and artifacts relating to Judaism and American life.

The museum's core exhibition "Visions and Values: Jewish Life from Antiquity to America" takes visitors to the journey Jewish people undertook four thousand years ago. Several thematic galleries feature multimedia installations incorporating artifacts and artworks, documents, films, photographs and sound recordings. The first gallery, "Beginnings," presents artifacts from the ancient Land of Israel. The second, "Journeys," focuses on the Diaspora and the Jews' adaptation to different lands and cultures. The "Holidays/Seasons" gallery features artifacts representing the Jewish holidays. The "Lifecycles" gallery illustrates the rituals associated with individual life. The "Synagogue" gallery features a reconstruction of the holy ark from Berlin's New Synagogue. The "Liberty and Immigration" gallery depicts immigrants' arrival in America and the struggle to attain liberty. The "Struggle and Opportunity" gallery shows how the Jews made their way in America and the evolution of their values. The Holocaust Memorial reminds visitors of European Jewry's tragic fate under the Nazis. Zionism and modern-day Israel are the subjects of the next gallery. Finally, "At Home in America" depicts the last half-century of Jewish life in America.

Liberty and Immigration Gallery

Scholar's desk, ink box with ink stone on top and brush holder (Choson Dynasty, late 19th century)

Korean American Museum (KAM)

3333 Wilshire Blvd, Los Angeles, 90010. ☎ (213) 388-4229. **Fax:** (213) 381-1288. **E-mail:** xkamerax@aol.com. **Thomas Guide:** 634 A2. 🚌 bus. **Hours:** Tue-Sat 11am-4pm. $ free. **Reservations:** recommended. P underground with KAM validation; metered on Catalina street. 📷 with permission only. **Membership:** available. **Year founded:** 1991. **Year opened:** 1995. **Primary focus:** to preserve and interpret the history, traditions, experiences, culture and achievements of Americans of Korean ancestry. **Research fields:** early Korean American immigration; Korean War (1950-53); furniture from the Yi Dynasty. **Special collections :** the Robert W. Moore Collection. **Major exhibitions:** "Generations: The Korean American Experience" (1994); "Comfort Women (1995); "Korean American Footsteps: Koreans in Hawaii since 1903" (1995); "Finding Family Stories" (1996). **Publications:** *Anthology of Korean American Life Histories; Maedup Art; Yangban Interiors; KAMera*, biannual newsletter. **Governing authority:** nonprofit. **Category:** history museum. **Activities/programs:** artist talks, changing exhibitions, classes/ courses, concerts, docent programs, educational programs, films, foreign language tours, guided tours, installations, internship program, lectures, multimedia presentations, outreach programs, performances, retrospectives, school programs, slide presentations, storytelling, summer programs, traveling exhibitions, volunteer programs, workshops. **Facilities:** audiovisual holdings, exhibit space/ gallery, gift shop, lecture hall, research library, slide registry. ♿ parking, wheelchair accessible. **Collection focus:** Asian art, folk art, folk life and traditions, folklore, furniture and interiors, social conditions.

Founded in 1991, the Korean American Museum is the nation's first museum dedicated to Korean Americans and their contribution to the American society. Through exhibits of photographs, documents, clothes, utensils, furniture and other objects, the museum focuses on the last hundred years of American history from a Korean American perspective, exploring the continuities and the changes that have occurred over time in the public and private sphere.

Graduation portrait of Young Soon Choo from Oberlin High School in Ohio, June 6, 1916

INDEX

Organizations by City

Organizations by Category

Days Open/Free Admission

Governing Authority

Activities/Programs

Facilities

Handicapped Facilities

Garden/Zoo Features

Collection Focus

General Index

ACKNOWLEDGMENTS

The publisher would like to thank many museums, companies, organizations and individuals for their contribution and assistance in the preparation of this book.

Photography Permissions

All photographs taken especially for this book are by Borislav and Mihailo Stanic. Grateful acknowledgments is made to the following for their kind permission to photograph on their premises:

Adamson House/Malibu Lagoon Museum; Adobe de Palomares; Air Force Flight Test Center Museum; Alhambra Historical Society Museum; All Cadillacs of the Forties; Amateur Athletic Foundation of Los Angeles — Paul Ziffren Sports Resource Center; American Military Museum; American Society of Cinematographers (ASC); The Ancient Biblical Manuscript Center; Angels Attic Museum; Antelope Valley Indian Museum; The Arboretum of Los Angeles County; Arcadia Historical Museum; Bailey House; Baldwin Park Museum; Banning Residence Museum; Beverly Hills Cactus Garden; Beverly Hills City Library — Art Collection; Bolton Hall Museum; Botanical Garden — CSU Northridge; Cabrillo Marine Aquarium; California Heritage Museum; California Museum of Science and Industry; Centinela Adobe; Chatsworth Museum; The Clarke Estate; County of Los Angeles Fire Museum; Covina Valley Historical Society Museum; The Craft and Folk Art Museum (CAFAM); Descanso Gardens; The Doctors' House; Doheny Library — Special Collections; Dominguez Ranch Adobe; Downey Museum of Art; Dr. Blyth's Weird Museum; Drum Barracks Civil War Museum; Duarte Historical Museum; Earl Burns Miller Japanese Garden; El Alisal; El Dorado Nature Center; El Molino Viejo (The Old Mill);

El Monte Historical Museum; El Pueblo de Los Angeles Historical Monument; Exposition Park Rose Garden; The Fantasy Foundation; Finnish Folk Art Museum; Fisher Gallery; Fort MacArthur Museum; UCLA Fowler Museum of Cultutal History; Franklin D. Murphy Sculpture Garden; Frederick's of Hollywood Lingerie Museum; Freeman House; Gamble House — USC; Gene Autry Western Heritage Museum; George C. Page Museum of La Brea Discoveries; Glendora Historical Society Museum; Goez Art Studio; Gordon R. Howard Museum; Greystone Park; Grier-Musser Museum; Guiness World of Records Museum; Hathaway Ranch Museum; Heritage Junction Historic Park; Heritage Park; Heritage Square Museum; Hill-Palmer Cottage; Hollyhock House; Hollywood High School Alumni Museum; Hollywood Studio Museum; The Hollywood Wax Museum; Holyland Exhibition; Homestead Acre and the Hill-Palmer Cottage; Huntington Library, Art Collections and Botanical Gardens; International Buddhist Progress Society; International Child Art Collection (ICAC); The Japanese Garden; Jet Propulsion Laboratory (JPL); John Panatier Nature Center; John Rowland Home and Dibble Museum; Juan Matias Sanchez Adobe Museum; Kaizuka Meditation Garden; Kenneth G. Fiske Museum of Musical Instruments; Kidspace Museum; Leonis Adobe/Plummer House; Life Science Museum and Nature Center; Lomita Railroad Museum; Long Beach Firefighters Museum; Long Beach Museum of Art; Los Angeles Children's Museum; Los Angeles County Museum of Art (LACMA); Los Angeles County Sheriffs' Museum; Los Angeles Maritime Museum; Los Angeles Poodle Museum; Los Angeles Public Library — Art, Music and Rare Books Department; Los Angeles Temple Visitors' Center; Los Angeles Zoo; Los Encinos State Historic Park; Manhattan Beach Historical Museum; Martyrs Memorial and Museum of the Holocaust; Max Factor Museum of Beauty; McGroarty

Arts Center; The Mildred E. Mathias Botanical Garden; Milestones of Flight Air Museum; Mole-Richardson Moletown; Monrovia Historical Museum; Mountains Education Program — Sooky Goldman Nature Center; Muller House; Museum in Black; Museum of Contemporary Art (MOCA); Museum of Flying; Museum of Jurassic Technology; My Jewish Discovery Place; Natural History Museum of Los Angeles County; Near East Institute and Archeological Foundation; Neff Home; Norton Simon Museum of Art; Old Masonic Hall; Orcutt Ranch; Pacific Asia Museum; Pageant of Roses Garden; Pasadena Historical Museum; The Petersen Automotive Museum; Petterson Museum of Intercultural Art; Phillips Mansion; Pio Pico Mansion; Point Vicente Interpretive Center; Ralph W. Miller Golf Library/Museum; Ramona Museum of California History; Rancho Los Alamitos; Rancho Santa Ana Botanic Gardens; Raymond M. Alf Museum; Redondo Beach Historical Museum; Richardson House; Ripley's Believe It Or Not!; Roundhouse Marine Studies Lab & Aquarium; San Fernando Mission; San Gabriel Mission; Santa Monica Historical Society Museum; Schindler House; Social and Public Art Resource Center (SPARC); Sondra and Marvin Smalley Sculpture Garden; South Coast Botanic Garden; South Gate Civic Center Museum; South Pasadena Preservation Foundation Museum; SS Lane Victory; Sunny Slope Water Co.; Torrance Historical Museum; Travel Town Transportation Museum; UCLA Athletic Hall of Fame; Vincent Price Gallery; Virginia Robinson Gardens; Wattles Mansion; Watts Towers of Simon Rodia; Wells Fargo History Museum; Western Museum of Flight; Whittier Museum; Whittier Narrows Nature Center; Will Rogers State Historic Park.

Credits and Copyrights

The position of photographs on a page has been abbreviated in the following manner: t = top; tr = top right; tl = top left; tc = top center; tb = top bellow; c = center; cr = center right; cra = center right above; crb = center right bellow; cl = center left; b = bottom; br = bottom right; bl = bottom left; bla = bottom left above; bc = bottom center.

Every effort has been made to contact copyright holders and we apologize for any errors and omissions. Museon Publishing would be pleased to insert appropriate acknowledgments in future editions of this guide.

We would like to thank the following institutions and individuals for permitting the reproduction of their photographs in this book:

Used with permission of the Automobile Club of Southern California: 196cl; Air Force Flight Test Center Museum: 153tl; Amateur Athletic Foundation of Los Angeles: 92br; photo by Joel Mark 92tc, 92cl; Antelope Valley Indian Museum: 154tr, 154cl, 154cr, 154bl; Banning Residence Museum: 120tl, 120br; Beverly Hills Historical Society: 44br; Biola University Art Gallery: 225br; by permission of Barbara Bloom: 180cl; by permission of Eugenia Butler: 125bl; California Heritage Museum: 24t; California Museum of Ancient Art: 65; Carole and Barry Kaye Museum of Miniatures: 48; © 1981 Center for Creative Photography, Arizona Board of Regents: 58br; Charmlee Nature Preserve Study Center: 12b; Chilao Visitor Center: photo by Gerald Reponen 169tc; City of La Mirada — Historical Heritage Comission: 225t; City of Los Angeles — Department of Cultural Affairs: photo by Thomas K. Meyer 214cr, 214br, 215tr; City of Walnut — Recreational Department: 229br; Courtesy of the Homestead Museum: 227; photo by Julius Shulman 227t, 227cl, 227b; The Craft and Folk Art Museum: 53tr, 53c, 53bl; photo by Michael Powers 53br;

© 1986 Peter David: 177br; Descanso Gardens: 139t, 139cl, 139b, 140tc; photo by April Gasci 139cr; Downey Historical Society Collection: 217b; Ennis-Brown House: photo by Tim Street-Porter 76t, 76cr; photo by Scott Zimmermann 76bl; © 1995 Dan Flavin/ARS, New York: 182br; Forest Lawn Memorial Park — Glendale: 136br; Forest Lawn Memorial Park — Hollywood Hills: 78tl; Fort MacArthur Military Museum: 116t; Franklin D. Murphy Sculpture Garden: 30tc (gift of Mr. and Mrs. Arthur C. Caplan, Mr. and Mrs. Donald Winston, and Mr. and Mrs. Walter Mc Maitland, 1968); photo by Grey Crawford 30tr (gift of David E. Bright, 1967); Gamble House — USC: photo by Marvin Rand 162cr, 162b; Gene Autry Western Heritage Museum: 83, 84t, 84c, 84bl, 84bc, 85; George C. Page Museum of La Brea Discoveries: 61c; © 1995 Robert Gober/Paula Cooper Gallery: 183tl; Golden State Mutual Life Art Collection: 93cl; by permission of Robert Graham: 30b; Griffith Observatory: 82cl; photo by E. C. Krupp 82t; photo by Robert Webb 82b; Grunwald Center for the Graphic Arts at UCLA: 29; by permission of Maren Hassinger: 125br; Hebrew Union College Collection, Skirball Museum, Skirball Cultural Center: 243cr (gift of Rabbi Ralph H. Blumenthal); photo by Timothy Hursley 243t, 243b; photo by Lelo Carter 243cl (gift of Joel Malter, Robert Abell, Louis Fischer and Melvin Wank); Hermosa Beach Historical Museum: 108b; The Historical Society of Pomona Valley: 232cr; Hollywood Bowl Museum: 70t; Hollywood Studio Museum: 69t, 69b; Hotel Bel-Air: 37; Huntington Library, Art Collections and Botanical Gardens: 170cl, 171cr, 172t, 172bl, 173bc, 175bl; The J. Paul Getty Museum: 13-17; Japanese American National Museum: photo by Norman Sugimoto 184tc, 184bc; photo courtesy of G. Nemura 184cr; Korean American Museum: photo by Michael Reinschmidt 244; by permission of Barbara Kruger: 181cl; L. Ron Hubbard Life Exhibition: 74cr; © 1981 Lili Lakich: 177tl; Lannan Foundation: 106; photo by Susan Einstein 106tl, 106bl, 106br; photo by Grant Mudford

106tr; © Roy Lichtenstein: 182tc; Little Learners Children's Museum: 208tl; Long Beach Museum of Art: 121cl, 121cr; LBMA, Video Annex: 121bl; Los Angeles County Museum of Art (LACMA): 54t; photo by Peter Brenner 55t; 56tc, 56tr (Gilbert Collection), 56bc (Carl Holmes Collection), 56br (gift of Mr. and Mrs. John H. Nessley), 57tl, 57tc (The Edwin Binney, 3rd Turkish Collection), 57bl (gift of the Ahmanson Foundation), 57bc, 57br (gift of Anna Bing Arnold), 58tl (B. Gerald Cantor Collection), 58tr (gift of Mrs. Lucille Ellis Simon), 58bl (bequest of Mrs. Fred Hathaway Bixby), 58br (anonymous gift), 59tl (Museum acquisition by exchange from David E. Bright bequest), 59bl , 59br, 60tr (The Mr. and Mrs. Allan C. Balch Fund), 60bl, 60br; Los Angeles County Sheriff's Museum: 224cra, 224crb; Los Angeles Public Library — History Department: 178cr, 178b; Los Angeles Zoo: photo by Neal Johnston 80t, 80cl, 80bl, 81t, 81cl, 81b; Martyrs Memorial and Museum of the Holocaust: 47cl; Max Factor Museum of Beauty: 71cr, 71cl, 71br; Montgomerry Gallery — Pomona College: 238t (Kress Study Collection), 238cr (Culley Collection), 238b (gift of Gerald Pomerat); photo by Schenck & Schenck 238cl; by permission of Kevin Mulvany and Susan Rogers 48cl, 48b; © 1995 Elizabeth Murray/Paula Cooper Gallery: 182tr; Museum of Contemporary Art (MOCA): 181t, 182tc, 182br; 183tl, 183tr, 183bl, 183bc; photo by Squidds & Nunns 182tr, 182bl, 182bla, 183br; photo by Gene Ogami 181cl; photo by P. Goldman 183cr; photo by Kira Perov/Squidds & Nunns 180b; Museum of Jurassic Technology: 89t, 89c; Museum of Neon Art (MONA): 177; The Museum of Television & Radio: photo by Grant Mudford 242c; photo by Globe 242b; NASA: 152, 153tr; © 1995 Estate of Louise Nevelson/Pace Wildenstein: 183tr; The New Otani Hotel Garden/Burks Hamner Associates: 184cl; Norton Simon Museum of Art: 157tl, 158t, 158bc, 158br, 159, 160t, 161tl, 161bl; © 1962 Claes Oldenburg: 183br; Olson See More Museum: 208bc; Pacific Asia Museum: 166tb; photo by Paul

Little 166t, 167tl; The Petersen Automotive Museum: 49b, 50, 51; Pico Rivera Historical Display: 212t; Placerita Canyon Nature Center: 150t; Plaza de la Raza: 197b; © 1995 Stephen Prina/Margo Leavin Gallery: 181b; Queen Mary: 118b; Rancho Los Alamitos: 123tl, 123cr, 123br; Rancho Los Cerritos: 126; © 1996 Robert Rauschenberg/ Licensed by VAGA, New York, NY: 183bl; © 1996 James Rosenquist/Licensed by VAGA, New York, NY: 182bla; Ruth Chandler Williamson Gallery: 239t (gift of General & Mrs. Edward Clinton Young), 239cl (Wagner Collection), 239bl; photo by Susan Einstein 239cr (gift of Fred and Estelle Marer); photo by Schenk & Schenk 239br (gift of Fred and Estelle Marer); San Fernando Valley Historical Society:144cr; San Gabriel Historical Association: 200t, 201b; © 1996 George

Segal/Licensed by VAGA, New York, NY: 183bc; Self-Realization Fellowship: 18t, 18r; by permission of Cindy Sherman: 182bl; © 1988 William Shipman: 177bl; Simon Wiesenthal Center's Museum of Tolerance: photo by Jim Mendenhall 45b, 46; Social and Public Art Resource Center: photo by A. Lopez 25bl; South Coast Botanic Garden: 111tc; Southwest Museum:189-192, 193cl; photo by Larry Reynolds 190t, 190br, 190bl, 191tc, 191tr, 192bl; photo by Donald Meyer 190bc, 191br, 191bl, 192bc; photo by Robert Curry 191tl, 192br; SS Lane Victory: 118t; Tournament of Roses: 156tc, 156cl; Travel Town Transportation Museum: 86t, 86cl; UCLA — Louise M. Darling Biomedical Library: History and Special Collections: 36t, 36c; UCLA at the Armand Hammer Museum of Art: 27-28; photo by Tim Street

Porter 27t; UCLA Fowler Museum of Cultural History: 31t; photo by Denis J. Nervig 32, 33tl, 33tr, 33bl; photo by Richard Todd 33tc; University Art Museum (UAM) — CSULB: 125; photo by William Nettles 125t; USC — Doheny Library: Special Collections: 103tr; USC — Fisher Gallery: 104; Vincent Price Gallery: 199cl, 199b; by permission of Bill Viola: 180b; © 1995 Andy Warhol Foundation for the Visual Arts/ARS, New York: 183cr; Watts Towers Art Center: 215tl, 215bl; Wells Fargo History Museum: 179b; Wildlife Waystation: 143br; Will Rogers State Historic Park: photo by Herm Falk 19bl, 19br, 19cr; William Andrews Clark Memorial Library — UCLA: 91cr; William S. Hart Museum: 148; World Wrestling Museum and Hall of Fame: 144bc; photo by Haruo Yamashiro: 214t.